ON THE MARGINS OF RELIGION

ON THE MARGINS OF RELIGION

Edited by
Frances Pine and João de Pina-Cabral

Berghahn Books
New York • Oxford

First published in 2008 by
Berghahn Books
www.berghahnbooks.com

© Frances Pine and João de Pina-Cabral 2008

All rights reserved.
Except for the quotation of short passages for the purpose of criticism and review, no part of this book may be reproduced in any form or by any means, electronic or mechanical, including photocopying, recording, or any information storage and retrieval system now known or to be invented, without written permission of the publisher.

Library of Congress Cataloging-in-Publication Data

On the margins of religion / edited by Frances Pine and João de Pina-Cabral.
   p. cm.
Includes bibliographical references and index.
ISBN 978-1-84545-409-8 (hardback : alk. paper)
1. Anthropology of religion. 2. Religion and sociology. I. Pine, Frances, 1952- II. Pina-Cabral, João de.
GN470.O65 2008
306.6--dc22
                            2008008517

British Library Cataloguing in Publication Data

A catalogue record for this book is available from the British Library

Printed in the United States on acid-free paper

ISBN 978-1-84545-409-8 (hardback)

CONTENTS

List of Figures   vii

Acknowledgements   ix

1. On the Margins: An Introduction   1
   João de Pina-Cabral and Frances Pine

Part I: Anthropology and Religion

2. Homeless Spirits: Modern Spiritualism, Psychical Research and the Anthropology of Religion in the Late Nineteenth and Early Twentieth Centuries   13
   João Vasconcelos

3. The Abominations of Anthropology: Christianity, Ethnographic Taboos and the Meanings of 'Science'   39
   Simon Coleman

Part II: Space and Religious Marginality

4. Religious Logistics: African Christians, Spirituality and Transportation   61
   Thomas Kirsch

5. Contested Spaces: Temple Building and the Re-creation of Religious Boundaries in Contemporary Urban India   81
   Ursula Rao

6. Bosnian Neighbourhoods Revisited: Tolerance, Commitment and *Komšiluk* in Sarajevo   97
   Cornelia Sorabji

Part III: Power and Relative Centrality

7. Revival of Buddhist Royal Family Commemorative Ritual in Laos 115
    Grant Evans

8. Centres and Margins: The Organisation of Extravagance as Self-government in China 135
    Stephan Feuchtwang

Part IV: Religious Options and Identitary Claims

9. Allies and Subordinates: Religious Practice on the Margins between Buddhism and Shamanism in Southern Siberia 153
    Galina Lindquist

10. On Celibate Marriages: Conversion to the Brahma Kumaris in Poland 169
    Agnieszka Kościańska

Part V: Modernity and the Transmission of Religion

11. Elders' Cathedrals and Children's Marbles: Dynamics of Religious Transmission among the Baga of Guinea 187
    Ramon Sarró

12. Geomancy, Politics and Colonial Encounters in Rural Hong Kong 205
    Rubie S. Watson and James L. Watson

13. The Sacrifices of Modernity in a Soviet-built Steel Town in Central India 233
    Jonathan P. Parry

Notes on Contributors 263

Index 267

LIST OF FIGURES

7.1.	Cover of the funeral booklet: 'History of His Majesty the King Sisavang Vong, King of the Lao Kingdom.'	116
7.2.	Commemorative stamp produced at the time of King Sisavang Vong's funeral in 1961.	117
7.3.	Commemorative stamp produced at the time of King Sisavang Vong's funeral in 1961.	118
7.4.	Pomp of a royal cremation.	120
7.5.	Ritual of commemoration at Vat That Luang.	124
7.6.	Royal family ritual in Luang Phrabang.	126
7.7.	The message on this offering reads: 'I, Tiao Soukthivong, aged 70 years, come yearly to pay my respects to the Buddha, the dharma, and the sangha. I request that I will not be possessed by evil, not be sad, and will not be ill. That I will not encounter ill-intentioned others, that I will not sicken, and I hope for success and happiness, and that I will get whatever I wish for. In truth.'	127
7.8.	That Haysokarath at That Luang temple that contains the remains of King Sisavang Vong. People are making offerings around the That before the ceremony begins.	128
7.9.	The 'master of ceremonies'; behind him is the small statue of Sisavang Vong and the offerings to the monks.	129
7.10.	The two young princes Saisana and Thanya are received by Satu Kham Chan.	129
7.11.	The two princes Thanya and Saisana are inducted into the temple.	130
7.12.	The commemorative ceremony in France. From the left, Prince Soulivong, the Prince Regent Sauryavong and his wife Princess Daravong.	131

ACKNOWLEDGEMENTS

The editors especially wish to thank Chris Hann for his encouragement and his help in promoting the debate that gave rise to this book. We are also grateful to the Max Planck Institute for Social Anthropology (Halle/Saale, Germany) for having provided us with an admirable venue for our meeting and for all the subsequent help in promoting this book; to the Institute of Social Sciences of the University of Lisbon; and to Marion Berghahn for her special dedication to the promotion of social anthropology.

Chapter 1

On the Margins: An Introduction

João de Pina-Cabral and Frances Pine

One lesson we have all had to learn in the past few years is that objects and practices, and beliefs and aesthetics, which might appear 'marginal' always have the potential to transform into powerful forms and processes; the things which for long periods exist and take place quietly in the margins, away from the apparent centres of power, can suddenly reconfigure, and go on to undermine, challenge and radically destabilise these very centres. As crises and political upheavals throughout the world are increasingly seen not as clashes between competing political ideologies, as they were so clearly during the cold war, but between rival religions, it becomes more and more difficult to make a straightforward equation between modernity and secularism, or to relegate religion to the position of 'tradition' or to a private world of faith. Nor is it possible to ignore the ways in which the centrality of religion in political and social discourse challenges twentieth-century ideas of secular politics and to some extent of civil society in all parts of the world, including the former socialist countries of eastern Europe and central Asia and of course the United States.

The authors of this series of essays do hope to further the anthropological study of religion but, more significantly, they aim to explore the way in which marginality functions in relation to religion. Even though the kind of practices and statements that most people around the world today would recognise as 'religion' are a constant of human existence, contexts and events often arise where movements formed and acts committed in the name of religion themselves come to challenge the very notion of religion as a clearly defined domain.

For anthropologists, the idea that religion is hard if not impossible to define and, even more so, to define in universal terms, is by no means new. To some extent, the enormous range and variety of beliefs and practices bunched together under the term 'religion' led to a confusion in definitions which was compounded by anxieties about problems of translation and ethnocentrism surrounding terms and concepts. Perhaps unsurprisingly religion, like kinship (see Carsten 2004), fell from grace as a field of anthropological study. Thus, in his handbook on the anthropology of religion, Stephen Glazier reports on a generalised feeling that religion has been 'marginalized' in anthropology (1997: 1).

Ten years on, we believe such an assessment is no longer possible – the ethnographic evidence of the importance of religion has re-imposed itself. Recently we have witnessed a dramatic rise in the anthropological study of new evangelical movements in Europe, North America and Africa, and of the rebirth of traditional religion long considered spent in the regions of Europe and central Asia previously dominated by the Soviet Union, as well as of the spread of new religious movements in the same regions. Through the social sciences, of course, as well as in the media and popular press, there has been an increasingly politicised interpretation and reading of Islamic religious practices at a worldwide level. While this re-emergence of religion as a proper and indeed essential field of study should be noted, it is not the sense in which, in this book, we explore the role of marginality for an anthropological understanding of religion.

Rather, we are motivated by a conviction that the grey areas are the best place to study both what we call religion and the place which it holds in the larger social context. One of the best tools of ethnographic interpretation – often used as a method for interviewing – is to assess the meaning of a category by testing the limits of its applicability. When analytical categories such as 'religion' are applied by anthropologists, one mode of judging their use as analytical tools is to evaluate how far they can take us in analysing phenomena that, originally, might not have seemed to fall within their reach.

What is at issue here, therefore, is not to break with the more common understandings of mainstream anthropology concerning religion by focusing on somehow 'odd' aspects of the religious experience – that would be puerile. To the contrary, we aim to engage with anthropological tradition and its time-honoured understandings by exploring the way in which religion works 'on the margins'. Marginality, understood as a factor of hegemony, thus becomes a gauge for assessing the meaning of religion and the role it plays in social life.

I

For the past two decades, and more, anthropologists have found it impossible to give a satisfactory definition of religion (Lambek 2002: 8–12). This is partly because the boundaries separating religion from other social domains can rarely be agreed upon, but also because the category itself appears to most of us to be so deeply grounded within the Judeo-Christian tradition that it is not easy to defend it against accusations of ethnocentrism.[1] Despite this lack of definitional clarity, however, religion has continued to be inscribed on the margins of most of what we write about other areas of socio-cultural life. And so it seems increasingly important to confront it directly, and to unravel what lies behind this shadow life of religion in anthropological writing.

As has happened with so many of the analytical concepts that modernity wrought for us, this one has survived its deconstruction. As an anthropological concept, its origins in early modernist responses to the Christian tradition were relatively easy to identify and deconstruct. What we had not accounted for, however, was that, much like kinship,[2] in the meantime religion had acquired so much analytic resonance within the social sciences – and the social sciences had had such a deep impact on the way our world is made – that we were not able simply to do without it.

When we decided to call a group of colleagues to debate at the beautiful setting of the Max Planck Institute for Social Anthropology in Halle (Saale, Germany), we immediately saw that it was wisest to avoid the tyrannies and perplexities of definition. Although it might have seemed problematic to base a debate, and then a book, on a minimally defined concept, we reckoned that with religion, as with other historically inherited categories of our discipline, it is most fruitful to think in terms of Wittgenstein's 'family resemblances'. In other words, even though between the first and the last chapter in this collection there may not be a unitary or coherent use of the concept of religion, each individual chapter contains ideas and theoretical trajectories clearly connected to those of the others.

Certain themes, which in these chapters appear in slightly different guises, have been recurrent throughout the history of anthropological debate. In particular, the chapters illustrate the ways in which religion inhabits the margins of other socio-cultural areas; the ways it delineates groups and defines power; the ways in which, in its most marginal expressions, it often provides a powerful site of dissent or protest; and the ways its silencing or suppression fail to lead to its eradication. During our discussions, it became all too apparent that, indeed, any attempt to capture the central essence of religion inevitably led us away from faith towards its margins: the practices of submission and transmission of power that daily constitute religious life.[3]

The second broad parameter for our book – the notion of margins – generated among our colleagues a similar multiplicity of responses. Although marginality has been clearly addressed by all of the authors, the manner in which the concept is formulated and understood varies widely from paper to paper. In the social sciences, the idea of marginality/centrality has had a long and diverse history.[4] Over the past fifty years or so, anthropological thinking about marginality has been shaped within three broadly defined domains: as an aspect of space/time, as a marker of categorical distinctions which surround inequality, and as a conceptual basis for the idea of moral communities.

So, although neither religion nor margins is an easily definable concept, the two consistently interrelate in anthropological theory. In this sense, concentrating on the margins of religion allowed us to think in terms of places/spaces where overlap and fuzziness of categorical distinctions is not only unproblematic but is in fact anticipated and even integral to the complex processes of sociality.

II

As anthropologists began to work on class, gender, ethnicity and on personal and collective violence and trauma, they were forced to look beyond the 'centres' of religion, kinship, politics and power. It has become impossible to divorce the concept of margins from those areas of political and cultural life where religion is implicit and embedded: where it is written on the body, inscribed on built spaces and landscapes, or where it is present in a silenced or silent mode. Some of the most forceful examples of challenges to political and economic domination by subaltern or penumbral voices are to be found at the margins of religion – most of the chapters in this collection give evidence to that.

Focusing on places, objects, bodies, narratives and ritual spaces where religion may be found or inscribed, the authors in this book reveal the role of religion in contesting rights to places, to knowledge and to property, as well as access to resources. The chapters address the major problems engaging anthropologists working on religion in the twenty-first century: the association between religion, belief and power; religion and the state; religion and science; and religion and violence. Their ethnographic examples highlight the embodiment of religion and its location in landscapes, built spaces and religious sites which may be contested, physically or ideologically, or encased in memory and often in silence. Finally, they focus on religion as a set of knowledge practices, identifying different registers and genres within its history, and probing the boundary between religion and science.

Several chapters directly address issues of political and economic change in relation to religion, and all focus on situations of transition or change where participation and belief are marked by heteroglossia; the voices of the powerful meeting those of the subaltern in increasingly complicated ways. Taken together, they show the importance of religion as a resource to the believers: a source of solace, spiritual comfort and self-willed submission.

What the concept of margins evokes is that, in the process of construction of sociality, the appropriation of the world (time/space), social power, and symbolic constructs describing the world are all intimately linked. This conjunction (which is not absolute and which is highly differentiated contextually) is what the concept of hegemony[5] attempts to capture: that is, the notion that sociality is constructed through an appropriation of the world which involves the attribution to some of a capacity to speak in the name of others.

What must be noted, however, is that centrality and marginality, as understood in this context, cannot be seen in any bipolar fashion: 'margins' come in all shapes and sizes, as do 'centres', of course. Stephan Feuchtwang's chapter in this collection, for example, provides a good instance of the way in which margins and centres are mutually produced, being determined by categorical processes of differentiation that are not all of the same nature. There is no marginality without centrality but neither can ever be absolute.[6]

Marginality/centrality is a strikingly structural notion. The structural implications of the concept of marginality/centrality are useful precisely because they allow us to start thinking structurally again while escaping the formalist strictures of our earlier structuralisms. The idealist romance that enthralled anthropology in the 1990s, manifesting itself in all forms of discursivity, has revealed itself to be profoundly depressing to our work.[7] We will have to rediscover a way of dealing with structure in sociality that allows us to grasp processes of conjugation between areas of sociality as they are constructed.

Approached from this perspective, the concept of 'margins of religion' can be interpreted in a number of ways. Primarily, there is the distinction between being 'a margin' of something or 'on a margin' between things. This difference depends on the level of reckoning chosen: the thing observed, in the first case; or a higher level of relatedness, where things exist in relation to each other, in the second case. In process, therefore, the two perspectives are not mutually exclusive. Then, religion can either be treated as the object of consideration – the 'thing' – or it may be treated adjectivally – a quality of the 'thing'. Again the two cases are not logically exclusive, as they depend on perspective of observation. And, finally, there is the matter of temporality or, better still, process. If marginality/centrality is a structural notion, it is necessarily in flux.

This being the case, it should come as no surprise that our authors did not feel bound to separate these distinct uses of 'margins'. In fact, the concept of marginality/centrality was used by all of them, sometimes more explicitly, sometimes more implicitly, in a highly plastic and processual manner. Toying with levels and perspectives is precisely what must be done to carry out good ethnography, as this unrelenting process of shifting is of the very nature of social 'things'. For this reason, we choose to talk here of 'things' in order to convey nothing more than the simple fact that social life, being quintessentially a play on rationality, operates in propositional fashion.[8]

III

The book starts and ends with sections dealing with the wider reflexive issues of the relation between religion and anthropology and between religion and modernity. The central sections address the issue of the marginality of religion by relation to the three axes of marginality that we identified above: space/time, social power and categories of identity.

Part I starts the debate with two chapters addressing the central issue of the margins between religion and anthropology. João Vasconcelos looks at the way in which, at the turn of the nineteenth century, the mutual exclusiveness between science and religion constituted a problem for some of the most central figures of the social sciences at the time. In turn, Simon Coleman's essay dealing with 'gospel ethnography' highlights the way in which contemporary conservative Protestantism powerfully challenges the social sciences. He shows how this challenge, which in many ways constitutes a margin between different fields of discourse, is hardly marginal to the understanding of our contemporary world. These two papers highlight shifting discourses around the paired concepts of science and rationality and of religion and irrationality, and the ways in which contesting these pairings challenges the very concept of modernity (and hence of the pre-modern) – an issue to which we return at the end of the book.

The debate is then continued in Part II by three chapters dealing with the multiple ways in which religious marginality relates to spatial-temporal marginality. Here the authors reveal the role of religion in contesting rights to places, to knowledge and to property, as well as access to resources. Thomas Kirsch's essay on what he calls 'religious logistics' in a prophet-healing church in southern Zambia is a fascinating ethnographic counterpoint to Coleman's chapter. He explores the implications of the relation between modern roads and road transportation and the spread of religious faith, highlighting the ambiguities and marginalities implicit in that movement. Ursula Rao's chapter on temple building in urban India shows how the creation of religious spaces in ambiguous settings functions as a margin of negotiation of community boundaries and rights of belonging. Cornelia Sorabji's contribution introduces us to the complexities of ethno-religious politics and everyday practice in post-war Bosnia. Focussing on the war-torn neighbourhoods in Sarajevo, she suggests that the Islamic moral duty underpinning *komšiluk* (neighbourliness) may provide a key to reconciliation and a return to some kind of tolerance after the traumas and betrayals wrought by neighbour upon neighbour during the war years.

The chapters in Part III address the issue of the margins of religion from the angle of relative centrality and its relation to political power. They do this in highly differentiated ways. Whilst Grant Evans' essay on the revival of Buddhist royal family rituals focuses on the way in which formulations of religious centrality are politically challenged and negotiated in contemporary Laos, Stephan Feuchtwang's chapter on extravagance, vulgarity and pomp in rural festivals in China (southern Fukien) examines the political consequences of the way in which centrality is constituted by those who know themselves not to be central. In these contributions we see poignantly exemplified the way in which all centrality is relative, thus consequently implying that marginality is pervasive.

Religious options have deep implications in identity claims, opening spaces of ambiguity that are also spaces of creativity. In Part IV, Galina Lindquist follows this trail by dealing with the way in which emerging political identities in the post-Soviet period interacted ambiguously with religion in the southern Siberian Republic of Tuva. Lindquist shows that the field of 'religion' is occupied by more than one claimant in Tuva and its margins are hardly decipherable.

In contrast to this chapter – but as a further exploration of the relations between margins, identity, and power – Agnieszka Kościańska's essay deals with a startling example of how religion can be used to work on identity in the field of gender relations. She studies female converts to a New Age movement of Hindu inspiration who are committed to strict sexual abstinence and inflexible dietary practices, even when they are married and have a family. The new attitudes of these converts contrast violently with established Polish notions of motherhood and femininity. This radical religious challenge to gender stereotypes provides us with a fascinating example of how gender relations are negotiated 'on the margins of religion'.

Finally, Part V closes the book with three chapters where the transmission of religious beliefs and dispositions is seen to be operating in relation to discourses on modernity in surprising ways. Ramon Sarró's chapter on the Baga of coastal Guinea-Conakry shows how the transmission of religion works on many fronts, some of which are only apparently marginal to it. The Baga's recent conversion to Islam (1956/7) is seen by them as part of a process of entering modernity. They feel deeply engaged with Islam, yet on closer inspection their religious landscape encloses a wealth of material that originates within traditional religious belief, and is transmitted in a silenced way, on the margins of religion.

The issue of modernity and its confrontation with the transmission of religious dispositions is yet again central to the essay on Chinese geomancy in colonial and post-colonial Hong Kong, written by Rubie and James Watson. Geomancy (*fengshui*), itself on the margins of religion, was and has remained deeply intermeshed with communal politics and the social constitution of space in southern China. Yet, the authors conclude that the tough restrictions on the use of space in Hong Kong's cramped environment will probably lead to a collapse of the social centrality of geomantic practices.

The book ends with a striking exercise on the way in which religious dispositions can mediate in marginal ways the access to modernity – providing modes of relating to the momentous changes that it brings along. Jonathan Parry dissects the tales he heard concerning the practice of human sacrifice in the building of large industrial infrastructures in central India. His study deals with a Soviet-built steel plant and the beliefs concerning human sacrifice that surrounded its construction. Parry concludes with a debate on sacrifice as a means through which humans 'accomplish immortal deeds by transcending their mortal limits' – an example par excellence of the way in which marginality constitutes power in human concerns.

IV

In short, rather than engaging directly the institutions of mainstream religions or the grand theories concerning magic, science or religion, the authors in this book focused on the politics of religion, on epistemologies and paradigms of spirituality and science, and on those areas of silence, ambiguity and forgetting, where religion and belief are hidden, subdued or suppressed. They all chose to look beyond the dominant texts of world religion to the notes and alternative scripts written in the margins. Moving away from Durkheimian assumptions concerning religion, as a morally binding force for collective identification and identity, their emphasis shifted to the far more uneasy and less conciliatory terrain of relations of hierarchy, conflict and exclusion. Even when cohesion and equality are stressed, the authors avoid a socio-centric perspective, locating the practices and beliefs they describe in open and constantly reflexive processes of communication that reinforce power as much as they create it.

As a whole, this collection of chapters aims to contribute towards a renewed interest in anthropological comparativism, suggesting a 'lateral' approach to universalism. In his essay concerning the meaning of the concept of religion, Rodney Needham (1981, Chap. 4) identified three main hurdles that must be overcome if one is to engage such issues comparatively: (a) the 'Aristotelian tradition of classification', which incites us to look for a 'common essence' to the phenomena we study, instead of approaching their resemblance as being of an indirect or sporadic nature; (b) a 'stress on inner states', which leads us to expect to find 'a peculiar cast of mind' among the adherents; and (c) a tendency to use 'a ceremonial aesthetics' that may not be the appropriate one to judge other traditions (1981: 90). Looking back on our debates, it would seem that the strategy of focusing on the margins yielded good fruit, allowing us to stay clear of some of the central problems these hurdles would pose.

What strikes us as surprising, however, is how the issue of the relation between science and religion has not lost any of its actuality today, more than a century after the debates concerning spiritism that Vasconcelos identifies. A quick search through the Internet will show how, after twenty years, Needham's critique of the concept of religion continues to rankle on as a source of contention, with the correspondent attempts at derision. Indeed, as Simon Coleman's essay shows, anthropology today faces new challenges from the forms of globalised religion that increasingly mark our world in the twenty-first century.

The fact is that there has been a deep change in the terms of the debate. When Needham approached these issues, his implicit unitary 'we' was constituted by 'Western scientists' and his implicit 'them' by the polymorphic ethnographic register. Today, such bipolarity is no longer valid and the play of power that implicitly backed it is not in place. Many of us (anthropologists) do not claim to be 'Western' and, in any case, it is not at all clear that 'Western' scientists are the most likely to embody the ethnocentric strains of the Judeo-Christian historical background of our scientific debate. Furthermore, the demands made by 'believers' on scientists are being backed by power claims that can hardly be identified simply as 'Western'.

The contributors to this volume do not focus their debates on the traditional tropes of doctrine, faith and ritual. Instead, they look at the margins of religion and between religions. Their work focuses on processes, on change and on power relations. Repeatedly, they show that in relation to religion the issue of modernity continues today to be of central concern.

The issue of modernity and its ambivalences pervades the whole book, from Vasconcelos' essay on spiritualism and Coleman's study of conservative Protestantism to Sarró's essay on the silent survival of Baga's pre-modern religion or Parry's chapter on human sacrifice at a modern construction site. Through analyses of specific historical processes in terms of responses to socio-economic and political change, the chapters consider, implicitly or explicitly, the problematic relation between science (including social sciences and anthropology in particular) and religion, and the ways that this connects to the new religious globalisation of the twenty-first century.

Notes

1. Cf. Needham 1981, esp. Chap. 4 'Characteristics of Religion' or Asad 1983.
2. Cf. Needham 1974 and Carsten 2004.
3. It seems worthwhile to note that 'power' is here used as the opposite of 'violence' in the sense proposed by Hanna Arendt when she claims that 'power needs no justification, being inherent in the very existence of political communities; what it does need is legitimacy' (1970: 52).
4. Cf. Pina-Cabral 1997.
5. Cf. Kate Crehan's (2002) useful study of the Gramscian concept of 'hegemony' and its relations to the anthropological concept of 'culture'.
6. In this sense, the relationship between margins and centre is asymmetrical, much in the same way as the relationship between alterity and identity (cf. Lévinas 1996: 34–38). For the contradictoriness of centrality see Derrida (1967: 410); for an ethnographic operationalisation of the notion see Pina-Cabral (2001: 220–21).
7. Cf. Pina-Cabral 2005. Observations of this kind are starting to do the rounds: e.g., 'one cannot simply continually respond to the unknown, and make absence and the non-relational as the only relationship with the world' (Gafijczuk 2005: 31).
8. Cf. Gafijczuk's discussion of the notion of 'thing'. He starts from Durkheim's comment in *The Rules of Sociological Method* that 'to treat facts of a certain order as things is … not to place them in this or that category of reality; it is to observe towards them a certain attitude of the mind' (quoted in 2005: 24). Then he argues that 'A "thing" … in its closest, most intimate definition, is not an object (even though as an empirical construct of its own kind it also presents *resistance*), is not dead or inert matter; it is not something, which faces us mutely, but rather a general way of connecting and corresponding with the world via a response, which allows us access to the structure of a reality as the effect and form of signifying representation.' (2005: 30).

References

Arendt, Hanna. 1970. *On Violence*. New York: Harcourt Brace and Co.
Asad, Talal. 1983. 'Anthropological Conceptions of Religion: Reflections on Geertz', *Man* 18(2): 237–59.
Carsten, Janet. 2004. *After Kinship*. Cambridge: Cambridge University Press.
Crehan, Kate. 2002. *Gramsci: Culture and Anthropology*. London: Pluto Press.
Derrida, Jacques. 1967. *L'écriture et la différence*. Paris: Seuil.
Gafijczuk, D. 2005. 'The Way of the Social: From Durkheim's Society to a Postmodern Sociality', *History of the Social Sciences* 18(3): 17–33.
Glazier, Stephen. 1997. 'Introduction', in S. Glazier (ed.), *Anthropology of Religion: A Handbook*. London: Greenwood Press, pp. 31–52.
Lambek, Michael. 2002. 'General Introduction', in M. Lambek (ed.), *A Reader in the Anthropology of Religion*. Oxford: Blackwell, 1–16.
Lévinas, Emmanuel. 1996. *Basic Philosophical Writings*. Eds A. Peperzak, S. Critchley and R. Bernasconi. Bloomington: Indiana University Press.

Needham, Rodney. 1974. *Remarks and Inventions: Sceptical Essays about Kinship*. London: Tavistock.
———. 1981. *Circumstantial Deliveries*. Berkeley: University of California Press.
Pina-Cabral, João de. 1997. 'The Threshold Diffused: Margins, Hegemonies and Contradictions in Contemporary Anthropology', in Patrick McAllister (ed.), *Culture and the Commonplace: Anthropological Essays in Honour of David Hammond-Tooke*. Johannesburg: Witwatersrand University Press, pp. 1–5.
———. 2001. *Between China and Europe: Person, Culture and Emotion*. London and New York: London School of Economics Monographs in Social Anthropology/ Continuum Books.
———. 2005. 'The Future of Social Anthropology'. *Social Anthropology* 13(2): 119–28.

Part I

Anthropology and Religion

Chapter 2

Homeless Spirits: Modern Spiritualism, Psychical Research and the Anthropology of Religion in the Late Nineteenth and Early Twentieth Centuries[1]

João Vasconcelos

Spiritism is the new science which has come to reveal to mankind, by means of irrefutable proofs, the existence and nature of the spiritual world and its relationship with the physical world. It appears not as something supernatural, but on the contrary, as one of the living and active forces of Nature, source of an immense number of phenomena which still today are not fully understood, and because of this they are relegated to the world of fantasy and miracles. (Allan Kardec, 1864, *The Gospel According to Spiritism*)[2]

How often has 'Science' killed off all spook-philosophy, and laid ghosts and raps and 'telepathy' away underground as so much popular delusion? Yet never before were these things offered us so voluminously, and never in such authentic-seeming shape or with such good credentials. The tide seems steadily to be rising, in spite of all the expedients of scientific orthodoxy. It is hard not to suspect that here may be something different from a mere chapter in human gullibility. It may be a genuine realm of natural phenomena. (William James, 1909, 'The Confidences of a "Psychical Researcher"')[3]

Introduction

Ambiguous objects are a good tool through which to examine the foundations of discreet categories. Spiritism, the spiritualist movement based on the doctrine established by the French educator Allan Kardec in the 1850s, is one such object. It announced itself as a 'scientific religion' or 'religious science', the 'science of the spirits'. Yet neither established sciences nor established religions recognised it as a legitimate relative. Another of these eccentric objects is psychical research, a tradition coeval with Kardecism, which reached its peak around 1900 and came to be what is now called parapsychology. In this essay I aim to identify some reasons for the sense of strangeness these objects provoke.

To this effect, I shall discuss the circumstances under which so-called modern spiritualism, psychical research and Kardec's spiritist doctrine have emerged within the context of the *pax moderna* between science and religion, accepting some of its terms while contesting others. Our modern state of affairs is founded on the presumption that different domains of reality correspond to specific modes of evidence, and on the attribution of different kinds of social power and dignity to those distinct modes. The natural world can be the object of *scientific experiments*, while spirits and divinity may be the object of *religious experiences*. I will argue that spiritualism, and most especially Kardecism and psychical research, put so much faith in the scientific mode of producing evidence that they wished to extend it to the world of spirits, hoping that it would reveal itself, as William James imagined, as 'a genuine realm of natural phenomena'. But the idea of a science of spirits seems to violate a constitutional principle of our modernity: how can we pretend to know scientifically that which must be excluded from consideration in order to produce scientific knowledge?

In the first part of the chapter, I will present a short summary of the early history of modern spiritualism and psychical research. I will emphasise the fact that many followers of both movements longed for reconciliation between science and religion and they saw in the naturalisation of the spiritual the means to achieve it. 'Spiritual' phenomena might well not be supernatural phenomena; they could belong instead to a still unknown nature. In the second part, I will speak about how the modern abyss between science and religion came about. I will argue that the social marginalisation of spiritualism and psychical research – that is to say, their homelessness – partially stems from both of them wanting to apply science's mode of evidence to matters that have remained, by very definition, on the other side of the wall, on the side of religion. This discussion will be continued and particularised in the third part of the chapter, where I will examine the way in which one of the founding works of the anthropology of religion, Edward Burnett Tylor's *Primitive Culture*, was criticised by two of the founding fathers of modern sociology and psychology, Émile Durkheim and Sigmund Freud, as well as by anthropologists and psychical researchers Alfred Russel Wallace and Andrew Lang. In the fourth part, I will examine Allan Kardec's spiritist doctrine and focus on two questions: the question of scientificity and the question of proof.

There is considerable terminological variation within the studies on spiritualism. For this reason, and also since I will be dealing here with texts written originally in different language traditions, I must start by making the adopted terminology clear so as to avoid misunderstandings. I use the expressions 'spiritualism' and 'modern spiritualism' alternatively to refer to a set of practices of communication with spirits and associated theories that have developed since the mid-nineteenth century. I have decided to use these terms following the current English usage, although I am aware that some confusion may arise. 'Spiritualism', for instance, is often used in contrast to 'sensualism' and 'materialism', but the philosophical discussions in which these antinomies make sense are not exactly the point in modern spiritualism.[4]

The word 'spiritism' was coined by Allan Kardec (1804–1869) to designate the doctrine whose basic principle is, in his words, 'the relation of the material world with spirits, or the beings of the invisible world'. 'For new ideas' Kardec wrote, 'new words are needed'. To speak of 'spiritualism' to refer to the experience of communicating with spiritual entities would easily give rise to confusion and misunderstanding. 'Everyone is a spiritualist who believes that there is in him something more than matter, but it does not follow that he believes in the existence of spirits, or in their communication with the visible world'.[5] Kardec's *spiritisme* is only one of the spiritualist traditions that emerged in the second half of the nineteenth century. I will refer to it as 'Spiritism' or, alternatively, as 'Kardecism'. Followers of modern spiritualism and subjects related to that movement will be named 'spiritualist', while followers of Kardec's Spiritism and anything concerning that doctrine will be referred to as 'spiritist' or 'Kardecist'. Now with the matter of terminology settled, let us pass on to the history.

Modern Spiritualism, Psychical Research and the Naturalisation of the Supernatural

The origin of modern spiritualism is usually traced back to a number of events that occurred in 1848 in the United States. That year, a family of farmers who had just moved into Hydesville, a small village near Rochester in the interior of New York State, was disturbed by the sounds of rapping and of objects being dragged about. Kate and Margaretta, the Fox's teenage daughters, came to the conclusion that the noises were communicating some kind of intelligence. By asking questions out loud and establishing codes for the raps as answers (one for 'no', two for 'yes'), the Fox sisters learnt to communicate with the entity that was allegedly producing the sounds. It turned out to be the spirit of a man who had been murdered in that house five years before and whose body had been buried in the cellar by the murderer. In young America, just as in old Europe, noisy manifestations attributed to spirits or ghosts were far from being a novelty. The episode with the Fox sisters might not have developed much further had they not invented a code, a basic language to communicate with the spirits. As Arthur Conan Doyle wrote, 'however humble the operator at either end, the spiritual telegraph was at last working'.[6]

Experiments with communicating with the other world spread like wild fire throughout North America and every continent. The diffusion of spiritualism went together with the establishment of psychical research, later to be known as parapsychology. Spiritualists and psychical researchers came close in that they were both interested in the same phenomena, but diverged in the reasons for doing so. At first, spiritualism was a fashion that swept through middle-class homes, very often through the women in the household. Later it grew popular, mainly in urban centres. People would get together and invite friends to meetings around three-legged tables that might end up levitating, turning and rapping out answers to questions put to them. Meanwhile, the number of women and men who emerged as mediums kept growing. Many people sought them out in order to communicate with the spirits of deceased family members, to hear the testimonies from beyond the tomb brought by the spirits of celebrities, or else to find solutions to problems called 'psychic' – a word that had a more ecumenical meaning at that time than it usually has now. In Britain, spiritualist churches flourished, usually organised around some charismatic medium.[7]

Among the psychical researchers, there were more or less confident spiritualists and there were also people who attended the séances to observe the mediums' performance from a position of scepticism as to the existence of spirits, and who looked for the origin of the phenomena they registered in the mediums' own psychism. This attitude prevailed, albeit not exclusively, in parapsychology from the 1930s onwards, and nowadays can be seen in a variety of approaches that range from the field of psychoanalysis to that of the neurosciences.[8] However, in the second half of the nineteenth century and the early twentieth century, the central concerns of psychical research were the soul's existence and immortality, and the existence of immaterial worlds or planes of the material that momentarily eluded the instruments of objectification hitherto developed by science. And, as the historian Janet Oppenheim puts it, 'some psychical researchers were as eager as the spiritualists to force the methods of science into the service of an unseen, immaterial world'.[9]

Within the spiritualist hypothesis, various subsidiary ones existed about the nature and characteristics of that spiritual world of which the phenomena produced by the mediums afforded a glimpse. The most popular seems to have been that which we could call the animist hypothesis. The Italian psychiatrist and criminal anthropologist Cesare Lombroso (1835–1909) was one of its adherents. In a book he wrote towards the end of his life, he tried to demonstrate that neither telepathic communication nor the eruption of the unconscious sufficed to explain some of the phenomena of which he had gathered eyewitness accounts or of which he actually testified during spiritualist sessions. These hypotheses failed to explain, for instance, the alleged fact that mediums temporarily lost up to half their body weight when helping the spirit materialise and immediately recovered it afterwards. Lombroso argued that phenomena such as this could only be understood by accepting the intervention of spiritual entities. He also maintained that the soul outlived the body's demise and that it was accompanied by a 'fluid material, visible and tangible in certain cases' and 'whose molecular constitution must be the same as that of the radiant bodies'.[10]

William James (1843–1916), the American philosopher and psychologist, was another distinguished intellectual who was a supporter of psychical research. He devoted the last twenty-five years of his life to it.[11] Whereas Lombroso concerned himself mostly with questions of the soul surviving death and the mechanics of mediumship, James was more enthusiastic about the possibility of the existence of a universal pan-psychism. This would be a kind of 'cosmic consciousness' or 'common reservoir of consciousness', which mediums managed to penetrate intuitively without knowing the mechanisms that allowed them to do so nor the real nature of this occult territory.[12] One can recognise in this hypothesis ideas reminiscent of mesmerism or animal magnetism, a theory outlined by Franz Anton Mesmer (1734–1815), an Austrian physician who had postulated the existence of an imponderable magnetic fluid that kept in relation all sorts of bodies and beings in the universe. The Mesmeric theory of the magnetic fluid and the practice of healing passes were also two of the most important sources of modern spiritualism.[13]

James's speculations owed a great deal to the work of Frederic Myers (1843–1901), an English scholar who, together with a group of fellow academics from Cambridge University, founded the British Society for Psychical Research. Myers introduced the notion of 'subliminal self' to designate that magma unattainable to usual consciousness which surged in 'the disintegrative streams of consciousness that were manifested in hysteria, the personality absorbing cosmic metetherial energy in sleep, and the personality rising to new spiritual awareness in ecstasy and sleep'.[14] Myers's ideas influenced most members of the British Society for Psychical Research, including James, who was president of the society between 1894 and 1895.[15] It does not necessarily follow that the author of *Pragmatism* and *The Varieties of Religious Experience* was a spiritualist in the strict sense of the word. Shortly before he died, James defined his position in relation to the so-called psychic phenomena in the following manner: 'I personally am as yet neither a convinced believer in parasitic demons, nor a spiritist, nor a scientist, but still remain a psychical researcher waiting for more facts before concluding'.[16]

Lombroso and James were just two of a number of scientists and intellectuals who between the second half of the nineteenth century and the early twentieth century became interested in the 'psychic' or 'spiritic' phenomena that had caused such a furore among the middle class, and who set themselves to investigating their credibility and identifying the forces that produced them. The names of those men of science are still recalled in spiritualist and spiritist circles whenever the scientificity of their respective cosmologies is at stake.

The historian Jenny Hazelgrove claims in her book about the implantation of spiritualism in British society between the first and second world wars that most people who adhered to the movement did not do so exactly 'to shore up failing faith in a metaphysical universe. For many, the supernatural realities of their lives were omnipresent; for some, they were burdensome. What Spiritualism offered to such individuals was a way of organising supernatural experiences and assumptions in relation to existing cultural realities'.[17] It so happened that one of the 'existing cultural realities' that often framed the reorganisation of experiences and ideas relating to the *supernatural* within intellectual and scientific circles was, paradoxically, the rejection of the idea of such a realm. Hence James's hope that, in place of the mysterious wonders until then observed, a new realm of *natural phenomena* was on the brink of being discovered.

In order to disclose the world of spirits as a true realm of natural phenomena, the spirits had first to be taken to the laboratory and submitted to procedures of proof designed to produce scientific facts. Scientific knowledge is produced within a particular regime of comprehension which, adopting Élisabeth Claverie's suggestion, we can call the 'regime of proof'. The possibility of understanding by means of proof depends on the ability to objectify what we want to prove. Objectification is 'a process of demonstration which may be reproduced at any stage within a similar Cartesian 'space'.[18] The regime of proof is a regime of factualisation which produces ponderable, measurable and calculable facts. The investment of great expectations as well as major human and material resources into the comprehension of the world by means of the regime of proof is one of the distinctive features of modernity. This investment stimulates the invention of techniques and instruments of objectification, from statistics to radioscopy, which continuously stretches the limits of the ponderable.

In the second half of the nineteenth and the start of the twentieth century, the prospect of spirits – possibly under new names – being understood within the framework of the scientific regime of factualisation did not seem perhaps as extravagant as it was to seem later. The world at that time was one in which science was developing everyday new techniques and instruments that could give objective reality to beings, materials and forces until then ignored, and that could capture in the web of ponderability beings, materials and forces which had hitherto marvelled humankind. It was in no way implausible that, sooner or later, the soul and spirits could also be objectified. This was the hope of people such as James and the firm conviction of others such as Lombroso. Most scientists and most religious minds, however, thought that those who nurtured these hopes and convictions could not possibly be in their right minds. What were the reasons for this prejudice?

Homeless Spirits in the Age of Science and Religion

In a book about the twilight of the entities called *exotiká* (hauntings, demons and fantastic beings) in contemporary everyday life in rural Greece, the anthropologist Charles Stewart states that the reason why Greek peasants tend to despise 'folkloric models' for understanding the world is not that they weigh them on the same scale of merits as they do to the 'scientific models':

> In my view it seems unlikely that this should be the sole mechanism, or even the most important one. On a daily basis ridicule and affectivity are more apparent and probably more immediately felt forces prompting the suppression of the *exotiká* as a vital body of thought. In practice, the *exotiká* are vanishing amidst sounds of mockery; they are being blotted out by emotions such as embarrassment, *not* by the action of silent contemplation leading to enlightenment.[19]

In the seemingly far distant land of the scientific institutions and universities of a hundred years ago, the dread of shrieks of laughter also helped to keep certain unwelcome *exotiká* at bay, inhibiting the investment in certain sorts of research. Lombroso was very clear about it in the preface to his book *Hypnotism and Spiritism*:

> When I planned to write a book about the so-called spiritic phenomena, after an entire life devoted to the development of psychiatry and criminal anthropology, my best friends harassed me with objections, saying that I was going to ruin my reputation. Despite that, I did not vacillate and kept on, for I thought it was my duty to crown my career of fights for the progress of ideas fighting for the most contested and baffled idea of the century.[20]

Lombroso was not the only reputed anthropologist of his time to give credit to the spiritualist hypothesis. Alfred Russel Wallace, for instance, the British anthropologist and naturalist who I will speak about later and who became famous for having presented concurrently with Charles Darwin the theory of the evolution of species through natural selection, was also a psychical researcher and a convinced spiritualist. And just as Lombroso had, he was also to know the stigma that hang over those men of science who allowed themselves to be seduced by the possibility of naturalising the spirits. The first pamphlet he wrote on the subject, 'The Scientific Aspects of the Supernatural' (1866), was received by his colleagues 'with deep disappointment'.[21]

My aim in this section is to seek some reasons why spiritualism was 'the most baffled idea' of the age of science and why scientists who were interested in it were looked at askance by their peers. In order to answer these questions, the path I will follow here consists in placing the emergence of spiritualism and psychical research within the context of the modern separation between science and religion. Of course, this is just one of many possible ways to account for the social marginalisation of spiritualism and psychical research, and by no means do I want to argue that it is a sufficient approach. But I will feel satisfied if I manage to convince the reader that it is a good way, a pertinent and fruitful way to tell the story.

We can begin by calling to mind a well-known passage by Max Weber (1864–1920) about the 'rationalisation' and the concomitant 'disenchantment of the world', which were for the German sociologist two of the most characteristic features of Western techno-scientific modernity. In a lecture he gave in 1918 at Munich University, Weber discussed the meaning of the so-called modern 'intellectualist rationalisation' in the following manner:

> Does it mean that we, today, for instance, everyone sitting in this hall, have a greater knowledge of the conditions of life under which we exist than has an American Indian or a Hottentot? Hardly. ... The savage knows incomparably more about his tools. ... The increasing intellectualization and rationalization do *not*, therefore, indicate an increased and general knowledge of the conditions under which one lives. It means something else, namely, the knowledge or belief that if one but wished one *could* learn it at any time. Hence, it means that principally there are no mysterious incalculable forces that come into play, but rather that one can, in

principle, master all things by calculation. This means that the world is disenchanted. One need no longer have recourse to magical means in order to master or implore the spirits, as did the savage, for whom such mysterious powers existed. Technical means and calculation perform the service. This above all is what intellectualization means.[22]

This extract from 'Science as a Vocation' has been endlessly cited and commented on. I just want to highlight here the penetrating statement that modern techno-scientific rationalisation is based on a belief which is itself exempted of rational and scientific fundamentation: the belief according to which 'there are no mysterious incalculable forces that come into play'. Spirits, magic and divinity itself are the paradigms of these mysterious and imponderable forces. What Weber teaches us is that the demise of such forces – or, in other words, the 'disenchantment of the world' – is not a consequence of scientific knowledge. On the contrary, it is an expectation that precedes it and is one of the conditions of its production.[23]

These ideas of Weber's can be read as a symptom – more than a diagnostic – of a certain kind of experience of modernity. In fact, I believe they gain by being thought of as expressions of the peculiar cognitive separation between nature, society and divinity which, as Bruno Latour argues, is constitutive of Western modernity. In Latour's terms, nature, society and divinity were set up in modernity not merely as realms appended to separate institutions (science, state and church), but more radically as distinct ontological realms, 'three regions of Being'.[24] Latour also argues that the separation of these three domains was well succeeded inasmuch as it was carried out along with the institution of a set of guarantees that prevented them from being thought of together. Questions relating to divinity were separated from those concerning nature, and both were kept away from questions dealing with society. 'Nobody is truly modern unless he accepts to separate God from the game of natural laws as well as those of the Republic'.[25] This is the foundation of modern secularism. And this is the condition under which divinity can exist in modernity. Divinity only becomes comprehensible and acceptable in metaphysics (a realm of theoretical speculation in which proof through objectification plays no part and hence does not compete with science) and in spirituality (as revealed in 'the intimacy of heart' of each person). These are thus the general conditions of the pax moderna between religion, the state and science.

But modern secularism is not only based on the separation between science, religion and politics. It also implies that the state ascribes different levels of legitimacy to the knowledge produced and transmitted by scientific and religious institutions. Scientific knowledge became the standard of what can be considered 'knowledge', knowledge based on objective facts. Religious knowledge, not observing the regime of proof, was integrated in modern life as a 'belief'. As Talal Asad wrote, 'where knowledge is rooted either in an a-Christian everyday life or in an a-religious science, the Christian apologist tends not to regard belief as the conclusion to a knowledge process but as its precondition'.[26] The fact that religious men and women are commonly called 'believers' – and that they describe themselves as such – illustrates very well how intimate the association between 'belief' and 'religion' has grown. By the peculiar arrangement of powers that shaped modern lay states, 'religious belief' turned into a matter of individual choice and religious institutions were left in competition in a nominally free market, whereas 'scientific knowledge' turned into a matter of public interest promoted by the state and collectivised through school education.

That which Asad and Labour point out is the hegemonisation of the public domain by laicism and the privatisation of religion, its nominal transformation into a question of individual consciousness. This in no way means that people are less religious in modernity than in other civilisational settings. The suggestion is that they are religious in a different manner. They learnt, we all learnt 'a totally individual and totally spiritual religion [that] allowed a critique of both the prominence of science and that of society, without forcing to bring God into none of them. It became possible for moderns to be lay and devout at the same time'.[27]

We also learnt that scientific knowledge is, unlike religion, a fair source for common knowledge. But, of course, most of us have not learnt to know scientifically, and none of us has learnt to know scientifically even the tiniest part of the world we live in. As Weber pointed out, the hegemony that science has conquered in the public domain does not mean that most people have grown to understand the world in scientific terms. Being produced in a regime of factualisation that entails extremely specialised languages, instruments and procedures, scientific knowledge is generally accepted as true on the basis of the credibility ascribed to the specialists and institutions that produce it. The moderns who are not scientists only learn – and learn before all else in the lay schools set up and supervised by the state – to rely on science and its procedures as the source of secure knowledge and to realise that spirits, deprived of the security that science can give, are not part of hegemonic vocabulary. This learning of secularism did not stop people from continuing to learn to be religious. The disenchanted worlds that Weber spoke of are the world of the exercise of science and the world of the conventions of modern citizenship. We may continue to be religious, but religious life is placed formally in a world apart.

Now it was precisely this state of affairs, just as it was becoming established, that spiritualism and psychical research in the second half of the nineteenth century came to challenge, with their erratic quest to naturalise the world of sprits. Psychical research and spiritualism (especially in its Kardecist variant) were decidedly modern intellectual undertakings in that they derived from a keen awareness of the separation between science and religion. They accepted the hierarchy of knowledge that establishes scientific proof as the hegemonic criteria of credibility and the private interest and controversial character of religious knowledge. And they took science so much to heart that they wanted to draw the soul, spirits, magic and divinity towards it and free them from the yoke of religion. By taking that step, however, they violated a prohibition. The idea of removing spirits from their environment and bringing them into the laboratory could not but seem impertinent, ridiculous or disturbing to most of those who had interiorised the premises of the modern constitution, be they atheist or religious. After all, didn't the sprits belong by definition to the realm of 'religious belief'? Wasn't to know scientifically by definition to know without appealing to the spirits and to divinity?

As we shall see in the fourth part of this chapter – when we speak about Kardec's ideas on what could be a 'science of the spirits' – this sentiment of absurdity was not the only obstacle hindering the scientific objectification of the otherworld. But it was undoubtedly an important obstacle in that it consigned psychical research to a thoroughly marginal and even dubious place in the field of the sciences. This marginalisation has obvious consequences of a practical nature. It makes it difficult to raise funds for investigation and recruit brains willing to take up a seemingly lost cause. In Britain, for instance, where a Society for Psychical Research has existed for over a century, the contemporary panorama of parapsychological research is not very heartening. The majority of the Society's members who devote themselves to investigation are autodidacts with no connection to academia who group themselves in regional associations.[28]

The homelessness of the spirits in the world of science is a correlate of the homelessness of the scientists who are committed to the research on 'spiritual' and 'paranormal' phenomena. They all speak in low tones and creep around on the margins of the socially visible.[29] In the field of social and human sciences, however, some paths have opened up for spirits to be integrated as scientific objects. This is what we shall see now as we look into some debates over the status of spirits and other religious ideas that took place during the dawning of the anthropology of religion.

On the Margins of Anthropology: Modern Spiritualism and Animism

In the world of science, and even in the narrow world of the social sciences and humanities, anthropology still holds the reputation of having an overpowering compulsion to seek out extravagant objects and suspicious company. There often is some fire where there is smoke. It is true that, among other social scientists, anthropologists are notoriously the most interested in spirits, witchcraft and rituals – matters of interest as well to parapsychologists and spiritualists of various sorts. And it is even true that there are anthropologists who are interested in these things not only as objects of cultural comprehension and sociological analysis, but also as possible gateways into new paradigms of understanding human life and the universe. We need not even call to mind the anthropologist-shaman Carlos Castañeda, that mysterious and liminal figure. Suffice to remember that the veteran anthropologist Margaret Mead was also a trustee of the American Society for Psychical Research and a member of its research committee.[30] Alternatively, read for instance the unconventional interpretation of ritual healing that Edith Turner recently presented in her book *Experiencing Ritual*.[31]

These cases, however, are more the exception than the rule. Most anthropologists who study subjects such as witchcraft, possession and spiritual healing are only too familiar with the border that separates anthropology from barmylogy and they keep the commandment: 'Thou shalt not bring spirits into thy office'. Or rather, you can bring them only under certain conditions. Let us look at an example. In an article in which he examines in a very interesting manner a number of poltergeist cases that involve teenage girls, the anthropologist David Hess explains his perspective in the following terms:

> The approach adopted here brackets the question of the mechanisms that could explain the various incidents: children's pranks, neighbours' attacks, dissociated behaviour, exaggerated reporting, telergy, psychokinesis, spirits, and so on. Whatever the mechanisms, the family members' discussion of the case reveals how in their minds it is linked up with domestic conflicts ...[32]

The epistemology of the social sciences has firmly anchored in itself this methodological decision, which consists of setting aside examination of the mechanisms at play in the phenomena attributed to the action of spiritual forces, as well as the prior question of their objective reality, and instead to accept them on face value and examine their intersubjective reality (that is, to examine within various theoretical frameworks the ways the phenomena exist 'in the minds' and life forms of the 'natives'). This epistemology determines which questions make sense in the social and human sciences' language games and which ones do not. 'So, do spirits exist or not beyond the lives of the people you are studying?' is an example of what is very likely a pointless question to put to a contemporary social scientist. However, things were not always quite like this. As we shall see, at the end of the nineteenth century when anthropology of religion was in its infancy, there were still a few snipers who managed to fire across the barricade that separated questions that could be asked in the social sciences from those that could be asked in psychical research.

In 1871 Edward Burnett Tylor (1832–1917) published his book *Primitive Culture: Researches into the Development of Mythology, Philosophy, Religion, Language, Art and Custom*. Tylor is considered the founding father of British anthropology and *Primitive Culture* is generally regarded as a founding work of the anthropology of religion. Using his encyclopaedic knowledge of beliefs and myths collected among primitive peoples and written traditions of ancient civilisations, Tylor defended the thesis that belief in spiritual beings (which he called 'animism') is the embryonic, minimum and universal nucleus of religion. No culture has existed that does not hold the idea that human beings, living beings in general as well as even inert objects are animated by a diaphanous double, or the idea that these spiritual forces can make themselves independent of their bodies and the idea that they have a life of their own and survive death or destruction of their physical sustainers. Tylor also advanced a speculative intellectualist theory to explain the origin of animism. The idea of soul – from which the ideas of spirit and divinity were to evolve later – was the result of the thoughts sparked by the awe early man felt when he saw his companions and familiar beings and objects doubled in his dreams, during trance or in other altered states.

Not only is *Primitive Culture* a key work because of its great breadth and its aim to construct a general theory of religion, but also because the most influential works in the anthropology and sociology of religion that appeared in the following decades were manifestly produced in critical dialogue with Tylor's theses.[33] The most famous response to Tylor, and the one with longer-lasting effects on the history of the social sciences was presented by Émile Durkheim (1858–1917) in *Les formes élémentaires de la vie religieuse* (1912). Apart from including a chapter entirely devoted to refuting Tylor's intellectualist speculations, the French sociologist's book can be regarded in many aspects as a kind of negative form of the English anthropologist's book. What most concerned Durkheim in Tylor's work was his theory about the origin of the idea of soul, ordinarily known as the 'dream theory', which reduced religion to 'a system of hallucinatory representations with no objective fundament'.[34] Durkheim could not admit that a system of representations without an objective basis could have lasted for thousands of years and still be operative in the age of science.[35] If religion persisted, it was because it was fulfilling some essential function in society.

His emphasis on social function led Durkheim to shift the essence of religion from belief to ritual and from the individual to the collective. It also led him to find the elementary forms of religious life in the collective rituals of some Australian aboriginal peoples. The emotion and, with it, the idea of divinity would have been born out of the states of 'collective effervescence' generated by ritual action. Divinity was nothing but the other name for society, the true source and object of religious life. Religion thus had an 'objective fundament' and could only be said to be an 'illusion' if by that one meant that religion expressed its object, for convenience, in a symbolic form. Moreover, Durkheim believed that 'there is in religion something eternal destined to survive all particular symbols in which religious thought successively enwraps itself. There cannot be a society that doesn't feel the need to preserve and consolidate at regular intervals the collective sentiments and collective ideas that make its unity and personality'.[36] In good French republican fashion, patriotism and civic cults were for Durkheim the modern forms of religious life.

The sociologism in the Durkheimian approach has a close counterpart, albeit symmetrical, in the psychologism that marks the attack on religion launched by Sigmund Freud (1856–1939) in *The Future of an Illusion* (1927). We should not be taken in by this book's title. When Freud states that religious ideas are illusions, he is not so far from Durkheim as may at first appear. 'Illusions' are for Freud those ideas which, although not based on trivial evidence, are not pure errors of interpretation or speculative delirium either – as were the animist ideas of Tylor's savage philosopher. 'We call a belief an illusion' Freud wrote, 'when a wish fulfilment is a prominent factor in its motivation, and in doing so we disregard its relations to reality'.[37] This is not the occasion to specify which are the desires that religious ideas satisfy for Freud, nor the way that he sought to demonstrate this. Suffice it to call to mind that among them looms a supposed universal yearning for a father-figure. The point

I would like to stress is simply that for Freud, as for Durkheim, religious 'illusions' have objective fundaments – unconscious drives for the first, society for the second – and subsequently that for both of them, religious 'illusions' have a kind of reality, a symbolical reality.

Symbolism, in the wide sense of the word, is thus the device that allows twentieth-century social and human sciences the possibility to take spiritual and religious ideas as objects of scientific knowledge without having to raise the issue of their respective objective reality. The strategy consists in accepting them in their intra- or intersubjective reality, as the ostensive symbols or expressions of the psychological, social and cultural phenomena that are identified by science.[38] One has only to consult the anthropological literature on spiritual possession or on witchcraft, for instance, to realise that what we do nowadays with the spirits is something more sophisticated – and at times more complicated – but not so very different from what the founding fathers of modern sociology and psychology did with them. We owe the ability to deal with the symbolic reality of religious ideas to intellectuals such as Durkheim and Freud. Durkheim redeemed them as sociological objects, refusing to discredit them as the result of gross errors in reasoning, as Tylor had.[39]

Sociologised or psychologised, the spirits conquered a place among the objects of the sciences. But apart from these two strategies of de-spiritualisation of the world by science, there opened a third – naturalisation. Alfred Russel Wallace and Andrew Lang were two British anthropologists and psychical researchers who battled for it. Their ideas, unlike those of Durkheim, have left no trace – and both men have become, at least in this particular aspect, excluded ancestors from the conventional history of anthropology. This is a good reason why it is worth spending some time on them.[40]

Andrew Lang (1844–1912) was a prolific Scottish scholar with a wide range of intellectual interests: a classicist and folklorist, a well-known author of volumes of fairytales and books about the history of Scotland, he was also an anthropologist and a psychical researcher. He was a founder member of the British Society for Psychical Research and the British Folklore Society, and was president of the latter in the 1870s and 1880s. Lang was close to the position held by his American contemporary James with regard to his interest in the 'supernormal' – which he also called the 'X region', an archipelago of phenomena unexplained by science, such as clairvoyance, fortune-telling, premonition or possession. He was a hopeful sceptic, always ready to unmask the cases of trickery that were by no means unusual in spiritualist séances, but who also believed that there were worlds beyond those that sciences of the material could reveal.

One of the books in which he wrote about the X region is *The Making of Religion* (1898).[41] Here Lang presents two distinct theses. The first is that 'the savage theory of the soul may be based, at least in part, on experiences which cannot, at present, be made to fit into any purely materialistic system of the universe'.[42] The second is that 'the idea of God, in its earliest known shape, need not logically be derived from the idea of spirit, however that idea itself may have been attained or evolved'.[43] This is a degenerationist thesis according to which religion at first took on a purely theist form (based on the idea of an immortal creator), which was contaminated by animist beliefs of a later origin. A proliferation of divinities along with 'fetishism' ensued, and finally a new monotheism (Israel's theism, from which Christianity emerged) developed which is, in genetic terms, a purified outcome of animism.[44]

Let us now focus on Lang's ideas about the birth of animist ideas. Besides challenging the tenet that animism had been the elementary form of religion, Lang refutes Tylor's theory on the origin of the idea of soul. Lang devotes the fourth chapter of his book to showing that in the vast amount of literature about the beliefs of savages, there is no sign that even the most savage of them all had confused a dream during sleep with a 'vision' or 'hallucination' while awake. He argues that it was in experiences of the latter and not of the former kind that the savage philosopher had come to the idea of soul. The reason why Lang insists on separating Tylor's 'dream theory' from his 'hallucination theory' and on stating that the latter deserves credit while the former does not stems from the central thesis in the first part of *The Making of Religion*. If they were based on visions, animism, as in fact modern spiritualism, could well have wrong hypotheses, but at least they would rest on solid bases: 'facts do not cease to be facts because wrong interpretations have been put upon them by savages'.[45]

Lang is relentless in his criticisms about the way Tylor neglected to investigate the possible objective facticity of the X phenomena the savages and modern spiritualists had experienced, instead limiting himself to stating that these were mere 'relics' of ancient animist beliefs. Lang also regrets that Tylor, by using the convenient notion of 'survival', dismisses the awkward question of modern spiritualism's contemporaneity. Lang, on the contrary, proposes to do

> what neither anthropology nor psychical research nor psychology has done: to put the savage and modern phenomena side by side. Such evidence as we can give for the actuality of the modern experiences will, so far as it goes, raise a presumption that the savage beliefs, however erroneous, however darkened by fraud and fancy, repose on a basis of real observation of actual phenomena.[46]

And as can only be expected, he does, in effect, discover what he takes as the evidence he is looking for. For Lang, the fact that supernormal experiences referred to in the beliefs of savages as well as in popular European superstition were remarkably similar to those which, in civilised cities at the end of the nineteenth century have been 'attested in many hundreds of depositions made at first hand by respectable modern witnesses, educated and responsible', grants them twice the credibility.[47] At the end of his book he suggests that '"we are not merely brain"; that man has his part, we know not how, in we know not what – has faculties and vision scarcely conditioned by the limits of his normal purview'.[48] For these faculties, 'modern science has still to find an explanation consistent with recognised laws of nature, but "spirits" we shall not invoke'.[49]

Lang's comments closely resonate with the contents of a review of *Primitive Culture* that Alfred Russel Wallace (1823–1913) had published long before, in the year 1872. Wallace, who was a naturalist and anthropologist besides a devoted psychical researcher, also thought that it was 'at least a possible solution to the problem of animism, that the uniformity of *belief* is due in great part to the uniformity of the underlying *facts*'.[50] It is noteworthy that Tylor took Wallace's criticism seriously enough to bother to leave 'his accustomed armchair in Somerset to come up to London for a month to engage in a kind of anthropological fieldwork'.[51] During that month he attended more than ten séances, but he wasn't convinced of the spiritual origin of the phenomena he observed.[52]

Both Wallace and Lang believed in the naturalness of so-called 'spiritic' facts and proposed that the anthropology of religion should draw closer to psychical research. But both men were also aware that theirs were voices crying in the wilderness and their aim difficult to achieve. Lang, in particular, understood that British anthropology at the end of the nineteenth century, recently emerged from 'that limbo of the unrecognised' in which it had floundered with psychical research and other dubious sciences, would hardly take a step back at the risk of being stigmatised again.[53] 'Though but recently crept forth ... from the chill shade of scientific disdain', Lang goes on in sarcastic vein,

> Anthropology adopts the airs of her elder sisters among the sciences, and is as severe as they to the Cinderella of the family, Psychical Research. She must murmur of her fairies among the cinders of the hearth, while they go forth to the ball, and dance with provincial mayors at the festivities of the British Association. This is ungenerous, and unfortunate, as the records of anthropology are rich in unexamined materials of psychical research.[54]

But Lang is not satisfied to locate the obstacles that hamper a dialogue between anthropology and psychical research within these matters of current scientific politics. He digs deeper and steps back further in time, seeking to understand how official science, under whose umbrella emerging anthropology sought to shelter, banished on principle the inclusion of the X region in its scope of investigation. And he finds one of the most expressive formulations of this principle of segregation in the work of his fellow countryman, the eighteenth century philosopher David Hume – and especially in what he sarcastically calls his *a priori* theory of the impossible.[55] Hume, as is known, was one of the first and most vehement promoters of the exclusion of questions relating to spirits and divinity from the sphere of knowledge worthy of that name. Hume argued against the followers of the 'natural religion' theory – according to which the existence of a providential, omnipotent and omniscient creator could be inferred from the contemplation of the design and order of the universe – that the impressions (knowledge acquired through the senses) represented the limit of acceptable knowledge, and that spirits and divinity, as they were not objects of impression, were outside the sphere of the knowable and that thus all questions raised about them were vain.

Focussing his criticism on Hume in the essay 'Of Miracles', published in *An Enquiry Concerning Human Understanding* (1772), Lang writes the following:

> Hume derided the observation and study of what he called 'Miracles', in the field of experience, and he looked for an *a priori* argument which would for ever settle the

question without examination of facts. In an age of experimental philosophy, which derided *a priori* methods, this was Hume's great contribution to knowledge. His famous argument ... is a tissue of fallacies which might be given for exposure to beginners in logic, as an elementary exercise.[56]

The problem, as Lang explains it, is that Hume defines a miracle as 'a violation of the laws of nature'. And by law of nature, the philosopher means

a uniformity, not of all experience, but of such experience as he will deign to admit; while he excluded, without examination, all evidence for experience of the absence of such uniformity. That kind of experience cannot be considered. 'There must be a uniform experience against every miraculous event, otherwise the event would not merit that appellation.' If there be any experience in favour of the event, that experience does not count. A miracle is counter to universal experience, therefore no event is a miracle. ... Therefore there can be no valid evidence for 'miracles'.[57]

Lang contrasts Hume's prejudice with the interest Kant showed in the visions of his contemporary, Emmanuel Swedenborg, when 'in the true spirit of psychical research' he wrote the latter a letter 'asking for information at first hand' – a letter the visionary received but never answered.[58] The question that Lang poses is that not all 'miracles' nor all 'supernormal' phenomena can be withdrawn from scientific consideration by means of the simple application of the empiricist criterion of 'impressions', because some of them, although uncommon and covered in mysticism, have manifestations that can be verified through the senses. To withdraw them from science, Hume must add that only ordinary impressions – and not extra-ordinary ones – should be credited as sources of knowledge.

'Miracles' and 'supernatural' phenomena such as clairvoyance and premonition were hybrid phenomena: although generally experienced and interpreted as 'revelations', religious or spiritual experiences, they outrageously overwhelmed the peaceful interiority that should characterise these kinds of experiences coming to trouble the tranquillity of the separation between the affairs of God and the affairs of nature. It is thus hardly surprising that ideologues of science should ban psychical research. As it was hardly surprising that ideologues of religion did so too. Established churches, wrote Lang, have an interest in Hume's definition. Because if miracles were to reveal themselves as subject to natural laws, churches would lose the basis of their authority: 'our notions of the possible cease to be a criterion of truth or falsehood, and our contempt for the Gospels as myths must slowly die, as 'miracle' after 'miracle' is brought within the realm of acknowledged law'.[59] In France, forty years before Lang published *The Making of Religion*, a Lyonnese teacher who was to become famous as the founder of Spiritism held very similar ideas about this and also believed that the naturalness of spirits had already been revealed. How? This is what we shall now see.

Science and Proof in Allan Kardec's Spiritism

The Spirits' Book was published in France in 1857. The subtitle explains that the book provides an explanation of 'the principles of spiritist doctrine on the immortality of the soul, the nature of spirits and their relations with men, the moral law, the present life, the future life and the destiny of the human race, according to the teachings of spirits of high degree, transmitted through various mediums, collected and set in order by Allan Kardec'.[60] Allan Kardec was the name the French educator Léon Rivail began to use when he abandoned his career as a teacher and writer of pedagogic books in order to devote himself entirely to the codification and dissemination of *'spiritisme'*, a term he himself invented to designate his doctrine.[61] During the 1850s, Rivail became interested in the fashion of talking and dancing tables that had gripped French middle-class homes. He soon set up a network of mediums he trusted and began to collect the teachings that several 'superior spirits' passed on through these mediums. And thus according to Kardec appeared *The Spirits' Book*, followed by *The Mediums' Book* (1861), *The Gospel According to Spiritism* (1864) and *Heaven and Hell* (1865).

I will focus here on the way that he defended Spiritism's scientificity and how he dealt with the question of proof for spiritic phenomena. Kardec called his doctrine 'the third revelation' – a revelation to surpass those of Christ and Moses. He also viewed it as a system that would forge an alliance between science and religion by proving that the narrow materialism of the first and the magic supernaturalism of the second were both mistaken. God's existence was not in question, neither was the existence of the soul, of angels, archangels and cherubs, of good and bad spirits, of lost souls and black magic. The question is that the understanding, religious and superstitious, people had of these phenomena and entities was wrong. The ignorance of the people together with the obscurantism, which the clergy fostered, led to believers accepting all these things as marvels and mysteries. Mysteries were for Kardec what ensured the clergy's authority; the clergy legitimated its role by its possession of the esoteric knowledge, which allowed it to mediate between the world of man and the other world. By naturalising the spiritual world, Spiritism would put an end to mysteries; it would disenchant the world without exterminating the spirits – making them instead comprehensible and acceptable to the very advanced and independent spirits of the republic of the Enlightenment.

Catholic clergy in Kardec's time did all they could to stick rigorously to their role of guardians of the mystery which the modern constitution granted them. While Kardec announced the coming of Spiritism, with its unique proposal to naturalise and rationalise religion, Pope Pius IX (1792–1878) in the heart of Roman Catholicism, which was then threatened by secularism, rationalism, scientism and the loss of the Papal States, advanced his unique proposals to irrationalise religion.[62] In 1854 Pius IX established the dogma of the Immaculate Conception of Mary. In 1858 the Virgin Mary appeared in Lourdes, in Kardec's own country, and revealed herself to the clairvoyant Bernardette Soubirous with the words 'I am the Immaculate Conception'. In 1870 Pius IX fixed the dogma of papal infallibility and the words of the Virgin in Lourdes were presented as proof of the pope's novel faculty. By the infallible mouth of Pius IX, Roman Catholicism defined itself as a religion in the modern sense of the term, stressing its foundation on irrational beliefs certified by an authority with extra-worldly prerogatives. Remarkably enough, however, even this claim of religion's identity had to appeal to a certain kind of *proof* – at least if we accept that one of the important social aspects of Marian apparitions that abounded between the mid-nineteenth century and the early twentieth century was its interpretation as proofs of the supernatural.[63] And through the words of Kardec, in their turn, minds converted to reason and science that could not stop believing in spirits could find a way to reconcile that faith with this conviction. Positive science, in the historical process of expanding its hegemony, did indeed threaten a radical despiritualisation of the world. Neither Pius IX nor Kardec would accept getting rid of the other world, but each of them integrated it in modernity in very different ways.[64]

In the excerpt from *The Gospel According to Spiritism* with which I began this text, Kardec defines his doctrine as a 'new science' which has come to show 'by means of irrefutable proofs' the relations of the physical world with the spiritual world, and that the latter is not a supernatural realm, but rather 'one of the living and active forces of Nature'. Kardec insists in all his books on the need for 'proof by experiment' of the existence of spirits and their relationship with mankind in order to establish Spritisim as a 'science' – 'religious science' and 'scientific religion' are two of the terms he uses. However, when the question of proof is looked at a little more deeply, it is clear that the proof under consideration does not depend exactly on the procedures of objectification that are used in conventional sciences. By qualifying Spiritism as a science, Kardec was well aware that he was speaking about a peculiar science and not 'science properly called':

> The positive sciences are based on the properties of matter, which may be experimented upon and manipulated at pleasure; but spiritist phenomena are an effect of the action of intelligences that have wills of their own, and that constantly show us that they are not subjected to ours. The observation of facts, therefore, cannot be carried on in the latter case in the same way as in the former one, for they proceed from another source, and require special conditions; and, consequently, to insist upon submitting them to the same methods of investigation is to insist on assuming the existence of analogies that do not exist. Science, properly so called, is therefore incompetent, as such, to decide the question of the truth of Spiritism; it has nothing to do with it; and its verdict in regard to it, whether favourable or otherwise, is of no weight.[65]

That the objects of 'spiritist science' are 'intelligences that have wills of their own' makes it difficult to apply a regime of comprehension designed to produce soulless non-volitional facts. But this is only part of the problem. The other is that the instruments through which the spirits have been objectified since the early days of modern spiritualism – the mediums – are themselves intelligent beings with their own volition. Spiritist vocabulary mechanises the mediums when it speaks of them as 'instruments' and compares them to 'telegraphic devices'. But obviously their human condition cannot be concealed. If both the objects and the instruments of spiritist science are intelligent creatures with their own will, how can we ensure that neither one nor the other will deceive the researcher? How can we ensure that some 'mischievous spirit' will not pretend to be a 'superior spirit' and take advantage of the medium's good faith? And how too can we ensure that mediums do not mix up or accidentally confuse the 'intuitions' they get from a spirit with their own 'intuitions'? And how can we ensure that the mediums do not do it consciously? These issues configure the problem of 'mystification' which Kardec and spiritualists in general have thought deeply about since the start without finding a secure way to avoid it. Kardec himself wrote in *The Spirits' Book* that 'we could fill a volume with most curious instances of spirit-hoaxings that have occurred within the circle of our own personal observation'.[66]

Well aware that the spirits' and mediums' intelligence and volition were an obstacle to the admittance of spiritualism and Spiritism into the republic of the sciences, yet intent on surmounting it, many psychical researchers began to experiment with mechanical instruments of objectification. Between the end of the nineteenth century and the early twentieth century, a number of techniques were developed aimed at bringing the spirits into the realm of scientific knowability – techniques such as the measurement of the medium's body weight during a state of trance, which convinced Lombroso, wax moulds with alleged imprints of ectoplasmatic forms or spirit photographs, all of which raised enormous expectations.[67] None of these techniques managed to produce results that convinced scientists on the whole, but they produced convincing enough results for spiritualists and spiritists.

Concluding Remarks

A number of anthropologists have presented theories concerning regimes of comprehension in which ideas such as those of soul, spirits, witchcraft, evil and divine grace attain an experiential facticity they have not achieved in the regime of production of scientific facts. Jeanne Favret-Saada, for instance, says that discourse of witchcraft – which is something different from discourse *about* witchcraft – can only be understood within what she calls the regime of 'affection'.[68] Élisabeth Claverie, in her analysis of the way Roman Catholics certify the Virgin Mary's intervention in their lives during group pilgrimages, speaks of the facticity that spiritual experiences intersubjectively shared acquire in what she calls the 'regime of faith'.[69] Bruno Latour, in turn, argues that religious speech can only be properly understood if situated in a regime of enunciation that is not referential nor communicational in the usual sense of the word – a regime whose archetype is that of lovers' speech and whose object is not to inform but rather to address people by moving them.[70] All these proposals can be understood as drafts for 'programmes of truth and interest' at stake in the sphere of religiosity or spirituality. And in people's lives there generally coexist many programmes of truth and interest which operate according to the situation.[71]

However, in the historical conjuncture and social contexts through which we have wandered in this essay, there has been a programme of truth that threatened to stifle all others. Within this conjuncture and these contexts, the idea that scientific knowledge was the paradigm of acceptable knowledge tended to hold sway over consciousnesses. Proof came to be considered an indispensable criterion of credibility, and believing out of its regime of factualisation could be held as a sign of ignorance or insanity. Freud was among the intellectuals who left us one of the most perfect formulas of this scientistic belief when he asserted that 'an illusion it would be to suppose that what science cannot give us we can get elsewhere'.[72] Even psychical researchers who rebelled against the canons of 'materialist science' did so in the name of 'science' and of the 'scientific spirit'. Kardec's Spiritism is an outcome of that state of affairs. Although Kardec himself was very clear that spiritist science was not a science like others, many of his followers ignored his caution and battled to achieve a status of parity. The battle, however, was lost, and Spiritism was left either in a kind of limbo between religion and science or ended up being socially defined as a religion. This is, for instance, what happened in Brazil, the country in which the spiritist movement has a long history and its largest following. Furthermore, the polarity between science and religion got so entrenched within Spiritism itself that it still provides an idiom periodically resurrected in internal quarrels and schisms.

Notes

1. This chapter derives from a doctoral project in course at the Institute of Social Sciences of the University of Lisbon. Research was funded by the Portuguese Institute for International Scientific and Technological Co-operation (ICCTI, process PFAEA/4.1.6) and the Foundation for Science and Technology (FCT, process SFRH/BD/4765/2001). I want to thank Carole Garton for her careful translation and João de Pina-Cabral for his insightful editorial suggestions. An earlier and extended Portuguese version of this essay was published in the Brazilian journal *Religião e Sociedade* 23(2): 92–126 (2003).
2. Kardec 1987 [1864]: 25.
3. In James 1986: 363.
4. It should be noted that some authors writing in English have preferred the word 'spiritism' to 'spiritualism' for that very reason (see, for example, Lang 1898: 66 n. 1), but this option has failed to make its mark in the English-speaking world.
5. These three quotes are taken from Kardec (1996 [1857]: 21).
6. Conan Doyle 1975 [1924]: 63. See Conan Doyle (1975 [1924]: 60–118) for a detailed description of the Hydesville case. Shorter accounts can be found in Kerr (1972: 3–9) and Nelson (1969: 3–7). Arthur Conan Doyle (1859–1930), the Scottish writer, best known as the creator of Sherlock Holmes, was also a doctor and, from 1917 onward, a convinced spiritualist. He presided over the London Spiritualist Alliance and published in 1924 *The History of Spiritualism*, championing spiritualism though a very rich source of information.
7. See Nelson 1969.
8. See Hess 1991: 110–111.
9. Oppenheim 1985: 3.

10. Lombroso 1911 [1910]: 6, 279; my translation.
11. Between 1886 and 1909 William James wrote several articles and reports for the British and American Societies for Psychical Research. These texts were collected and republished in James (1986). This aspect of James's work is examined by Cho (1996) and Croce (1997). Croce stresses the impact that the spiritual concerns of Henry James (father of William and novelist Henry James) had on his philosopher son. Henry James senior was a great admirer of the Swedish mystic and scientist Emmanuel Swedenborg (1688–1772), whose books were in circulation by the middle of the nineteenth century in European and American milieus, where spiritualism spread (see Conan Doyle 1975 [1924]: 11–24; Kerr 1972: 10). On the Swedish visionary and his doctrine of correspondences see Needham (1985: 117–48).
12. James 1986: 374.
13. In fact, modern spiritualism did not suddenly land on earth like a meteor, and Mesmerism was one of its primary sources.
14. Frank Miller Turner, 1974, *Between Science and Religion: The Reaction to Scientific Naturalism in late Victorian England*, New Haven, Yale University Press, p. 124; cited in Cho (1996: 16). On the influence of Myers' ideas over James see also Croce (1997: 215).
15. See Hazelgrove 2000: 194. Frederic Myers was also a source of inspiration for Lombroso (see Lombroso 1911 [1910]: 146).
16. James 1986: 374.
17. Hazelgrove 2000: 23.
18. Claverie 1990: 66; my translation.
19. Stewart 1991: 116; author's italics.
20. Lombroso 1911 [1910]: 5; my translation.
21. Wallace, quoted in Pels 2003: 250.
22. Weber 1948 [1919]: 138–39; author's italics.
23. The demise of spirits and magic matches just one of the senses the expression 'disenchantment of the world' has in Weber's writings. That sense is the one anthropologists usually focus on (for two recent examples see Lambek 1996 and Schneider 1991), but it is not the only one. As is well known, Weber borrowed the expression 'disenchantment of the world' from the poet and play-writer Friedrich Schiller (who had spoken more precisely of the 'de-divinization of the world'), and in the German sociologist writings that phrase kept the polysemy which is proper of poetical images. In its more radical sense, the 'disenchantment of the world' refers to the loss of the meaning of death and the meaning of life that allegedly goes after the colonisation of modern spirits by techno-scientific rationalisation and by the ideology of progress (see Weber 1948 [1919]: 139–40).
24. Latour 1991: 60; my translation.
25. Latour 1991: 51; my translation.
26. Asad 1993: 47.
27. Latour 1991: 51–52; my translation.
28. See Smith 2001.
29. See Tiryakian 1974.
30. See Lett 1991: 307.
31. Turner 1992. Other recent 'alternative' approaches to the spirit world may be found in Young and Goulet (eds) 1994 and Willis 1999.
32. Hess 1990: 430.
33. See, for example, Marett 1909 and Lowie 1925.
34. Durkheim 1960 [1912]: 97; my translation.

35. Durkheim makes this very explicit when he writes: 'Our entire study rests on the postulate that this unanimous feeling of the believers from all the ages cannot be purely illusory' (Durkheim 1960 [1912]: 596).
36. Durkheim 1960 [1912]: 609–10.
37. Freud 1985: 213. See also Palmer 1997: 33–35.
38. This means, in Latour's terms, to replace an old transcendence with a new one (see Latour 1996: 26–27).
39. Or, as Dan Sperber (1974: 13) phrases it, as 'illicit inferences drawn from insufficient data' (my translation).
40. See Handler (ed.) 2000 about other excluded ancestors and their respective processes of exclusion.
41. *The Making of Religion* is a sequel to *Cock Lane and Common Sense*, a book that Lang had published four years before. An abridged account of this book can be found in Stocking (1995: 56–57).
42. Lang 1898: 2.
43. Lang 1898: 2.
44. Both theses directly counter two aspects of Tylor's theory about the origin of religion. George Stocking (1995: 50–63) calls our attention to the circumstance that led to *The Making of Religion* culminating in a 180° turn in Lang's intellectual trajectory and also a rebellion against his mentor Tylor. He also suggests that this turn follows 'a pattern that was by no means unusual among Victorian intellectuals at the end of the nineteenth century: an exposure to conventional religion during a pre-Darwinian childhood, a period of rationalistic doubt in the early heyday of evolutionary naturalism, and then a movement back toward supernaturalism, either of the conventional religious or the spiritualist variety – in a context of impending personal mortality, unease about the progress of European civilization, a reaction against "positivism" and "materialism", and a heightened intellectual interest in irrational psychological phenomena' (1995: 56). For further reading on this subject see also Turner 1993.
45. Lang 1898: 70. It is important to notice that Lang did not hold the spiritualist *theory* in much better account than the animism of the savages. Whilst defending the reality of X phenomena such as clairvoyance, he vehemently criticises 'the mid-Victorian spiritualists, who, as usual, explained the phenomena, in their prehistoric way, by "spirits"' (1898: 93).
46. Lang 1898: 50.
47. Lang 1898: 8.
48. Lang 1898: 334.
49. Lang 1898: 9.
50. Wallace's review of *Primitive Culture* was originally published in 1872 in the journal *The Academy*. This text can be found at http:/www.wku.edu/~smithch/S207.htm., where I got the passage quoted here.
51. Stocking 1971: 88.
52. The plot of this backstage episode in the history of anthropology has been reported and examined by George Stocking (1971) and more recently by Peter Pels (2003).
53. Lang 1898: 43.
54. Lang 1898: 47–48. The British Association in question is the British Association for the Advancement of Science, created in 1831.
55. Lang 1898: 326.
56. Lang 1898: 18.
57. Lang 1898: 18.
58. Lang 1898: 28.

59. Lang 1898: 25.
60. Some of the superior spirits that transmitted the teachings collected by Kardec are identified by him, such as those of St John the Baptist, St Augustine, St Vincent of Paula, St Louis the King of France, the Spirit of Truth (occasionally identified as the spirit of Jesus), Socrates, Plato, Fenelon, Benjamin Franklin or Emmanuel Swedenborg.
61. Allan Kardec is the name of a Gaul from the time of the druids who, according to a revelation made to Rivail, had been one of the previous incarnations of his own spirit. Aubrée and Laplantine (1990: 29) relate this identity change to the nationalist fascination regarding the Celtic past that spread in the spiritist, occultist and esoteric milieus of late nineteenth and early twentieth century France.
62. By using 'rationalise' and 'irrationalise' in this context, I refer to rationalism not in the strong sense of the exclusive trust in reason as source of knowledge, but in the wider sense of accepting as valid knowledge only that which is possible to pass rational examination.
63. The cycle of modern Marian apparitions I refer to began in La Salette, France, in 1846 and closed in Fátima, Portugal, in 1917. For more on this cycle see, for example, 'Apparitions, Messages, and Miracles: Postindustrial Marian Pilgrimage', in Turner and Turner (1978).
64. For more on Pius IX's pontificate and the height of the conflict between religious authority and that of science see, for instance, Turner (1993: 195–96).
65. Kardec 1996 [1857]: 37–38.
66. Kardec 1986 [1861]: 387.
67. For spirit photography see Charuty 1999 and Tucker 1997.
68. See Favret-Saada 1977 and 1990.
69. See Claverie 1990.
70. See Latour 2002.
71. On the notion of 'program of truth and interest' see Veyne 1987 [1983]. As Veyne writes, 'our spirit is not vexed when it surreptitiously changes its program of truth and interest, apparently contradicting itself. This happens all the time. It is not ideology; it is our ordinary way of living' (Veyne 1987 [1983]: 106).
72. Cited in Palmer 1997: 76.

References

Asad, Talal. 1993. *Genealogies of Religion: Discipline and Reasons of Power in Christianity and Islam*. Baltimore: Johns Hopkins University Press.

Aubrée, Marion and François Laplantine. 1990. *La table, le livre et les esprits: naissance, évolution et actualité du mouvement social spirite entre France et Brésil*. Paris: Jean-Claude Lattès.

Charuty, Giordana. 1999. 'La 'boîte aux ancêtres': photographie et science de l'invisible', *Terrain* 33: 57–80.

Cho, Tracey. 1996. 'The Psychologizing of Religion in William James' *Varieties of Religious Experience*', *The Harvard Brain* 3(1): 14–18.

Claverie, Élisabeth. 1990. 'La Vierge, le désordre, la critique: les apparitions de la Vierge à l'âge de la science', *Terrain* 14: 60–75.

Conan Doyle, Arthur. 1975 [1924]. *The History of Spiritualism*. New York: Arno Press.

Croce, Paul Jerome. 1997. 'Between Spiritualism and Science: William James on Religion and Human Nature', *Journal for the History of Modern Theology* 4(2):197–220.

Durkheim, Émile. 1960 [1912]. *Les formes élémentaires de la vie religieuse: le système totémique en Australie*. Paris: Presses Universitaires de France.
Favret-Saada, Jeanne. 1977. *Les mots, la mort, les sorts*. Paris: Gallimard.
———. 1990. 'Être affecté', *Gradhiva* 8: 3–9.
Freud, Sigmund. 1985. *Civilization, Society and Religion*. London: Penguin Books.
Handler, Richard (ed.). 2000. *Excluded Ancestors, Inventible Traditions: Essays Toward a More Inclusive History of Anthropology*. Madison: University of Wisconsin Press.
Hazelgrove, Jenny. 2000. *Spiritualism and British Society between the Wars*. Manchester: Manchester University Press.
Hess, David. 1990. 'Ghosts and Domestic Politics in Brazil: Some Parallels between Spirit Possession and Spirit Infestation', *Ethos* 18(4): 407–38.
———. 1991. *Spirits and Scientists: Ideology, Spiritism, and Brazilian Culture*. Pennsylvania: Pennsylvania State University Press.
James, William. 1986. *Essays in Psychical Research*, ed. Frederick H. Burkhardt et al. Cambridge, Mass.: Harvard University Press.
Kardec, Allan. 1986 [1861]. *The Mediums' Book*, trans. Anna Blackwell. Rio de Janeiro: Federação Espírita Brasileira.
———. 1987 [1864]. *The Gospel According to Spiritism*, trans. J.A. Duncan. London: Headquarters Publishing.
———. 1996 [1857]. *The Spirits' Book*, trans. Anna Blackwell. 2nd ed. Rio de Janeiro: Federação Espírita Brasileira.
———. 2003 [1865]. *Heaven and Hell*, trans. Anna Blackwell. New York: Spiritist Alliance for Books.
Kerr, Howard. 1972. *Mediums, and Spirit-rappers, and Roaring Radicals: Spiritualism in American Literature, 1850–1900*. Urbana: University of Illinois Press.
Lambek, Michael. 1996. 'Afterword: Spirits and Their Histories', in Jeannette Marie Mageo and Alan Howard (eds), *Spirits in Culture, History, and Mind*. New York: Routledge, pp. 237–49.
Lang, Andrew. 1898. *The Making of Religion*. London: Longmans, Green and Co.
Latour, Bruno. 1991. *Nous n'avons jamais été modernes: essai d'anthropologie symétrique*. Paris: La Découverte.
———. 1996. *Petite réflexion sur le culte moderne des dieux faitiches*. Paris: Les Empêcheurs de Penser en Rond.
———. 2002. *Jubiler, ou les tourments de la parole religieuse*. Paris: Les Empêcheurs de Penser en Rond.
Lett, James. 1991. 'Interpretive Anthropology, Metaphysics, and the Paranormal', *Journal of Anthropological Research* 47: 305–29.
Lombroso, Cesare. 1911 [1910]. *Hypnotisme et spiritisme*, trans. Charles Rossigneux. Paris : Ernest Flammarion.
Lowie, Robert H. 1925. *Primitive Religion*. London: Routledge.
Marett, Robert R. 1909. *The Threshold of Religion*. London: Methuen.
Needham, Rodney. 1985. *Exemplars*. Berkeley and Los Angeles: University of California Press.
Nelson, Geoffrey. 1969. *Spiritualism and Society*. London: Routledge and Kegan Paul.
Oppenheim, Janet. 1985. *The Other World: Spiritualism and Psychical Research in England, 1850–1914*. Cambridge: Cambridge University Press.
Palmer, Michael. 1997. *Freud and Jung on Religion*. London: Routledge.
Pels, Peter. 2003. 'Spirits of Modernity: Alfred Wallace, Edward Tylor, and the Visual Politics of Fact', in Birgit Meyer and Peter Pels (eds), *Magic and Modernity: Interfaces of Revelation and Concealment*. Stanford: Stanford University Press, pp. 241–71.

Schneider, Jane. 1991 [1989]. 'Spirits and the Spirit of Capitalism', in Eric Wolf (ed.), *Religious Regimes and State-formation: Perspectives from European Ethnology*. Albany: State University of New York Press, pp. 181–219.
Smith, Matthew. 2001. 'An Overview of Psychical Research in Britain', *Paranormal Review* 10: 3–5.
Sperber, Dan. 1974. *Le symbolisme en général*. Paris: Hermann.
Stewart, Charles. 1991. *Demons and the Devil: Moral Imagination in Modern Greek Culture*. Princeton: Princeton University Press.
Stocking, George W. 1971. 'Animism in Theory and Practice: E.B. Tylor's Unpublished "Notes on Spiritualism"', *Man* 6(1): 88–104.
———. 1995. *After Tylor: British Social Anthropology, 1888–1951*. London: Athlone Press.
Tiryakian, Edward (ed.). 1974. *On the Margin of the Visible: Sociology, the Esoteric, and the Occult*. New York: John Wiley.
Tucker, Jennifer. 1997. 'Photography as Witness, Detective, and Impostor: Visual Representation in Victorian Science', in Bernard Lightman (ed.), *Victorian Science in Context*. Chicago: University of Chicago Press, pp. 378–408.
Turner, Edith. 1992. *Experiencing Ritual: A New Interpretation of African Healing*. Philadelphia: University of Pennsylvania Press.
Turner, Frank Miller. 1993. *Contesting Cultural Authority: Essays in Victorian Intellectual Life*. Cambridge: Cambridge University Press.
Turner, Victor and Edith Turner. 1978. *Image and Pilgrimage in Christian Culture: Anthropological Perspectives*. New York: Columbia University Press.
Tylor, Edward Burnett. 1876 [1871]. *La civilisation primitive*, trans. Pauline Brunet. 2 vols. Paris: Reinwald.
Veyne, Paul. 1987 [1983]. *Acreditaram os Gregos nos Seus Mitos?*, trans. António Gonçalves. Lisbon: Edições 70.
Weber, Max. 1948 [1919]. 'Science as a Vocation', in Hans H. Gerth and C. Wright Mills (eds and trans.), *From Max Weber: Essays in Sociology*. London: Routledge and Kegan Paul, pp. 129–56.
Willis, Roy. 1999. *Some Spirits Heal, Others Only Dance: A Journey into Human Selfhood in an African Village*. Oxford: Berg.
Young, David E. and Jean-Guy Goulet (eds). 1994. *Being Changed by Cross-cultural Encounters: The Anthropology of Extraordinary Experience*. Peterborough: Broadview Press.

Chapter 3

The Abominations of Anthropology: Christianity, Ethnographic Taboos and the Meanings of 'Science'

Simon Coleman

Unique Truths and Anthropological Taboos

In 1992, Ernest Gellner preached a sermon in King's College Chapel, Cambridge. His theme was 'The Uniqueness of Truth' (1992b). Gellner's Jewish origins and secular convictions hardly made him an obvious candidate for the pulpit, but his talk focused less on divine revelation than on a problem that had absorbed him all his life: the epistemological conditions under which Truth can be approached in the face of the treacheries of language and the pluralities of human culture. He published an expanded version of the sermon as a book, *Postmodernism, Reason and Religion* (1992a), of which the work of a Muslim scholar, Akbar Ahmedl, was originally planned to make up half. Gellner wrote (1992a: vii) that the intention had been 'to show that a full-blooded, committed believer and an intellectual adherent of Enlightenment doubt could face each other within the compass of a single volume, discussing, more or less, the same theme, and to do so with courtesy and in an amicable manner'. The proposed juxtaposition of views was finally abandoned, apparently not because of intellectual disagreements but because of a different, if equally powerful, force: the (presumably commercially influenced) whim of the publisher.

Gellner's arguments are concerned with the intersections as well as the conflicts between absolutism and its intellectual opponents. He explores the frictions and incongruities between religiously based language and anthropological discourse, describing three[1] claimants to modern cognitive authority that he sees as ironically – perhaps tragically – equidistant (1992b: 9): 'The [religious] Fundamentalist and the Enlightenment Puritan share a sense of and respect for the uniqueness of truth; the EP and the relativist, share a penchant for tolerance; and the relativist and the fundamentalist, share a reasonably well furnished, habitable world, as opposed to the arid emptiness of the world of the EP.' Gellner reckons that many anthropologists belong to the relativist camp. He describes himself, however, as a card-carrying, Enlightenment Puritan, a follower of 'rationalist fundamentalism' (1992a: 1) – not a holder of any substantive conviction but a follower of a much chillier doctrine: that all claims for cognitive authority must be judged by generic, procedural prescriptions about how disinterestedly and reliably to investigate the world. Thus, much of Gellner's most brilliant bile is directed against post-modernists – in his view, occupiers of a fashionable sub-set of relativism – who are dismissed as peddlers of 'narcissism-hermeneuticism' (1992a: 26) and a virulent form of 'conceptual intoxicant' (ibid.: 30). By contrast, as a self-styled Rationalist Fundamentalist who has immersed himself in the study of Islam, Gellner admires the seriousness of his religious counterparts[2] and their conviction that what they say both means something specific and might make a tangible difference to the world. He insists that while we might not consider fundamentalists wholly 'suitable for polite society', we should not allow our snobbery 'to stand in the way of our recognition of their importance' (ibid.: 6).

I want to use Gellner's sermon as a catalyst for considering some of the issues raised by the editors of this volume. I am particularly interested in the way he brings religious discourse into an apparently equal debate with social-scientific scholarship. If the supposed conflict between science and religion has been a foundational concern for modernity, one might add that the specific connections and tensions between anthropology (as modern social science) and Christianity (as contemporary faith) have been left relatively unscrutinised. It is true that specifically sociological predictions of global secularisation have mostly been ignored by the practitioners of our discipline, just as post-nineteenth-century anthropology has largely opposed the progressivist Frazerian myth of religion's replacement by science, but this is not to say that all religions have been granted equal status in the ethnographic pantheon. As Robbins (2001) has recently remarked, we have a well-established Anthropology of Islam (and of Buddhism and of Hinduism), but not – as yet – one of Christianity.

This is not the place to trace the historical links, both implicit and explicit, between Christian ideas and the development of the social-scientific theoretical canon (the constitution of anthropology by Christianity); nor do I intend to provide chapter and verse on the presence, or lack of it, of Christianity in past monographs (the constitution of Christianity as an ethnographic object); nor yet am I attempting to sketch out, or to argue for or against, the very idea of an Anthropology of Christianity. However, I do wish briefly to refer to some of the issues that are raised by our disciplinary neglect of this particular faith. Of course we might claim, along with Evans-Pritchard (1965: 15), that such neglect is far from benign, since many early scholars set the intellectual tone for our discipline by discovering in 'primitive' religions a weapon that they thought could be used with deadly effect against Christianity. We might also argue that Christianity bears some responsibility for its own peripherality within our discipline. The ideological separation of transcendent from mundane spheres of activity (cf. Stewart 2001) could be said to have encouraged Western anthropologists to assume that Christianity had little relevance in the public sphere of their own societies, even as they searched for intimate, immanent connections among religion, politics and economics in non-Western contexts. On the other hand, where Christianity is acknowledged in fieldwork contexts, it can too easily be dismissed as a form of 'intrusive' hegemony, associated not only with the evils of missionaries, capitalism and colonialism but also with a form of irrationality that is particularly to be chastised because, frankly, it should know better. Consider the following anecdote recounted by João de Pina-Cabral (2001: 330–31). Long ago he was at a seminar given by Peter Rivière, who was asked whether he found it difficult to understand the beliefs of the South American Indians he studied. Rivière responded that he regarded such beliefs as recognisable stuff held in clear-headed ways by reasonably tolerant people. However, what Rivière simply could not understand was the intolerant Biblical literalism that American Baptist missionaries were trying to impose on the Trio. In this story, conservative Protestants perhaps embody an unholy trinity of anthropological taboos: lack of openness to alternative worldviews; an intrusion of the powerful West not for purposes of observation, but in order to effect ideological transformation (and thus also disrupt our ethnographic illusions of bounded contexts); and an apparent literalism, a simple-minded basing of Truth in a single text. An inconvenient tendency to travel to the places also inhabited by fieldworking anthropologists is therefore combined not with constructing monographs *out of* exotic cultural experience, but with retranslating such exotic culture *into* the familiar terms of a book (*The Book*) whose premises are regarded as unalterable. Gellner remarks (1974: 26) that anthropologists have tended to be charitable in their acts of interpretation and translation, attempting to convey the coherence that is assumed to be found in 'primitive thought'. However, in his view (ibid.: 31–32), ethnographers who are roughly liberals in their own society seem to become Tories when speaking on behalf of the society they are investigating, showing understanding and tolerance to 'the tribesman' but summarily condemning the Western missionary.[3]

Rivière's frustration with meddling Baptists is a long way from Gellner's rather more abstract imagery of a civilised symposium devoted to discussing the nature of Truth. However, any attempt to exclude Christians of whatever stripe from our ethnographic purview now looks like a lost cause. As Stewart remarks (2001: 325), the current epistemological environment in which a degree of reflexivity has become *de rigueur* encourages 'us' (presumably, in his terms, Western anthropologists) to examine our own religious convictions before we engage in research, and to consider the extent to which they should – or ever could – be set aside.[4] Moreover, the Christian 'field' has started to come towards 'us' in at least two ways. Not only do Western ethnographers increasingly carry out fieldwork 'at home' but Christianity itself has in certain respects become more visible. Conservative evangelicals occupy public discourse – have become a political religion – not only in classical areas of fieldwork but also in contemporary American political arenas and even, occasionally, in the UK (Coleman and Carlin 2004).[5]

Christianity, then, is coming increasingly on to the fieldwork agenda, in Western and non-Western contexts. But, even now, there are significant gaps in our coverage. We have quite a few studies of popular Catholicism, but far fewer of Catholic elites. Many ethnographic accounts of 'sympathetic' evangelicals[6] (ethnically distinctive, poverty-stricken, resistant of hegemony, in need of our advocacy) exist, but far fewer focus on the 'unsympathetic' variety (white, rich, Western, unashamedly ambitious in their pursuit of ideological hegemony, often disdainful of secular anthropologists).[7] Thus, Susan Harding, author of a book on Jerry Falwell (2000), has traced the contradictory position of many scholars to the existence of Christian fundamentalists. Harding argues (ibid.: 374), that academic inquiry regards such Christians as displaying behaviour that is sufficiently 'unreasonable' as to require social-scientific explanation. Yet, the anti-orientalising tools of cultural criticism have their ideological limits:[8] Christian fundamentalists often constitute an area of ethnographic taboo, a decidedly 'repugnant cultural other', in the eyes of fieldworkers. Harding found that her colleagues wondered why she wasn't choosing some other, *any* other, ethnographic object. She was subjected to policing academic discourses, involving inquiries that posited a link between personal conviction and academic curiosity and boiled down to the question: 'Are you now or have you ever been a born-again Christian?' (ibid.: 375). And so Harding makes a plea (ibid.: 392) for ethnographic study not only of 'politically sympathetic' but also of so-called 'repugnant' cultural objects.[9]

Note how Harding's choice to work in her own country, the U.S., leads to the assumption that she must be 'one of them'. How, we are forced to ask, is fieldwork to be managed in this ethnographically (perhaps still doubly) taboo area? After all, participant observation often depends on a kind of mimesis, an appropriation of the other that is sufficiently comprehensive to allow for cultural 'understanding' to occur (cf. Coleman 2002) – or so we often like to tell ourselves. Hastrup notes (1993: 174), for instance, that since Malinowski 'there has been an expectation that ethnographers learn to think, feel and often even behave like a native', so that (ibid.): 'To "know" another world, one must associate with the natives, even possibly become one of them, at least temporarily. In anthropology, the claim to knowledge remains based in a personal experience.'

This is not to deny, of course, that 'participation' itself is a flexible concept, or that varying theoretical paradigms might inform different methodological practices. Admittedly, also, the argument is occasionally made that such a state of ethnographic revelation is especially hard to achieve with religious topics. Stewart (2001: 327) asks how one can reveal the mystical secrets of 'their' religion if one neither believes in those secrets nor in the mystical power of any faith. I confess that I do not feel this query gets at the heart of the problem. Why should we assume in rather liberal Protestant fashion that our own forms of inner mystical experience somehow give us access to theirs? Such an argument falls into the trap of assuming that we are all potentially seekers in our different ways after the same ineffable Truth (McCutcheon 1997). Asad, indeed, worries that seeing religion as a transhistorical and transcultural phenomenon runs the risk of separating it conceptually and analytically from the domain of power (1993: 28–29).

Rather more important from my point of view is another perspective explored by Stewart, that (2001: 328): 'It is alright to get initiated as a shaman or other sort of religious practitioner so long as one does not really believe in such a religious system, or so long as one renounces such belief later.' The separation between the field and home must, in this example, be maintained. But what happens when the field is located physically and (albeit only in certain respects) epistemologically very close to home? What do we risk when we attempt to gain proximity to a religious 'Other' who already has a well-defined identity within arenas of public discourse that surround us in our everyday lives?[10] Lurhmann remarks (2001) that in most settings, going native is an indulgent fantasy; but dealing with Christian evangelicals can be psychologically risky, and one can argue that there are a number of reasons for this danger. For a start, conservative Protestants – at least in the West – are often aware of the categories 'anthropologist' and 'social scientist', and have developed ways of assimilating the ethnographic project into their own activities. An obvious example of this home-grown form of colonisation is provided by the Word of Life, the charismatic ministry I study in Sweden: not only does the group run its own university, it has even taught its own version of anthropology to its students, incorporating in its library the work of Ernest Gellner.[11] More broadly, so-called translation of culture (Rubel and Rosman 2003) can work both ways, and believers are often expert at producing their own texts and narratives of social reality. I found that many Swedish charismatics were prepared to listen to my stated reasons for fieldwork while assuming that – whether I acknowledged it or not – God had a plan for my life, and that the words I would soon be producing would be contained not in an ethnographic monograph but in a witness of God's power to save anybody, even me. According to its rhetoric, evangelical discourse depends on the ability to colonise personal consciousness and experience with sacred language and perception whose true meanings can supposedly only be penetrated by those who have committed themselves to the faith. In effect, a form of 'double-knowledge' is ideally cultivated, according to which consciousness 'in the natural' is superseded by supernaturally derived forms of conviction. Anthropological writings do not merely describe evangelicals, they often compete with them in attempts to define and describe religious and even apparently secular realities.

So, as Spickard and Landres pose the question (2002: 6), one can study the Nuer without becoming Nuer, but can one study evangelical Christianity without somehow 'getting inside' the faith that defines it? This query is more precise than Stewart's earlier question about whether one needs to be generally religious to understand the religion of others because it is faith-specific: it is saying that evangelicals seem to regard the colonisation of consciousness as being their central constitutive practice, and so the ethnographer has to work out how to get to grips with such practice as part of the process of translating ethnographic experiences of religious discourse into anthropological texts – whether those texts are written on a page, presented at conferences, or even preached in chapels. Thus, another way of phrasing the question might be: should one study such Christianity by letting the faith 'get inside' oneself?[12]

Much of the rest of this chapter is about some scholars who have negotiated the tensions between conservative Protestantism and the social sciences in the production of what Elisha and Erzen have (2001) called 'gospel ethnography'.[13] I am particularly interested in studies, carried out in Western contexts, which have raised the issue of how the anthropologist does – or does not – connect with the faith. Encounters between anthropology and evangelicalism are occurring at a time when evangelicalism is once again contesting Western (and other) spaces of public, intellectual and civil discourse with politicians, journalists, scientists and social scientists.[14] However, my hope is that the following will say as much about the culture of Anglo-American anthropology as it does about that of evangelicalism. I therefore focus not only on fieldwork but also on assumptions about texts, and indeed assumptions about what makes a social science.

Apollonians versus Dionysians: Between Gellner and Harding

I started by invoking Gellner's sermon in King's College Chapel, and I want to begin this section by revisiting his position on rationality, science and religion. The aim here is not to look at the detail of his argument but to examine the assumptions it reveals, to see what it might tell us as we attempt to develop an anthropological perspective on conservative Protestantism. My basic point is that Gellner's world-view seems reasonable (in a clubbable sort of way) and yet also deeply totalising in its assertions of equality of voice and tolerance of dialogue – even 'trialogue'. Religious Fundamentalism, *Rationalist* Fundamentalism and Relativism are honoured by being granted entry to Gellner's global field of epistemological competition. But there is a problem here for any ethnographer. To qualify, each ideological system is reduced to a set of textualised positions that appear to be commensurate rivals for the same goal, ultimate cognitive authority.[15] And what is significant is not just the metaphorical location of Gellner's argument – where he's 'coming from' intellectually – but also the *literal* location of his original pronouncements. King's College Chapel is a place of worship, but it is hardly, say, Thomas Road Baptist Church;[16] Akbar Ahmed is a 'full-blooded' Muslim, but he is also a professor of anthropology who has spent a long time working in Western universities. The discursive playing field employed by Gellner to frame his presentations of competing systems of conviction is set up to favour certain assumptions about how and why to present one's views (cf. Asad 1986), while ignoring the power relations that would be involved in cultural translation between 'unequal' contexts (Asad 1993: 179). Overall, intellectualism prevails (Tambiah 1990).

Of course I have to concede that the presence of 'anthropology' in a university such as that run by the Word of Life – and the presence of Gellner's work on its bookshelves no less – do seem to come pretty close to the image of a symposium. Moreover, the willingness of conservative Protestants to engage with secular opponents on such issues as creation/evolution and the state of the economy does imply, if not civilised debate, at least some level of communication on common issues. However, we simply cannot assume that engagement in 'conversation' implies common understandings of the rules and meanings of what is going on. I shall provide just one example of what I mean from my own fieldwork. Particularly during the 1980s, the pastor of the Word of Life, Ulf Ekman, regularly responded in the secular press to criticisms that he brainwashed followers into irrational beliefs and actions, extorted money from the poor and promoted unrealistic views on healing. Ekman usually presented his defence through a persona that was entirely reasonable in secular terms, saying that the group's finances were managed in accordance with Swedish law, that people could make a choice over whether to join and when to leave, and so on. However, on occasion to fellow believers, he also reinterpreted his statements in the light of charismatic ideology representing himself as 'fighting with the devil' as he responded to the criticisms of journalists and academics; as plugging into God's immutable laws of prosperous increase while ostensibly discussing the detail of tax returns; and more generally invoking 'the mind' and talking at the level of 'the natural' for the sake of his unregenerated readers, even while he could draw on supernatural convictions derived from 'the spirit' and 'revelation knowledge'. It is too simplistic to say that Ekman was therefore being dishonest in his more public pronouncements; however, he was certainly not drawing on exactly the same assumptions about meaning, truth and human commonsense as his journalistic interlocutors.[17]

There are more fundamental and long-standing debates about rationality, language and cultural comparison that are being unearthed here. Winch's famous disputes with MacIntyre raised the question of whether there was shared space, shared notions of intelligibility, between informant and fieldworker (Wilson 1974). While Gellner's position has generally been to assume with MacIntyre that standard tests of rationality can be applied across cultures, the Winchean question remains relevant as we consider whether we can follow Gellner's lead in visualising a debate between three apparently equal interlocutors without making the category mistake of dealing with religion as if it were a quasi-(social-) scientific view (see, e.g., Wilson ibid.: xvi). And if this problem seems difficult to resolve when comparing Western thought with that of 'primitives', it is made even more intractable when the 'primitives' can themselves claim (using our own language) to be scientists, to be skilled purveyors of politically and culturally informed argument in secular public discourse, and indeed to be able to trace intellectual ancestry from the foundation of many of the academic institutions that have been assumed to contain the higher reaches of Western rationality.

I do not intend (yet) to address these problems directly, but I do want to compare Gellner's image of dialogue/trialogue with work that has focused more directly on conservative Protestantism in its ethnographic encounters. Gellner and Harding agree that 'fundamentalism' is not to be dismissed as an irrational, irrelevant opponent of modernity: rather it is constituted by, and contributes significantly to, modern discursive practices. The work of both of these anthropologists encourages us to explore the frictions and incongruities between religiously based language and anthropological discourse. However, the rhetorical and intellectual pathways they take to reach such conclusions are radically different. We have already seen that Gellner's tone is often detached, ironic and largely dependent on the texts of other scholars to make his case.[18] His work moulds fundamentalism into an apparently generic discourse, adapted to a civilised, transcultural conversation about Truth. As we shall see, Harding's translation of Christian fundamentalist language into more full-blown ethnography apparently ditches the ironic detachment and confronts the reader with the unvarnished words of the believer – the repugnant other.[19] She puts her ethnographic self in the front line as an object of performative, proselytising language, in effect producing a phenomenology of the faith by showing how words are *experienced* and not 'merely' read, spoken or heard. Juxtaposed, Gellner's and Harding's disjunct textual strategies almost embody Apollonian versus Dionysian approaches to the scholarly representation of religious discourse: rhetorical sobriety opposed by a more passionate, virtually possessed, engagement with the cultural object: symposium is opposed by ecstasy.

Harding's possibly best-known work, her paper 'Convicted by the Holy Spirit: The Rhetoric of Fundamental Baptist Conversion' (1987), appeared in *American Ethnologist* and was then reprinted, with some editing, in her *The Book of Jerry Falwell* (2000). The piece is dominated by Harding's account of an interview with a Baptist pastor, and before we examine it a few prefatory remarks should be made. Most students of conservative Protestantism have experienced fieldwork events where they have felt that the project of ethnography has been counterbalanced by one of equal and opposite evangelisation. The interview is one of the prime catalysts for such battles of discursive appropriation, since it ironically involves anthropologist and informant in a situation where fieldwork methodology and missionary habitus complement each other almost to perfection. Active speaker is invited to communicate with passive, apparently receptive listener, and even to talk in the personalised, rhetorical genres that constitute most forms of witnessing. Alan Peshkin (1986: 1) writes of how his interview sessions with a fundamentalist pastor usually opened with a prayer; Vincent Crapanzano (2000: 54) soon learned not to refer to his own life in conversation with religious conservatives since that would set off a kind of missionising reflex in his interlocutor; I have had an interview about creationism with a Professor of Material Science turn into something much closer to personal witness, despite the apparently unpromising context of a busy, secular, academic office.

Harding's paper is the classic account of this kind of encounter. What interests me about her piece is the way it deals with the ambivalent intersections between ethnographic and evangelising voices, in the process coming to question the extent to which the repugnant other remains purely 'other', but also perhaps redrawing the boundaries between a text to be read and one to be 'experienced' by scholars consulting her work. An introductory section giving some general background on Fundamentalist uses of language leads into something very different: an extended account of the results of her fieldwork encounter with Reverend Cantrell in the liminal space and time of dusk in a church on the outskirts of Lynchburg. She regards herself as being 'invaded by the fundamental Baptist tongue' (ibid.: 169), and juxtaposes personal reflections with very large extracts of Cantrell's witness to her.

The effectiveness of Harding's paper is dependent upon her inhabiting an implicit liminal space and time in between fieldwork and ethnography – a strategy that enables her to act as a mediating vehicle in conveying the language of the preacher to the consciousness of the reader. The long, dramatic quotes from Cantrell are engaging, as is the shaping of the paper as a rite of passage, seemingly conveyed almost in real time. Most powerful is Harding's use of herself as a human index of the power of Cantrell's language (Tannen 1989): she apparently loses control of the interview, just as she comes to realise that born-again believers regard non-believers, those who cannot deploy fundamentalist language, as by definition unable to understand the faith (1987: 171; Favret-Saada 1980; Harding 2000: 39). The question then becomes: how can ethnographic understanding be attained?[20]

Let us look more closely at the paper to see how this question might be answered. Cantrell addresses Harding throughout much of the central portion of the text, but Harding's mode of address in relation to the reader is also highly significant. Pronominal shifts echo Harding's fieldwork experience: initial, third-person generalisations about fundamentalism are converted in the next section into a gripping tale of attempted conversion, in which the 'I' of Harding the ethnographer is juxtaposed and sometimes comes close to merging with the 'I' of Cantrell as personal witness.[21] Then, in the final section of the paper, the conclusion that seemingly restores Harding's explicit ethnographic voice, she actually combines third person, declarative statements ('witnessing is an orthodox Protestant rite of conversion' [1987: 178]) not only with first person reflections ('I was caught up in Reverend Cantrell's stories' [ibid.: 179]) but also with a number of more direct, second person appeals to the reader, such as: 'You cannot both believe and disbelieve' (ibid.: 178). Just as Cantrell turns his mode of address from 'I' to 'You', so Harding does too, and if, as she states, her intention is 'to show' as much as 'tell' what conversion and belief are (ibid.: 171), she demonstrates her ethnographic mastery of the language of evangelism at the very point where she shows how easy it is for herself, and perhaps others, to surrender to its seductions. Harding's *listening* to Cantrell slips with rhetorical ease into our *reading* of his words: the supposedly repugnant other draws close to us as well as to Harding through the very close interweaving of evangelising narrative with ethnographic text.

Harding's highly effective rhetorical strategies are also evident in her oral presentations of fundamentalist language. In May 2001, at the American Ethnological Society conference in McGill,[22] she presented a paper on 'Word Power' at a panel (to which I also contributed) called 'Divine "Texts" in Performance'. Harding noted that her intention was to read from 'The Book of Oral Roberts', and her initial remarks prefaced the playing of an extended recording of Roberts's immensely powerful sermon on 'The Fourth Man', based on Daniel Chapter 3. Webb Keane has noted (1997: 61) that the different ways in which quoted words are framed by quoting speech can have entailments for their respective authority. Direct quotation is more deferential to the original speaker than indirect quotation, and in Harding's case we see how a conference performance actually allows her to reproduce the intonation, the rhythm, one might even say the verbal charisma of Roberts in a new context. The purposes of two language ideologies converge here: Harding, I assume, wants to convey a vivid and memorable piece of ethnography; Roberts is a master of presenting narratives that combine intimacy with an ability to be entextualised, lifted out of any particular interactional setting (Csordas 1997: 206; Keane 1997: 62). As far as I am aware, nobody in the audience at McGill was converted into an evangelical, but I am pretty sure that we were engaged in a way that was qualitatively different to a more normal, perhaps more comatose, conference attitude.

These mediations between preacher and audience do not mean that Harding is acting as an evangelist; rather, ethnographic form and missionising message are allowed to complement and even echo each other in ways that exemplify Harding's analysis. An important point made in her *The Book of Jerry Falwell* (2000: 24) is that preachers are not bound by intellectual property rights: verbal borrowing without citation is regarded as a Christian virtue, not a vice (Crapanzano 2000: 58).[23] Thus, Falwell, in common with Roberts, is both a powerful personality and, curiously 'a man without a center' (Harding 2000: 273), embodying tensions between an officially singular authorial voice in the foreground and multiple authors – other preachers, ghostwriters, the Bible itself – in the background. And rather similar, equally fertile, predicaments are evident for Harding as ethnographer. Anthropology might be seen to have inherited the Romantic-humanist tradition of what Rice and Waugh, responding to Roland Barthes, call the 'egotistical sublime' (1989: 253): cultures are created and owned by their ethnographers in a way that makes authors active and subjects passive (Marcus and Fischer 1986: 1). In contrast to this stereotype, Harding presents a picture in which heteroglossia and double-voicing are located in both fundamentalist and ethnographic texts (Harding 2000: 183 and note her references to Bakhtin 1984).

Giving voice to the other is hardly new in itself as an ethnographic strategy (Csordas 1994: xi), but the point is that as a strategy it can take many different forms. It is Harding who chooses what to quote, when and how, but one can argue that she recontextualises evangelising discourse in such a way as to retain something of the power of its original mode of address. Harding lets herself be authored by preachers in a way that might sometimes be said to accept the autonomy of the Bible-based word as a performative force. She becomes a metonym for a secular culture that itself is being colonised/missionised by such Christians. Perhaps *The Book of Jerry Falwell* 'belongs' to Falwell as well as to Harding; and, according to the same 'gospel' logic, maybe the fact that Roberts's sermon was replayed at McGill meant that Harding's paper was as much an evangelical as it was an ethnographic event.[24]

However, we need also to be aware of the predicaments inherent in this approach. Part of the power of Harding's ethnographic encounter with Cantrell inheres in what it implies about agency. Harding appears to have little choice in relation to the verbal invasion directed at her, and of course what Cantrell is trying to do is to make Harding speak, and reply to him, not in the voice of the ethnographer, but of a believer. Mimesis, in a sense, is forced upon her. The final verbal affirmation, signalling the conversion of Harding from a sceptical listener into a believing speaker, never comes. But in seeming to lose control, however temporarily, of Professor Harding the interviewer, she is also simultaneously authenticating the ethnographic 'I', the persona that can claim to 'understand' gospel culture. Anthropological agency is actually reinforced through its being put at risk in this fieldwork context; and just as Cantrell located Harding in an oral, narrative frame for an afternoon, so she locates him very successfully in her own, written, narrative frame. This is of course a form of textual negotiation that is not confined to studies of evangelicals. Hastrup (1993: 177) describes and remains critical of an automatic provision of textual space for native voices in the sense that such voices are inevitably edited, and perhaps even subjected to a Western form of logocentrism.

The ambiguities and shifts of voice in the ethnographic performance that Harding choreographs can also, as I have implied, become representationally risky tools in the study of Western Christianity since they expose social-scientific taboos. Quite a few years ago, I attended a British conference of sociologists and anthropologists of religion. I was due to deliver my first ever paper on charismatics, and was nervously wondering how it would be received. The speaker scheduled just before me was an equally young ethnographer, a woman, who gave a talk about her work in a gay evangelical church in the U.S. As we listened, it became clear that what she was calling Geertzean thick description was also something else: a form of 'coming out' in an academic setting, and perhaps even a form of unvarnished missionising. To this day, I have never seen such a hostile response from an audience to an ethnographic presentation, and the aggression came even from people who were previously acquainted with and evidently liked the ethnographer. The obvious comment on this event is to say that the response reflected a deep unease with homosexuality, or with the mixture of homosexuality and evangelicalism. Knowing the people involved, I think that it is equally plausible to consider another, more professionally specialised form of taboo: the sense that what was being presented had *entirely* merged ethnographic and evangelising voices. As a form of witness, the paper lacked any analytical framing through which the speaker could reclaim a professional form of personal identity.

In the example I have just given, the dangerous affinities between the pulpit and the academic podium might seem to be evident. Both provide access to what appears to be the main means of communication of both evangelicals and anthropologists: the Word (or word). Let me therefore develop my comments about the language ideologies in both of these sub-cultures by providing one more extended ethnographic example of a contemporary fieldworker dealing with conservative Christians, before I make some more general, comparative comments. R. Stephen Warner's *New Wine in Old Wineskins* (1988) is increasingly seen as a classic social-scientific account of a contemporary Protestant congregation.[25] In the text, he notes that numerous factors drew him to Mendocino Presbyterian Church in California, in particular the fact that his former wife and eight-year-old son had 'come to Jesus' and joined its congregation (ibid.: 67). The news came through a jolting form of verbal exchange – and one that brought together his personal, work and fieldwork lives: in response to a letter he sent to his former wife, expressing his disappointment over having been denied promotion, he received not a reply expressing sympathy, but a tape of an evangelical sermon.

The issue of language and its use then became central not only to Warner's understanding of what was going on in the church but also to his personal negotiation of how to define the boundaries between his fieldwork and private identities. He notes (1988: 73): 'In truth, unlike the stock anthropologist among the aborigines, I knew there were no barriers of race, ethnicity, or language to my going native, and I had plenty of improbable models, new Jewish Christians among them, to show that there was only the verbal confession of faith separating "them" from me.' This thin verbal barrier came to be seen as all-important. Thus: 'My rule was not to say anything I did not believe, and therefore I never offered a prayer.' He soon learned how to use evangelical idioms, but when they entered his own speech they came complete with 'oral quotation marks' (ibid.: 81). In contrast, Warner had few qualms about *physical* actions (with the exception of communion)[26] that allowed him to fit in unobtrusively with what others were doing: he joined hands in prayer circles, looked like a normal member of the congregation at meetings, did what others did (ibid.: 74).

Warner, a long-lapsed Presbyterian, clearly shared with his informants a cultural recognition of the power of the spoken word to express authentic, sincere, interior experience. Keane (1997: 65) has remarked on the possibilities that language contains for mediating between the eminently social (as a pre-existing medium of communication) and the deeply subjective (as an apparent medium of inner thought). It seems significant that Warner did not mind joining in songs, as he sensed that such behaviour represented, compared to spoken prayer, the lowest level of personal religious commitment. Songs can be seen as preformed, collective, addressed to nobody and everyone – in Keane's terms the social predominates over the subjective; prayer is more spontaneous, associated with the individual, addressed to God, and thus risks mixing the interior personal self with the ethnographically 'presented' self.

The central importance of language to Warner's management of his fieldwork experience is revealed in a further, less obvious way. Making notes, subsequent to experiences of fieldwork, became much more than a means of recording data: his writings became a kind of 'secular confessor' (1988: 74). Of course all ethnographic diaries have this quality of letting off steam, but surely what is significant is the precise nature of the confessional steam that is produced. In this case it is as though the act of converting church encounters into social-scientific language functioned specifically as a process of de-evangelisation.[27]

Warner called his overall strategy 'ambivalent participation' (1988: 74) and in my view he acted as many other fieldworkers would have done – indeed pretty much as I have done in my own work. Yet his remarks highlight an important predicament for gospel ethnography. I have argued that anthropological fieldwork usually contains traces of an embodied theory of action in its assumed effects on the data-gathering self: it is not so much that ritual precedes belief, à la Robertson-Smith, but that participation is assumed to feed observation: strategies of mimesis often act as a means, if not of blending self with other, at least of giving privileged access to ethnographic appropriation of exotic culture.[28] However, a refusal – or an inability – to deploy religious language in a certain way necessarily removed Warner from possibly the most central act of evangelical participation.[29]

Having left Warner snared on the horns of an ethnographic dilemma, let me briefly compare the constituent parts of my triad of perspectives on the intersections between religion and ethnography. Gellner's symposium implies the possibility of a dialogue with religionists in discussing not only the nature of religion but also reality and rationality in a wider sense; Harding's piece is actually about the conversion of dialogue into monologue, a surrender of the self to the words of a pastor and an apparent – if only initial – yielding of ethnography to religious language. In fact, her work (oriented toward linguistic anthropology) in this piece and in *The Book of Jerry Falwell* focuses far more on words and narratives than on people, and we learn little about the effects of such language on anybody other than herself. It seems to me that Warner's approach lies somewhere between that of Gellner and Harding. His work is peopled by a more varied and everyday selection of characters and activities, and while he is not involved in debates about Truth with his informants he does engage them in extended conversations about many aspects of their beliefs and habits. It may be no coincidence that, of the three presented here, he is also the ethnographer whose personal and fieldworking lives are most densely intertwined: not only is his entry into the field mediated by his son and former wife but he ends up marrying a fellow choir member of the church as real life intrudes on to the ethnographic persona.

If we look at the problematic relationships between religious and ethnographic languages that are revealed in these works, Warner's basic fieldwork problem is speaking in a way that retains an authentic but not alienating sense of the distanced ethnographer; Harding's is listening in a way that enables her to keep hold of a sense of that distance; Gellner's is how to present the possibility of dialogue or civilised argumentation between points of view. Gellner's view is tempting if we are to accept that fundamentalism is itself a part of modernist discourse, but his sermonising involves a narrative encapsulation of his interlocutors quite as effective as that practised by religious believers. His story becomes an epic tale of the search for Truth, and strips away what are seen as the extraneous cultural and ritualised features of the three intellectual options that are available. Whatever Gellner's intentions, that way does not lie contemporary ethnography. But we need to bear in mind, of course, that his position was first developed some forty years ago and bears a considerable philosophical imprint, whereas Warner's and particularly Harding's approach assimilate the numerous subsequent crises of ethnographic representation that have occurred in recent decades. Implicit in Harding's ethnography are concerns over the voice of the informant and the subject position (and also the gender) of the ethnographer.

Whatever their differences, the three authors provide us with a common predicament concerning the power of language and the intersections of academic with religious language ideologies. We see how the gospel ethnographer produces a text, and usually assumes that his or her informants are also concerned with texts, albeit in a different way. Both are peoples of the Book (or books). But does the placing of such emphasis on words fall into a trap that is particularly evident in works on conservative Protestantism: the assumption that language, spoken or written, is the only 'true' or valid expression of a religious commitment that itself is assumed to be unitary in character (Percy 1996)?[30] Protestant unease with ritual has classically focused on whether the demands of mediating forms are by definition opposed to the expression of pure meaning, and therefore on the extent to which material, fleshly signs can or cannot reveal authentic experience without distortion. Literalist understandings of language have therefore apparently stressed the referential or semantic dimension of language rather than its pragmatic, context-relating aspects (Crapanzano 2000; Coleman, in press) or indeed how it can be embodied: the meaning of a text is taken to be ultimately decidable and able to be traced to original, authorial intention.

Such assumptions may lead to good evangelical theology but ultimately they are unlikely to produce fully convincing anthropology. Is not literalism itself a 'lived reality' as much as an expression of textual dogmatism (Forstorp 1992: 18)? Without wishing to resurrect old dichotomies between intellectualist and symbolist positions, I simply note that we need to bring the non-verbal back into our purview if we are to understand evangelical culture in the round (Coleman 2000). For example, Harding's book (2000) includes a wonderful picture of Falwell taken in September 1987. In his role as temporary chief of Heritage U.S.A. (the Christian Disneyland newly relinquished by the disgraced Jim and Tammy Bakker), he is reluctantly taking a publicity plunge and allowing himself to be photographed slipping down Heritage Island's three-story Typhoon water slide. His body language – arms folded across chest, feet clasped firmly together, unsmiling – is rather less than ecstatic (Coleman 2001). This buttoned-up picture is intriguingly counterbalanced by another illustration of Falwell staring confidently at the camera, arms outstretched, occupying the pulpit of his Thomas Road Baptist Church. Yet, the contrasts in bodily rather than verbal language are not highlighted by Harding, who has other concerns. Or, to quote from my own work (Coleman, in press), one can argue that distinctions between truthful propositions and bodily disciplines begin to break down when we see how charismatic language ideology is translated into specific forms of action relating to words. Swedish listeners explicitly perceive themselves as 'receiving' language by applying so-called 'spiritual ears' to what is said, and 'spiritual eyes' to the heavily scored and noted Bibles that virtually everybody brings to services. Proper 'reception' can also involve highly disciplined private assimilation of the Word through combinations of Bible reading, prayer and tongues, with physical attitudes such as walking, kneeling and sometimes even running. Reading or listening, to be effective, should ideally be translated into forms of speaking, and the latter is often seen as physically speaking out performatively charged words that have been stored within the self. Literalism may also be translated into a form of meta-linguistic practice, since preachers are very fond of quoting verses that are themselves commentaries on language use, and which in effect provide templates for appropriation not merely as *words* but as actions *in relation to* words. Such 'meta-literalism' involves deployment of scripture to focus reflexively on the iconic value of 'the literal', and then the conversion of such iconic reading into speaking or acting. In this language ideology, if the Bible verse tells us that faith, mediated by language, can move mountains, it is also providing us with instructions as to how we should physically deploy language ourselves, as words are translated into means of transforming the world.

In using a stereotype of the evangelical or fundamentalist as one-dimensionally chained to referential views of sacred language we may be in danger ourselves of taking the ideology of literalism rather too literally. But by examining the ways in which language ideology is embodied we address one predicament but create another: can we still maintain with Warner that it is ethically consistent to hold hands in a prayer circle, but not to speak the words of a prayer? Are not both actually central to the constitution and presentation of 'authentic' evangelical identity?

(Conservative) Christianity Away from the Margins

My assumption has been that anthropological study of a certain branch of Christianity is important not only because it increases our ethnographic coverage but also because it can pose questions about the anthropology of religion as a cultural practice. While the argument is often made that religion is a problematic category in itself because many cultures have no strictly equivalent term in their languages, I have been attempting to show that, even where languages are ostensibly shared by believers and non-believers, significant and difficult issues of translation and comparison arise.

My focus has been on conservative Protestantism, so that specific questions relating to Catholicism, Orthodoxy and so on remain to be considered. However, I would not be willing to accept the view that by looking at evangelicalism and related ideologies I am thereby looking at the extreme margins of Christianity. Martin (2002: 1) notes that Pentecostalism and the wider charismatic movement alone currently occupy perhaps a quarter of a billion people, perhaps one in twenty-five of the global population, so that they can be compared with other massive religious mobilisations such as those within Islam. More pragmatically, we can hardly forget that military events are currently being orchestrated by a U.S. government whose moral and geo-political impulses are undoubtedly influenced by evangelical assumptions. One of the exciting aspects of an approach that is located 'on the margins of religion' and seeks a middle ground between the inscribed practices of daily life and the formal rituals of religion is that it refuses to accept the peripheralisation of religion as a set-apart and therefore potentially irrelevant sphere of activity and concern. Although I have not looked at everyday practices as such, I have attempted to show the value of acknowledging some of the ways in which Christianity can inscribe itself within the daily life of the anthropologist.

Notes

1. Cf. Klass's (1995: 149ff.) parallel discussion of post-rationalists, 'scientistics' and fundamentalists.
2. Gellner does note (1992a: 7) that the West has its own fundamentalists 'at home', even if they are not in quite such a dominant position as their Muslim counterparts.
3. Again, almost twenty years later, Gellner (1992a) claims that relativists are particularly intolerant of non-relativists in their own society, while he notes (somewhat hyperbolically) that the absolutism of other cultures 'receives favoured treatment, and a warm sympathy which is very close to endorsement' (ibid.: 73). We should not of course forget that some fieldworkers have also been missionaries – see, for example, Sundkler's (1961: 15–16) reflections on his fieldwork as a Christian in South African churches.
4. This is not of course to assume that most Western anthropologists are committed Christians. They will, however, have had extensive exposure to Christian assumptions.
5. See, for instance, my later comments about creationism in a British school.
6. In this essay, I shall use 'evangelicals' as a blanket term for conservative Protestants in general. The nomenclatural debates concerning the relations between Christian fundamentalism, evangelicalism, Pentecostalism and the neo-charismatics continue (cf. Coleman 2000), as does the debate as to whether it is valid to consider Christian and, say, Islamic fundamentalism as even remotely comparable (cf. Martin 2002: 1).
7. As Spickard and Landres (2002: 7–8) note of U.S. ethnographers, while the religions of the marginalised are no longer seen as just an irrational response to social dislocation, there is still a tendency to think of them as problematic. There are more ethnographies of African American Pentecostalism than of mainstream churches.
8. Crapanzano (2000: 19) notes that American fundamentalists are themselves fond of pointing out that liberals are hardly liberal in their treatment of religious conservatism. In Sweden, I found that some theologians could rationalise my wish to study the Word of Life on the grounds that one needed to 'keep track' of what such a 'dangerous' organisation was doing. One anthropologist asked why I wanted to study 'those nuts'.
9. Her appeal is especially poignant because she is referring to cultural 'others' who belong to and are attempting to find a voice within her own society, that of modern America. Contrast Luhrmann's (1989: 343) depiction of contemporary witches in the UK: she notes that the larger cultural order largely tolerates magical practice and sees it as unthreatening.
10. For the purposes of this chapter, 'us', as stated earlier, refers primarily to a broadly Western cultural identity, in keeping with the ethnographies and ethnographers chosen. This approach is taken for the purposes of focussing the argument, and not to deny the important issues involved in other forms of encounter.
11. *Encounters with Nationalism* (1994) has been placed on the Humanities Reading List.
12. This paper explores this issue in relation to evangelicalism, but that is not to say that variants of the methodological dilemmas posed are not evident elsewhere in ethnographies of religious topics. Favret-Saada (1980) famously wrestled with the need to participate in native discourses of witchcraft in the Bocage.

13. Invited Session of AAA, 2001: 'Gospel Ethnography: Predicaments of Fieldwork in the Cultures of Protestant Evangelism.'
14. This is not to deny that other religions are doing the same, of course, but they are beyond the scope of this chapter.
15. In one of Gellner's images, each position represents a point on a triangle (1992a: vii): each can be seen to constitute part of a closed system.
16. The location of Christian 'fundamentalist' Jerry Falwell's ministry.
17. Moreover, my suspicion is that the presence at the Word of Life of Gellner's book on nationalism is related to the attempt to construct – and teach – the most efficient conditions for religious revival.
18. Of course in the texts mentioned here Gellner is not writing ethnography as such, although he draws on ethnographic information.
19. I assume, nonetheless, that Harding would resist any Gellnerian charges of relativism. She argues that studies of repugnant cultural others lead not to moral relativism but towards making 'liberal notions painfully unsustainable', not least because 'our sense of political choice is sharpened by deconstructing the totalising opposition between "us" and "them"' (1991: 393).
20. Harding's encounter with Cantrell did make me recall a half-forgotten afternoon of fieldwork, from 1987. I was attending a large conference of charismatics in Uppsala. A visiting American preacher was speaking to the massed congregation, and after about half an hour I felt a novel sensation of disquiet. After a few more minutes I decided not to stay, and left the hall in the middle of the sermon. In retrospect, this sounds like a bad case of what Crapanzano (2000: 19) calls 'a sort of cognitive-emotional claustrophobia and, not to polish the point, desire to flee'. What I want to point out, however, is the ambiguities that are possible in interpreting this incident. My rejection of the sermon felt to me like irritation and ennui, an indication that it might be time to return home; but from a different, believers' perspective it might have been taken to illustrate that the verbal invasion had finally started, that charismatic language was chipping away at a fieldwork habitus. In such terms, my fleeing merely indicated a triumph of anthropological flesh over a newly evangelically receptive spirit.
21. Thus (1987: 178): 'Cantrell received ... peace in his soul, an eager willingness to give still more. The same gifts, he concluded, awaited me, if only I too would accept Christ.'
22. Panel organised by Matthew Tomlinson.
23. If a preacher such as Falwell is a master of imitation, especially of speech mimesis (Harding 2000: 25), this skill reflects a widespread assumption that a famous preacher is a character in stories that extend beyond his own person. For instance, Jerry Falwell inhabits a world generated by Bible-based narratives and characters, and he invites his followers to engage with, appropriate to themselves, perhaps even imitate the words of his narratives. The conventional anthropological taboo against plagiarism, the appropriation of another's words as one's own, reveals a rather different attitude to authorship but focuses mostly on student essays. The merger between the ethnographer's and the informant's voice is more ambiguously negotiated.
24. Although Harding's extensive merging of ethnographic and preacherly voices is unusual in its degree, such use of 'gospel' text is a common ethnographic trope. Nancy Ammerman's *Bible Believers* (1987: 1) starts with a statement from Falwell, asserting the infallibility of the Bible; my own book (2000: 1) on charismatics begins with a web-based invitation from a Swedish youth preacher to contact him for intercession. More subtly, textual metaphors and images insinuate themselves

into theoretical perspectives – hence Warner's *New Wine in Old Wineskins* (1988), a title which refers both to a biblical verse and to a theoretical analysis that deals with issues of change. Even Steve Bruce, in certain respects the sociological equivalent of Ernest Gellner in his attempt to provide a positivist framework for the assessment of the social and political effects of conservative Protestantism, structures the chapters and analysis of *The Rise and Fall of the New Christian Right* (1990) around books of the Bible, moving from Genesis to Revelations.
25. Perhaps I am cheating here, as Warner is a sociologist, but his book was conceived, and in my view succeeds, as a piece of ethnography.
26. Neitz, a lapsed Roman Catholic (2002: 39), regards her strategies of participant observation among Charismatic Catholics as being broadly similar to Warner's, and adds: 'Neither Warner nor I took communion with the people we studied. To me, taking communion signifies belonging. It also signifies believing.'
27. Though even away from the immediate context of the field, Warner retained his awareness of the mutual permeability of evangelical and secular cultures: his therapeutic notes on his state of mind could also be seen as 'a source of data on the anxieties felt by the convert' (1988: 81).
28. Thus, the imitative magic of fieldwork may not give us unmediated access to what 'they' believe (Luhrmann 1989: 14; Coleman 2002), but the self is still usually deployed as a fieldwork tool.
29. Of course not all forms of qualitative data gathering involve mimesis, but it is nonetheless frequently a key component of participative approaches.
30. Cf. Luhrmann's more general comment (1989: 353) that beliefs are not propositional commitments held consciously and claimed consistently and in a logical relationship to such commitments.

References

Ammerman, N. 1987. *Bible Believers: Fundamentalists in the Modern World*. New Brunswick: Rutgers University Press.

Asad, T. 1986. 'The Concept of Cultural Translation in British Social Anthropology', in J. Clifford and G. Marcus (eds), *Writing Culture: The Poetics and Politics of Ethnography*. Berkeley: University of California Press, pp. 141–64.

———. 1993. *Genealogies of Religion: Discipline and Reasons of Power in Christianity and Islam*. Baltimore: Johns Hopkins University Press.

Bakhtin, M. 1984. *Problems in Dostoevsky's Poetics*. Minneapolis: University of Minnesota Press.

Bruce, S. 1990. *The Rise and Fall of the New Christian Right*. Oxford: Clarendon.

Coleman, S. 2000. *The Globalisation of Charismatic Christianity: Spreading the Gospel of Prosperity*. Cambridge: Cambridge University Press.

———. 2001. 'Review of the Book of Jerry Falwell', *American Anthropologist* 103(3): 867–68.

———. 2002. '"But Are They Really Christian?": Contesting Knowledge and Identity In and Out of the Field', in J. Spickard, J.S. Landres and M. McGuire (eds), *Personal Knowledge and Beyond: Reshaping the Ethnography of Religion*. New York: New York University Press, pp. 75–87.

———. (in press) 'Why Silence Isn't Always Golden: Charismatic Speech and the Limits of Literalism', in M. Engelke and M. Tomlinson (eds), *Christian Ritual and the Limits of Meaning*. Oxford: Berghahn.

Coleman, S. and L. Carlin (eds). 2004. *The Cultures of Creationism: Antievolutionism in English-Speaking Countries.* Aldershot: Ashgate.

Crapanzano, V. 2000. *Serving the Word: Literalism in America from the Pulpit to the Bench.* New York: New Press.

Csordas, T.J. 1994. *The Sacred Self: A Cultural Phenomenology of Charismatic Healing.* Berkeley: University of California Press.

———. 1997. *Language, Charisma and Creativity: The Ritual Life of a Religious Movement.* Berkeley: University of California Press.

Evans-Pritchard, E. 1965. *Theories of Primitive Religion.* Oxford: Clarendon.

Favret-Saada, J. 1980. *Deadly Words: Witchcraft in the Bocage.* Cambridge: Cambridge University Press.

Forstorp, P.-A. 1992. *Att Leva och Läsa Biblen. Textpraktiker i Två Kristna Församlingar.* Linköping: Linköping University Press.

Gellner, E. 1974. 'Concepts and Society', in B. Wilson (ed.), *Rationality.* Oxford: Blackwell, pp. 18–49.

———. 1992a. *Postmodernism, Reason and Religion.* London: Routledge.

———. 1992b. 'The Uniqueness of Truth', A Sermon Preached on May 31 1992 before Cambridge University (King's College), pp. 3–11.

———. 1994. *Encounters with Nationalism.* Oxford: Blackwell.

Harding, S. 1987. 'Convicted by the Holy Spirit: The Rhetoric of Fundamental Baptist Conversion', *American Ethnologist* 14(1): 167–81.

———. 1991. 'Representing Fundamentalism: The Problem of the Repugnant Cultural Other', *Social Research* 58(2): 373–93.

———. 2000. *The Book of Jerry Falwell: Fundamentalist Language and Politics.* Princeton, NJ: Princeton University Press.

Hastrup, K. 1993. 'The Native Voice – and the Anthropological Vision', *Social Anthropology* 1(2): 173–86.

Keane, W. 1997. 'Religious Language', *Annual Review of Anthropology* 26(1): 47–71.

Klass, M. 1995. *Ordered Universes: Approaches to the Anthropology of Religion.* Boulder: Westview Press.

Luhrmann, T. 1989. *Persuasions of the Witch's Craft: Ritual Magic and Witchcraft in Present-day England.* Oxford: Blackwell.

———. 2001. Discussant's Comments. AAA Conference in Washington DC, November 28–December 2, 2001 Session on 'Gospel Ethnography: Predicaments of Fieldwork in the Cultures of Protestant Evangelism'. Saturday, December 1.

Marcus, G. and M. Fischer. 1986. *Anthropology as Cultural Critique: An Experimental Moment in the Human Sciences.* Chicago: Chicago University Press.

Martin, D. 2002. *Pentecostalism: The World Their Parish.* Oxford: Blackwell.

McCutcheon, R. 1997. *Manufacturing Religion: The Discourse on Gui Generis Religion and the Politics of Nostalgia.* New York: Oxford University Press.

Nietz, M. 2002. 'Walking between the Worlds: Permeable Boundaries, Ambiguous Identities', in J. Spickard, J.S. Landres and M. Mcguire (eds), *Personal Knowledge and Beyond: Reshaping the Ethnography of Religion.* New York: New York University Press, pp. 33–46.

Percy, M. 1996. *Words, Wonders and Power: Understanding Contemporary Christian Fundamentalism and Revivalism.* London: SPCK.

Peshkin, A. 1986. *God's Choice: The Total World of a Fundamentalist Christian School.* Chicago: Chicago University Press.

Pina-Cabral, J. de. 2001. 'Three Points on Secularism and Anthropology', *Social Anthropology* 9(3): 329–33.

Rice, P. and P. Waugh (eds). 1989. *Modern Literary Theory.* London: Arnold.

Robbins, J. 2001. 'What Is a Christian? Notes towards an Anthropology of Christianity' AAA Conference in Washington DC, November 28–December 2, 2001 Session on 'Gospel Ethnography: Predicaments of Fieldwork in the Cultures of Protestant Evangelism'. Saturday, December 1 on 'Gospel Ethnography: Predicaments of Fieldwork in the Cultures of Protestant Evangelism'.

Rubel, P. and A. Rosman. 2003. 'Introduction: Translation and Anthropology' in P. Rubel and A. Rosman (eds), *Translating Cultures: Perspectives on Translation and Anthropology*, pp. 1–22.

Spickard, J. and S. Landres. 2002. 'Whither Ethnography? Transforming the Social-scientific Study of Religion', in J. Spickard, J.S. Landres and M. Mcguire (eds), *Personal Knowledge and Beyond: Reshaping the Ethnography of Religion*. New York: New York University Press, pp. 1–14.

Stewart, C. 2001. 'Secularism as an Impediment to Anthropological Research', *Social Anthropology* 9(3): 325–28.

Sundkler, B. 1961. *Bantu Prophets in South Africa*. London: Oxford University Press.

Tambiah, S. 1990. *Magic, Science, Religion, and the Scope of Rationality*. Cambridge: Cambridge University Press.

Tannen, D. 1989. *Talking Voices: Repetition, Dialogue, and Imagery in Conversational Discourse*. Cambridge: Cambridge University Press.

Warner, R.S. 1988. *New Wine in Old Wineskins: Evangelicals and Liberals in a Small-Town Church*. Berkeley: University of California.

Wilson, B. 1974. 'A Sociologist's Introduction', in B. Wilson (ed.), *Rationality*. Oxford: Blackwell, pp. vii–xviii.

Part II

Space and Religious Marginality

Chapter 4

Religious Logistics: African Christians, Spirituality and Transportation

Thomas Kirsch

Introduction

Spreading a religion like Christianity poses logistical problems: it implies traversing space; determining points of departure, crossings and destinations; specifying media, channels and go-betweens; constructing social and technological networks; managing acts of translation; and securing access to means of transport.

However, there are different views regarding what 'spreading Christianity' actually involves. Some Christian organisations aim to diffuse the Christian *message*, in other words, 'religious propositions', which are then thought to stimulate the recipients' faith. A well-known historical example of this type of Christian organisation is the British and Foreign Bible Society of the early nineteenth century, which, according to Leslie Howsam, pursued a text-centred logic of evangelicalism and presumed that:

> since the scriptures held the key to salvation, it was up to serious Christians to make them widely available, in English and translated into foreign languages, at affordable prices, in appropriate formats. Such was the duty of human agency: the Bible text would do the rest. (Howsam 1991: xiv)

Here the Biblical text was claimed as being endowed with a certain agency in itself.[1] The logistical problem thus lay in the translation, printing and circulation of the Bible. In more recent decades, the distribution of audio and videocassettes, transmission by radio and television, and use of the internet have come to serve as a similar depersonalised and spatially unbound means of diffusing the *Word* (e.g., Buckser 1989; Alexander 1994; Launay 1997; Hackett 1998; Eickelman and Anderson 1999).

For other Christian organisations, however, such emphasis on propositional content is not sufficient. In these cases, spreading Christianity implies disseminating some *spiritual quality* going decisively beyond the subject matter of Christian doctrines. These organisations, many of them commonly subsumed under the category of Pentecostalism, consider it their duty to bring people into contact with the Holy Spirit and to make them experience, even embody, its divine power. This objective poses its particular logistical challenges, necessitating what might be called the 'logistics of the spirit'.

There are several religious communities which achieve this by promoting the spiritualistic use of the mass media. Some faith-healers encourage their audiences to touch their television screens during broadcasts. The American evangelist Benny Hinn, for example, who claims to be a channel for God, stated during a TV show on the Trinity Broadcasting Network in 1999 that Christian television programmes might even raise the dead:

> I see something quite amazing. I see rows of caskets lining up in front of this TV set and ... I see actually loved ones picking up the hands of the dead and letting them touch the screen and people are getting raised as their hands are touching that screen.[2]

Another example of this spiritualistic use of the mass media is a bi-monthly publication put out by the Apostolic Faith Church, whose imprint states that 'Before these magazines are sent out, they are always prayed over for the healing of the sick and the salvation of souls.'[3] Some members of this church whom I met therefore assumed that touching a copy of the magazine would somehow bring them closer to the Holy Spirit.

Other religious communities, however, remain sceptical of such claims, stressing instead more or less personalised acts of spiritual mediation. These communities usually claim to have originated from a sudden inpouring of the Holy Spirit that occurred to the founder of their church without human intervention. Nevertheless, the dissemination of the Holy Spirit beyond such originating moments requires communities to develop some idea of how the social mediation of spiritual empowerment might be achieved. When they enter into a state of possession during crusades and church services, for example, Pentecostal evangelists transfer the Holy Spirit through such actions as the laying-on of hands, blowing at people, or throwing the Holy Spirit like a baseball at the congregation. What these procedures have in common is a view that the diffusion of the Holy Spirit presupposes temporal and spatial co-presence, as well as tangible interactions between religious experts and the laity. It is at this point that the strong connection between spiritual religious practices aimed at the personal experience of transcendence in the here-and-now and (rather worldly) logistical issues becomes most apparent.

By examining religious logistics, this article will offer a new perspective on the anthropology of religion. In general, this approach is based on the assumption that the metaphysical, experiential and meaning-making dimensions of religious discourses and practices are closely connected to how religious communities are organised (cf. Davis 1982). More particularly, it concentrates on the ways in which religious practitioners establish connections with one another in order to initiate or facilitate religious encounters, communication and empowerment. The focus on 'religious logistics' accordingly implies taking account of the roles of physical space, infrastructure, means of transport, the movement of people, communication media and religious intermediaries when examining the social construction of communal, yet spatially dispersed religious life.

In the following, this approach is exemplified through an analysis of the relationship between spirituality and logistics in a contemporary African-initiated prophet-healing church in the rural areas of southern Zambia.[4] In the Spirit Apostolic Church, divinely ordained religious practice was seen as necessitating a close association with the Holy Spirit (*muuya usalala*).[5] This spiritual entity was not thought to be transmissible by means of physical objects such as 'fetishes' or communication media (Kirsch 2002b). Rather, the empowering relationship was felt either to originate in a personal, solitary encounter with the Divine or – in most instances – to be attained through acts of mediation by someone who was already thought to enjoy such a privileged association.

As will be shown below, the connection of spiritual intermediation and logistics entails a certain ambiguity for members of the Spirit Apostolic Church. Several senior leaders of the Church worked as truck-drivers, which allowed them to combine their occupation with their evangelising activities and their efforts to spread the Holy Spirit. When these leaders toured the branches in their trucks, their visits were locally associated with imageries of imminent welfare and modernisation. However, people in my research area also associated driving as an occupation with the consumption of alcohol, prostitution and a reckless search for profit. The 'logistics of the spirit' in the Spirit Apostolic Church thus involved a peculiar paradox: for many members, the means of spreading Christianity that their leaders used to some extent contradicted the spiritual quality that should be spread with it.

In order to examine how this paradoxical constellation was handled within the Spirit Apostolic Church, this article begins by outlining the connection between the development of the Church, general infrastructural developments and processes of modernisation in the Southern Province of Zambia. Then, an excursion through different religious geographies, both historical and contemporary, in my research area will help set the stage for a discussion of the ambivalences concerning the truck-driving activities of the senior leadership of the Spirit Apostolic Church. Finally, the article deals with the 'logistics of the spirit' proper. Here it will be argued that it was almost impossible to resolve the feelings of ambivalence mentioned above with regard to journeys from the 'wilderness', where solitary encounters with the Divine were sought, to the centres of communal religious practice. Since the 'outside' and the 'inside' were separated here by roads and their potential dangers, the possibility of the 'uncontaminated' importation of the Holy Spirit became questionable. In the case of the intercongregational 'logistics of the spirit', by contrast, the ambivalences were partly resolved by conjoining imageries of spirituality with imaginaries of modernity.

Roads and Routes

In the early 1950s, when Rabson, the Bishop of the Spirit Apostolic Church in 1999, was still a child, he and his parents lived in the rugged hills of the escarpment between the Central African Plateau and the Gwembe Valley.[6] At that time, access to the Valley and the thinly populated hills was difficult (cf. Colson 1962: 611). Some minor footpaths led through the escarpment, which were used by the Gwembe Tonga in bartering with the Tonga on the Plateau, small-scale trading and seeking labour in the towns and commercial farms adjacent to the railway line connecting Lusaka with Livingstone and with the mines of Southern Rhodesia (now Zimbabwe), South Africa and on the Northern Rhodesian (now Zambian) Copperbelt.[7] Most of the scattered villages on the escarpment and in the Gwembe Valley were only accessible using such paths. The homestead of Rabson's parents, however, was located close to the Old Road, the only road in this area allowing one to travel from the Plateau to the Gwembe Valley by motor vehicle. Narrating his life-history to me in 1999, Rabson recalled:

> I really enjoyed watching the cars and trucks passing by. There were not many cars in these years, but whenever I heard the noise of engines, my friends and I made sure to stand close to the road. I guess it was at that time that I started having the wish of becoming a driver.

The Old Road had been built by the British colonial administration in the 1930s, when yet another drought-induced famine had struck the Gwembe Valley (Scudder 1962: 215–47; Colson 1979). It reached from the railway line to a settlement close to the Sinazeze creek, where a depot for famine relief had been constructed, and then to the mission station of the Primitive Methodist Missionary Society at Kanchindu (Read 1932: 18), a British mission society that had started to evangelise in the Gwembe Valley around the turn of the nineteenth century. Up to the mid-1950s, only a small number of European traders were active in the Gwembe Valley, and even the missionaries periodically shifted their mission station from the Valley to the better climate of the Plateau.[8] Apart from some limited initiatives in growing cash crops like tobacco and cotton, it was mostly labour migration that provided the Gwembe Tonga with the money they needed to pay the hut taxes and purchase at least some of the highly valued commodities of the whites.[9]

While the Gwembe Valley had thus long been one of the remotest parts in this region of south-central Africa, this situation altered drastically when the Kariba Dam was built in the mid-1950s. Constructing the dam, which created what at that time was the largest man-made lake in the world, necessitated the resettlement of about 57,000 people and led to rapid infrastructural developments (Colson and Scudder 1975: 194). An accelerated influx from the outside world, the increased incorporation of the area into systems of market economy and the initial stages of urbanisation were all aspects of this rapid change, which also caused the disintegration of many customary ways of living.[10]

Rabson grew up during this time of marked socio-cultural, economic and religious transformation. When in 1999 he stressed having been deeply influenced by the existence of the Old Road, he presented it as a symbol foreshadowing not only the development of the Gwembe Valley as a whole but also of what seemed to be his personal future as a driver, as well as a Christian whose efforts in proselytism linked the Gwembe Valley and the Plateau. In the 1960s, Rabson became a member and eventually pastor of the Full Gospel Church of Central Africa, a small African-initiated church founded by a Tonga migrant who had returned from working in the mines of Southern Rhodesia. This was the church from which the Spirit Apostolic Church separated three decades later, with Rabson being one of its founding members.

When his father died in the mid-1960s, Rabson moved away and joined the crew of a British construction company in the township of Batoka on the Plateau near the escarpment. This company was building the new road from Batoka to Maamba in the Gwembe Valley, where open-cast coal-mining had recently begun. While being employed as a construction worker and moving along with the tarmac road as it was gradually extended, Rabson learned how to drive and eventually obtained a driving licence. He stopped working for the construction company, subsequently finding employment with a number of different companies. He worked as a lorry-driver for a garage in Choma on the Plateau, as a driver for a development aid organisation in the Gwembe Valley, and periodically as a taxi-driver shuttling back and forth every day between the Plateau and the Valley. Wherever he went, Rabson tried to establish new Christian communities. From the 1960s onwards, he thus succeeded in setting up twenty-eight branches of the Full Gospel Church of Central Africa. When, later on, he founded the Spirit Apostolic Church, whose headquarters came to be situated near Batoka on the Plateau, eight of these congregations joined him.

Besides Rabson, several other senior leaders of the Full Gospel Church and later of the Spirit Apostolic Church also worked as drivers. Others were supported by Rabson while they were trying to obtain a driving licence, and yet others worked as his assistants.[11] Among the leaders of these churches, therefore, were a comparatively high number of people whose occupation had something or other to do with vehicles and motor transport. Their employment provided opportunities to spread the Church more widely than other African-initiated denominations could even dream of.

Nevertheless, as will be demonstrated in a later section of this article, the driving activities of the senior church leadership were treated with ambivalence. Before discussing this further, however, I would first like to take a step back into history and describe the antecedent religious geographies into which the Spirit Apostolic Church came to be embedded.

Religious Geographies and Ambivalences

Richard Gray has succinctly pointed out that the transformation of African societies through Europeans 'began, not with colonial rule, but with the steamers, railways, telegraph, vernacular bibles, and newspapers of the nineteenth century' (1975: 1).[12] Being scattered throughout the territory, the first missionary societies, which started to settle in Northern Rhodesia towards the end of the nineteenth century, faced difficulties of logistics and communication, which they sought to solve through the introduction of infrastructures and technologies linking them to some of the other newly developing Christian centres.[13] Simultaneously dividing the whole territory into various exclusive 'spheres of influence' (cf. Henkel 1989), the missions and the colonial authorities attempted to prevent competition among religious communities.[14] What thus evolved in the first decades of European missionary activity was a complex constellation of territorially more or less neatly separated religious divisions connected to each other by an ever-increasing network of infrastructural and communication measures, such as roads, postal services and shared book rooms.[15] Taken together, these measures established a 'new moral topography on African soil [that] struck out into the wilderness, linking it to the noble empire of the spirit' (Comaroff and Comaroff 1991: 173).

In the Gwembe Valley, the first mission station of the Primitive Methodist Missionary Society was established close to the Zambezi River at Siccoba in 1901.[16] A nearby post of the colonial administration facilitated and protected the missionaries' activities, while the wagon road from Bulawayo to Kalomo in the north, which forded the river at Siccoba, secured provisions and communications. After the construction of the railway bridge over the Zambezi at Livingstone in 1905 (Vickery 1986: 56) this ford lost its importance, so the missionaries decided to shift the mission station eighty kilometres further downstream to Kanchindu. Among the main criteria for the choice of the new permanent location were 'population density, favourable conditions for the health of the missionaries, and access to supplies' (Ulrich Luig 1997: 88). In subsequent decades, this mission station became a centre of religious, economic, medical and educational life in the area. In contrast to some other denominations, however, the Primitive Methodist Missionary Society never attempted to draw local Christians into one spatially bounded community.[17] Rather, the mission station served as a starting point for the missionaries' tours of the surrounding areas, as well as for the construction of out-stations which were staffed with African teacher-evangelists. These activities were confined to a particular 'sphere of influence', which had been demarcated in order to forestall conflict with the Pilgrim Holiness Church, the Salvation Army and the Jesuits operating in other parts of the Gwembe Valley (Colson and Scudder 1980: 49–60).

The evolving religious geography of the Primitive Methodist Missionary Society to some extent relied on infrastructural and politico-administrative structures that had been established previously by colonial agencies. At the same time, the mission society itself engaged in the development of a new infrastructure in the Gwembe Valley. Setting up mission stations and out-stations went along with claims to a religious monopoly in particular areas. Constructing gravel roads with the help of local workers thus promised improvements in accessing and controlling these areas.

This involvement in building infrastructure left a strong impression on the local population. In my interviews with elderly men who, during their youth in the Mweemba area of the Gwembe Valley, had witnessed such road construction, it was repeatedly stressed that the newly built roads were among the most substantial results of the missionaries' presence in the area, affecting not only converted Christians but also the non-Christian majority. Its impact, however, was not always seen in a positive light. Whereas some of my interviewees regarded the roads as a fundamental step in the overall improvement of their lives, since they made commodities and markets more easily accessible and labour migration more convenient, others felt that they had opened up their respective residential areas to harmful influences pouring in from the outside. Several of my interlocutors even asserted that there had been a considerable increase in witchcraft after roads had been built close to their villages.

Thus, as far as early infrastructural development in the Gwembe Valley is concerned, there appear to have been mixed feelings with regard to the association of missionaries and the building of roads. Two major trends can be distinguished. Roads as a way to *leave* the Gwembe Valley (for trading, purchasing commodities, labour migration, etc.) usually had positive connotations for those I interviewed. Roads as a way for people, objects and ideas to *enter* the Valley, by contrast, were frequently regarded much more critically. After all, people going about on the roads might be immoral or even malicious. But it is also possible to differentiate my interviewees' views according to another criterion: whereas some regarded the roads as intrinsically having some kind of influence, whether positive or negative, others maintained that they can be used by individuals with particular deliberate aims in mind, whether good or bad. For the latter, it was thus personal motivations for going on the roads that really mattered. We shall encounter similar conflicting assessments and ambivalences towards roads and everything having to do with them – like motorised transportation – at a later point in this article, when discussing the logistics of the spirit in the Spirit Apostolic Church.

The evolving religious geography of the Primitive Methodist Missionary Society negated pre-existing religious geographies.[18] Among the non-Christian religious practices of the Gwembe Tonga, in pre-colonial times appeasing the ancestors (*mizimu*) played a significant role in securing the well-being of family and lineage members (Colson 1955, 1960: 122–61); although to a much lesser extent, this is still of some importance today (Price and Thomas 1999: 521). Because of the relative freedom that men enjoy in choosing where to live (Colson 1960: 98–101), religious practices addressing ancestors evolved into extensive networks spanning different villages and neighbourhoods. Rain shrines (*malende*), conversely, were the centres of cults with local and occasionally regional catchment areas (Colson 1977). They were usually resorted to by neighbouring villagers for matters to do with the agricultural cycle, epidemics or droughts. Each shrine was thought to be 'responsible' for a particular spatial area. Nonetheless, at times people successively approached different shrines when their quest for help at a particular shrine proved ineffective. The rain shrine in Monze on the Plateau attracted supplicants from far afield (Colson 1977: 125; O'Brian 1983); in the mid-1990s, many of my interlocutors considered this shrine to have been particularly powerful.[19] For them there existed an asymmetry, the rain shrine in Monze on the Central African Plateau being ascribed a somewhat superior status to those in the Gwembe Valley.

Some of these non-Christian religious practices were also characterised by particular ambiguities. People were quite aware, for example, that spirit mediums might feign possession by the spirit of the shrine (Colson 1969: 76). And even when a particular spirit manifestation was deemed genuine, its actual identity was a matter of interpretation, those witnessing the event feeling free to decide for themselves whether they had witnessed a benevolent or malevolent being (cf. Kirsch 1998, 2002a).

An even more pronounced ambiguity could – and still can – be found in *masabe* possession cults, a form of religious practice that presumably originated in Zimbabwe, from where it spread into the 'land of the Tonga' (*butonga*) in the 1920s (Jaspan 1953, Colson 1971). *Masabe* spirits usually have an ailing effect until their existence is accepted by the afflicted. This acceptance is expressed by more or less regular participation in meetings of a loosely associated cult group, where the spirit takes control of the afflicted in a possession dance. Once accepted in this way, *masabe* spirits can be helpful to and protective of the individuals associated with them. Three aspects of *masabe* possession cults are of particular relevance for the present analysis. First, the pantheon of *masabe* spirits has changed over time; whereas in the early twentieth century they mostly represented spirits of the wild, that is, animals like lions and baboons, or the spirits of neighbouring tribes, like the Shona and Ndebele, the experiences of colonialism and resettlement brought forth new types of *masabe* associated with Europeans, technologies and urban culture. *Masabe* spirits now represented, for example, soldiers (*maregimenti*), trains (*citima*), airplanes (*indeki*), bush-clearers (*siacilipwe*), European dancing (*madance*) and accordions (*cilimba*).[20] By the 1980s, however, spirits symbolising material achievements had lost much of their relevance, and *masabe* mostly now stood for rather abstract ideas about 'civilisation' and modern empowerment (Luig 1993: 112). Secondly, despite the apparent divergences, the different types of *masabe* spirit have in common the idea that they represent powers originating from 'outside' of the immediate social *Lebenswelt* of the Gwembe Tonga, powers that were conceived as enticing, but also as potentially menacing (Luig 1992: 119). Thirdly, this ambivalence towards entities and influences from 'outside' in *masabe* possession cults was accommodated through a process of bodily incorporation. Their spirits being 'modernizing agents' (Luig 1994: 43), the *masabe* were therefore intermediaries between 'inside' and 'outside', between 'tradition' and 'modernity'.

Concerning religious geographies in the Gwembe Valley, I have so far described two forms of ambivalence: that expressed in *masabe* possession cults, and that articulated by my interlocutors with regard to the early missionaries' efforts at road construction. Both had in common the fact that the ambivalence at some point referred to Western artefacts and 'modern' lifestyles, and both also dealt decisively with the strained relationship between what were locally conceived of as the 'inside' and the 'outside'.

These two aspects have interesting parallels in the Spirit Apostolic Church. In describing the religious geography of this Church and local ambivalences with regard to motorised transport, two factors emerge. Firstly, it can be shown that ambivalence relating to the driving activities of the senior leadership of the Church had pronounced similarities with that concerning the roads built by missionaries. Secondly, part of this ambivalence was resolved in a manner that was similar to the *masabe* cults' method of dealing with the 'outside', namely, through the idea that it is possible to convert potentially negative (modern) influences into something beneficial by making them a part of one's life. This, in turn, required linking imageries of spirituality with imageries of modernity.

Motorised Proselytism

Like the early mission societies in the Gwembe Valley, the religious geography of the Spirit Apostolic Church can be described as encompassing a centre and various 'out-stations', namely, the branches.[21] In contrast to the former, however, from its very beginning the spatial configuration of the Spirit Apostolic Church overlapped with networks of other Christian denominations. In one of my major research areas, a comparatively sparsely populated area of forty-nine square kilometres surrounding the small market centre of Sinazeze, for instance, the congregation of the Spirit Apostolic Church was competing with seventeen other denominations of various kinds. Awareness of religious competition therefore provided crucial momentum for the working of the Church. Attempts to stabilise church activities were also exacerbated by the fact that many local Christians were quite willing to change their denominational affiliation if they were not satisfied with the performance of the church they had previously attended (Kirsch 2004). The church elders thus had to struggle continuously in order to maintain a following.

When compared to other African-initiated churches in the area, the Spirit Apostolic Church had some characteristics which appear to have made it easier for it to resist interdenominational competition. Among these was particularly its pattern of spatial distribution and its extraordinary forms of transportation, which influenced how it was perceived by outsiders. With its headquarters on the Plateau and its branches in the Gwembe Valley, the Church's spatial configuration reflected the distribution of the rain shrines (*malende*), the rain shrine in Monze on the Plateau being ascribed a religious status superior to those in the Valley by many of my interlocutors.[22] In religious terms, the Church centre accordingly stood for privileged access to spiritual revelation, as well as for the prospect of divinely ordained well-being. Given the relative remoteness of the Gwembe Valley up to the mid-1950s, the spatial location of the headquarters also made it a symbol of modernity, including all its technologies, desirable commodities and prestigious lifestyles.

The senior church leaders' occupation as truck-drivers combined these elements in an intricate fashion. The man behind the steering wheel shuttling in between the Plateau and the Gwembe Valley came to deliver sermons, utter prophesies and treat the afflicted, the very means of transportation he used holding out the promise of economic success and prosperity to his local followers. The fact that Rabson, Bishop of the Spirit Apostolic Church from 1996 to 2002, had even been involved in constructing the tarmac road that opened up the Gwembe Valley to the rest of the world decisively enhanced this imagery of the senior leaders as the pioneers, representatives and heralds of modernisation, even though the church never explicitly preached any form of 'Gospel of Prosperity' associated with such imagery.[23]

It can be assumed that some of the interest in the Spirit Apostolic Church resulted from its senior leaders' association with modern forms of transportation. A comparable constellation emerged when Sinazeze became electrified in 1999. Most construction workers of the Zambia Electricity Supply Corporation (ZESCO) belonged to the Pentecostal Word of God Ministry based in Lusaka. While proceeding along the gravel road from Sinazongwe to Sinazeze, where they set up posts for electrical cables, these workers engaged in proselytism and in establishing new branches of their Church. An electric organ and a megaphone, which none of the other denominations in the area used, became heralds of the new (electrified) era and attracted spectators – presumably not only because preaching by megaphone could hardly be ignored.

That such performances of modernism left a strong impression on the local population is due to the fact that most Gwembe Tonga today live on the edge of poverty. Since the mid-1970s, the local impact of the Zambian economic recession, failing opportunities for wage labour and labour migration, and repeated droughts have had a deteriorating effect on the Valley's economy (Scudder 1985). For the majority in my area of research, it was therefore even difficult to obtain their daily food. Regarding the employment of their leaders, members of the Spirit Apostolic Church hence felt admiration or even envy. For boys and young men in particular, working as a driver offered a highly desirable life perspective, associated with wealth, social authority and some kind of knowledgeable 'cosmopolitanism'. Having a close relationship to the senior church leaders thus meant becoming involved in a beneficial way of life.

At the same time, however, the behaviour of drivers passing along the roads of the Gwembe Valley – transporting coal, fish, cattle or other goods – was often regarded critically. It was well known that some drivers engaged in illegal activities such as smuggling drugs or misusing their vehicles for purposes other than those their employers intended. It was also no secret that many drivers and their assistants were regular visitors to the taverns close to the road. Accidents occurred frequently because of their careless and occasionally intoxicated driving, and when drivers accidentally ran pedestrians down, they rarely showed any remorse but simply compensated for the deaths unemotionally by making financial payments. In addition, drivers were associated with prostitution in two ways. Taverns and bottle stores were frequented by younger women offering sexual services in exchange for money or sometimes merely a drink. And for business women, who pursued small-scale trading and depended on motorised transportation, a driver's demand for sexual services was not unusual. It was therefore particularly the relationship between drivers and women which was seen as highly precarious.

Such unfavourable perceptions also had an impact on how the senior leaders of the Spirit Apostolic Church were conceived. Some people suspected that the immoral aspects of driving for a living might have rubbed off on these leaders. Allowing one's daughter to hitch a lift on a church leader's truck to go to a choir meeting was thus not always deemed appropriate. People were not entirely sure whether their leaders could be trusted and whether – despite their claims to the contrary – they actually kept away from illegal businesses, girlfriends and taverns when on the road. Imaginings and prejudices concerning the driving profession seriously called into question the morality of the church leaders, and thus their capacity as channels for spiritual powers.

On the whole, members of the Spirit Apostolic Church were entangled in a pronounced dilemma: they expected their leaders to engage in the dissemination of the Holy Spirit while harbouring ambivalent feelings regarding the means of transport that were used for this end. When seen in a positive light, driving a truck stood for modernity, prosperity and expanding horizons; seen negatively, it simply stood for immorality writ large. Let us now examine different forms of this ambivalence and how these were handled with regard to the Church's logistics of the spirit.

Logistics of the Spirit

As in many other African-initiated churches in southern Africa, members of the Spirit Apostolic Church considered the Holy Spirit to be associated with particular non-social realms.[24] Short periods of meditative seclusion in the wilderness were thus an important element of its religious practice. The elders and prospective church leaders were expected regularly to spend some time in spatially and socially remote areas in order to strengthen or, if they were said to have become spiritually weak, re-establish a privileged relationship with the Holy Spirit.

When they returned from the wilderness – usually hilltops in the escarpment between the Gwembe Valley and the Plateau – the religious experts were thought to have become exceedingly powerful in spirituality. Some of my interlocutors metaphorically compared the newly spiritualised state of the Church leaders with a 'battery' that had been 'charged' during seclusion and then 'discharged' through engagement in the spiritual activities of the community. Such activities, in turn, served for the spiritual empowerment of others: through healing, preaching, laying on hands and praying, the religious experts brought the laity into close association with the Holy Spirit.[25] In contrast to these procedures, achieving immediate contact with the Holy Spirit by reading the Bible was considered impossible. I was repeatedly told that, in their material form, the scriptural verses did not 'contain' the Holy Spirit. Whereas it was claimed that the 'physical' keeping of non-Christian spirits was possible, this possibility was rejected as far as the Holy Spirit was concerned. Instead, the Holy Spirit was conceived as an inevitably unbound and evanescent entity, which human beings could not control in its movements (*'takwe ukonzyakuyata muya waleza'*). Not even touching the Bible was assumed to have any healing power, unless the touching was mediated by a spiritually empowered religious expert.

The unbounded nature of the Holy Spirit also related to its association with human beings. According to the common understanding in the Spirit Apostolic Church, the body of an ordinary human person in its normal state resembled a *tabula rasa*. Yet if one led a proper Christian life and was assisted by a spiritually capable church elder, the Holy Spirit would start to come close to one's body and to surround it. And by means of communal efforts, like the singing of spiritual hymns, the Holy Spirit could be induced to enter the body (*kunjila mumubili*) of the person concerned. Then spiritual activities like witchfinding, prophesy or the exorcism of demons could be expected.

Despite the imagery of a 'battery', however, instances of the bodily incorporation of the Holy Spirit were rare. Spiritually, therefore, capability did not imply that the person concerned 'possessed' the Holy Spirit, in the sense of 'having it incorporated permanently'. Rather, it represented the likelihood that the Holy Spirit would use the particular individual as a channel for contacting others. The logistics of the spirit in the Spirit Apostolic Church thus did not mean 'transporting' the Holy Spirit as an entity, but rather transporting the *human channel* for it.

As already mentioned, a crucial dimension of such logistics of the spirit pertained to the perceived need for recurrent spatial movements from the 'outside' to the social 'inside', the word 'outside' here having the sense of 'wilderness', that is, a more or less remote, non-social realm.[26] In the 1960s, if one started out from the headquarters of the Full Gospel Church in the escarpment between the African Central Plateau and the Gwembe Valley, such unpopulated bush lands were not hard to find. In later decades, however, the leaders of the Spirit Apostolic Church faced serious problems in retreating from the social sphere. This was mostly because resettlement in connection with the construction of Lake Kariba and the general population growth in this region had led to an increased density of settlement, which made it increasingly difficult to find a solitary place where one would not encounter anyone for several days. In 1999, the 'wilderness' that people sought was still situated on a hilltop in the escarpment, but now it was no longer very far from human settlements.[27] Such hills were within walking distance of the tarmac road leading from Batoka to Maamba, along which villages had come into existence. Thus, retreating from the social no longer meant seeking absolute withdrawal in spatial terms. 'Remoteness' had become a more relative notion (cf. Ardener 1987) and was increasingly associated with 'secrecy'. Whereas earlier generations of church leaders knew the specific mountain where spiritual seclusions had previously been conducted successfully, later generations were frequently denied this information by their predecessors.

Church leaders' difficulties in retreating from the social sphere were also due to transport problems. Since the headquarters of the Spirit Apostolic Church had been established near Batoka on the Plateau – and hence quite far from any kind of mountain – the leaders had to travel quite a distance in order to find an appropriate place for spiritual seclusion. This journey by itself was not deemed to have any significance for the religious practitioner; the very process of withdrawing into the wilderness had no connotations of a religious pilgrimage (Turner and Turner 1978). And since the journey into the escarpment had to be undertaken by hitchhiking – given the impossibility of parking your employer's vehicle for several days in the middle of nowhere – the issue of retreating for spiritual seclusion into the 'wilderness' frequently boiled down to profane questions of scheduling and finance.

For the laity, such logistics of the spirit were characterised by ambivalence. It was not the case that their church leaders simply walked away into the wilderness and then came back some days later hungry and dirty, that is, just the way my interlocutors imagined people would be when returning from meditative seclusion in the bush. Instead, heading back home involved prolonged periods of waiting for a lift at the roadside, frequently enjoying a first bath and meal somewhere on the way, and eventually taking a ride in the back of a truck. It was these seemingly trivial instances of social involvement that members of the laity feared might have a diminishing effect on whatever the church elders had experienced on the hill that was religiously important for the congregation. In the words of one of my interlocutors, a 34-year-old female member of the church:

> You know, when they come back here, almost half of the message has got lost. When they sit on the trucks, they forget. Descending from the mountain, they are strong in the spirit; but once they reach here, they are almost back to normal.

This statement represents a strong version of a feeling shared by many members of the Spirit Apostolic Church, namely, that the means of personal transport used by the church leaders to reach and return from appropriate places for solitary prayers somehow might have a 'contaminating' effect on them.

Concerning the first dimension of the logistics of the spirit in the Spirit Apostolic Church, two major points can be discerned. First, 'wilderness' had become a scarce resource. Solitary seclusions there were thus relatively rare events and were, in addition, increasingly used for the construction of religious hierarchies. Second, the logistical means of journeying to and from the 'wilderness' were being judged critically. The means seemed to contradict the ends.

Feelings of ambivalence were also voiced with regard to intercongregational visits by senior church elders – the second dimension of logistics of the spirit in the Spirit Apostolic Church. Religious authority in the Church evolved in the form of an extended dispersal of charisma (Shils 1958). In 1999, all the church elders had brought about their association with the Holy Spirit through an act of mediation involving someone who had previously achieved a reputation for spiritual capacity. In the case of the senior elders, this mediation was traced back to the Full Gospel Church. In the case of the junior leaders in the branches, the mediation of the Holy Spirit was said to have been carried out by the senior members of the Spirit Apostolic Church. In this way, authorisation by the church elders was related to previous instances of spiritualisation, that is, to centres of origination where the particular dispersal of charisma was supposed to have started.

The senior leaders were well aware of the significance of touring the branches (*kuswaya mbungano*). When they arrived, they were celebrated and treated in a highly respectful manner by the members and junior leaders of the branches. Close contact with the senior leaders was prestigious and for many held out the promise of a spiritualising effect. Yet despite this obvious subordination, the branch leaders pursued their own interests in such encounters. During church meetings, for example, the division of labour between the junior and senior leaders entailed moments of mutual instrumentalisation. The junior leaders benefited from the presence of their superiors, who provided them with an authority that could be extended into the everyday religious practices of the branches. In order to achieve this end, the junior leaders promoted the authority of the superior church elders, elevating the latter in order to be elevated themselves. Religious authority evolved in a chain of translation (Callon and Latour 1981), in which the authority of the senior leaders was constructed by the junior leaders' instrumentalising and self-authorising references to it. The religious authority of the senior leaders thus relied crucially on the willingness of the junior leaders to use them for their own empowerment. The senior leaders, for their part, instrumentalised the junior leaders by allowing them to perform on the public stage at religious practices. By having the junior leaders deal with the minor activities of the meeting, the senior elders' own spirituality and religious activities were endowed with outstanding importance. Each group had a certain influence over the other, while simultaneously being dependent on it.

Given the junior leaders' tendency to instrumentalise the senior leaders according to their own interests, the association of the latter with the profession of driving was not interpreted as a problem when the senior leaders were present. Rather, they were introduced as heralds of modernity from a distant place and as being endowed with prodigious spirituality. During the absence of senior church leaders, however, the means of transport they used was regularly made an issue. Critically highlighting the dubious nature of their driving activities, speculation then arose, for example, whether they occasionally stopped at taverns, what illegal businesses they might be pursuing, and why a particular woman had been allowed to join the driver in his cab on a particular day. These speculations usually went along with derogative remarks about the spiritual capabilities of the senior church leaders. It was conceded that they might have been spiritually capable in the past, but it was also felt that their lifestyles had had a certain corrupting effect on them. Rhetorically distancing themselves from the headquarters, the branches then presented themselves as being autonomous in questions of spirituality.

Thus, with regard to the second dimension of the logistics of the spirit, reaction to the senior leaders' forms of mobility was two-edged, alternating between two lines of argumentation without conclusively dissolving the ambivalence. In one line of reasoning, the relationship between spirituality and motorised logistics was treated as being more or less antagonistic. This was based on the assumption that it is impossible to work as a driver and have a privileged relationship with the Holy Spirit at the same time. Roads and their associated lifestyle were seen as being endowed with an agency in themselves, which fundamentally contradicted Christian moralities. In an interesting inversion, references to the extraordinary mobility of the senior church elders thus concurred with claims to autonomy at the local level.[28] In the other line of reasoning, spirituality and motorised logistics were depicted as being compatible. Roads and driving trucks were not ascribed an agency in themselves; instead, it was religious motivation and personal morality that permitted a Christian driver to be distinguished from his more disreputable colleagues.

In contrast to the movements from the 'wilderness' to the 'inside' of communal religious practice, the inter-congregational journeys between the Plateau and the Gwembe Valley were also associated with imageries of modernity. Rather like the incorporation of *masabe* spirits described above, the senior leaders' positive acceptance and appropriation of forms of modernity were thus conceived as an act of conversion that turned potentially harmful forces into beneficial ones. Images of auspicious spirituality overlapped with images of auspicious modernity. In this line of argumentation, the motorised 'importation' of the Holy Spirit into the local context therefore became part of Christian spirituality – an implicit promise for prosperity.

Conclusion

In this analysis of 'religious logistics', I have argued that the complex configuration of the logistics of the spirit in the Spirit Apostolic Church evolved against a background of general infrastructural developments from the mid-1950s, which opened up the Gwembe Valley to the regional context of the Central African Plateau and beyond. That one of the founding members of this church, Rabson, had personally been involved in the construction of the particular road infrastructure invested the senior leadership in the eyes of the laity with the status of pioneers of modernisation. This image was further enhanced by the fact that many senior leaders worked as truck-drivers, shuttling back and forth between the Plateau and the Valley.

Nonetheless, the association of the church leadership with driving trucks for a living also had certain drawbacks. The actual behaviour of truck-drivers was often placed in a negative light. In the case of the leaders of the Spirit Apostolic Church, their driving activities raised doubts concerning their ability to serve as mediums of the Holy Spirit. For many members of the church, the (motorised) means of transportation used for the dissemination of the Holy Spirit contradicted the moral qualities of the spiritual entity that was to be disseminated.

These feelings of ambivalence were particularly pronounced when journeys back from spiritual seclusions in the 'wilderness' were concerned. Since by the 1990s the 'wilderness' had become a scarce resource – which, furthermore, was only accessible by way of road infrastructure – returning from the 'outside' to the 'inside' of communal religious practice usually implied involvement with the social that was deemed potentially corrupting for what had been experienced during spiritual seclusion. Between the wilderness and the religious community's location lay the road infrastructure and its concomitant, motorised transportation, which physically connected, yet morally disconnected, the two spheres.

These ambivalences were also felt in the case of the intercongregational journeys of the senior church leadership. In contrast to the logistics concerning spiritual seclusions, however, here it was possible to link notions of spirituality with the images of modernity associated with the Church's headquarters on the Plateau. The ambivalence with regard to the driving professions of the church leadership was thus converted into an implicit Gospel of Prosperity. The motorised means of physically connecting the two realms, the religious centre and the branches, became part of the message.

Notes

1. However, in the history of Christianity, it is rare for this notion of an autonomous agency of texts – where the Bible 'does the rest' – not to be accompanied by a range of activities aimed at enabling prospective Christians and neophytes to make divinely ordained use of the Bible, for example, by propagating particular 'literacy practices' (Street 1984). For an extended version of this argument see Kirsch (2002b).
2. This is a transcription of what Benny Hinn said on Paul and Jan Crouch's TBN television program (*Praise The Lord*, 19 October 1999).
3. *Higher Way Magazine*, 1998, Vol. 91, No. 6, p. 2.
4. Fieldwork on African Christianity in Zambia's Southern Province was conducted during a total of seventeen months in 1993, 1995, 1999 and 2001 and was made financially possible by grants from the Free University of Berlin (in 1993), the DAAD (in 1999) and the DFG (in 2001). This article is mainly based on data from my field research in 1999 and 2001; my use of the past tense has to be understood accordingly.
5. Personal names and the name of the church have been kept anonymous.
6. The Gwembe Valley lies about six to seven hundred metres below the Central African Plateau and extends from the so-called Devil's Gorge on the Zambezi to the confluence of the Zambezi with the Kafue, some 300 kilometres further down the river. The north-west part of the valley belongs to the Southern Province of Zambia, the south-east to Zimbabwe.
7. On the early inter-regional trading activities of the Plateau Tonga see Miracle (1959); on later developments in the relationship between the Valley and the Plateau see Colson and Scudder (1975).
8. According to Colson and Scudder (1980: 49), there were no Western missionaries in the Gwembe Valley from 1939 to 1954, though the African teachers and pastors remained even during these years. As for trading activities, a Gwembe Tour Report from 1952 states: 'There are no village stores in the area [of chief Sinazongwe; T.K.] and if they have to do any shopping, the people generally go to Siazwela or Batoka. At the present time, cash is not plentiful and all income is derived from those away at work' (Gwembe Tour Report No. 3, 1952; National Archive of Zambia: Sec 2/1016).

9. In 1956, more than 40% of the male taxable population had left the villages as labour migrants (Colson 1960: 32). On trans-Zambezi labour migration at the end of the nineteenth century see Makambe (1992); for a historical perspective on labour migration among the Gwembe Tonga see Ute Luig (1997); on contemporary Gwembe Tonga migration see Bond et al. (1996) and Cliggett (2000).
10. The socio-cultural and economic consequences of resettlement are discussed at length in, for example, Colson (1971) and Scudder (1969, 1993).
11. Some junior church leaders pursued small-scale businesses along similar lines. In 1999, for example, the pastor of the congregation in Nanyenda in the Gwembe Valley was running a 'filling station' consisting of two plastic containers and a tube. Lorry-drivers who transported coal from the mines in Maamba to the railway station in Batoka surreptitiously sold the petrol in their lorries, which was in great demand in this area, since the next proper filling station was almost eighty kilometres away.
12. For a similar argument see Headrick (1981, 1988).
13. One example of such infrastructure is the launching of the steamer *The Good News* by the London Missionary Society on Lake Tanganyika in 1885 (Henkel 1989: 31). A similar case is the construction, between 1882 and 1883, of the Stevenson road in Nyasaland, which linked the Livingstonia Mission to a station of the London Missionary Society.
14. Yet cases like the conflict between the London Missionary Society and the Catholic White Fathers, whose range of activities in some areas overlapped, meant that such attempts were not always successful (cf. Garvey 1994); for a similar competitive situation between the Catholic White Fathers and the Livingstonia Mission see Ipenburg (1992).
15. On the latter see Msiska (1986), Ragsdale (1986: 45), Shaw (1958).
16. For a history of mission Christianity in the Gwembe Valley see Ulrich Luig (1997).
17. According to Brian Garvey (1994: 40–45), for example, the Catholic White Fathers established 'Christian villages' close to their mission stations in north-eastern Rhodesia.
18. It can be assumed that this negation actually took the form of an ideological struggle concerning the definition of landscape, a type of conflict succinctly described by Terence Ranger (1999) for Christian reactions to Mwali shrines in the Matopo Hills in Zimbabwe.
19. Another rain shrine with an extensive catchment area was situated in Gokwe, in what today is Zimbabwe.
20. It is worth noting here that many of the gifts that *masabe* spirits expect from their human hosts also represent Western commodities like soap, perfume or even radios (Luig 1992: 117).
21. Although the spatial distances between these congregations do not seem great at first glance, given that the largest distance was seventy-one kilometres, travelling from one branch to another could take about a day. For most members of the church, journeys had to be undertaken by hitchhiking on the back of a truck and occasionally involved repeated changes of the means of transport in order to reach one's destination.
22. In a similar vein, after the mid-1950s *masabe* healers frequently came from the Plateau. As Ute Luig points out: 'They either belonged to the Plateau Tonga who settled in the valley in view of the new economic possibilities, or they were returning labour migrants from the towns or mines in South Africa. Some of them also worked in hamlets along the railway or in the newly established urban centres.

Thus, *masabe* possession became part of an increasing interrelationship between town and country' (1994: 38).
23. Paul Gifford defines the 'Gospel of Prosperity', which in Africa has increasingly been propagated by transnational – particularly from the U.S. – evangelists since the 1970s, as follows: 'The essential point of this Gospel of Prosperity is that prosperity of all kinds is the right of every Christian. God wants a Christian to be wealthy. True Christianity necessarily means wealth; it inevitably brings wealth. Conversely, poverty indicates personal sin, or at least a deficient faith or inadequate understanding' (1990: 375).
24. A good example of this is the Zimbabwean church called the 'African Apostles of Johane Masowe', here, the Shona name of its founder (Johane Masowe) already indicating the religious significance of 'wilderness' (*masowe*) (Dillon-Malone 1978).
25. According to the local understanding, these activities are expressions of particular 'gifts of god' (*cipego caleza*) (cf. Kirsch 1998).
26. The CiTonga term for 'wilderness' is *lusaka*, although some churches in the Gwembe Valley that have a historical background in Zimbabwe tend to use the Shona term *masowe*.
27. To my knowledge, the number of people moving from the Valley floor to the escarpment has significantly increased in the 1990s due to overpopulation, a shortage of fields and the (ensuing) increase in witchcraft accusations.
28. Similar inverse relationships have repeatedly been described in the literature on processes of globalisation; see, for example, R. Robertson's arguments concerning universalism and particularism in a globalised world (1994).

References

Alexander, Bobby C. 1994. *Televangelism Reconsidered: Ritual in the Search for Human Community*. Atlanta: Scholars Press.
Ardener, Edwin. 1987. '"Remote Areas": Some Theoretical Considerations', in A. Jackson (ed.), *Anthropology at Home*. London: Tavistock, pp. 38–54.
Bond, Virginia, Lisa Cliggett and Lyn Schumaker. 1996. 'STDs and Intrarural Migration in Zambia: Interpreting Life Histories of Tonga Migrants', *Relation to the Transmission of STDs and HIV*. Population Institute for Research and Training., Bloomington, Indiana: Working Paper HB880.I52 no.97-6.
Buckser, Andrew. 1989. 'Sacred Airtime: American Church Structures and the Rise of Televangelism', *Human Organization* 48(4): 370–76.
Callon, Michel and Bruno Latour. 1981. 'Unscrewing the Big Leviathan: How Actors Macro-structure Reality and How Sociologists Help Them to Do So', in K. Knorr-Cetina and A.V. Cicourel (eds), *Advances in Social Theory and Methodology: Toward an Integration of Micro- and Macro-sociologies*. Boston: Routledge and Kegan Paul, pp. 277–303.
Cliggett, Lisa. 2000. 'Social Components of Migration: Experiences from Southern Province, Zambia', *Human Organization* 59(1): 125–35.
Colson, Elizabeth. 1955. 'Ancestral Spirits and Social Structure among the Plateau Tonga', *International Archives of Ethnography* 47(1): 21–68.
———. 1960. *Social Organisation of the Gwembe Tonga*. Manchester: Manchester University Press.
———. 1962. 'Trade and Wealth among the Tonga', in P. Bohannan and G. Dalton (eds), *Markets in Africa*. Evanstone: Northwestern University Press, pp. 601–16.

———. 1971. *The Social Consequences of Resettlement*. Manchester: Manchester University Press.

———. 1977. 'A Continuing Dialogue: Prophets and Local Shrines among the Tonga of Zambia', in R. Werbner (ed.), *Regional Cults*. London: Academic Press, pp. 119–39.

———. 1979. 'In Good Years and in Bad: Food Strategies of Self-reliant Societies', *Journal of Anthropological Research* 35(1): 18–29.

Colson, Elizabeth and Thayer Scudder. 1975. 'New Economic Relationships between the Gwembe Valley and the Line of Rail', in D. Parkin (ed.), *Town and Country in Central and Eastern Africa*. Oxford: Oxford University Press, pp. 190–212.

———. 1980. *Secondary Education and the Formation of an Elite: The Impact of Education on Gwembe District, Zambia*. New York: Academic Press.

Comaroff, Jean and John L. Comaroff. 1991. *Of Revelation and Revolution, Vol. 1: Christianity, Colonialism, and Consciousness in South Africa*. Chicago: Chicago University Press.

Davis, John (ed.). 1982. *Religious Organization and Religious Experience*. London: Academic Press.

Dillon-Malone, Clive. 1978. *The Korsten Basketmakers: A Study of the Masowe Apostles*. Lusaka: University of Manchester Press.

Eickelman, Dale and Jon Anderson (eds). 1999. *New Media in the Muslim World*. Bloomington: Indiana University Press.

Garvey, Brian. 1994. *Bembaland Church: Religious and Social Change in South Central Africa, 1891–1964*. Leiden: E.J. Brill.

Gifford, Paul. 1990. 'Prosperity: A New and Foreign Element in African Christianity', *Religion* 20: 373–88.

Gray, Richard. 1975. *The Cambridge History of Africa*. Vol. 4. Cambridge: Cambridge University Press.

Hackett, Rosalind. 1998. 'Charismatic/Pentecostal Appropriation of Media Technologies in Nigeria and Ghana', *Journal of Religion in Africa* 28(3): 258–77.

Headrick, Daniel. 1981. *The Tools of Empire: Technology and European Imperialism in the Nineteenth Century*. Oxford: Oxford University Press.

———. 1988. *The Tentacles of Progress: Technology Transfer in the Age of Imperialism, 1850–1940*. Oxford: Oxford University Press.

Henkel, Reinhard. 1989. *Christian Missions in Africa: A Social Geographical Study of the Impact of their Activities in Zambia*. Berlin: Reimer Verlag.

Howsam, Leslie. 1991. *Cheap Bibles: Nineteenth-century Publishing and the British and Foreign Bible Society*. Cambridge: Cambridge University Press.

Ipenburg, A. 1992. *All Good Men: The Development of the Lubwa Mission, Chinsali, Zambia*. Frankfurt (Main): Peter Lang.

Jaspan, M.A. 1953. *The Ila-Tonga People of North-western Rhodesia*. London: International African Institute.

Kirsch, Thomas G. 1998. *Lieder der Macht: Religiöse Autorität und Performance in einer afrikanisch-christlichen Kirche Zambias*. Münster: LIT Verlag.

———. 2002a. 'Performance and the Negotiation of Charismatic Authority in an African Indigenous Church of Zambia', *Paideuma* 48: 57–76.

———. 2002b. 'Spirits, Letters, and Agency: Literacy Practices and Charisma in African Christianity', PhD thesis. Frankfurt (Oder): European University Viadrina.

———. 2004. 'Restaging the Will to Believe: Religious Pluralism, Anti-syncretism, and the Problem of Belief', *American Anthropologist* 106(4): 699–711.

Launay, Robert. 1997. 'Spirit Media: The Electronic Media and Islam among the Dyula of Northern Côte D'Ivoire', *Africa* 67(3): 441–53.

Luig, Ulrich. 1997. *Conversion as Social Process: A History of Missionary Christianity among the Valley Tonga, Zambia*. Münster: LIT Verlag.

Luig, Ute. 1992. 'Besessenheit als Ausdruck von Frauenkultur in Zambia', *Peripherie* 47/48: 111–28.

———. 1993. 'Gesellschaftliche Entwicklung und ihre individuelle Verarbeitung in den affliktiven Besessenheitskulten der Tonga', *Tribus* 42: 109–20.

———. 1994. 'Gender Relations and Commercialisation in Tonga Possession Cults', in M. Reh and G. Ludwar-Ene (eds), *Gender and Identity in Africa*. Hamburg: LIT Verlag.

———. 1997. 'Wanderarbeiter als Helden: Zwischen kolonialer Entfremdung und lokaler Selbstvergewisserung', *Historische Anthropologie* 4(3): 359–82.

Makambe, E.P. 1992. 'The Mobilisation of African Labour across the Zambezi for the Zimbabwean Colonial Market before the Chibaro Era, 1889–1903', *African Studies* 51(2): 277–94.

Miracle, M.P. 1959. 'Plateau Tonga Entrepreneurs in Historical Inter-regional Trade', in *Rhodes-Livingstone Journal* 26: 34–59.

Msiska, A. 1986. 'Early Efforts at Creating African Literature: Its Distribution, Local Authorship and Library Service in Northern Rhodesia (Zambia) and Nyasaland (Malawi)', *Libri* 36(3): 240–46.

O'Brian, Dan. 1983. 'Chiefs of Rain-Chiefs of Ruling: A Reinterpretation of Pre-colonial Tonga (Zambia) Social and Political Structure', *Africa* 53(4): 23–42.

Price, Neil and Neil Thomas. 1999. 'Continuity and Change in the Gwembe Tonga Family and Their Relevance to Demography's Nucleation Thesis', *Africa* 69(4): 510–34.

Ragsdale, John P. 1986. *Protestant Mission Education in Zambia, 1880–1950*. London: Associated University Presses.

Ranger, Terence. 1999. *Voices from the Rocks: Nature, Culture, and History in the Matopos Hills of Zimbabwe*. Bloomington: Indiana University Press.

Read, Gordon. 1932. *Report on Famine Relief: Gwembe, 1931–1932*. Livingstone: Northern Rhodesia Government Printer.

Robertson, Roland. 1994. *Globalisation: Social Theory and Global Culture*. London: Sage.

Scudder, Thayer. 1962. *The Ecology of the Gwembe Tonga*. Manchester: Manchester University Press.

———. 1969. 'The Ecological Hazards of Making a Lake', *Natural History* 78(2): 68–72.

———. 1985. *A History of Development in the Zambian Portion of the Middle Zambezi Valley and the Lake Kariba Basin*. Binghamton: Institute for Development Anthropology.

———. 1993. 'Development-induced Relocation and Refugee Studies: 37 Years of Change and Continuity among Zambia's Gwembe Tonga', *Journal of Refugee Studies* 6(2): 123–52.

Shaw, J.R. 1958. 'The Distribution of Books in Northern Rhodesia', *The International Review of Missions* 47(185): 90–95.

Shils, Edward. 1958. 'The Concentration and Dispersion of Charisma', *World Politics* 11(1): 1–19.

Street, Brian. 1984. *Literacy in Theory and Practice*. Cambridge: Cambridge University Press.

Turner, Victor and Edith Turner. 1978. *Image and Pilgrimage in Christian Culture*. New York: Columbia University Press.

Vickery, Kenneth P. 1986. *Black and White in Southern Zambia: The Tonga Plateau Economy and British Imperialism, 1890–1939*. New York: Greenwood Press.

Chapter 5

Contested Spaces: Temple Building and the Re-creation of Religious Boundaries in Contemporary Urban India

Ursula Rao

Introduction: Religion and the Public Life in India

Religion has a prominent place in the public life of contemporary India. People believe and worship in many ways. Religion also plays an important role in local and national politics, and there are extensive intellectual debates concerning the role of religion in the public life of a modern post-colonial nation. In India the majority of citizens are Hindu. There is also a substantial minority of Muslims and Christians and comparatively smaller groups of Jains, Buddhists, Sikhs and Parsis.[1] In this multi-religious setting, the effort to find an appropriate place for religion also focuses on how different religious communities should be accommodated within a singular political structure. In this chapter I will address questions of religion in the public life of India from the perspective of practice, and show how people shape the urban territory with respect to their beliefs, thereby defining as well as blurring boundaries between different religious as well as other social groups.

The study is located in the middle Indian city Bhopal and focuses on Hindu temples.[2] I will describe and analyse the building of 'illegal' temples and the struggles that result from this. The argument focuses on conflicts between religious activists – Hindus as well as Muslims – administrators and politicians. Why and when are temples made and destroyed? Who favours and who opposes them? Addressing these questions, I will give an account of the way people struggle for an appropriate place of religion and a space for divine actors in the city.

This brings into focus social demarcations that are brought about and made palpable during temple movements, while at the same time instrumental in shaping the conflicts. People create categories to make sense of their situation and bring about solutions. At a conceptual level, these produce irreducible contradictions between believers and non-believers in divine intervention, between a secular state and a religious majority, between Hindus and Muslims. However, people know that actual situations are more complex and they reformulate their judgments, differentiating and at times also crosscutting these categories by more concrete assessments about the intention of a particular person or situation. They distinguish between egoistic politics and genuine devotion, between divine intervention and religious pretence, between believers and non-believers, between secular and sacred territory, between tolerant and intolerant Muslims etc. Conflicts throw these boundaries into sharp relief, because they force actors to decide on which side they want to stand. Yet at the same time these boundaries are blurred in order to approach compromises. A secular state accepts religious claims, a priest allows police in the temple, Muslims acknowledge the religious claims of Hindus, etc. Every event forces the re-conceptualisation of preconceived notions of the "Other" and the preparation of a common territory for communication across these conceptions.

It is in this sense of boundary making and unmaking that I will talk about the margins of religion. Controversial religious practices focus the attention of participants on the margin of any concrete religion. People need to decide how far they can stretch their own conviction without losing their religion or the solidarity of their group. The negotiation of margins defines what makes the core and re-establishes it by drawing boundaries that define what is necessary, possible and acceptable.

Religious Appropriation of Space

Quite unlike their traditional counterparts, modern Indian cities are not planned according to religious consideration. In fact, it seems that today most urban planners are hostile to the inscription of religious meaning on the urban territory, because it poses a challenge to their ideal of rational city planning. However, this does not prevent the appropriation of urban space in religious terms. This takes place during the celebration of religious festivals, the outbreak of communal riots and through the construction of shrines and temples.

I received my first clue to the conflicts over urban territory when I went to the building authorities in Bhopal in order to get access to records of the religious buildings in Bhopal. Officially constructions on public land need prior permission from the city administration. If approval has not been obtained, such a building, for example a temple, is illegal and can be destroyed. Yet, there were hardly any records at all concerning religious constructions: no petitions, no inquiries, and only a few temples for which official permission had been given. This lack of documentation formed a striking contrast to the reality of continued work on devotional buildings all over the city – particularly of course on public land. It was here that I realised the wide gap that existed between city planning and construction reality.[3]

In order to draw a 'religious map' of Bhopal I was back on the streets, making my way from temple to temple to collect data from and stories surrounding the construction of the innumerable religious buildings. I gathered many different stories and learned of various motivations for building or supporting a temple. I met women who felt the need for a place of worship in their neighbourhood. Their desire was informed by perception of the distance they could travel alone from home without being called indecent or accused of wasting time. The need for a temple close by was an expression of their desire to reconcile religious and domestic duties. I learned of wandering ascetics who felt that they had become too old to travel and wanted to establish themselves as priests in a locality. They asked for divine help in choosing a site for a new temple that would become their home and support them. There were businessmen who joined hands to show their devotion to a deity and thereby facilitate the success of their enterprises. By building a temple the entrepreneurs wanted to return a proportion of their earnings to the divine power and hoped that in turn they would continue to prosper. A religious building in close proximity to their place of business promised to help them profit from the emanation of the divine energy, to communicate their religious attitude towards customers and demonstrate their importance in the area. I also came across caste groups, congregations and religious communities who wanted to create a place for community worship, become visually present in a locality and sometimes also to counter the presence of another religious group. Temples were also started by individuals who got possessed or had revelations and thus learned of a deity's intention to become present somewhere in the city. Others asked for a boon from a god or goddess and in return promised to build a new temple.

Common to all these stories is the determination of people to build a temple near the place they live or work. The deal is between them and the divine actors; the city administration does not figure as an agent that should have any power over the use of urban space for religious purpose. To probe deeper into this matter I asked one of the important Hindu leaders in the city why people did not approach the government first before starting to build a temple. His answer was simple and to the point: "The thing about legal and illegal [temples] is that they [city administration] do not give permission in advance. How can one then build a temple legally? All the temples were constructed as a response to the needs of people!" This statement reflects the popular attitude that people have a right to worship their deities and will do so if they feel the need. It also confirms the stereotypical perception of the state as an institution that is insensitive to the 'religious needs' of people, as put forward by many believers and made popular through the polemic of Hindu nationalist propaganda.

There is no doubt that a hostile attitude exists among many highly-placed officials towards what they call the 'mushrooming of temples', and they are outspoken about their disgust at a situation in which they seem to be unable to enforce the law. Often it is impossible to prevent the building of a temple, since people plan the activity secretly and install the idol during the night. Once a temple is built it is difficult to destroy it. Builders mobilise public support through word of mouth propaganda and newspapers to create opposition against the state in case there are plans to destroy the religious building.

There are various reasons why leading administrators oppose illegal temples. The unpredictable foundation of temples stands in the way of systematic city planning. Normally built in crowded places, illegal temples frustrate the administration's efforts to ensure unobstructed mobility. Once a temple is built it never stops growing. Devotees will continue to add new shrines, further rooms, a higher roof, a water tank, shops for devotional goods, etc. A tea and sweet shop may spring up to feed visitors and deities. The bigger a temple grows the greater will be its popularity. People come in large numbers in the mornings and evenings to worship, festivals attract big crowds and religious parades include popular holy sites in their program. Temples also host homeless religious servants and beggars. There is extensive ringing of bells daily and electronic transmission of devotional singing during festival times. All in all, the area around a temple becomes a place for dense and often noisy social activity that transforms the locality.

Often administrators question the religious intentions of builders. They believe monetary or political motivations to be paramount. Temples provide income for trustees, priests and vendors of devotional material and they give a home to ascetics, poor devotees and beggars. Politicians plan temples to win local votes. Hindu nationalists use temples to antagonise and marginalise residents of other faiths, especially Muslims, in a particular territory. In the latter case, a new temple can upset the social balance in a locality. Even a small shrine may lead to the mobilisation of large crowds in support of or in opposition to the religious building, which in turn can provoke inter-religious conflicts or even riots. Thus, some temples create new 'sensitive' spots in the city that pose problems of law and order. Devotees also acknowledge these dimensions. They discuss negative impacts of temples or egoistic ways of using and appropriating them. However, when weighed against the beneficial presence of a deity in a locality, such problems appear secondary. They are the negative side effects of an overall positive development.

While many believers assume that the administration as such is suspicious of and hostile towards religious activities, they nevertheless distinguish between individuals. They know who is more or less sympathetic towards 'Hindu interests' and use their access to bureaucratic power in order to bolster their demands. They may also plan the making of a new temple during a time when they feel that the administration is weak because of changes in personal or other activities that absorb their energy. If there are no useful ties to the administration, activists may rely on political contacts. Builders approach politicians to help realise or save a temple building. They seek the patronage of members of parliament or other well-known figures of Hindu nationalist background who can be easily convinced to support any religious project. However, there is a danger in involving powerful agents. Entrusting a personal project to leaders will diminish the influence of those who started the activity. What began as a local concern may then easily be absorbed into larger political struggles, which might in part even jeopardise the original aims. This way, a local struggle for a temple can suddenly turn into an activity supporting a Hindu nationalist agenda (Freitag 1989; Pandey 1990; Jaffrelot 1998; Rao, forthcoming).

What becomes apparent is that the appropriation of urban space for religious purposes is set within a social matrix that forces the renegotiation of religious boundaries in two senses. Firstly, there is an overlap of religious and political intentions and desires at two levels. The creation of new religious sites is related to political projects that are attempts to impose a particular role on religion in public life. Temple building activities are also embedded within local conflicts over status and influence. Secondly, the conflicts discussed here are carried out by human agents who act in the name of the divine. The struggles over religious territory relate to complex negotiations about ideas of non-human agency. The margin of religion as *human* activity is marked by a religious imagination that sees human influence in religious matters as limited by the autonomy of divine actors. The next two sections will explore these activities of boundary making and blurring during temple controversies.

Between Religion and Politics

Religious activities in India are embedded in social processes of politics and economy. The following two examples of processions that involve temple buildings show how deeply intertwined different aspects of urban life are in practice.

Mattison Mines (1996) observed an annual spring festival in Madras, during which the god Kandasami – whose temple is controlled by a caste group called Beeri Chettiars – is taken out from his temple and paraded through the streets, where his devotees live, offering people a chance to worship their god and pay respect to their leaders, the managers of the temple. The organisers of the festival are not free to take Kandasami wherever they want. Since a parade through neighbourhoods belonging to other (caste) communities would challenge the authority of their leaders – who have their own temples and marked territories – the congregation is led only through those streets in which the trustees and sponsors of the festival have a clientele. In recent years many Beeri Chettiars have left their traditional neighbourhood and settled in other parts of the city. This has forced the organisers of the procession to re-define the route again and again, adapting it to the new living pattern of the community. To retain a sense of caste-community even in times of dispersed living, the caste leaders increased the number of processions during the spring festival. There are now six processions, each heading in a different direction, which re-connect the scattered members of a caste to their religious centre. Together these processions demonstrate that the community still exists, if only symbolically, and legitimise the leaders as representatives of a definite group (Mines 1996: 65–83).

The Shivratri procession in Bhopal makes for another example in which religious and social meaning are closely intertwined. Every year at Shivratri the central Shiva temple in the old town – controlled by the caste group of Aggrawals (mostly dealers in jewellery) – takes out a procession through the streets of Bhopal. In the 1990s the meaning of this parade was changed due to a new social arrangement. A new Durga Temple had been constructed in the city centre by a group of Hindu cloth-traders who wanted to assert their presence in this Muslim dominated area. The temple had triggered a major controversy between the administration, the local Muslim population and Hindu traders. Mobilising massive support among the urban population, the Hindus succeeded and got their temple legalised. Because of the anti-Muslim bias of the temple the area around it has become a favoured place for Hindu nationalist political activities.[4]

In the 1990s the management of the Durga Temple agreed to marry goddess Durga off to Shiva from the nearby Shiva Temple. This transformed the annual Shivratri procession into a marriage procession which now annually re-enacts the connection between Shiva and Durga, Shiva Temple and Durga Temple, Shiva Temple Committee and Durga Temple Committee. This connection has two effects. It creates a close bond between bride givers and bride takers. Through the arrangement the already influential Aggrawals have increased their following in the city, while the local businessmen from the Durga Temple Committee have ensured powerful patronage for their own economic activities. The divine marriage has changed economic relations, creating a mutual dependence between otherwise competing business-houses.

The marriage also has political implications. It connects the Durga Temple – until today considered to be an anti-Muslim project – with one of the oldest and biggest temples in the city centre. The connection strengthens Hindu solidarity in a residential area dominated by Muslims and increases their negotiating power in the city. This solidarity is an expression of the dominant political mood in the city, where many people applaud the Hindu nationalist political project and want to see Hindus in power and Muslims marginalised.

Such a project is formulated against the backdrop of Bhopal's history as capital of an independent Muslim state that existed from 1722 to 1949, when the Muslim ruler submitted to the Merger Movement and Bhopal joined the India Union two years after India's independence from Great Britain (Mittal 1990). Today many people in Bhopal feel that it is time for Hindus to rule and counter the former Muslim domination. There are regular complaints about religious suppression during Muslim rule. Historical documents confirm that during the second half of the nineteenth century Hindus were not allowed to celebrate religious festivals publicly and were forbidden to erect *shikharas* (the typical pyramid-like roofs of North Indian temples) on their temples inside the walled city.[5] Building a prominent Hindu temple at the entry of the walled city is a political statement that acknowledges and furthers Hindu political and religious dominance in Bhopal today.

Because religious performances are so relevant for the organisation of social relations, they are highly contested. In Mines' example only careful spatial considerations can lead to a successful procession, while in Bhopal there is a constant undercurrent of tensions between celebrating Hindus and the Muslim population in the area. Today there is a permanent police post near the Durga Temple and no major festival at Pir Gate passes without provisions for police security. In very 'sensitive situations' – when a Hindu and Muslim festival fall on the same date, or when Hindus celebrate on a Friday, the day Muslims go to the mosque – the riot prevention force[6] is called in. Talking about festivals, organisers narrate with pride the number of policemen mobilised, which is taken to be an indication of the importance of the festival. Strict security measures arise from the experience (and historicised narrative) that festivals are typical places for religious strife to start. Many cities in India are studded with places in which the memory of riots is inscribed on the territory. Such memories are refreshed and kept alive by the extended negotiations which nowadays precede every religious celebration (see, for example, Brass 1998; Jaffrelot 1998).

It is against this reality of communal strife that many administrators project their dream of a 'clean' city. By imposing a modern, 'rational' order they hope to liberate society from religious conflicts, which are considered to originate from primordial loyalties. In a secular nation state the inscription of religious meaning onto the urban landscape seems not only ideologically problematic but socially dangerous, because it threatens peace in the city and disturbs a smooth political and economic development of the territory. Since a privatisation of religious matters or the secularisation of Indian society seems still out of sight, the Indian state has opted for allowing state agencies to interfere in public religious matters. The aim of this regulation is to ensure a balance between religious interests and economic necessities, and to ensure the peaceful coexistence of different religious communities.

However, such efforts to contain religious strife have not reduced tension, but rather have led to new frictions, about an appropriate role for religion in a modern state. Two versions of the secular state are debated. Some intellectuals and politicians argue for a complete and strict separation of religion and state, while others believe that the state has to interfere and regulate religious matters, especially since the majority of Hindus cannot depend on ecclesial structures to 'modernise' their practices.[7] A secular ethic should ensure that all religious groups are treated equally by the state (see, for example, Chakrabarty 1990; Vanaik 1997). There are others who argue against secularism. One sector of intellectuals believes that, in order to be just, politics needs to be informed by religious ethics (see, for example, Nandy 1985, 1990; Madan 1987). More radical is the position of some Hindu fundamentalists who want to build a Hindu Nation (see, for example, Hellman 1996).[8]

These intellectual debates are constantly fuelled by concrete conflicts in which the intersection between politics and religion seems highly problematic. The controversy about the making of a Ram Temple in the North Indian pilgrimage town Ayodhya is notorious. The temple is supposed to be built at the site of the former Babri Mosque, which was destroyed by radical Hindus on 6 December 1992. Hindu nationalists claim that the mosque stood on the ruins of a former Temple that marked the birthplace of the mythological God, King Ram. There is no archaeological evidence to support this thesis. However, supporters of the Ram Temple consider such scientific evidence unnecessary and defend their claim in terms of the divine desire of Ram to be present at his birthplace and the right of believers to worship their god at such a prominent and beneficial spot. The conflict has been stirred up by many politicians, foremost by members of Hindu nationalist organisations and the party BJP (Bharatiya Janta Party).[9] Leaders have mobilised voters in the name of the God

Ram in order to profit during election time. Today it is generally agreed that the enormous success of the BJP is also due to their radical political-religious stance in favour of Hindus. This politics has increased hostility between Hindus and Muslims in India, leading to many violent outbreaks and creating insecurity among members of religious minorities, not only Muslims but Christians as well, who have also started to feel the negative impact of Hindu chauvinistic politics.

In Bhopal too, there are many stories that explain religious tension in terms of egoistic politics. Here I just want to narrate three examples, each of which approaches the subject from a different point of view. In the first story, Hindu politicians are blamed for communal[10] politics. People of all backgrounds acknowledge that the foundation of the Durga Temple at Pir Gate involved political interests. This is because leading politicians favoured and supported a temple in the Muslim residential area in order to gain sympathy among the local population of Hindus. They still today use Pir Gate as a place to mobilise Hindu voters with an anti-Muslim agenda.

A second story focuses on a Muslim administrator who is accused of religious manipulation. Unlike other cities, Bhopal has hardly any history of violent religious conflicts. Thus, people search for an explanation for the riots which also erupted in Bhopal after the destruction of the Babri Mosque in Ayodhya. In one explanation the Collector, who at that time was a Muslim, is blamed. The day after the destruction of the mosque Muslims in Bhopal started to protest. The protests turned violent and involved Hindus and Muslims in communal strife that lasted several days. Hindus complain that the Collector was slow in deploying police force on that day because he was personally hurt by the events in Ayodhya and wanted Hindus in the city to suffer.

There is a third story that depicts politicians and administrators using an anti-religious stance in order to win support from former untouchables, especially those who fight against orthodox Hindu religious and political activities. This is a story about the Nilkantheshvar Mahadev Temple in Maha Pratap Nagar, a crossing in New Bhopal. Parts of the temple have been destroyed twice by the city administration. This happened each time during the night before the annual birthday celebration for the late political leader Ambedkar. Ambedkhar is celebrated as the father of the constitution and receives particular reverence from former 'untouchables' who hail him as the founder of a political movement for equal rights of former 'untouchables', also know as the Dali-movement.[11] In Bhopal the birthday celebration for Ambedkar includes a small ceremony at Maha Pratap Nagar, at the Ambedkhar statue, which has been permanently fixed in the centre of the crossing – and within sight of the temple. Every year on 14 April politicians climb up to the statue to garland the figure and thus honour the great founding father and famous Dalit. Supporters of the temple claim that the destruction of their site of worship just before the Ambedkar celebration was an effort of politically motivated administrators and policemen, who want to win the sympathy of those Dalits who define themselves in clear contrast to Hindu traditions, which they consider oppressive and which they blame for their terrible plight as oppressed people.

While each of these stories focuses on a different problem, they share one assumption: that power holders manipulate religious issues in their favour. They do this not because they are religious or want to further the religious interests of devotees, but rather for egoistic political reasons. The argument – typically found among leading administrators – that the religious activities of devotees create tension and strife is turned around. Politicians and administrators are depicted as the true culprits who manipulate the religious sentiments of believers in the interests of factional politics.

I do not mean to favour one or the other explanation. All accusations of religious manipulation by leaders could be countered by oppositional statements, and further investigation would reveal that these events are embedded in a complex net of intersecting interests and motivations, both religious and political. My aim here is not to recover various memories of these specific events or search for culprits. I rather want to draw attention to the fact that people do not perceive politicians and administrators as neutral agents, who can arbitrate in religious matters. Members of the elite are seen as following their own interests and not hesitating to use or fuel religious controversies for the sake of their own career development.

For religious activists this is not always negative, but may have positive dimensions. People play with the self-interest of leaders to win them over for their own religious projects. Yet, they also know that bringing in powerful actors may lead to a redefinition of their project in different terms and can have consequences they never anticipated nor intended. Thus, differentiation is necessary. This is how I understand a statement from one of my informants about politics and temples which first appeared contradictory to me. The interviewee claimed that it is the duty of a (Hindu) politician to support the construction of a local religious site but that it is evil if he participates in the mobilisation of Hindus for a Ram Temple in Ayodhya. While in the former case the construction of a temple appears as a necessity which helps to turn a neighbourhood into a home for people and as such is considered to be non-provocative in nature, the latter is perceived as a diabolic game sought by politicians to gain popularity at the expense of a peaceful and harmonious life for ordinary people.

In order to judge the legitimacy of religious projects, people contextualise them. Religious activists distinguish between situations in which a leader evinces, or does not evince, faith. They also keep track of the ways local movements are appropriated, knowing that leaders follow their own (hidden) agenda and thus use believers' unrest to further their own interests. The experience/conviction that religious engagement brings worldly returns does not necessarily diminish its merit, nor does it *a priori* call the sincerity of a person's belief into question. What counts is the motivation. Through gossip, participants try to assess the sincerity of people's motivation, which in the end remains inaccessible and thus leads to constant reshuffling of opinions.

However, negotiating an appropriate way of dealing with religion has a further dimension. While believers are aware of the political dimension of their struggle they rarely perceive it solely in terms of human actions, but rather as the implementation of a divine will. They resist the idea that the state has sole authority over its territory, by claiming that human agents can not contain divine activities. Thus, locating gods and goddess in the city also forces debates about the limits of the human world and how to contain divine actors.

Overruling Human Agency

Anyone who has done research on religion in India will have come across narrations of divine self-manifestations. They are part of a standard repertoire of believers (see Davis 1995: 629–30). A great number of stories about temples start with the observation that the statue (normally a stone) appeared from the ground miraculously and invited, if not forced, the construction of a temple by divine intervention. I also found written evidence for such stories.

> A *mata* [old lady] of the Bagware clan ... was grinding grain in a mortar at her house. ... While she was grinding, blood started appearing in the mortar. At the sight of the blood the *mata* got frightened. She took the remaining grain from the *kunda* [lid], put it on the ground, covered the mortar with the *kunda* and left the house. She told the event to the women and men of the neighbourhood. Hearing the news, people reached her house. When they uncovered the mortar they saw the blood emerging from the mortar and found that a small *pindi* [a representation of God Shiva] had appeared with a little ... wound from which blood streamed. ... Daily the *mata* poured *ghi* [clarified butter] on the wound for it to heal. The wound closed and the *pindi* started to grow day by day.
>
> When this news reached the reigning Raja Tikamgarh, he came to see the place. When he saw that in her house Shri Mahadevji personally had manifested himself, he told the *mata* and her family that he would have a temple constructed at this place in which she and her family could reside (Bhadakariya 1958: 56–58, my own translation).

It is easy to find other such stories, making similar claims about the foundation of almost every temple. When discussing self-manifestations, people seldom wonder whether such things really happen, but discuss where and when they took place. The more closely a person is involved in the construction of a temple, the less chance there is of his resorting to explanations of a miraculous manifestation. It is therefore not surprising that many middle-class people lament the fact that modern temples do not have the same aura as historical ones, since only the latter have their origins in divine manifestations. New temples, they say, are erected by humans in order to show off. Thus, while stories of self-manifestation find wide acceptance, their plausibility increases with growing temporal and spatial distance, as is normal with processes of mythical legitimisation.

Stories of divine intervention pose a challenge to the law enforcement agencies. People demand a 'right to worship' and defend a temple as being legitimate, even when in official terms it is illegal. For many believers the question of temple construction does not fall under the competence of the state, since divine manifestations cannot be controlled by a secular institution. This is not to imply that people ignore the claims of the state to sole authority over its territory, or do not understand them. But they may at times place divine authority above that of the state.

Representatives of the state have the law on their side when they want to prevent the 'illegal' building of religious sites. Yet, in concrete cases the situation is usually rather explosive and demands flexible strategies. When conflicts arise administrators, policemen and politicians are confronted with a number of competing claims, formulated by various social groups and agents who also may offer contradictory interpretation of a divine will. In order to solve a conflict over a temple, decision makers may then opt to take seriously the claims of believers and provide a forum for the negotiation of an appropriate interpretation of divine will. Two examples may demonstrate how this happens.

The first is taken from Ujjain, a pilgrimage site in Eastern Madhya Pradesh, which is famous for its Shiva Temple, considered to be one of nine major places of Shiva worship. The Mahakaleshvar Temple is one of three temples in Madhya Pradesh that fall under the jurisdiction of the state. The president of the Mahakaleshvar Temple Trust is *ex officio* the Collector[12] of Ujjain. In 1996 the Collector was confronted with a dramatic and very difficult situation. During the major pilgrimage season a stampede occurred in the temple that killed more than fifty people. After this event the Collector had to restore peace in the temple and trust in its management. A rumour circulated that the stampede was a sign of Shiva's anger, aroused by the decaying of the silver *yantra* (mystical diagram) in the sanctuary. On learning about this rumour, the Collector immediately sent people in search of an artist who could restore the *yantra*. He then called for donations, he himself contributing the first kilogram of silver, and encouraging all the other officials to follow suit. The restoration of the *yantra* was not the only measure he implemented. He had fences erected that would make people stay in queue when waiting. He introduced permanent security personnel who controlled the temple and he installed a camera and a set of televisions to transmit pictures constantly from the sanctuary to various places in the temple, thereby extending control over the innermost part of the temple as well. The pictures further entertained people and distracted their minds during the long hours of waiting. Now they could watch the *puja* (Hindu form of worship) taking place, which the Collector was convinced would have a disciplinary effect.

The implementation of all these measures was beset with controversy. Secular minded officials felt that it was wrong of a Collector to restore a *yantra* and thereby himself encourage 'superstition'. Some of the temple servants objected to the security personnel. They felt that they were out of place in a sacred site, the territory of the god. Several senior priests raised objections to the television set, saying that the importance of the sacred object was diminished through its constant availability on screen. Others feared that people would start entering the sanctuary for the wrong reasons, not out of religious devotion, but in order to appear on television. However, the Collector answered all these objections by drawing attention to the 'package', offering it as a well-balanced solution that addressed a wide range of concerns. He convinced people that the problem was only solved if all different involved groups believed so.

A different example where religious and official attitudes clashed was narrated to me by a state official from Bhopal who was Collector in 1982 when the Durga Temple was built first at Pir Gate crossing. He was determined to prevent this project, because he felt that the anti-Muslim bias of the temple would pose a great problem for the future of this central locality. He knew that removing the Durga statue would enrage many Hindus who believe that once it has been installed a consecrated statue can never be removed without provoking the anger of the goddess. In order to increase the legitimacy of his act in the eyes of Hindus and to prevent rumours about revenge by the goddess, he called a priest who agreed to support his cause. Together with the police they held a ritual at Pir Gate, lifted the statue and carried it in a procession to a nearby temple, where the Durga statue was re-installed. All this happened at night to avoid interference from a religious opposition.

This intervention did not prevent the making of a Durga Temple at Pir Gate. However, the removal of the statue initiated a debate over the re-negotiation of the spot. The initial plan had been to build the temple in the middle of the crossing. Taking a strong stance, the Collector forced Hindus, Muslims and the city administration to settle the issue unanimously. He assembled various leaders and made them sit together until they had reached a solution. After three days and two nights of negotiations, a plot towards one side of the crossing was identified and was given over to the Durga Temple Committee. The Collector agreed to reinstall Durga in her original place; from there she was taken in another religious procession to her new permanent home.

Both these cases demonstrate that state agents may opt to take people's religious claims into account, independent of their own beliefs. One of their tasks is to negotiate solutions for conflicts, also including those revolving around religious matters. In this context divine agents also have to be taken seriously, because they are introduced as real by some people who claim to represent their will. When solving religious controversies, these claims have to be addressed and negotiated with respect to various other interests. Like everyone else, deities also have to compromise and they do. Observing the practices of believers over a longer period, I learned that divine actors can be manipulated. In order to get to know the divine will and learn how it can be influenced, believers spend hours debating and discussing. They consider the opinion of ritual specialists, of scholars who know the scripts, of persons who get possessed, they recall family or caste traditions and consult individuals who have revelatory experiences. Understanding the divine will is a social process, in which those who can claim effectively to be close to gods and goddesses have more authority.

Thus, it is scarcely surprising that the Collector in Ujjain and the Collector in Bhopal co-opted respected religious leaders in order to increase the legitimacy of their intervention into the religious sphere. The reforms in Ujjain passed the trustee board of the Mahakaleshvar Temple before they were implemented. Among the trustees are state officials, renowned personalities of the city and important religious leaders. Their approval increased the legitimacy of the changes. In Bhopal the Collector accepted help from a priest and called together the Hindu leaders of the city for negotiations in order to make sure that the solution would hold.

Conclusions

Acting upon urban territory, people create a home for their deities. They often do so in opposition to official state policies. Thereby they claim a status as citizens who have a right to act in their city and on their city. The erection of illegal temples, and the appropriation of urban space for religious purposes, represent a form of resistance through which people intervene in order to shape the territory according to their needs and wishes. Such instances of resistance are not always liberating or emancipating, nor are they necessarily politically innocent. Mobilisation around a religious theme has religious and political reasons and implications. As agents who are actively involved in an effort to give supremacy to their reading of the city, protesters exploit the powerful impact the imagination of space has for social relations. Fighting over space, people try to gain power by symbolically inscribing identity on the territory and thus establishing, confirming or furthering their access to status, money, political influence and divine grace.

The analysis of such movements has highlighted two kinds of boundaries that are central for the way actors make sense of and position themselves in such struggles. I talked about the boundary between politics and religion and that between human and non-human activities. In India people often say that religion should be free of politics. Yet, they know that this aim is impossible to achieve, and while they voice a desire for a 'pure' spirituality they also actively renegotiate the border between acceptable religious politics and undesirable political manipulation of religious themes. Thereby they create a space for legitimate religious intervention in the political arena. These negotiations take into account people's interpretation of the divine will. Deities are introduced as independent of state authorities. They become present though self-manifestation and appear in dreams to communicate their wishes. To be able to respect the divine will, believers need to communicate across borders that divide the human and the non-human world. Localising religion in the city means learning to distinguish real from fake divine intervention and genuine from egoistic politics.

Activities in the name of divine actors also define social categories of believers and non-believers, Hindus and Muslims, good and bad politicians, etc. They are constructed and reconstructed in concrete conflicts, sometimes also against established stereotypes. In some contexts the 'Muslim Other' turns into a religious ally in a struggle against a hostile state, or a Hindu administrator is accepted as sharing interests with Hindu activists, even if he embodies a state that is constructed as antagonistic to Hindu interests. Similarly, a secular administrator may take religious beliefs into account in order to strengthen the confidence religious-minded people have in the state. Concrete negotiations thus blur boundaries by allowing for transgressions of social categories. At the same time they create particular experiences that enliven such categories – providing concrete experience of their existence – which are presented, recreated and given concrete meaning in the process of developing, understanding and solving conflicts.

In contemporary India these boundary negotiations are highly relevant for the definition of public religion, especially in the Hindu context. Hinduism is a term that subsumes a large set of very different practices and beliefs. People who are called or call themselves Hindus follow a wide rage of different traditions according to region, caste, family, religious sub-group, congregation, etc. There is no centre that binds all these practices and beliefs together, nor is there a single holy book or a central authority that would define the 'essence' of Hinduism (see, for example, Sontheimer and Kulke 1989; Malik 1996). Hinduism as a category exists foremost as a residual term that subsumes under it all those people in South Asia that do not belong to any other religion, like Islam or Christianity.[13] Since colonial intervention in India, Hinduism has become increasingly identified as a political category that defines Hindus as belonging to a separate community, potentially antagonistic to other religious communities. Today, some political activists have begun to draw on Huntington's (1998) concept of 'clash of civilisations' to explain the need for a unified and aggressive Hinduism that will face up to Christianity and Islam. Experiences of communality and intensified internal communication have also fermented the emerging of a popular and increasingly unified form of 'mainstream Hinduism' (see, for example, Thapar 1985; Das 1995; Ludden 1996).

In other words, the invention of a term and the practices evolving around it eventually lead to the definition and formation of a group within which people increasingly share a common ground. In this process the negotiation of boundaries is of major importance. Remaking boundaries in action, Hindus assert and define their religion in the public sphere in India today. Here they make claims about what is an essential part of their religion and thus needs to be taken seriously by political and administrative actors, who are the servants of a state that guarantees the freedom of religion. The mobilisation of Hindus in the name of divine intervention creates common experiences and a forum for the negotiation of essential parts of Hindu belief. It is here that the idea of a Hindu community becomes a social reality.

Notes

1. According to the census data from 2001, the distribution of religious affiliation is as follows: Hindus 80.5%, Muslims 13.4%, Christian 2.3%, Sikhs 1.9%, Buddhists 0.8%, Jains 0.4%.
2. I collected the material for this study during sixteen months of fieldwork in Bhopal during the years 1996 to 1999 (for more details see Rao 2002; 2003b)
3. Illegal religious buildings are constructed by all religious communities, also Muslims and Christians. Here I concentrate only on Hindu religious constructions.
4. For details about this controversy see Rao (2003b: 48–56; forthcoming).

5. This is why, even today, the majority of temples in the city centre are of a haveli (mansion) type, which means that they are built inside the houses and are not visible from the outside.
6. RAF – Rapid Action Force
7. Hinduism is a general term that signifies a whole set of different social and religious practices, traditions and beliefs that originate from the Indian subcontinent. There is no central holy book, no church and there are no central dogmas or practices that bind all these different and at times contradictory traditions together. For this reason some scholars prefer to talk of Hindu Religions (see, for example, Sontheimer and Kulke 1989).
8. For an extensive summery of the debate see Rao 2003a.
9. The party acts as the parliamentary wing of the Hindu nationalist movement (see, for example, Malik und Singh 1994; Jaffrelot 1996).
10. Communal here means politics that shows a favour towards one religious community and/or politics that increases the tension between different religious communities.
11. *Dalit* means 'downtrodden', 'oppressed', and was used by Ambedkar as a name for former 'untouchables' to force attention to their terrible plight.
12. The Collector is the chief administrative official of a district, who is in charge of development and maintaining law and order within the district.
13. In the case of Jains and Sikhs, opinions are divided. Some count them as Hindus while others see them as constituting separate religions.

References

Bhadakariya, Shyamlal. 1958. *Suryavansha 360 Gotriya Kshatriya Vanshavala*. Gwalior: Royal Printing Press.

Brass, Paul R. 1998. *Theft of an Idol: Text and Context in the Representation of Collective Violence*. Calcutta: Seagull.

Chakrabarty, Bidyut (ed.). 1990. *Secularism and Indian Polity*. Delhi: Segment.

Das, Veena. 1995. 'Communities as Political Actors: The Question of Cultural Rights', *Critical Events: An Anthropological Perspective on Contemporary India*. Delhi: Oxford University Press, pp. 84–117.

Davis, Richard H. 1995. 'The Rebuilding of a Hindu Temple'. In: Donald S. Lopez Jr. (ed.): *Religions of India in Practice*. Princeton: Princeton University Press.

Freitag, Sandra B. 1989. *Collective Action and Community: Public Areas and the Emergence of Communalism in North India*. Berkeley: California University Press.

Hellman, Eva. 1996. 'Dynamic Hinduism: Towards a New Hindu Nation', in David Westerlund (ed.), *Questioning the Secular State*. London: Hurst, pp. 237–58.

Huntington, Samuel. 1998. *Clash of Civilisations and the Remaking of World Order*. London: Touchstone.

Jaffrelot, Christophe. 1996. *The Hindu Nationalist Movement and Indian Politics, 1925 to the 1990s: Strategies of Identity-building, Implantation and Mobilisation*. Delhi: Viking.

———. 1998. 'The Politics of Processions and Hindu-Muslim Riots', in Amrita Basu and Atul Kohli (eds), *Community Conflicts and the State in India*. Delhi: Oxford University Press, pp. 58–92.

Ludden, David (ed.). 1996. *Making India Hindu: Religion, Community, and the Politics of Democracy in India*. Delhi: Oxford University Press.

Madan, T.N. 1987. 'Secularism in Its Place', *Journal of Asian Studies* 46(4): 747–59.

Malik, Aditya. 1996. 'Hinduism or Three-thousand-three-hundred-and-six Ways to Invoke a Construct', in Günther D. Sontheimer and Hermann Kulke (eds), *Hinduism Reconsiderd*. 3rd ed. Delhi: Manohar, pp. 10–31.

Malik, Yogendra K. and V.B. Singh. 1994. *Hindu Nationalists in India: The Rise of the Bharatiya Janata Party*. New Delhi: Sage.

Mines, Mattison. 1996. *Public Faces, Private Voices: Community and Individuality in South India*. Delhi: Oxford University Press.

Mittal, Kamla. 1990. *History of Bhopal State*. Delhi: Munshiram Manoharlal.

Nandy, Ashis. 1985. 'An Anti-secularist Manifesto', *Seminar* 314: 14–24.

———. 1990. 'The Politics of Secularism and the Recovery of Religious Tolerance', in Veena Das (ed.), *Mirror of Violence*. Delhi: Oxford University Press, pp. 69–93.

Pandey, Gyan. 1990. *The Construction of Communalism in Colonial North India*. Bombay: Oxford University Press.

Rao, Ursula. 2002. 'How to Prove Divinities? Experiencing and Defending Divine Agency in a Modern Urban Indian Space', *Religion* 32(1): 3–11.

———. 2003a. *Kommunalismus in Indien: Eine Darstellung der wissenschaftlichen Diskussion über Hindu-Moslem Konflikte*. Halle: Institut für Indologie und Südasienwissenschaften, Universität Halle.

———. 2003b. *Negotiating the Divine: Temple Religion and Temple Politics in Urban India*. Delhi: Manohar.

———. (forthcoming) 'Re-enacting Partition in Bhopal: Muslim History and Hindu-Muslim Relations in Middle India', in Smita Tewari Jassal, Eyal Ben-Ari and Burkhard Schnepel (eds), *Memory and the Partition Motif*. Delhi: Sage.

Sontheimer, G.D. and H. Kulke (eds). 1989. *Hinduism Reconsidered*. Delhi: Manohar.

Thapar, Romila. 1985. 'Syndicated Moksha', *Seminar* 313: 14–22.

Vanaik, Achin. 1997. *Communalism Contested: Religion, Modernity and Secularization*. Delhi: Vistaar.

Chapter 6

Bosnian Neighbourhoods Revisited: Tolerance, Commitment and *Komšiluk* in Sarajevo

Cornelia Sorabji

Since the 1992–95 war in Bosnia the concept of *komšiluk* (neighbourliness, neighbourhood) has attracted much analytical attention.[1] While there is general agreement that the concept is important there is far less about *why* it is so.[2] The prevailing trend in political science and sociology has been to treat *komšiluk* as a social mechanism or structure regulating or ordering relations between different ethno-national groups, primarily Bosnia's Serbs, Croats and Bosniacs. From this shared starting point, however, there is scholarly divergence over whether, in pre-war Bosnia, *komšiluk* was an aspect of a benignly tolerant pluralism which was to become a '*Tradition Betrayed*' (the subtitle of Donia and Fine 1994) or alternatively of a semi-coerced '*Antagonistic Tolerance*' ready to disintegrate into violence when circumstances permitted (Hayden 2002). This scholarly debate is associated with political disagreements over relative responsibility for the war and over the possibility of some form of post-war reconciliation.

This paper aims to rescue *komšiluk* from its role as handmaiden to the political debate and to return it to its primary, commonsense meaning as concerning human relations between physical neighbours living in proximity to each other who, in practice, often belong to the same ethno-nations as each other, not to different ones. I suggest that the prevailing tendency to view the concept primarily as one in the realm of Balkan ethno-nationalist politics mistakes the metaphorical meaning of the term for its primary one and that this perspective is, in part, a product of a scholarly 'ethnic coding bias' (Brubaker 2002) which tends to privilege questions of communal identity over other ways of interpreting material, and in so doing to obscure the complexity of everyday social processes and relationships. As Nowotny puts it: 'the more we focus on identity as the constitutive, though always frail and continuously changeable ultimate entity of social, political, religious, cultural and personal life, the more the social ties and bonds that make up cohesion become subjugated to and eclipsed by it' (2002: 354). I hope to elucidate some of the complexity of those social ties and bonds by examining the Sarajevo usage of the term *komšiluk* and by considering some practices within and feelings expressed about one particular, largely Bosniac neighbourhood in Sarajevo both before and after the 1992–95 war. I highlight the qualitative difference between *komšiluk* relations on the one hand and, on the other, a second characteristically Bosnian and conceptually reified field of relationships, that of *veze* or connections. In the case of *komšiluk* relations I suggest that moral duty, sanctioned by Islamic religious tradition, is understood as an important underpinning. In this sense, *komšiluk* can be understood as sited 'On the Margins of Religion'.

This paper focuses on Bosnian Bosniacs (and in particular on Sarajevo Bosniacs in the old neighbourhoods), and the place of religion in their understanding of the importance of *komšiluk*. It is not about Bosnians in general. Given the politicised nature of some of the scholarly debate around Bosnia,[3] I stress that in adopting this specific focus I do not intend either to argue that Bosnia's non-Bosniac populations did not value neighbourly relations in pre-war Bosnia or to insist that all Bosnians used to hold equally to *komšiluk* values but that Serb and Croat populations betrayed the tradition. That I do not consider Serb and Croat attitudes to *komšiluk* in the context of this ethnographic paper is largely because I have not undertaken in-depth fieldwork in Serb and Croat neighbourhoods. But it is also relevant to point out that, just as I do not see *komšiluk* as a system or mechanism regulating relations between ethno-nations, I also do not believe that relative Serb Orthodox, Croatian Catholic or Bosniac Muslim commitment to the idea of *komšiluk* is key to apportioning relative responsibility for the war. *Komšiluk* is an important cultural concept and practice but is not a determining force able either to prevent or to create war, or to rebuild multi-ethnicity in its wake. Whether *komšiluk* may have any *indirect* relevance for these important questions will be briefly considered at the end of the paper.

The Scholarly Debate around *Komšiluk*

Among those who interpret *komšiluk* as a positive political force is Sanguin, for whom *komšiluk* is a 'contract of citizens' (Sanguin 1998). Like Sanguin, Solioz places *komšiluk* as a value alongside citizenship: 'therefore the conflict in the 1990s became one of two value systems: the values of citizenship and neighbourliness (*komšiluk*) and the values of 'ethnic division' (Solioz 2002: 31). Both commentators associate *komšiluk* with citizenship as against nationalism and separatism. In Bulgaria scholars seeking both to explain and to maintain the avoidance of violent ethnic conflict in that country have highlighted the role of *komšiluk* (the Bulgarian variant of the term) and posited the existence of a related 'Bulgarian Ethnic Model' (BEM).[4] At one level, the phrase 'Bulgarian Ethnic Model' refers specifically to the political accommodation that has been reached between the Bulgarian state and the Bulgarian Turkish political party. At a more general sociological level, the BEM is understood as the totality of peaceful inter-ethnic relations which have prevented conflict in that country, with an emphasis on the bottom-up actions of ordinary people, and particularly on the role of *komšiluk*. The sociologist Antonina Zhelyazkova explains: 'Perhaps what is most characteristic of the Bulgarian ethnic model is that it is ruled and controlled from below – by the people living side-by-side. Despite attempts at destructive interference at times from politicians, ideologues or fundamentalists, the communities continue to work together to maintain peace and good neighbourly relations' (Zhelyazkova 2002; see also Georgieva 1995; Chukov 2001).

In Bulgaria this morally positive evaluation of the significance of *komšiluk* has been criticised as overly romantic (Iliev 2001). In the Bosnian case the romanticism has been yet more damningly cast as a 'weapon of war' in the arsenal of Bosniac leaders seeking to influence international public opinion (Bougarel 1999/2000: 27). One of the most serious and prolific scholars of contemporary Bosnia, Xavier Bougarel, argues that, far from being allied with the values of citizenship and democracy, *komšiluk* is a practice antithetical to democracy:

> the concept of democracy is presumed, in general terms, on that of citizenship. In fact, the principle which has given structure to the Bosnian political order has not been citizenship, but rather communitarian identity ... the informal institution of *komšiluk* (good neighbourliness) ... was based on a constant reaffirmation of community identities and codes, and not on their effacement ... In terms of the relationships it established between the public and private spheres, between communitarian identity and social bonds, it represented the inverse of citizenship, rather than its premise. (Bougarel 1996: 87–88)

This is arguably a particularly French view of the nature of citizenship and of democracy and was, for example, central to arguments in favour of 2004 legislation banning the wearing of conspicuous religious symbols, including hijab, in French schools (Bowen 2004a and b). More relevantly, for the purposes of this paper, it is a view which, like that of those Bougarel opposes, mistakes the primary meaning of *komšiluk*.

What is *Komšiluk*?

Bougarel notes that the term designates the entire realm of neighbourly relations, but opines that 'nevertheless, in the context of multi-community Bosnian society it applies above all to good neighbourly relations in between members of different communities' (Bougarel 1999/2000: 27). Other scholars go further, implying that its *only* denotation is inter-ethnic. Thus, Hayden says 'The institution of *komšiluk* ... established clear obligations of reciprocity between people of different "nations" living in close proximity' (Hayden 2002: 206) and Pouligny says 'it refers to two people from two different communities'

(Pouligny 2002: 21). However, a closer, ethnographic examination demonstrates that *komšiluk* is not understood in this way at the grassroots level, and ethnographers like Tone Bringa or Ivana Macek do not mistake the metaphorical for the primary meaning (see Bringa 1995, Macek 2000).

Komšiluk is a Turkish derived term, as is *komšija*: neighbour. It refers to neighbourly relations and to the physical environment of the neighbourhood. If you ask a Bosniac 'what does *komšiluk* mean?' (*šta znači komšiluk?*') the immediate, commonsense response will be about a physical neighbourhood location and the relationships within it. 'Neighbourhood' and 'neighbourhood relations' therefore seem reasonable translations for the term. Like the English term 'neighbourhood', *komšiluk* does not denote an officially bounded administrative district but an area whose boundaries are defined, in part, subjectively. A combination of distance and topology (for example the location of roads, shops or other non-households) provide the basic criteria for a subjective definition of the boundaries, but at the outer edges, degree of affection, approval, respect or sympathy also plays a role.

While the denotations of *komšija* and *komšiluk* may equate to those of English terms, their wider import is better grasped via a comparison with the British English use of the word 'home' (North American usage is slightly different). Like 'home', *komšiluk* is used to refer both to a physical place and to relations within that place and, again like 'home', '*komšiluk*' evokes a moral context which, at first blush, is understood as a positive one. One of Webster's Dictionary definitions of 'home' is 'the abiding place of one's affections' (quoted in Casenove 1994: 64). The default value of 'home' is positive despite our awareness that home is not always and for everyone a wholly positive experience. The same is true of *komšiluk* and, as I will discuss below, experiences within the *komšiluk* can be difficult or distressing. In contrast, the Ottoman, Turkish administrative word for a neighbourhood district – *mahala* – is more likely to be used in negative formulations. A *mahaluša*, for example, is a nosy neighbourhood gossip (female) absorbed in the minutiae of her geographically circumscribed life.

This brief discussion of linguistic usage illustrates that the scholarly tendency to view '*komšiluk*' as denoting inter-communal relations is an example of what Brubaker has called 'groupism: the tendency to take discrete, sharply differentiated, internally homogeneous and externally bounded groups as basic constituents of social life, chief protagonists of social conflicts, and fundamental units of social analysis' (Brubaker 2002: 164). As Brubaker notes: 'Coding and framing practices are heavily influenced by prevailing interpretive frames. Today, ethnic and national frames are accessible and legitimate, suggesting themselves to actors and analysts alike. This generates a "coding bias" in the ethnic direction' (2002: 174).

This is not to suggest that Bosnians do not identify themselves as belonging to ethno-national communities or that these identifications did not become 'chief protagonists' in the 1990s. But even at the worst of times the majority of individuals who self-identified as Serb Orthodox, Catholic Croat or Bosniac Muslim did not view everything, including *komšiluk*, entirely through an ethno-religious frame. Had they done so the words of Nikola Koljević, one of the four wartime Bosnian Serb political leaders, would have lacked rhetorical force. In May 1991 Koljevic tried to reassure Muslims in the town of Bileca that 'a neighbour is more than a brother'. Clearly his intention was that 'neighbour' be understood as 'Muslim' and 'brother' be understood as 'Serb', and thereby to suggest that 'we Serbs value you Muslims more than we value ourselves': such a statement would not work as a rhetorical device if *'komšija'* literally and primarily denoted 'Muslim' (or 'non-Serb'). In the immediate pre-war era the metaphorical use of *'komšiluk'* to refer specifically to intercommunal relations as opposed to ordinary neighbourhood relations became common. For example, Serbian speakers at a November 1990 rally in the Sarajevo suburb of Vogošća opined that Muslims there had 'always been good neighbours with the Serbs' (*Oslobodenje* 14.11.90 p. 13, quoted in Donia 2006: 261). The same appears to have been the case during the bloody Second World War. In 1944 Bosniac historian Muhamed Hadžijahić used a pseudonym to write to the Allied Forces to explain the Bosnian situation as he saw it. He wrote of an 'ideal system' of inter-confessional relations which 'is comprehended in the word *komšiluk (susjedstvo)* which in Bosnia has been raised to the level of a cult' (quoted in Filandra 1998: 181).[5] Given the social importance and the positive default value of the concept of *komšiluk*, it is unsurprising that Bosnians seeking to promise or to promote peace during volatile times would employ it as a powerful metaphor for harmonious inter-ethnic relations. I have argued elsewhere that this metaphor was readily understood by and self-evident to Bosnians during the recent war and that by first invoking and then sullying it (i.e., by killing and exiling the metaphorical neighbours), it was possible to convey with high emotional impact the message that metaphorical neighbours from other nations were not welcome (Sorabji 1994, 1995).

Islam and Neighbourhood

The importance of neighbourhood is well supported by hadith literature (literature reporting the sayings and practices of the Prophet and his immediate companions, as relayed by sources with verifiable pedigree) and by linguistic usages in the classical age of Islam. In Sarajevo in the mid-1980s the value of neighbours was explained to me via the tale of the Prophet's father-in-law, Abu Bakr, who sold a house worth X for the sum of twice X, explaining that the extra value derived from the quality of the neighbours.[6] Another hadith reports the Prophet saying 'The Angel Gabriel so impressed on me the importance of neighbourhood that I thought I was going to receive an order that neighbours should inherit from neighbours' (*Preporod* Feb 2003). The twelfth century Persian Quranic scholar Al-Zamakshari was nicknamed 'Jar Allah' – Neighbour of God (Karic 1999: 191). In the tribal and kin dominated context of seventh century Arabia, the growth of the initially small and persecuted Islamic community was perhaps bound to rely on the elevation of non-kin, neighbourhood ties and bonds as forms of moral community and mutual support.

In a study of pre-Soviet Central Asia, Geiss argues that while tribal membership had been based on kinship and descent, neighbourhood membership was acquired by consent of the existing neighbours to incomers buying or building property, and by participation in communal religious activities. Shari'a-based law shaped neighbourhood relations, for example by insisting on personal rather than group responsibility for crimes and by allowing for the fragmentation of property through inheritance (Geiss 2001). Within the Ottoman Empire administrative and penal law was to play a role in reinforcing neighbourhood bonds. Marcus suggests that the nosy neighbour syndrome of eighteenth century Ottoman Aleppo was encouraged by a legal system in which whole neighbourhoods could be held accountable for misdeeds within them (Marcus 1986).

During my fieldwork in Sarajevo in the socialist mid-1980s the importance of neighbourhood both as a physical space and as a moral environment and set of relations was clear (Sorabji 1989 Chap. 2; see also Bringa 1995). I lived in one of the neighbourhoods on the hills above the old Ottoman town centre called Baščaršija. It was a place of privately owned houses rather than apartment blocs and a large majority of the neighbours were Bosniacs. Some of the households were those of pre World War Two Sarajevo residents but many were headed by villagers who moved in during the socialist period, particularly during the 1960s and 1970s. The neighbourhood was made up of households (*kuće*) which either corresponded to nuclear families or were based upon them (for example, a nuclear family plus husband's mother). Each household fiercely guarded its privacy from others and each was made up of individuals who also fiercely guarded certain forms of privacy from each other, particularly with regard to money.

The neighbourhood was felt to be and was symbolically marked as distinct from the town below. Thus, people changed into house clothes when in their own home or visiting in the neighbourhood, and into town attire when they left it. In the neighbourhood people exchanged traditional Arabic and Turkish derived Muslim greetings: '*Merhaba!*' '*Akšam Hajrula – Allah Razula*', rather than the Slavic '*Dobar Dan*' '*Dobar Večer*' of the town. Neighbours were important for social purposes, including frequent coffee visits between women, and for practical ones; for learning new skills from, for borrowing tools, food and occasionally money, and so on.

The separation of the neighbourhood from social life beyond it was reinforced by the socialist self-managing system: 1980s socialist Yugoslavia did not experience levels of oppression similar to those of the Warsaw Pact countries but there was always some degree of danger that, depending on the political climate of the day, a person's words or deeds could be deemed counter-revolutionary or nationalist. This buttressed a desire to preserve realms of relative privacy, including the neighbourhood, separate from the public domain. There was also a specifically religious basis for the neighbourhood, its discrete status and its internal coherence. During Ramazan many neighbours would gather at the local mosque after the evening break-fast (*iftar*) to pray the thirteen rekats of the *Jacija namaz*, the last of the five daily prayers, followed by the twenty rekats of *Teravija*.[7] Most of these local mosques were closed for prayer throughout the rest of the year but during Ramazan many people who were otherwise minimally observant would increase their efforts to fulfil religious duties. The feast of Ramazan *Bajram* which followed the fast was an occasion on which neighbours would visit each other with Ramazan greetings and to eat Turkish style cakes: baklava, kadaif, ružica. The other major festival of the Muslim year, *Kurban Bajram*, was understood specifically as a neighbourhood festival. *Kurban Bajram* commemorates Abraham's willingness to sacrifice his son at God's command, and God's last minute decree that he should sacrifice a ram instead. In the 1980s (and far more so today) several of the neighbourhood families would sacrifice a sheep in the garden (few of the households felt wealthy enough to sacrifice one sheep per adult member, as is the Islamic ideal). Some of the meat was kept back for the household and some distributed to friends or family outside the neighbourhood, but the majority was distributed by the children or women of the household to other neighbourhood households. Even those households that did not sacrifice would receive meat, and during the four days of the *Bajram* festival there was constant visiting throughout the neighbourhood.

Another important neighbourhood-centred event was the women's death ritual known as the *tevhid*, the Bosnian language variant of the Arabic term *tawhid*, meaning the perfect uniqueness and unicity of God (see Sorabji 1989, Chap. 6). *Tevhids* are traditionally held by women and led by female Quranic reciters on five separate occasions after a death. The bereaved do not invite other women to a *tevhid*; women are supposed to find out about the death (from newspapers and the grapevine) and to come of their own accord. In the case of the first *tevhid*, which is held simultaneously with the burial, it was the neighbours who were most likely to be able to know of the death. Throughout the early days of bereavement, neighbours visit regularly, bringing food, coffee and sugar. Failure to attend a neighbour's *tevhid* would, in the 1980s, have been seen as reprehensible in a way that the absence of more geographically distant kin and friends would not.

In contrast to Muslim women's death rituals in most parts of the world, and indeed to women's death rituals generally (Bloch and Parry 1982), Bosniac Muslim women pride themselves on their calm and stoical demeanour. To cry, wail or contest the death is understood as a refusal to accept God's will. The *tevhid*'s stated purpose is prayer for the soul of the dead and the efficacy of such prayer is understood as depending in part upon the ability of participants to control negative emotions, the expression of which would defy God's will. There is no sense that women should not *feel* anguish and it is fully understood that the bereaved will find it extremely difficult to sit through the *tevhid* ceremony, particularly the first in the series of five, which occurs simultaneously with the burial. However, those who cry are admonished on the grounds that they are failing to do the best for the departed. At one *tevhid* I attended in 2003 the sniffles of the widow whose 42-year-old husband had died only forty days earlier were met with a scornful 'Huh! You couldn't hold out at the last one either!' (i.e., at the *tevhid* held seven days after death) 'Get out if you can't stop that! What's the benefit of that?' Other women, albeit with less ferocity, backed up the first: 'There's no benefit from that ... It's hard, it has to be hard ... Think of your son ...' I will return to this emphasis on self-control and endurance.

Commitment and the Pros and Cons of Neighbourhood

The role of secrecy and suspicion in the Balkans has been commented on by several ethnographers (see, for example, Du Boulay 1976; Rheubottom 1987; Brown 2003: 228–30) and was also brought home to me. My fieldwork milieu taught me valuable lessons about trust and sharing that I had not learned in England, but in doing so it also sent me into occasional spells of frustrated claustrophobia. These were occasioned by the tensions and suspicions that existed between different households and by those household members' vigilant preservation of their corporate privacy. Remarks that I found innocuous could be indignantly understood by others as clearly offensive, yet when I sought explanations they often left me none the wiser. Sometimes I felt that my neighbours were a little over sensitive. At other times I realised that their suspicions were justified, for example when one household would try to extract information from me about another. I became familiar with interactions in which a neighbour would attempt to exploit my lack of skill in the conversational art of replying-without-replying honed by local adults. I suspect that my own attempts at this art sometimes descended into a hopeless case of 'acting English' (*praviti Englez*), the apposite Bosnian phrase, meaning to behave as though one doesn't understand the situation. However, it was in the spirit of the place that no one would ever have suggested such a thing to my face.

The very existence of this phrase – 'acting English' – and the occasional denunciations of third parties for doing so, illustrate that the neighbours themselves could feel irked by the pressures associated with seamless concealment of information and second-guessing of motives. Like me, and despite their greater social skill, the neighbours suffered the claustrophobic and suspicious aspects of *komšiluk*. In exasperation, women would occasionally assert their wish to cut themselves off from the nosy, meddling neighbours or advise each other to '*pusti ti njih!*' – 'just let them go/ignore them'. But only one neighbourhood household, one in which the housewife was a non-Yugoslav and a non-Muslim, really did cut itself off from the network of coffees, *tevhids*, loans, gifts, *kurban*, gossip, and so on. I suggest that this is not because, in the mid-1980s, the social and material benefits of *komšiluk* outweighed the costs (although this was probably true) but because the call of *komšiluk* is not heard through a cost/benefit filter but as a duty with religious overtones, a duty that is sometimes pleasurable and profitable, sometimes painful and testing, but never a morally neutral choice. This degree of moral commitment is lacking from another characteristic and conceptually reified field of social relations in Bosnia, that of *veze* – connections.

Veze are similar to the *blat* relationships Ledeneva describes for Russia (Ledeneva 1998), but while the word '*blat*' is used infrequently in Russia, and generally as something that other (dubious) people do, the word '*veze*' was and is heard constantly in Sarajevo. *Veze*, like *blat* relations, exist between individuals rather than households, although people close to the individual with the connection may of course feel the benefit of them. In *komšiluk* relations, on the other hand, individuals act both as individuals and as representatives of their household. Whereas in Soviet Russia *blat* was an absolute necessity due to the lack of a market economy, in the 1980s Yugoslavia had a limited form of market under the system known as Socialist Self Management, and Sarajevo was not characterised by Moscow-style shortages and queues. But *veze* were needed for other purposes, for example to acquire clothing or fabric beyond the often limited range available in shops, to organise a plumber, a butcher for *kurban*, or to gain employment. They enabled a higher standard of living and, as in Russia, were a source of personal pride: the individual's ability to draw on his or her *veze* network to resolve a problem or satisfy a wish was experienced as a personal success, as was the individual's ability to help others in their turn. The term '*veze*' could be used disapprovingly of third parties to suggest they had procured something unfairly ('he got that job via *veze*') but could also be used positively to allude to one's own social agility and nouse ('how did you get that?!' – 'I have *veze*!'). Unlike *komšiluk* relations, *veze* connections are not a matter of commitment or duty. If a person consistently fails to return or acknowledge a favour the *veze* relation ends. Thus, one woman I know, 'Amira', had procured a particular document from the council for a friend, 'Mirza', of a friend, 'Kanita'. Mirza thanked Amira at the time, but one year later he failed to recognise or acknowledge her when they met again via the intermediary friend, Kanita. Amira vowed never to help Mirza again. In contrast, I suggest that *komšiluk* relations share with *tevhid* the responsibility to control and rise above painful or negative emotions.[8]

This became clearer to me in the post-war period. During the 1992–95 war most people spent most of their time in the neighbourhood. Due to the lack of arms and military infrastructure, even men of military age were deployed on a rota system and therefore spent considerable periods at home. Under conditions of cold, hunger and anxiety, *komšiluk* became both more important and more challenging. In many cases neighbourhood relations became stronger and closer, but bonds could also become severely strained, as in the following three cases.

1. One of the wealthier families in my neighbourhood, a family with a relatively long urban pedigree and thus a claim to higher social status, had a good sized cellar but during the war made clear that they did not want it filled with neighbours sheltering from the shelling. This household was perceived as reluctant to share its relative wealth, and coolness towards its members was exacerbated by the fact that they had managed, via *veze*, to have their son excused from military service. At the same time their links with the Islamic Religious Establishment made it far easier for them both to obtain humanitarian aid, and to remain in wartime employment.
2. A woman kept a goat which produced milk, thus providing her with a wartime income. The neighbour who told me this story had a small granddaughter who, after months of stoical deprivation, one day asked if she could have some milk, 'even just a *fildžan* of milk' (a small, traditional Bosnian coffee cup). The grandmother recounted this pitiful request to the goat owner, who demanded five Deutschmarks (the only usable currency in wartime Sarajevo) for a litre. Her husband reprimanded her and successfully insisted she give the milk for free, but the incident remained a painful one in the grandmother's mind. For her the inability to feed or provide security and

pleasure to her grandchildren was the worst aspect of the war and the neighbour's refusal to assist her was not forgotten in the peace.
3. A third and graver example of damaged neighbourhood relations revolved around a tomato patch and a plum tree. This story was told to me during the war by the plum tree owning household. The tomato owner claimed that his next-door neighbour's plum tree was casting shade over his plants, thereby inhibiting their growth. An argument ensued and the tomato grower fetched an axe and tried to attack the plum owning man. The attacker was restrained by his own family.

Years after these events the various neighbours in question were clearly ambivalent or hostile towards those by whom they felt injured. But only in the case of the axe attack was contact between the households (almost) severed. Even in this case the women of the households remained in low-key interaction, aware of each others' presence over the garden fence, avoiding each others' gaze as far as possible but occasionally mumbling the routine enquiry 'How are you?' – 'Fine, you?' when eye contact was inadvertently made. The plum tree household resumed the despatch of *kurban* meat to the tomato patch household, but wrote the housewife's name on the package, rather than that of the axe-wielding husband, thus symbolically denying his existence in their moral world. The axe wielder himself was entirely avoided and ignored by members of the plum household, and ignored them in return.

Such a visible rent in the fabric of the *komšiluk* is rare and was occasioned by something as grave as a potentially fatally attack. In the other two cases I have cited, the neighbours attempted to rise above the negative and continue with the duty of *komšiluk*. Thus, when I asked the grandmother how she felt about receiving a traditional *Bajram* visit from the goat owning neighbour whose behaviour had hurt her so, the answer was '*to je red*' – that is in order, that is the way it should be. As in the *tevhid*, where faith in God demands that painful feelings of bereavement, although accepted as natural, must be suppressed in the interests of the deceased's soul, so in *komšiluk* painful feelings are put aside in the interests of the religiously sanctioned residential community.

Tolerance and Re-integration

The war radically altered the ethnic demographics of Bosnia. In the cause of ending inter-ethnic bloodshed, the peace agreement widely known as 'Dayton' embedded ethno-national identity in the country's constitutional structure, for example through the creation of a three person Presidency: one Serb, one Croat and one Bosniac. Ten years later there have been both refugee returns and some modifications to the state structure established by the peace deal but no one believes that Bosnia's pre-war demographics could now be fully restored. Many of the displaced no longer want to return to their pre-war homes, even were it safe or practical for them to do so.

For those who understand *komšiluk* as denoting or at least referring primarily to inter-communal relations, the de facto high degree of ethnic division and the painful memories suggest that '*komšiluk* has ceased to be a central reality' in Bosnia (Bougarel 1999/2000: 28). In a thought-provoking article, Robert Hayden cites Bougarel on *komšiluk* and argues that the tradition was only ever one of 'negative tolerance' as opposed to 'positive tolerance'. He associates the former with the philosophy of John Locke, casting it as a pragmatic restraint from interference for reasons of self-interest, and the latter with John Stuart Mill whom he describes as advocating tolerance as a 'celebration of diversity for its own sake' (Hayden 2002: 217). Considering syncretic shrines and religious practices in South Asia and the Balkans, Hayden proposes a concept of 'competitive sharing' in which worshippers from different communities simultaneously share and are in conflict over religious sites. 'This competitive sharing is compatible with the passive meaning of "tolerance" as non interference but incompatible with the active meaning of tolerance as embrace of the Other' (2002: 205). Hayden links this analysis to his view that the international community is misguidedly seeking (an implicitly Western) 'positive tolerance' and ethnic re-integration in Bosnia.

I want to suggest that a more fine-grained examination of *komšiluk* than is offered in much of the recent literature will demonstrate that Hayden has taken his argument one step too far to bear the weight of real life. I hope the preceding pages have illustrated that the term refers primarily to physical neighbours and their relations, regardless of those neighbours' ethno-national identities, and that it is an ethnic 'coding bias' which suggests otherwise. *Komšiluk* is not, therefore, definable as an 'institution' which 'established clear obligations of reciprocity between people of different "nations" living in close proximity' (Hayden 2002: 206). Those neighbourly relations are both enjoyed and benefited from – through coffee visits and conversation, the comfort of condolences, the satisfaction of religious duties performed, the assistance of loans, etc. – and are a source of irritation, upset or worse – through nosiness, gossip or wartime refusal to help. The otherness of neighbours' temperaments, aspirations, personal habits and social standing are experienced at different times as positive and as negative. Hayden's division of tolerance into two types along a positive/negative axis therefore implies an either-or choice which sits ill with the complexity of everyday life.

A different distinction, drawn by the philosopher Bernard Williams, between tolerance as a practice and tolerance as a principle or virtue casts more light on social reality (Williams 1996). Williams' tolerance as a practice sounds something like Hayden's negative tolerance. Tolerance as a practice may be based on Hobbesian calculations of self-interest or on 'broad church' views; the idea that there are many paths to God. Tolerance as a practice is unstable because calculations may change or a broad church outlook evolve into simple indifference (which logically rules out tolerance since we can not be said to tolerate things which cause us no discomfort whatsoever). Williams' tolerance as a virtue is an ideological commitment which forms part of a liberal, pluralist philosophy. This philosophy poses tolerance as a virtue in and of itself, and claims that this virtue is self-evident and 'rises above the battle of the values'. But ultimately it is forced to admit that tolerance is grounded in the value of each individual's personal autonomy (i.e., tolerance is necessary to make space for the value of personal autonomy). At first glance this second form of tolerance appears to equate to Hayden's 'positive tolerance', but on closer examination the fit is more questionable. For Hayden implies a geopolitical distinction while ignoring the distinction between practice and virtue. In his formulation people in countries not dogged by inter-communal conflict manage to *practise* positive tolerance/ tolerance as a virtue, whereas in South Asia or Bosnia they are limited to practising negative tolerance/tolerance as a practice. He thus mixes Williams' categories of practice and virtue.

I suggest that keeping practice and virtue conceptually separate, as Williams does, helps us to comprehend a more plausible reality in which ordinary people, whether in Sarajevo, Delhi, London or Halle, experience some negative feelings about others and in response deploy (or do not deploy) 'toleration and its awkward practices' (Williams 1996: 26). (They may perhaps also move progressively towards a state of indifference in which tolerance is unnecessary and logically impossible.) In contrast, Williams points out that tolerance as a virtue has a 'very specific form, which limits the range of people who can possess it' (1996: 19). It is a philosophical or ideological commitment, not an everyday behaviour. Further, Williams evokes a (Western) scenario in which toleration

> has to be sustained not so much by a pure principle resting on a value of autonomy as by a wider and more mixed range of resources ... [including] an active scepticism against fanaticism and the pretensions of its advocates, conviction about the manifest evils of toleration's absence and, quite certainly, power, to provide Hobbesian reminders to the more extreme groups that they have to settle for co-existence. (1996: 26–27)

In other words, Williams suggests that those of us living within societies, like the U.K., which lack a recent history of inter-communal violence on the scale of Bosnia or South Asia nevertheless for the most part practice tolerance in what, from Hayden's perspective, counts as a 'negative' rather than a 'positive' way. In comparison, Hayden's geopolitical distinction between a negative, 'antagonistic' practice of tolerance in certain places (Bosnia, South Asia) and a 'positive', celebratory one in others (U.K., U.S.) seems unpersuasive, and certainly too weak a premise on which to build a case for the maintenance or dismantlement of states.

If *komšiluk* can not give us any direct answers to questions about post-war reconciliation, can it shed any indirect light? There have been few incidents of violence against Serb returnees, but in general Sarajevo Bosniacs do not actively welcome them, largely because of the painful memory management processes that such returns entail (Sorabji 2006). However, the examples I have offered of emotionally difficult post-war neighbourhood relations show that, as in the *tevhid*, religious values and teachings underpin the moral imperative to forebear, endure and tolerate. This suggests the possibility that, while Bosniacs do not welcome Serbs to return to live in the city which Serb forces so ruthlessly besieged, they could in practice find that it goes against the grain to refuse *komšiluk* actively with any who nevertheless do so.[9] It is certainly true that, in the post-war neighbourhood I know best, there is emotional investment in the idea of the continued existence of *komšiluk*. In the wake of the war there is far less visiting and mutual material support than before because households are busier making ends meet, in most cases poorer, sometimes psychologically depressed, and often embarrassed by the state of their homes and furnishings. But when I have questioned neighbours as to whether *komšiluk* traditions are dying under the weight of new socio-economic circumstances, one common response has been denial and an explanation that I am focusing only on the symptoms of *komšiluk* (coffee visits, exchange) whereas the essence is alive and manifested at times of need like bereavement, and at religious festivals. The level of investment in this idea suggests that Bosniacs might, in daily reality, find it hard wholly to exclude returnees. It is at least theoretically possible that, having failed wholly to exclude, they might then find in the category of *komšija* a way of defining returning Serbs which takes the focus off the latter's ethnicity. Conversely, of course, it can be noted that the moral demands of *komšiluk* may be precisely part of the reason for which re-integration is not desired: 'if they come back we will be obliged to be their *komšije*'.[10] It is also the case that, in the apartment blocks of the newer parts of town, as opposed to the old neighbourhoods of which I write here, it is slightly easier to avoid the neighbour's eye and thus to ignore the demands of *komšiluk* without having to violate them actively. These points illustrate the dangers, flagged at the beginning of this paper, of overloading *komšiluk* with the responsibility of explaining the causation, maintenance or reversal of complex, multi-faceted phenomena such as war and post-war re-integration.

Notes

This paper is based on fieldwork done before, during and after the war, from 1985 to 2003. That work has been supported, *inter alia*, by grants from the Economic and Social Research Council and the British Academy. Three academic institutions have hosted my efforts: the Centre for Policy Studies, Central European University; the Department of War Studies, King's College London; and the Anthropology Department of University College London. I am grateful to Frances Pine and Michael Stewart for reading versions of this paper, and to the Foreign and Commonwealth Office for allowing me time to write it up. The views expressed are mine alone.

1. The official name of the country is now 'Bosnia and Herzegovina' but this is unwieldy and I have used plain 'Bosnia' instead. In late 1993 a decision was made by the Congress of Bosnian Muslim/Bosniac Intellectuals to rename the former 'Muslim' population 'Bosniac'. This decision was internationally reflected in the Washington Agreement in March 1994, and later enshrined in the General Framework Agreement on Peace (GFAP, commonly known as 'Dayton' after the place where the peace was negotiated). I use 'Bosniac' except in those cases where I am indicating specifically religious affiliation, but readers should bear in mind that prior to the war 'Muslim' was the correct terminology and that even today it is common in ordinary conversation.
2. The titles of several works about Bosnia attest to this common observation, for example: *We Are All Neighbours* (Christie and Bringa 1993), *The Key to Thy Neighbour's House* (Neuffer 2002), *Love Thy Neighbour* (Maass 1997).

3. See, for example, the exchange of views in the journal *Anthropological Theory*, volumes 2004: 4(1) and 2005: 5(4) (Cushman 2004, Cushman 2005, Denich 2005, Friedman and Robbins 2005, Hayden 2005, Kapferer 2005, Kideckel 2005 and Wilson 2005).
4. I am grateful to Dimitrina Mihaylova for drawing my attention to the Bulgarian debate.
5. '*Susjedstvo*' is a standard Slavic word for neighbourhood and neighbourly relations used in Serbia, Montenegro, Croatia and Bosnia. Hadžijahić's use of it to explain the term '*komsiluk*' to foreigners (who would not know either word) illustrates that the latter phenomenon is felt by him to be somewhat different in quality, specifically Bosnian and less immediately comprehensible than '*susjedstvo*'.
6. In her ethnography of wartime Sarajevo, Macek records this story told not of Abu Bakr but of someone from 'an old Sarajevan Muslim family'. Perhaps this is a case of religion slipped even further into the margins? (Macek 2000: 126)
7. Bosnian default custom is to pray both the religiously obligatory and the 'sunna' or desirable *rakats*, unless the worshipper is particularly pressed for time. The wartime emergence of a new wave of Arab-inspired Bosnian Muslims whose default setting is the opposite – to pray only the obligatory *rakat* unless they are particularly at leisure – has occasioned irritation on both sides.
8. Laidlaw has argued that Durkheim is responsible for the widespread anthropological sense that all culturally prescribed behaviours are 'moral', and for the consequent dissipation of the meaning of morality within anthropology as a discipline (Laidlaw 2002). Arguably, this comparison of two important, culturally reified sets of relationships, *veze* and *komšiluk*, may help illustrate the interpretive danger of an anthropological urge to spread morality too thinly and broadly.
9. The challenge of going against the grain was vividly depicted in a May 1992 entry in journalist Zlatko Dizdarević's wartime diary column in *Oslobodenje* (see Dizdarevic 1994: 15–17). He wrote of the man whose three-year-old daughter was shot by a sniper and who announced that he wanted to invite the killer for coffee and ask him, human to human, why he had done it. Dizdarević despairs of those who cannot recognise evil for what it is and instead invite it for coffee. This theme of exasperation with their own perceived passivity is not infrequently heard from post-war Sarajevo Bosniacs.
10. It is also the case that some new trends of Islamic thought which have emerged in Bosnia since the war downplay the traditional Bosnian Muslim veneration of *komšiluk* in favour of other values claimed to have a stronger Islamic mandate.

References

Bloch, M and J. Parry. 1982. *Death and the Regeneration of Life*. Cambridge: Cambridge University Press.

Bougarel, X. 1996. 'Bosnia and Hercegovina: State and Communitarianism', in D. Dyker and I. Vejvoda (eds), *Yugoslavia and After: A Study in Fragmentation, Despair and Rebirth*. London: Longman, pp. 87–115.

———. 1999/2000. 'Retour sur le Bon Voisinage', *L'ARA (Association Rhone-Alpes d'Anthropologie)*, special issue on *Regards sur les Europe: une anthropologie impliquee dans les Balkans* 44: 26–28.

Bowen, J. 2004a. 'Muslims and Citizens: France's Headscarf Controversy', *Boston Review* Feb./March issue. http://bostonreview.net/BR29.1/bowen.html

———. 2004b. 'Does French Islam Have Borders? Dilemmas of Domestication in a Global Religious Field', *American Anthropologist* 106(1): 43–55.

Bringa, T. 1995. *Being Muslim the Bosnian Way*. Princeton: Princeton University Press.

Brown, K. 2003. *The Past In Question: Modern Macedonia and the Uncertainties of Nation*. Princeton: Princeton University Press.

Brubaker, R. 2002. 'Ethnicity Without Groups', *Arch. Europ. Sociol* XLIII(2): 163–89.

Casanova, J. 1994. *Public Religions in the Modern World*. Chicago: University of Chicago Press.

Christie, D. and T. Bringa. 1993. *We Are All Neighbours*. Granada TV documentary.

Chukov, V. 2001. 'Bulgarian Ethnic Model: A Pragmatical National Version of the Multi-ethnic Dialog'. http://crcs0.tripod.com/lgivl.html

Cushman, T. 2004. 'Anthropology and Genocide in the Balkans: An Analysis of Conceptual Practices of Power', *Anthopological Theory* 4(1): 5–28.

———. 2005. 'Response to Hayden and Denich', *Anthropological Theory* 5(4): 559–64.

Denich, B. 2005. 'Debate or Defamation? Comment on the Publication of Cushman's "Anthropology and Genocide in the Balkans"', *Anthropological Theory* 5(4): 555–58.

Dizdarević, Z. 1994. *Sarajevo: A War Journal*. New York: Henry Holt.

Donia, R. 2006. *Sarajevo: A Biography*. London: Hurst.

Donia, R. and J. Fine. 1994. *Bosnia and Hercegovina: A Tradition Betrayed*. London: Hurst.

Du Boulay, J. 1976. 'Lies, Mockery and Family Integrity', in J.G. Peristiany (ed.), *Mediterranean Family Structures*. Cambridge: Cambridge University Press.

Dyker D. and I. Vejvoda (eds). 1996. *Yugoslavia and After: A Study in Fragmentation, Despair and Rebirth*. London: Longman.

Elkana, Y. et al. (eds). 2002. *Unravelling Ties: From Social Cohesion to New Practices of Connectedness*. Frankfurt: Campus.

Filandra, S. 1998. *Bošnjaćka Politika u XX Stoljecu (Bosniac Politics in the 20th Century)*. Sarajevo: Sejtarija.

Friedman, J. and Robbins, J. 2005. 'Statement of Editorial Principle', *Anthropological Theory* 5(4): 405.

Geiss, P. 2001. 'Mahallah and Kinship Relations: A Study on Residential Communal Commitment Structures in Central Asia of the 19th Century', *Central Asia Survey* 20(1): 97–106.

Georgieva, T. 1995. 'Co-existence as a System in the Everyday Life of Christians and Muslims in Bulgaria', in Zhelyazkova, A (dir.), *Relations of Compatibility and Incompatibility Between Christians and Muslims in Bulgaria*. Sofia: International Centre for Minority Studies and Intercultural Relations & Intercultural Relations Foundation, pp. 151–72.

Hayden, R. 2002. 'Antagonistic Tolerance: Competitive Sharing of Religious Sites in South Asia and the Balkans', *Current Anthropology* 43(2): 205–31.

———. 2005. 'Inaccurate Data, Spurious Issues and Editorial Failure in Cushman's 'Anthropology and Genocide in the Balkans', *Anthropological Theory* 5(4): 545–54.

Heyd, D. (ed.). 1996. *Toleration: An Elusive Virtue*. Princeton: Princeton University Press.

Iliev, A. 2001. 'Participation of Bulgarian Roma in the 2001 General Elections and Prospects for Political Representation', *Roma Rights* 4(21). http://www.errc.org/cikk.php?cikk=1232

Kapferer, B. 2005. 'In Positions to do Great Damage: A Comment on the Cushman, Denich, Hayden and Wilson Debate', *Anthropological Theory* 5 (4): 577–81.

Karic, E. 1999. *Essays on Behalf of Bosnia*. Sarajevo: El Kalem.

Kideckel, D. 2005. 'The "Tar Baby" Revisited: War in Former Yugoslavia and Anthropological Discourses and Responsibilities', *Anthropological Theory* 5(4): 571–75.

Laidlaw, J. 2002. 'For an Anthropology of Ethics and Freedom', *Journal of the Royal Anthropological Institute* 8(2): 311–32.
Ledeneva, A. 1998. *Russia's Economy of Favours: Blat, Networking and Informal Exchange*. Cambridge: Cambridge University Press.
Maass, P. 1997. *Love Thy Neighbour: A Story of War*. New York: Vintage.
Macek, I. 2000. *War Within: Everyday Life in Sarajevo Under Siege*. Uppsala: Acta Universitatis Upsaliensis.
Marcus, A. 1986. 'Privacy in Eighteenth Century Aleppo', *International Journal of Middle Eastern Studies* 18: 2.
Neuffer, E. 2002. *The Key to Thy Neighbour's House: Seeking Justice in Bosnia and Rwanda*. New York: Picador.
Nowotny, H. 2002. 'Reconnecting Ties', in Y. Elkana et al. (eds), *Unravelling Ties: From Social Cohesion to New Practices of Connectedness*. Frankfurt: Campus, pp. 351–62.
Parkin, D. (ed.). 1987. *The Anthropology of Evil*. Oxford: Blackwell.
Peristiany, J.G. (ed.). 1976. *Mediterranean Family Structures*. Cambridge: Cambridge University Press.
Pouligny, B. 2002. 'Building Peace in Situations of Post-mass Crimes', *International Peacekeeping* 9(2): 181–201.
Rheubottom, D. 1987. 'The Seed of Evil Within', in D. Parkin (ed.), *The Anthropology of Evil*. Oxford: Blackwell, pp. 77–91.
Sanguin, A.-L. 1998. 'Sarajevo avant et après le siège: les mutations culturelles d'une capitale multiethnique', *Geographies et Cultures* 27: 41–62.
Solioz, C. 2002. 'From Protectorate to Partnership: Bosnia and Herzegovina on the Road to Sovereignty', in D. Solioz and S. Dizdarevic (eds), *The Ownership Process in Bosnia and Herzegovina*. Baden-Baden: Nomos (Democracy, Security, Peace Vol. 159), pp. 19–49. Also on www.christophesolioz.ch.
Sorabji, C. 1989. 'Muslim Identity and Islamic Faith in Sarajevo', PhD thesis. Cambridge: University of Cambridge.
———. 1994. 'Une guerre très moderne: mémoire et identité en Bosnie-Hercegovine', *Terrain* 23: 137–50.
———. 1995. 'A Very Modern War: Terror and Territory in Bosnia-Hercegovina', in R.A. Hinde and H. Watson (eds), *War: A Cruel Necessity?: The Bases of Institutionalized Violence*. London: Tauris, pp. 80–95.
———. 2006. 'Managing Memories in Post War Sarajevo: Individuals, Bad Memories and New Wars', *Journal of the Royal Anthropological Institute* 12(1): 1–18.
Williams, B. 1996. 'Tolerance: An Impossible Virtue?', in D. Heyd (ed.), *Toleration: An Elusive Virtue*. Princeton: Princeton University Press, pp. 18–27.
Wilson, R. 2005. 'Towards an Open Debate on the Anthropology of Genocide', *Anthropological Theory* 5(4): 565–69.
Zhelyazkova, A. (dir.). 1995. *Relations of Compatibility and Incompatibility Between Christians and Muslims in Bulgaria*. Sofia: International Centre for Minority Studies and Intercultural Relations & Intercultural Relations Foundation.
Zhelyazkova, A. 2002. 'Bulgarian Ethnic, Religious Communities Co-exist Side-by-side', *Southeast European Times*, 9 January 2002. http://www.setimes.com/cocoon/setimes/xhtml/en_GB/features/setimes/articles/2002/01/020111-BULGARIA-001

Part III

Power and Relative Centrality

Chapter 7

Revival of Buddhist Royal Family Commemorative Ritual in Laos

Grant Evans

King Sisavang Vong of Laos died on the '29th day of October 1959 at 5 minutes past 10 p.m. at the age of 74 years 3 months and 15 days, after being on the throne for 55 years, 3 months and 14 days,' as reported by an astrologically sensitive commemorative volume published at the time of his funeral in April 1961. At his death he was the longest reigning monarch in Asia, perhaps the world, and this in itself was evidence of his great merit. His reign has subsequently been matched only by Emperor Hirohito of Japan, and the current Thai King. Readers of the commemorative volumes produced for his funeral, however, were all reminded that everyone 'is born, ages, sickens and dies', even kings. Impermanence is all, Buddhism counselled mourners throughout the Kingdom.

Crowned in 1905 by the French Resident Superieur in Laos, Sisavang Vong saw his northern Kingdom of Luang Phrabang expand gradually until, after World War Two, he became the constitutional monarch of the whole Kingdom of Laos. He was deposed briefly by an enthusiastic, but small, nationalist movement at the end of the war, but this is never mentioned in official histories. In 1949 the Kingdom became an independent part of the French Union, and in 1953 became completely independent. He was the one credited with this achievement, and not unfairly. No sooner had this happened than the city of Luang Phrabang was threatened by a Viet-Minh invasion in one of the final manoeuvres of the anti-French war in neighbouring Vietnam. The King refused to budge from his indefensible capital. *Nouvelles du Laos* (30/10/1959) reported the consequences of this decision in its edition announcing his death and which recounted his achievements: 'The impact was considerable. There was an increase in Royal Prestige both domestically and internationally. Everyone exalted the King's courage and his high civil virtues. The Sovereign's tough stance in face of the Viet-Minh's threats reinforced the country's unity.' At the time of his death he was mourned as the unifier of modern Laos, as a

Figure 7.1. Cover of the funeral booklet: 'History of His Majesty the King Sisavang Vong, King of the Lao Kingdom.'

person steeped in Lao culture, and as a defender of Buddhism. Even today, Lao who see his photo will say he exudes '*boun barami*', the power of great merit. But already in 1959 the storm clouds of the Cold War were gathering. By the time of his funeral in 1961 the country was rent by civil strife from which communist forces benefited, and the country was staring into the vortex of the coming Vietnam War that would finally engulf and destroy the Royal Lao Government and the monarchy in December 1975.

Every year after his funeral an official commemorative ceremony for King Sisavang Vong was held at the That Luang temple in Luang Phrabang where his ashes had been interred in a rebuilt stupa (*That*), founded by a former Queen in 1820 and renamed That Haysokarath.

This ceremony was presided over by the new King Sisavang Vatthana and the Queen, and was attended not only by members of the Royal Family but also by leading figures in the government, including the long-time Prime Minister, Prince Souvanna Phouma, member of another key royal lineage in Luang Phrabang. These events were sometimes accompanied by the issue of commemorative stamps, and always by notices in the newspapers which contained a brief account of his reign (see Figure 2 and 3). The last official celebration was on 29 October 1975, and the last notice was printed on the front page of the newspaper *Xat Lao* (Lao Nation), already in the hands of the revolutionary forces, who by that time had almost completely dismantled the Royal Lao side of the coalition government that had been formed with the communists (under U.S. pressure) in 1973. Until December 1975 they remained publicly committed to maintaining the monarchy.

But on 2 December 1975, the Crown Prince, Vong Savang, had to deliver his father's abdication to the communist party congress, which then announced the formation of the Lao People's Democratic Republic. The former King was appointed 'advisor' to the President of the new Republic, but it was a task he ignored. Thenceforth, all official royal ceremonies vanished.

Figure 7.2. Commemorative stamp produced at the time of King Sisavang Vong's funeral in 1961.

Figure 7.3. Commemorative stamp produced at the time of King Sisavang Vong's funeral in 1961.

In late 1975 the emerging new Stalinist-style regime had already begun to encourage members of the 'old regime' to go off to 're-education camps', for a few months they were told, but in fact many were away for years, or forever. After December, others were rounded up and sent off, including many members of the Royal Family. The King's eldest daughter and her husband had fled into exile, as had his other daughter, whose husband had been rounded up, and also his youngest son and his wife. The Crown Prince and his wife Princess Manilai stayed, as did the King's second son, Prince Sisavang and his wife Princess Ratsami. The King, who by now had handed the palace over to the new regime and moved to his private residence beside the Mekong River, insisted that he would die on Lao soil. Thus, it was a much diminished Royal

Family that gathered for a quiet, private commemorative ceremony on 29 October 1976, and it was the last time for the King. In March 1977, he, the Queen and his two sons, as well as other leading members of the Royal Family, were arrested and imprisoned in the camps established by the regime in the mountainous province of Hua Phan, bordering northern Vietnam.[1] From the middle of 1979 the health of the three prisoners began to deteriorate. One day at the beginning of January the Crown Prince was confined to his bed seriously ill (he died two weeks later).[2] Prisoners wrapped the cadaver in a sheet and took it to be buried just north of the camp. The King and Queen tried to follow but the soldiers would not allow it. The King himself died in mid-March 1980 and the Queen was also not allowed to attend his burial.[3] She was soon transferred to a camp for all female prisoners at Phafaek, where she is believed to have died in 1982.[4] The LPDR government has never given full details of their demise, and only under pressure from the French Government did the communist party leader Kaysone Phomvihane say during an official visit to Paris in December 1989 that the King had died of malaria. The Ministry of Interior in Vientiane are still tight-lipped.[5]

Death and Commemoration in Lao Buddhism

At whatever level of the social structure it occurs, death causes a rupture. In the case of a King's death the rupture is global, but the appointment of Crown Princes ensures a rapid transition. Thus, *Nouvelles du Laos* on 30 October 1959 proclaimed: 'The King is Dead! Long Live the King'. In fact, Prince Savang Vatthana had already been appointed Regent in August 1959, and he was immediately recognized as the new King. Indeed, Quaritch Wales (1931: 162–63) has drawn attention to the ritual similarities between rites of coronation and rites of cremation in Siam (and Cambodia and Laos), both entailing a supreme elevation and 'rebirth'. But Wales' further remarks are worth noting:

> It is particularly important that a Royal Cremation should be celebrated with the greatest possible pomp, because death is the greatest danger that the idea of divine kingship has to combat ... with the spread of western education, and the shadow of communism, the Royal Cremation plays an even bigger part than formerly in impressing on the people that the king is not dead, but has migrated to a higher plane, where he will work out his destiny as a Bodhisattva for the good of all beings. (1931: 166)

It also, he says, sets an 'example to the people in filial piety' (1931: 166). And, indeed, the funeral of King Sisavang Vong was carried out with all the pomp available to the Lao monarchy.

Ordinarily a decaying corpse (*saak sop nao*) is the source of a potentially dangerous spirit (*phi*) until it is properly disposed of, usually within days, by cremation presided over by Buddhist monks.[6] *Phi*, therefore, is an essence that survives death until, along with the corpse, it is sent on its way through ritual

Figure 7.4. Pomp at a royal cremation. (Photo: Grant Evans)

cremation. The essence that remains thereafter to be reborn is the *duang vinyaan*, a term derived from Pali *vinnanya*, 'consciousness'. With highly meritorious lay individuals, monks and royalty, however, their bodies may be kept for months or years before cremation. They are believed to be especially pure or meritorious and therefore their deaths are not necessarily associated with *phi*, and hence there is less haste in sending off their remains. After ritual bathing and other purificatory rites a King is placed in a funeral urn which is then the site of ritual offerings and prayers by monks to help ensure the assumed elevation to nirvana, *nipaan muang kaew*, of the King following cremation. This assumption about the elevation of Kings to nirvana is a fundamental difference between ordinary Lao Buddhist expectations, where the cycle of rebirth is taken as given, and royal death, where that cycle is transcended.

A central ritual practice for the dead in Theravada Buddhism involves merit transference from the living to the dead to try to ensure a more exalted rebirth in the future for the person who has passed away. The sharing of merit in this way would appear to contradict Buddhist doctrine inasmuch as each individual is supposed to be morally responsible for one's actions. But, as Charles Keyes (1983: 271) has observed: 'Without the inclusion of the conception of merit-transfer within the theory of karma, it would be difficult, if not impossible, for those who lead the lives of householders – as distinct from the life of the *bhikkhu* – to make karmic theory the basis of an ethos or orientation toward action.' Merit is transferred through the medium of the *sangha*, who are a 'field of merit' for lay Buddhists. Offerings are made to the sangha and the merit made as a result of such moral actions is transferred to the dead, typically during prayers offered by monks while each individual pours a libation from a vessel containing scented water symbolizing the transfer. The prayers offered are called in Lao, *sut sak anijaa*.

Whenever anyone dies among the Lao it is usual that at least a son or a grandson, or other male relatives, enter the monkhood to become a 'field of merit' for the family. They enter usually for a short time, perhaps one week, until after the cremation. But, in the case of royalty the period of mourning is longer, at least 100 days. The entry of young men into the monkhood in this way is centrally informed by the idea that younger generations have reciprocal duties to older generations, and in particular parents. The relationship is especially important between mothers and sons, for women cannot participate in this supreme moral act of entering the monkhood, but a mother can sponsor her son's entry and in this way he becomes a field of merit for her, just as he or his son can become a field of merit for her again by entering the monkhood when she dies. The ordination of a monk, however, is a communal affair not only participated in by the immediate family but by friends, neighbours and whoever else wishes to *dai boun*, make merit, through their participation. The reciprocity expressed is simultaneously specific, family reciprocity, and general in that the new monk is also a field of merit for the whole community. Indeed, the amount of merit generated by an occasion is more or less perceived as exponential according to the number of people who join in, and thus it becomes a supreme display of communal solidarity and individual merit making.[7]

Various memorial rituals are held for the dead after cremation, the most important being 100 days after when the remains are usually placed in a small *that* in the temple grounds. Thereafter, offerings are made to the dead at the New Year, where, for example, a new set of clothing may be offered to the deceased by better-off families. After the ritual is finished these are taken by the monks and then given by them to poor parishioners. In this way the Lao say they *dai boun song teu*, make merit twice over. Rituals are also often held on the date of their death, called *boun bang sakun*, or when a long departed son, for example, wishes for whatever reason to enter the monastery to transfer merit to his parents and simultaneously gain merit himself. In Buddhism the rebirth of the *vinyaan* of the deceased is indeterminate and, therefore, there is no known point at which commemoration should come to an end. Furthermore, I would argue that such 'theological' issues are not uppermost in the minds of the majority of Lao. The ritual is seen as an act of devotion, a kind of filial piety, whose primary object is to enact these cultural values as both a cultural model of Lao family relations and a model for family relations, directed at all concerned but especially the younger generations. Thus, I would suggest that the offering of clothing, for example, is an expressive act, an iconic statement of family concern, which does not entail any strong belief that they are somehow transferred to the dead, as in Chinese ancestor worship, for example, or indeed among the upland non-Buddhist Tai whose practices are described as *teu phi*, ancestor worship.[8] And, this description, *teu phi*, is used precisely to mark the difference between Buddhists and other groups in Laos. Belief in *phi* of various kinds is, of course, widespread among the Buddhist Lao, and anthropological discussions of Theravada Buddhism have pointed out that this helps in everyday life to resolve the indeterminacy of one's karma, *kam* in Lao, through a belief in active unseen agents, either benign or malevolent. These beliefs, however, are either kept separate from Buddhism, or are encompassed by it.[9]

Indeed, the commemoration of ancestors among the Lao is not of the kind where ancestors are believed to have a continuing interest in the world. Speaking of northern Thai, Keyes has remarked that the belief in rebirth 'aborts a tendency ... to think of the dead as ancestors' (1987: 185). This, he also argues, is related to 'the lack of interest in genealogy' (1987: 199) among these people, and we can include the Lao. But in this respect Lao royalty (like royalty everywhere) is radically different from ordinary Lao in their intense interest in and knowledge of genealogy because, naturally, their status depends on it. In other words, there is a clear knowledge of, and pride in, known ancestors stretching back for generations. But are they ancestors who have a continuing interest in the world?

Quaritch Wales was one of the first to write about the significance of royal commemorative ceremonies in the Thai context. Writing in the late 1920s, he remarks on a practice begun only at the turn of the century which was to represent kings in life-like statue form. This broke with a tradition in the region whereby kings may be disguised as *Bodhisattvas* (e.g., Angkor Thom in Cambodia), but otherwise only Buddha images or those of angels or gods were made. In keeping with modern kingship, this brought Siamese Kings out into the public gaze, secularising their image. But these images themselves have become fields of merit for the populace and, moreover, they have attracted their own spirit mediums. Besides these, lifelike golden statues are kept in the Grand Palace, and at New Year (the Coronation Anniversary) and Chakri Day on 6 April, which celebrates the founding of that dynasty, the King, nobles, officials and the public offer prayers before these statues. Wales also comments on the new custom which had just come into being at that time of making offerings before royal portraits, something which is now common.[10] Prayers to the actual relics of the former monarchs, however, are only offered by the Royal Family and nobles, and in a clearly Buddhist context. By the 1930s, busts of King Sisavang Vong, his father and grandfather had been made and were kept in the palace in Luang Phrabang, but I do not know if they were a centre of ritual activity. The first public statue of a King was that of the sixteenth-century monarch Sethathirath, constructed in 1957 in front of the famous stupa he built in Vientiane, the That Luang. His likeness was divined by a medium. In January 1973 a statue of King Sisavang Vong himself was erected in front of one of the main temples in Vientiane, Vat Simuang, and a replica placed in the palace grounds two years later. However, it was too late for them to become established as a site of ritual offerings, and subsequently people are wary of being seen making such offerings, although it happens occasionally. As we will see, a small bust of Sisavang Vong is used in contemporary commemorations of him. In January 2003, the 're-traditionalised' communist state in Laos sponsored the erection of a statue of the King who founded the first major Lao Kingdom, King Fa Ngum, and it was erected with full Brammanical rites, including, it was reported, an invitation to the spirit of his wife to attend the ceremony.

This brief consideration of the place in commemoration of public statues of Kings in modern Thailand and Laos does highlight, I think, an ambiguity in popular perceptions of the fate of dead Kings.[11] The ability of spirit mediums to embody briefly these Kings and offer advice to the living certainly suggests that they are treated as general 'ancestors' who can be entreated to maintain an interest in the living. Offerings made at the equestrian statue of King Rama V of Thailand on Chulalongkorn Day (23 October), by many thousands of Thai, makes it especially *saksit* (magically, spiritually potent) on that day. However, it is ambiguous whether by making merit that day people expect better future outcomes because of accumulated merit, or whether they expect direct intervention by the spirit of the King in the manner of an ancestor. Similarly, the Buddhist protective amulets, including pictures of royal figures in both Thailand and Laos, protect their wearers through the exceptional merit manifest in the amulet. The ambiguities in these various practices, however, dissipate when played out in an overtly Buddhist context where commemoration brings one into communion with a being of exceptional merit in a setting that provides a field of special merit for all concerned. In this respect, I think one has to argue that despite royalty's interest in genealogy and ancestry, it does not in the Lao or other similar cultural contexts translate into an ancestor cult.[12] Furthermore, I have no evidence that members of the royal family approach spirit mediums with the aim of communicating with ancestors.

Revival

From 1977 until the late 1980s the wives of the King's sons were under virtual house arrest, and of course deeply distressed by the arrest of their husbands and the absence of any news from them. Princess Manilai remained in the Crown Prince's residence in the centre of the city facing a police station directly across the road. Princess Ratsami, who had been living in the King's residence until the arrests, had moved back to live with her mother. They took refuge in Buddhism. Many years later, in 1997, Princess Manilai told me of the guidance she received from the abbot of Vat Phone Phao, *Satu* Mouk:

> He taught us to forget all our grief. I took his words to heart and so I did not have any grief or sadness. He said that we have to be aware of everything around us, and just remember that there are people worse off than us but they still survive. Nothing is certain for both the rich and the poor. Our fingers are not all equal. When we are poor or in grief, we have to accept it. We are all born alike and end alike in death. Thinking too much shortens one's life. Nothing is like the Buddha's teachings. Whatever he teaches is right. He tells us not to worry too much about this life, and when we die is determined by our karma.

Until the early 1980s commemoration of King Sisavang Vong had fallen to Princess Khamphin, one of his unmarried daughters, who had fled to Vat

Figure 7.5. Ritual of commemoration at Vat That Luang. (Photo: Grant Evans)

Phone Phao on the outskirts of the city to become a nun immediately after the revolution because she feared for her life and felt that only the temple, the Buddha, could protect her. Each year she alone had carried on the commemoration of her father in small, private rituals at Vat That Luang until 1983 after which she was gradually joined by others, some of whom had begun to return from the camps. I still recall her shock when I first approached her at the temple for an interview in 1996, her frail voice echoing in the empty room, 'I cannot remember anything. What should I do? Your questions do not refresh my memories. In 1976, when the revolution took over, I fled right away.'[13] But by the mid-1990s much had already changed in Laos.

The collapse of communism globally after 1990 was alarming for the surviving communist–party-led regimes in Asia. Most of them (except North Korea) had begun important economic reforms in the 1980s, but the collapse accelerated marketisation, now accompanied by legal reforms (primarily to accommodate foreign investment) and a dramatic loosening of the state's control over everyday life. By the turn of the twenty-first century everyday life in Laos, Vietnam and China was almost unrecognisable compared with only a decade before. All of these regimes turned to the past and a strident form of cultural nationalism to smooth over the shredded and tattered orthodoxy of communism, which they could not fully relinquish without calling their own legitimacy into question. In Laos this 're-traditionalising' of the communist state entailed closer identification with Buddhism (the state religion under RLG, while under the LPDR it had been marginalised), and rituals formerly presided over by the King found communist state officials attempting to fill his shoes. Other rituals and cultural practices have been revivified, if only for the purposes of cultural tourism, such as with the 'royal ballet' and its dances from the *Ramayana*, formerly held in the palace grounds at New Year. Indeed, the direct appeal to the tourist dollar that is being made is underlined by the fact that 'royal ballet' is written thus in English, while in Lao it is the national ballet, and the Royal Theatre is simply The Theatre.

This highlights some of the ambiguities surrounding this revival, because many cultural practices point to a monarchical presence, if only implicitly. Indeed, the vicissitudes of attempting traditionalist revivals was shown during the erection of a statue of a fourteenth-century monarch, King Fa Ngum, by the regime in early 2003. It led to such intense speculation about the country's royal past that a disclaimer was published on the front page of the English language paper, *Vientiane Times*.[14] The regime simply wished to present him as a national hero and the founder of the first Lao Kingdom, but they were unable to control the meanings that ricocheted around the event.[15]

In the 1990s ordinary Lao villagers found that practices that had previously been frowned upon or actively suppressed as 'superstition' were now accepted as part of the 'beautiful ancient Lao culture' that had to be 'nurtured and protected'. Elaborate offerings at temples for the commemoration of ancestors (which by now also included many of the leading revolutionaries who had passed on) have become common, along with ostentatious displays of support for the temples. The former Royal Family was able to capitalise on this revival of tradition, not by an appeal to royalty (that had to be left to tourist promoters!), but by an appeal to the fact that their family ceremonies were no different from other Lao and were part of the 'beautiful ancient Lao culture' too. Thus, since the mid-1990s the royal family, centred on King Sisavang Vong and his descendants in Luang Phrabang, have gathered publicly at Vat That Luang on 29 October to commemorate him, and they are increasingly joined by relatives who fled overseas but have returned for the ritual.[16] Perhaps one could say that the first major post-1975 ritual was held in 1996 when Princess Khamphin sponsored a *kathin* ceremony, an offering of robes, for the monks.[17]

I first attended the ceremony in 2001, and again in 2002, which was an important occasion because it was combined with a *boun khong bouat*, the induction of two young 'princes' into the monkhood, Princess Manilai's son Thanya,[18] and Princess Ratsami's son. The day before was taken up with preparations, naturally at the houses of the two princes, but also at the house of the only remaining son of King Sisavang Vong in Laos, who in fact was too old to attend the ceremony the following day. This house which is adjacent to the palace is by now a run-down large house which is visually an immediate reminder of 'old' Luang Phrabang, as the tourist brochures would have it. The men gathered in the garden to construct the *phasat pheung*, beeswax stupas, which would be covered with money and offered to the *sangha* at the temple the following day. Anybody (not from Luang Phrabang) passing by would have

Figure 7.6. Royal family ritual in Luang Phrabang. (Photo: Grant Evans)

seen little to distinguish these activities from any other household ritual activity in Laos. People in Luang Phrabang, however, are acutely aware that this is a royal family ritual, involving only that family and other people 'close to the palace' in the past.[19] In contrast to pre-1975 public royal ritual, it is seen by outsiders as a 'private' ritual (Figure 6). Inside the house, women were preparing some of the food for the following day, while much of it would be prepared early the following morning for the repast that would follow the ceremony. They and some men were also platting together other objects for making offerings, such as the offering in the photo below by Tiao (prince) Soukthivong and his family.

People began to gather at Vat That Luang between 8 a.m. and 9 a.m. on the 29th, some chatted outside before joining those who were already seated on the floor inside the temple waiting for the rituals to begin. Some would make small offerings at the base around Sisavang Vong's stupa before entering, some would do it later (Figure 8). Inside the temple women gathered in the back half, men in the front closest to the monks who are seated in front of the main altar and main Buddha statue. At the front of the men is a 'master of ceremonies', and to his right a table on which sits a small bust of King Sisavang Vong and robes being offered to the *sangha*.

The ritual proceeded in two stages, first the induction of the young novices and then the ritual of commemoration. It began at 9 am with the two young men, their heads shaven and dressed in white robes, taking their leave from their mothers and presenting themselves to the gathered *sangha*. The ritual, it

Figure 7.7. The message on this offering reads: 'I, Tiao Soukthivong, aged 70 years, come yearly to pay my respects to the Buddha, the dharma, and the sangha. I request that I will not be possessed by evil, not be sad, and will not be ill. That I will not encounter ill-intentioned others, that I will not sicken, and I hope for success and happiness, and that I will get whatever I wish for. In truth.' (Photo: Grant Evans)

should be remarked, is presided over not by the abbot of Vat That Luang, but by the supreme patriarch of Luang Phrabang, Satu Khamchan, who comes from another former royal temple, Vat Saen. It is no small matter. Over the next three quarters of an hour the young men become part of the *sangha* and can then join the other monks for the prayers of commemoration.

In his leading of these prayers, Satu Khamchan proclaims that these prayers are offered for Sisavang Vong and his descendants. No mention is made of Savang Vatthana, his wife and sons, although this could be reasonably inferred

Figure 7.8. That Haysokarath at That Luang temple that contains the remains of King Sisavang Vong. People are making offerings around the That before the ceremony begins. (Photo: Grant Evans)

from the term 'descendants'. From my discussions with participants, it is certainly understood that merit is being made for the former King and Queen and their sons, but failure to mention this explicitly in the prayers is presumably because the commemoration is on the day of Sisavang Vong's death, and is understood as such by the authorities. Furthermore, it is likely that it is still politically problematic to refer publicly to King Sisavang Vatthana's death.

Figure 7.9. The 'master of ceremonies', behind him is the small statue of Sisavang Vong and the offerings to the monks. (Photo: Grant Evans)

Figure 7.10. The two young princes Saisana and Thanya are are received by Satu Kham Chan. (Photo: Grant Evans)

Figure 7.11. The two princes Thanya and Saisana are inducted into the temple. (Photo: Grant Evans)

The only public memorial ceremonies that have been held for King Sisavang Vatthana and the others have been by the Royal Family in exile in France. A Regency council was established there in 1979, and in 1984 the King's youngest son, Prince Sauryavong, assumed the title of Regent following intimations of the King's death in 1983. But it was not until Kaysone's announcement in Paris on 14 December 1989 that the Lao community finally acknowledged that the King was dead.[20] In September 1990 the Royal Family in exile, other members of the nobility and the Lao community at large gathered at the Pagode du Bois de Vincennes – built for the 1931 Exposition Coloniale – for a Buddhist memorial ceremony for the King and the others who had perished in the camps. Interestingly, *Point de Vue* (20/9/1990) reported that, 'After the Buddhist ceremony, representatives of the Hmong ethnic group celebrated an animistic rite before a cenotaph [outside the temple]. For them the King was the single most important line attaching them to other Lao. He was for them like a god (*demi-dieux*)'.[21]

Figure 7.12. The commemorative ceremony in France. From the left, Prince Soulivong, the Prince Regent Sauryavong and his wife Princess Daravong.

Commemoration at the Margins

Commemoration of King Sisavang Vong, which had been an important event in the ritual calendar of the Royal Lao Government, almost disappeared altogether after 1975. Banished to the margins of society, it was for a short time only the lonely figure of a nun in her white robes, Princess Khamphin, who was able to observe the rituals. After 1983 the rite was slowly reconstituted, and in the more liberal atmosphere of the 1990s it has become a central part of the ritual calendar of the surviving members of the Royal Family. The ritual is presented as a private one, but as it takes place in public space in one of the main royal temples of the city. It also gives royalty a ritual presence it has been denied since the revolution.[22] It is a slender and marginal presence, and one which the government is keen to contain.

It is understandable too that the ritual is focussed on Sisavang Vong rather than his son, Sisavang Vatthana, and not only for political reasons or the fact that the exact date of the latter's death is unknown. Sisavang Vong had a long and successful reign, and his vinyaan was sent on its way after the completion of all the proper rites. He therefore continues to represent an ideal of royalty in its fullness and splendour, rather than the tragedy and sadness attached to the memory of Sisavang Vatthana. Only when and if the latter's remains are ever returned to Luang Phrabang will some of the pall that surrounds the demise of the last King begin to lift. Today the ritual's leading sponsor is still the aged but sprightly nun, Princess Khamphin, the last remaining daughter of Sisavang Vong. She has been a key link in the chain of commemoration, but an increasingly fragile one. It is through this commemorative ritual that royal descendants are able to reaffirm their royal status, and it is sure to be practiced for at least another generation. But after that, it may slip over the margin of social memory into the well of impermanence.

Notes

1. In fact, the Queen went voluntarily, refusing to be separated from her husband. Princess Manilai and Princess Ratsami were both pregnant, and this plus the fact that they had young children, meant that they stayed behind.
2. Khamphan Thammakhanthi, (n.d.) 'La Vérité sur le Camp-Prison No.1, ou Camp de la Mort au Point 438–745', unpublished manuscript.
3. They were not cremated as would be normal and fitting because it wasted wood!
4. See Kremmer (2003: 220).
5. For the broad historical context of the events described above see Evans (2002b).
6. Interestingly, I have been told that it is good luck to have heard the last breath of a person, presumably because one has briefly glimpsed the threshold between life and death.
7. If asked, Lao will, however, simply say that more people makes it a happy, *mouan*, occasion, while fewer makes it sad, and by implication less meritorious.
8. For a discussion of funerals among upland Tai see Evans (1991). These groups in Laos are Black, White and Red Tai, whose languages belong to the Tai family, as do Lao and Thai.
9. Lao attitudes are perhaps aptly illustrated by a Lao medical doctor I know whose wife is sino-Lao. In her paternal household an altar for her dead Chinese father is maintained by the family who make offerings to him according to what they understand to be Chinese practice. It should be pointed out that all the members of this family are active Theravada Buddhists. Before a written examination at one time the husband asked his wife to make an offering at her father's altar to help him succeed. In other words, he drew on her access to an ancestral *phi* to assist him, just as Lao may approach other *phi* for help in everyday life – with love affairs, for example.
10. The only publicly displayed portraits since 1975 of King Sisavang Vatthana, his Queen Khamphui and the Crown Prince are in the former palace, now a 'Museum'. The paintings done then by Soviet painter, Ilya Gazurov, in 1967 were the only images on display for most of the 1990s when the palace was finally opened to the public. As I have speculated elsewhere, the paintings and the statues done by the once 'fraternal' Soviets could not be discarded after the revolution. And nor could they be discarded following the Soviet collapse and the revival of tradition – such are the ironies of history! In the past two years several photos have also been displayed. Needless to say, these are not available for veneration. However, in 2002, it was said to me that Lao who visited the palace were sure that the eyes of the Queen have *vaew*, they follow you, evidence of *vinyaan*.
11. For a longer discussion of related issues see Evans (2002a).
12. Elsewhere (Evans 1998a) I have argued that attempts in Laos to construct a political cult around the communist party leader, Kaysone Phomvihane, are aborted by the same Buddhist cultural practices that abort ancestor worship. This is by way of contrast with East Asia, with its cults of Mao, Ho Chi Minh and Kim Il Sung. Interestingly, a linguist colleague reports that in the south of Laos she has witnessed one highland minority group who normally practice a form of ancestor

worship, approaching one of the busts of Kaysone that have been placed around the country (made in North Korea!) in much the same way as they would approach their ancestors.
13. In subsequent interviews she told me she was frightened, but felt she had to answer truthfully because she was in a state of *sin* ('holiness'). Indeed, she wrote to relatives in Australia to see if she should speak with me again, and they replied that she should. And, she did.
14. Somsack Pongkhao, 'Fa Ngum not a revival of monarchy', *Vientiane Times*, 14–16 January 2003.
15. For a book-length discussion of this process of 're-traditionalisation' see Evans (1998b).
16. These are usually women, or grandchildren, because the surviving older men who were part of the 'old regime' feel that it is still too dangerous for them to return.
17. This described briefly in Kremmer (1997: 58–60).
18. Thanya, at the age of 17, had fled to Thailand in August 1981 with his brother Soulivong, and then onto France. Thanya then went to Australia. Soulivong is still in exile and is considered to be the 'Crown Prince'. Thanya, whose role overseas was never as political as his brother's, came back to Laos in 2001. Part of his motivation to return appears to have been his filial responsibilities to his mother.
19. Ordinary Lao will joke that people who have only *dam maak houng* ('close to the palace') may pretend to be royalty or have royal connections. *Dam maak houng* is a common Lao dish sold at roadside stalls, made up of shredded green papaya, fiery chillies and a pungent fish paste, *paa daek*, and denotes a lowly and common occupation. This jesting in itself is indicative of the collapse of a central arbiter of who is or is not royal. In a related vein, children brought up on communist propaganda about the 'feudal' past are surprised to encounter now impoverished aristocrats. They have coined a savage appellation for them, *Tiao khi tuk*, 'royal beggars'.
20. Information coming out of Laos in the early years after the revolution was confusing and often misleading. For example, in January 1981 five refugees from Laos in Thailand claimed to have been present some five months earlier at the cremation of the former King, along with Prince Souvanna Phouma and his brother, President (Prince) Souphanouvong. However, refugee claims, such as this one, were often considered unreliable. As for the LPDR, its spokesman said: 'King Savang Vatthana of Laos is in seminar in Viengsay [Huaphan] Province. He is strong at work. He is well now. He is not dead.' *Bangkok Post*, 9/1/1981. As we have seen, the King was already dead, which the regime would have known well.
21. The Hmong, organized in patrilineal clans, are ancestor worshippers.
22. Royal funerals, where the corpse is kept for many months and is an object of prayers, have disappeared from Laos entirely. The 'Red' Prince Souphanouvong, the remaining public figure of royal ancestry in the new regime, was accorded the same rites as other party leaders on his death in 1995. Individuals of royal ancestry follow the same rites as ordinary Lao these days.

References

Evans, Grant. 1991. 'Reform or Revolution in Heaven? Funerals among Upland Tai', *Australian Journal of Anthropology* (formerly *Mankind*), April 1991: 81–97.

———. 1998a. 'Political Cults in Southeast Asia and East Asia', in L. Summers and Ing Britt-Trankell (eds), *Culture and Politics in Asian Societies*. Uppsala Sweden: Uppsala Studies in Cultural Anthropology.

———. 1998b. *The Politics of Ritual and Remembrance: Laos Since 1975*. Chiang Mai: Silkworm Books/Honolulu: Hawaii University Press.

———. 2002a. 'Immobile Memories: Statues in Thailand and Laos', in Shigeharu Tanabe and Charles F. Keyes (eds), *Cultural Crisis and Social Memory: Politics of the Past in Thailand*. London: Routledge/Curzon.

———. 2002b. *A Short History of Laos: The Land In Between*. Sydney: Allen and Unwin/Chiang Mai: Silkworm Books.

Keyes, Charles F. 1983. 'Merit-transference in the Kammic Theory of Popular Theravada Buddhism', in Charles F. Keyes and E. Valentine Daniel (eds), *Karma: An Anthropological Inquiry*. Berkeley: University of California Press.

———. 1987. 'From Death to Birth: Ritual Process and Buddhist Meanings in Northern Thailand', *Folk* 29: 181–206.

Kremmer, Christopher. 1997. *Stalking the Elephant Kings*. Chiang Mai: Silkworm Books.

———. 2003. *The Bamboo Palace*. Pymble, NSW, Australia, Flamingo (HarperCollins).

Wales, Quaritch. 1931. *Siamese State Ceremonies: Their History and Function*. London: Curzon.

Chapter 8

Centres and Margins: The Organisation of Extravagance as Self-government in China*

Stephan Feuchtwang

Like all people, Chinese are centric. The very name for China in Chinese is, as we have been endlessly informed, the Central kingdom (Zhongguo). As a civilisation, it is the Central florescence of culture (Zhonghua). It is famous for having had – for longer than two millennia – in aspiration and more often than not in fact, a single political centre that was also conceived to be the cosmological centre. This is not simply an imagined centre, it is also the capital of a fiscal administration and of a system of ritual, jural and educational authority.

Anthropologists rarely if ever gain access to political centres, not anyway to those as large in scale and extent of dominion as China's centre. Nearly all fieldwork has to deal with relative centricity, which is also relative marginality, carrying with it such connotations as heterodoxy.[1] Most of the people in our field sites know themselves to be relatively central or relatively marginal – usually in relation to more than one conception of a centre. Yet they also conceive themselves to be centres. I shall, for instance, be concerned with how people in such a place make it into a centre, both politically and cosmologically. In China such places are where, according to a cliché of the Chinese empire, the heavens are high and the emperor is far away.

In dealing with this centrality and marginality, we face questions of perspective and of scale. By rituals, particularly those derived from the Daoist ritual of offering and cosmic adjustment (*jiao*), a bounded territory becomes the centre of the universe through the bodily transport of the master officiating at its centre, a merging of microcosm with macrocosm (Schipper 1982: 125–26, 134–35). I shall argue that a similar process occurs in the extravagant festivities outside and around the ritual centre. For the ritual occasion, a place whose inhabitants in another perspective know themselves to be remote from the centre becomes a centre on the same cosmological scale as the empire.

Rural Civil Society and Democracy?

Territorial festivals, variously called temple assemblies (*miaohui*), tours of the boundaries (*xunjing*), or receiving incense (*yingxiang*), are times for a general celebration that has some of the qualities of late medieval European pageants – carnival, charivari or revel. Chinese territorial festivals do not feature a central ritual of reversal such as in sixteenth-century France, where for a carnival a king (equivalent to the English lord of misrule) was 'elected' by bidding for the privilege with donations to the local saint (Le Roy Ladurie 1980: 303). But, like late medieval European plebeian pageants, Chinese territorial festivals are occasions for theatre, for procession, for mixing of genders and ages and for extravagant noise and excitement (*renao*), which have always been denounced as heterodox and wasteful. Medieval European pageants included young men in confraternities who mimicked and shamed transgressors of local custom and also organised local defence (Davis 1971, cited in Bristol 1985: 43). Territorial festivals in China do not centre on shaming and sexual mockery. They stress protective display and the use of demonic power to cleanse the area of malign forces. But like European pageants they give prominence to bands of youth, which in everyday life act as village militia, crop-watchers, fire-watchers and defenders. And they go further than European pageants in self-organisation. Instead of the guilds, churches and other associations of rule and patronage that organised the Europeans' pageants, Chinese territorial festivals have their own organisation and leadership.[2] In principle it is open to anyone who has proved by their good fortune, devotion to the public good and capability to have what might, if it did not have such Christian connotations, be called divine grace or charisma. Equally remarkable is the fact that Chinese territorial festivals have been maintained in Taiwan and revived in very many parts of mainland China. I will return to that important political fact. But first I want to introduce a further element.

Divine Selection

I ask you to consider divination as a mechanism for a collective choice of leaders that provides the outcome with authority. I will introduce such a mechanism as I observed it most closely in Shiding, a small town in northern Taiwan. It is also practiced in Meifa, a village in the mainland county of Anxi, opposite Taiwan in southern Fujian.[3] The mechanism is a ritual selection of leaders by a play of chance that endows the leader with charisma. Weber had good reasons to call 'charisma' the conferring of dictatorship upon a leader by recognition, that is, by 'the grace of those who follow him' (Weber 1947: 386). Charisma is too often authoritarian and sectarian. But this example shows that this is not always true. I observed it at a time when a republican state formation had been in existence for several decades. But I want to describe the practice first in isolation, without consideration of political regime.

It is a system of suffrage by the (nearly always male) heads of established households in a territorially defined and ritually sanctioned association.[4] Each festival of such an association defines what Taiwanese anthropologist Lin Meirong and others have called a 'ritual sphere' (Lin 1986). A festival procession defines its own ritual sphere.[5] It is an urban neighbourhood or a rural territory in which there is peer pressure of neighbours to participate, covering a great range of interpretations and commitments to the festival and the divine protector that it celebrates. Its ritual focus is an incense burner, and the master of the incense burner changes every year, selected by means of divination at the festival of the previous year. In the most thorough cases, divination is first used to select the head household (*toujia*) of each neighbourhood or sub-section and then to select the master and vice-master of the incense burner from them. In the poorest associations, the master is chosen in this way from a list of all the established households. 'Established' means all households that have opened a domestic altar. The residents without established domestic altars will be guests at the feasts of the established. The list is a census of all established households, each named by its head. Against it is the number of the head's sons, because one of the duties of the master of the incense burner is to collect tithes from each household at a standard rate per male member. Recently in Shiding, the small town in Taiwan where I first observed this practice, women have been included.

The mechanism of divination is throwing the two halves of a split bamboo root, with one side rounded, the other flat. The blocks are thrown to the ground after being shown respectfully in front of incense burning to an image of the deity. If one rests flat side up and the other rounded side up, a positive answer is signified and recorded. This procedure is repeated for each household listed in the section, barring last year's section head household. The name against which the longest sequence of positives has been marked is the section's head household. Then the same is done to choose the next master and vice-master of the incense burner from the section heads. Every household on the list has, therefore, an equal chance of being selected by divine suffrage.

Other principles of organisation may modify this basic principle of equality before an authorising god. For instance, where the expenses of being selected are great, poorer households are excluded. The wealthier donate their resources and name in a display of wealth for the public good. But this is an acknowledged variation of the principle of divine suffrage being open to all.

Besides census and choice by a random process of divination, another principle of participation is rotation. When the association is made of a number of hamlets or neighbourhoods it is usual to rotate among them the responsibility of selecting the head for the festival uniting them all. Rotation is a system of holding shares of responsibility. Similar share-holding rotas are organised after there has been a family division, for taking responsibility for the care of surviving parents (Hsieh 1985). Share-holding rotas are also used in mutual savings associations and in larger commercial associations. This involves a contractual agreement, often but not always written. Here the long history of non-governmental literacy is important to note. Such contracts did not depend on prior recognition by the magistrates of imperial rule (Cohen 2002).

Along the same lines, it should also be noted that many territorial liturgical associations were also responsible for the rotation of responsibility for the upkeep of paths and bridges, as well as for the upkeep of incense, candles and minor offerings for their deities throughout the year. That this fact is strongly associated with territorially based universality surely gives it a claim to something like a tradition of self-government, if not of democracy.

The festival that marks out a territorial association sets the boundaries of local loyalty and its contiguity with similar associations of local sovereignty with whom there is a rivalry of hospitality and display. Festivals to the same god in other places in the region, or to other gods as territorial guardians in neighbouring territories, are times when the performers of this place are invited to join in the displays of neighbouring places. In other words, festivals set each place as a territorial community in relation to other, close and similar places. Rivalry and hospitality can turn from generosity into flares of violent conflict between competing bands displaying their martial and musical arts. They can either be mediated quickly or escalate like a feud as they did in both Fujian and Taiwan, along lines of dialect-group affiliation, which are also affiliations to the gods favoured by the group. They may verge on communalism but they are not informed by any difference of doctrinal truth or ethnicity. Such explosions involved imperial troops in their suppression, who took one side to suppress the other and thus restore peace. Since the establishing of strong states in Taiwan and the mainland in the late nineteenth and early twentieth centuries, such conflicts have ceased to escalate. But festivals remain acts of territorial solidarity and rival generosity.

The popular religious culture of southern Fujian may be exceptional for territorial universality of divine suffrage and for funding by tithes. An example from northern China brings out a comparative lack of democracy, but not lack of self-government. The great annual assembly of the Dragon in Fanzhuang in the province of Hebei is organised, not by the politically authorised leadership, but by nineteen heads of the assembly who elect a leader from their number. The nineteen represent the Dragon to the villagers, not the other way around. They do not represent sections of the village. The privilege and responsibility for organising the festival is inherited. The nineteen are families who in the past showed their devotion to the Dragon and to the village public. They are helped by *retired* officials who had in office won a good reputation among the villagers (Liu 2000: 281–83). The festival fund comes from donations and voluntary payments by worshippers, not from tithes.

In Hebei, as in Fujian, public good is manifest in extravagant festivity, the word for which is *renao*. *Renao* translates literally as heat and noise, exemplified by explosions of firecrackers. But it implies a great deal more: liveliness, social excitement, the care of display on offering tables, the colourful inventiveness of decorations and festival procession contingents, including those of the musical and martial arts bands. The quality of *renao* on one hand and the solemnity of the ritual of cosmic adjustment in the temple on the other make up the respect in which the god is held and the blessings he or she is presumed to have bestowed. But of course it is a performance of the villagers. They perform the nearest approximation to a time of plenty (a vision of abundance). They put on the munificence of the response of the gods of the festival to wishes for peace and prosperity. What they observe in their own performance is a proof or failure of charisma, making a judgement that reflects on themselves, their leader and on the god that chose him. Their leader and they have succeeded (or failed) in acquiring blessing. The god has (or has not) protected them against misfortune because they have not (or they have) given her or him offence, or because she or he is no longer efficacious. The fact that a deity represents the territorial community it has chosen for efficacious protection does not detract from its members observing and judging the conduct of its selected leader and god. If over a period of many years the god is no longer considered to be efficaciously responsive (*xing, ling* or *ganying*), it will be abandoned or augmented by another god that has been proved over a number of years and gained a local following. Nor does divinity detract from financial accountability to members of the territorial association. Accounts of the donations and how they were spent are posted in public, both in Fanzhuang and in Meifa and Shiding.

In sum, within the confines of presenting the territorial association as 'blessed', leadership capacities of both god and charismatic leader are tested and proved by members' observations and by the judgements of all members eligible for divine selection. Among the criteria of judgement are benevolent responsiveness and meritorious virtue (*gongde*). They are at the same time criteria by which local leaders who have been selected by other principles, such as central state appointment, can be and are judged.

A territorial liturgical association is a kind of sovereignty that is neither the delegated sovereignty of the local government of an imperial state nor the sovereignty of a local electorate. The deity and the rites of a festival describe and centre an area. Its protector is a chosen deity, whose festivals are a tradition that has been inaugurated and modified in the history of that named place (Feuchtwang and Wang 2001: Chap. 2 and 5). The festivals and the temple that houses its local deities, with the records of its periodic refurbishment, together constitute that place as a history of fortune made and sustained by its households. It includes the addition and substitution of more effective and appropriate deities for those that were chosen earlier. In short, a festival describes and narrates a territorial sovereignty which refers to a universe that includes it but that is not the same as the political state. It is therefore a qualified alternative to the political state and a base from which to criticise it, implicitly or explicitly, as we shall see.

Between State and Territorial Association: The Local Temple

The temple built to house one or more deities of local liturgical associations is a public good whose funding comes mainly from large donations. They are commemorated in permanent inscriptions, not just in accounts written on paper and posted on walls. One among the main donors is likely to be the manager who raises the funds and oversees its building or rebuilding and refurbishment. What is more, the management of the temple building is also likely to lead to management of the temple's financial assets, its land and any other property. All this, including the donated funds and furnishings, is corporate, belonging to the overarching liturgical association. Even so, temple leadership is not chosen by divine selection but by willingness to contribute to the public good and by an already achieved reputation for being a capable manager. The temple's manager may seek confirmation from the main god by some form of divination, but he is a member of the local elite, however that is constituted in the historical circumstances of access to official status, to a ruling class, and to the means for acquiring wealth. The local temple is therefore an institution that mediates local liturgical associations and government. Its manager turns to both kinds of authority, that of established status and rule and that of the local divinity and its festival association.[6] The same can be said of a festival like the Dragon assembly in Fanzhuang. Its manager and reviver in the 1980s was not one of the nineteen assembly heads, but a much respected old villager who was an army veteran. He has been followed by others who combine respect in both directions, from local government officials and from the local population (Liu 2000: 281–82).

The Local Temple under a Republican State

It is now time to insert this institution of collective self-governance and its liturgical associations into the particular historical circumstances of the People's Republic of China (I shall only be able to allude to the different political context of republican Taiwan). The restoration of local temples and festivals, leaving some previous gods and adding some new ones such as Mao Zedong, has occurred in every province of China, in cities as well as small towns and villages, although certainly not in all. There is much more to be said about this restoration, suggesting why it has occurred here but not there, and how much is restoration, how much is new. Here I want to concentrate only on the way that political context has changed the significance of the restoration from the way in which festivals and temples functioned under the dynastic, imperial state.

Under the imperial state, local temples were one of a number of institutions of self-government (including lineages, trade associations and merchant guilds), with nothing of centralised state administration at that local level. Where once local elites mediated imperial rule at several levels from county to village and organised their own militia and schools, now representative assemblies, government administration, Party branches, schools and police stations reach down to villages. The Chinese states on either side of the Taiwan straits are secular states, rejecting the cosmology and deities of the imperial state as well as their variants among common people. Mao Zedong did recognise a form of peasant self-government in community temple associations (*shetanhui*) in the area of Xunwu, on the border between Fujian and Jiangxi provinces (Thompson 1990: 127). But he used such institutions as models for peasant associations that were locations of mass participation in Party-led campaigns, not forms of self-government. The communes and brigades that were, under Mao, the forms of local government have been succeeded by townships and administrative villages, their assemblies, heads, and Party Secretaries, all introduced from above. So local temples, their festivals and their residents' eligibility for ritual leadership are now a parallel institution to the institutions of state, including elected assemblies and leaders. Elections to village and township assemblies on the mainland are closely supervised by the only Party of government and are administered by the Ministry of Civil Affairs. But, as a result of political reforms in the 1990s, non-Party candidates can and do get elected.

Consequently, where festivals have been restored, the same population that has been turned by a republican state into citizens who take part in elections of representatives in local assemblies also belongs to an alternative ritual constituency of divine selection. This fact turns the alternative, divine constituency into a counterpoint citizenship. The judgement of proof of good leadership for its collective blessing is available as an independent base for judging leadership in the local political state.

To see how this works, I turn to a veteran leader who switched from political to ritual leadership.[7]

Meifa

Each year the festival of the main local deity of Meifa village confirms a territorial association in which the head of the incense burner is chosen from one of the sections of the village. The sections share responsibility in an annual rotation of four years. Once selected, the head of the incense burner association is responsible for organising next year's festival. It was remarkable how the task transformed the person from a rather retiring demeanour to a much more confidant one in the year that my friend and colleague Wang Mingming and I observed him.[8] But he also had at his disposal the manager of the temple. That manager, whose name was Chen Wansheng, had a history of negotiating the tensions between local loyalty and loyalty to the central political authority in ways that gained him the trust and respect of villagers.

Chen Wansheng was respected for having been a bold and forceful cadre.[9] The Party Secretary, Chen Decai, in office during our research, admitted this but then discounted it. 'Many villagers listen to him and not to us cadres. His disguise deceives them. By nature, Wansheng is a feudal sectarianist (*fengjian zongpai*)'. Decai used this item of Maoist denunciation in 1995, nearly twenty years after Mao's death and fifteen years after the Party's repudiation of Maoist mass mobilisation politics. Both he and Wansheng had become cadres in the Maoist era, and both of them still supported the Maoist ideal of advancing the collective good, even as each of them also advanced his own career in commercial enterprise. But to Decai the collective good is identified with the state: 'In the past sectarianism was criticised by Mao Zedong who saw it as a danger to society. I still believe sectarianism is a form of opposition to the state's basic power. Now, the government tends to be less strict about it. But it still is a danger.' His accusation of sectarianism came because Wansheng as a cadre had supported the collective welfare of the people of the village in a 'feudal', that is to say, ritual mode that 'disguised' him as a popular hero. In doing so he had sacrificed his Party career, and this was precisely what villagers respected.

As one of Wansheng's neighbours explained to Wang Mingming, in each neighbourhood (*kakle* in Southern Fujianese) there is someone who in a conflict is known by both sides and whose words they could respect. For Meifa it was Wansheng. 'He is upright and concerned for the public good (*kongka* – literally "the public family") and not just for his private self (*sulan*)'. It is to Wansheng that people turned when they had grievances against the county and township officials in charge of road building and the poor compensation they received for the destruction of their houses. In turn, he had used his connections and his local support to insist that a new enterprise located on land appropriated by the county from the village should, if the owner wanted to avoid trouble, employ him as its site manager and at least 100 fellow villagers as workers.

Whether for his own glory or not, Wansheng had shown himself to be responsive in the same mode in which the local god is thought to be responsive and efficacious. He combined willingness to listen and capacity to act forcefully. He was in possession of the blessing of relative wealth, showing his innate capacity, resilience and resourcefulness. In putting himself out, in spending so much of his time in the management of the public affairs of the ancestral hall and the temple, Wansheng was making an offering to the village and he thought of it as self-sacrifice. From the villagers' point of view his self-sacrifice described his responsiveness to calls upon his loyalty to the locality, whose identity and history are celebrated by the festival of its local deity.

Village elections in Meifa have made almost no difference to this state of affairs. The man elected head of the village for the third time in 2001 was a close associate of Wansheng. In other villages, elections have been a means of getting rid of unpopular cadres, but in Meifa Wansheng was simply there as an alternative authority.[10] The mechanism of divine selection has not been used to appoint Wansheng to his position of authority. But the voice authorised by divine selection is the voice of the respect in which he was held as local temple manager and by which he judged himself. It is the same voice that judges a deity and a master of the incense burner for their performance of collective blessings. It does not have a party. Nevertheless, it functions caustically and protectively, as a resort of moral judgement, in relation to the local politics of central state and party authority.

Fanzhuang – An Instructive Contrast[11]

Responsibility for housing the tablet, which is the spiritual seat of the Dragon, and for being host to the annual assembly in Fanzhuang rotated, as I have pointed out, around nineteen assembly heads (*huitou*) that are hereditary households.[12] But the contrast with Meifa is instructive because despite the differences we can still find some elements in common with the far greater democracy of the selection of masters of the incense burner in Fujian and Taiwan. In Fanzhuang, as in Meifa, there is an ethic of equality and of acting for the public good among the nineteen representatives. They elect one of their number to be the manager of the festival each year, and if he is domineering and partisan, they depose him and elect another. Households of Fanzhuang which have shown over years their devotion to the imperial Dragon that is the local deity can be accepted by the current assembly heads to join them. Their number is not fixed. Devotion to the Dragon is indirectly, through the Dragon, a devotion to the general good of the village.

The north-eastern Chinese regions are much affected by syncretic traditions, labelled White Lotus by ruling regimes (ter Haar 1992). They have a strong Buddhist element, and convey a more pious festival mode than those in the south. The Dragon festival is much less carnal than territorial festivals in Fujian and Taiwan. There is no feasting on meat for the households of Fanzhuang, as there is in Meifa. On the contrary, abstinence from meat marks the sanctity of the occasion, although visiting bands are fed generously with meat. Whereas in Meifa, plays performed on an open-air stage gather great crowds in front of the temple, in Fanzhuang there is no theatre. But there are other costs and an account of income and expenditure is displayed and burned in offering to the Dragon. The income is not from a tithe but from a variety of other sources. They include gifts from villages linked to this festival, in a network of temples, visiting Fanzhuang with their bands. They also include peace and security incense (*pingan xiang*) and oil money put into the large box in front of the Dragon tablet, the main site of pious obeisance. In addition, there are pledge offerings for response to a prayer to the Dragon, and special donations of money or services, such as truck transport for the supplies to the restaurants that host the visitors.

Despite these pieties, the occasion remains an extravaganza. The assembly is a great display of music, theatrical tableaux, drum bands and martial artists from Fanzhuang and the network of villages to whose own festivals it is linked. And the displays of the bands are as spectacular and noisy with exploding firecrackers, drums and cymbals as any in Fujian. They are similarly described as *renao*. The annual temple assembly is a very special occasion, in which the representation of the imperial Dragon, a large and ornamented tablet carried in procession to the marquee, becomes a centre as great as that of the state. Inscribed on the tablet are the words: 'Seat of the spirit of the Dragon, true commander of the ten sections and the three regions of the universe'. Across the front of the temple a great red banner proclaims the 'Great assembly of the Dragon tablet transmitted down the ages whose awesome fame shakes the four quarters'. A stone inscription tracing the Dragon to the origins of the Chinese people has recently augmented this extravagant description of local sovereignty, as the centre of the Chinese universe. The power of this pomp is demonstrated in the many performances of martial art. They are not removed to a stage but make their places within the crowds of onlookers. As they reach the huge expanse, normally a market, now thronged with onlookers, they use their arms to clear a space. I remember being thrust back by young men wielding metal tipped lances. They were members of a troupe bearing the motto of the loyal bandits of the marshes, the subject of an episodic novel (*Shuihu Zhuan*), and many plays. Their performance was a ritual display of imperial might that is also a fairly chaotic display of local strength and pride.

Other displays had the potential for mockery of the current political order, just as in European revels.[13] In one a woman was in the position of an ox pulling a roller. She wore headgear with long paper ears. Behind the roller walked a man dressed in slick city wear and dark glasses. He had a whip that he snapped so close to her head that it tweaked her paper ears, obviously a display of skill. I asked an onlooker what he was enacting, and was told with a smile: oh, he's a cadre. The symbolism is indirect, shielded by the grotesque mix of the contemporary and the archaic, and by the general context of an imperial mythology.

Territorial Liturgical Association in the Current Situation

The festival is a public sphere. For the moment of its occasion it is juxtaposed with secular, electoral citizenship. Its invocation of totality is not the same as a state's territorial sovereignty. It is that of a local sovereignty as great or greater than that of the central state, but only cosmologically, not in the geography of its organisation. That is its political weakness in the sense of its having a potential for social transformation.

But there is good reason to see the celebration of local sovereignty as strength, and that is by contrast with the populism of mass movements. I have already made the point that even in southern Fujian the institution of festival leadership is that of finding charisma by divination. In the Hebei example, you could say that it has already been found and is transmitted by patrilineal descent. In both, however, the ethic of local loyalty is paramount. In Chinese and European peasant rebellions and other mass movements, the leader was also charismatic – the preacher-prophets that Weber mentioned. Such examples raise what I think is a central political question in and for Weber: how to distinguish good from bad charisma. Weber describes charisma as the election of a dictator, in which the gift of grace is given and found in a leader. Its recognition can be withdrawn by a devoted following. In a modern state, the most common example of this is the party leader, which Weber (1947: 388) describes as 'a type of charismatic authority in which the authoritarian element is concealed'. Weber was referring to radical party leaders who emerge in times of crisis, leaders of followers in a movement that creates or responds to an explosive situation. They are like prophets, proving to have the desired attributes of certainty in making choices between incompatible ends and bearing, or claiming to introduce, a normative order.

Schnepel (1987) ingeniously argues an elective affinity between charismatic authority and democracy from Weber's writing on charismatic kingship and his opinion of the political incompetence of Kaiser Wilhelm II, who asserted his divine right even as his blunders led towards the war that would engulf Europe. What was needed was a politically competent statesman and innovative politician who emerges 'by virtue of personal trust in him expressed by his followers in elections', but 'once the political leader has been recognised ... he may treat this freely given trust in him as a duty on behalf of the ruled to follow him' (Schnepel 1987: 44–45). I want to treat such a vocational politician as an ideal of what I think Weber would agree is good charisma. Applying the same discrimination to followership, good charisma retains accountability, in testing and demanding proof of leadership qualities. Bad charisma is the *Führerprincip* of hypnotised or terrorised dependence on the leader.

Here it seems to me that celebrations of local sovereignty win over the populism of radical movements because what they celebrate in their god and her or his representatives, whether inherited or divined, is responsiveness to the local population in a territorially defined place. Local loyalty can be tested and found wanting just because it is local. The charisma of more distant leaders is less accountable.

Festivals also help to form and transmit criteria for making political and moral judgements. They sustain a collective voice outside a central authority that wields power. Of course they have not been acknowledged as a model on which to build civil society and the mechanisms of democratic representation. But in China, as in parts of Europe such as Andalusia (Gilmore 1998), they live on as an element of civil society despite urbanised intellectuals and the snobbery of theories of modernisation.[14] Their pomp, vulgarity and extravagance preserve their autonomy. And here I reach three anthropological conclusions.

Pomp, Vulgarity and Extravagance

On pomp I am borrowing Clifford Geertz's notion of a theatre state: 'mass ritual was not a device [in Negara, Bali] to shore up the state, but rather the state, even in its final gasp, was a device for the enactment of mass ritual. Power served pomp, not pomp power' (1980: 18–19). But festival ritual does not create the power of the central state. It creates an alternative centre of an imaginary and cosmological state. And it authorises not a steep and multilayered but a shallow hierarchy of accountable leadership.

On vulgarity, I am comparing and contrasting the grotesquerie of demon-quellers, portrayed as the most vivid pictures, statues, dancers and puppets in a territorial festival, which protects by exorcistic dances and displays. I am also thinking of the mockery of the present from the mixed costumes of the archaic and the modern, both in China and in European carnival ambivalence. Festive vulgarity can, of course, be hijacked politically. It is not a guarantee of autonomy.[15] It is particularly vulnerable in a political culture of rival mass followings, or populism, rather than as in the People's Republic of China (PRC) a single party that still professes to have a mission even if it is no longer mobilising for revolution. In Taiwan, which has the same festival culture but which since 1987 has had a political culture of rival parties seeking a mass base, there has been political cultivation of local festivals. Rival parties do organise local festivities but they are rather tame affairs of staged entertainment and they are not held at the time of the local carnivals. Politicians like to be photographed in well-known temples. There is also a tradition of local hoodlums laundering their wealth in donations and in participation in the local carnival-festivals. Men who represent a party in local elections sometimes lead such hoodlums. But they do not try to organise or even appropriate gods' festivals for a party as do communalist parties in India.[16] They just use them to appear as prominent and powerful individuals.

In China, as everywhere, the more populist, or should I say powerfully appealing, forceful if not bullying politicians, have a facility to be vulgar. And in that sense vulgarity is a political resource by which authority can be gained. But its very ambivalence encourages many potentially diverse choices of lead to be followed and many recombinations to be possible at a local level of vulgarity. They cannot easily by mastered by a central command except by terror. It is more usual, I think, for central and more peaceful authorities of education and of the industries of culture to extract, abstract, refine and keep a distance from the vulgar. It is more likely that governments and their parties in Taiwan and the mainland will take steps, as they have in the past, to reduce and improve local festivals. But I doubt whether in Taiwan – or in a future PRC of more open political rivalry – there will be any attempt to take over the vulgarity of the festival. This is because politics is not ethnic-religious in either Taiwan or the PRC. In the meantime, vulgarity is still a distancing fact from higher levels of political authority.

On extravagance, as distinct from both gift and sacrifice, a Chinese festival is a public performance of bounteousness. It is a performance of public good fortune. More than in other acts of generosity, the emphasis is on collective sharing.

Chinese territorial festivity, like carnival, enacts what Gilmore (1998: 209) nicely calls 'a timeless parochialism of place' that at the same time appropriates to itself themes and objects of what is right and true from a Great Tradition, including, in rural Andalusia, Christian charity and compassionate judgement. Chinese territorial festivity is less about sex and gender, more about protection of fortune, military and musical prowess, colourful and noisy display and eating well. But like the Chinese festival, the Andalusian carnival also performs what I would call a political cosmology. By tableaux of grotesques beside solemn invocations of a deity and his or her armed guards, both kinds of territorial festivity negate the present in favour of ideals set in archaic time. What is perhaps peculiar to (or perhaps it is just that I am stressing this characteristic of) the Chinese festival is that it replaces current institutions of maintaining order administered from a remote centre with a present organisation of force and a display of effective divine protection.

There is asymmetry between the receivers and the givers of bounty, who are the gods on the other side of the boundary of mortality, represented by donors. But festivity also emphasises two other things: one is rivalry of display and of hospitality to outsiders, a rivalry between potentially hostile but generous equals; the other is sharing among receivers who as enjoyers of bounty are placed on an equal footing. 'We are all equal around a feast table,' as I was told. Revellers are aware that wealthy donors sponsor the festival but also that they are donations to the public good in which donors and recipients share in common gratitude. Their donation converts gains made in short-term cycles of exchange into the long-term cycle of feeding the community (Parry and Bloch 1989). But it is more than that. Gratitude is turned into celebratory enjoyment to the point of challenging the very authority that permits and grants the revelry: a god, ancestors, a local leader and hero, or the state and its leaders. Since the object of authority, capable of judgement, is also by definition in a hierarchical relation to the subject of judgement, a subject's desire to be unified with authority or to claim identity with it is judged negatively. But moments of exuberant license are releases from that negation.[17]

Desire to be in the place of authority can be displaced onto the reconstruction of a lost authority (a god, the collectivity of ancestors) as a way of admitting it is lost but also as an act defiant of current authority (the state). It can also be enjoyment of the bounty of God, a saint, an ancestor or a deity by almost ignoring its existence (but not quite – something we could call positive negation) realising that it is 'our' not 'its' bounty we enjoy. We then enter a new kind of negation, exuberant near-destruction of desired authority. This sentiment is startlingly expressed by a Sardinian proverb 'Even God is frightened by the enriched poor'.[18] It is true that this can become violent, mob conservatism – as it often was in Medieval Europe – or as in nineteenth-century and earlier Fujian and Taiwan it can escalate into feud. But where accountability and organisation are more independent of state and religious orthodoxy, as in Chinese festivals, the charisma of exuberance is better, more independent if also conservative in appearance and motivation. It is, of course, politically silent or hidden, kept within a local religious or cosmological or traditional and customary casing, in comparison with extensive pilgrimages and Maoist mass mobilisation. But this simply raises the interesting question of when and how the low and the local explodes from its containers and becomes articulated as a more general aspiration to abundance and joy.

Notes

* Many thanks to the participants in the conference on Margins of Religion in Halle, Germany, May 2003 for their comments and suggestions – particularly Cornelia Sorabji, Galia Valtchikova, Chris Hann, Galina Lindquist, Julia Eckert and Burkhart Schnepel. They caused me to rethink and rewrite various parts of this chapter.

1. I have deliberately formulated this situation so that it cannot be assimilated to relativism. Edwin Ardener (1989) offers a theoretical treatment of remoteness.
2. The leaders of festivals have different titles in different parts of China: incense leader (*xiangtou*), master of the incense burner (*luzhu*), assembly leader (*huitou*).
3. The only difference is that in Meifa the master Daoist arranges the divination (of eight head households and from them the master of the incense burner), whereas in Shiding it is the current master of the incense burner who oversees the divination.
4. They have been named liturgical associations by Schipper (1977). He includes two other kinds of liturgical association, those based on common interest and those based on common origin. His focus is on territorial liturgical associations in a city, mine on similar associations in small towns and villages.
5. A local temple may house the incense burners and images of deities for a number of such festivals. But they are usually congruent, so that it is possible to speak of the ritual sphere of a local temple and its festivals and thus to speak of the association of all its deities' liturgical associations. The attempt to use this for administrative control by the Japanese colonial regime made combinations of liturgical or festival associations attractive, and it was Japanese folklorists who coined the term 'ritual

sphere'. But they have no other basis of institution than the organisations of festivals themselves.
6. For an example of the tensions involved in this combination see Robert Weller (1987: 56–59).
7. A fuller account is given in Feuchtwang and Wang 2001.
8. The quotations that follow come from Wang Mingming's field notes and tapes.
9. Unfortunately he was killed in a road accident in 2003.
10. In fact, Decai retired after the end of our research, and was replaced by one of Wansheng's sons. The village head, elected for yet another time, continued to associate himself closely with Wansheng. So Wansheng's status as authoritative elder and manager of the village's temple and its festival associations was consolidated, and the village head acted in partnership with both him and his son.
11. Profound thanks to Zhao Xudong for sharing the following information, based on his fieldwork over a number of years between 1997 and 2002.
12. In 2004 a permanent temple had been built to house the Dragon tablet and the *huitou* lodged in the temple instead of lodging the Dragon tablet in his house for the year between festivals. Until then, the tablet was kept for the year in the house of the elected *huitou*.
13. Underdown (1985: 55) describes a pageant in Wells, Somerset (England) put on to raise money for a new bell for St Cuthbert's church in 1607. It included standard items such as Robin Hood, Noah's Ark, a Lord of the May, Morris dancers and giants. But it also included a very local figure. Revellers had constructed a spotted cow carried by a satyr. Everyone knew that it shamed the mistress of a Puritan constable of the city who had tried to prevent maypole festivities, denouncing them as a 'painted calf'.
14. The Andalusian carnival is not as deliberately a celebration of abundance as the Chinese territorial festival. It is more a time of license that has stressed sexual lewdness in its songs and acts. It is a time of extravagant ambivalence, combining misogyny and ribaldry about men hoodwinked and buggered by transsexuals, when all the women in the procession are anyway men dressed as women. Skits and rhymes combine the persecution of female deviance in the medieval European tradition with the upholding of chivalry and laments about the victimisation of women. The old anticlerical tradition continues. It is not now accompanied by fierce clerical condemnation. But Gilmore makes the valid point that interpretations of carnival as rituals of rebellion or as resistance were anyway reductive and inadequate. Carnival heightens the ambivalence of wishes and fears normally blunted and intermingled (1995: 207).
15. My thanks to Julia Eckert for making this point so emphatically in her study of the Shiv Sena hijacking of festivals in Mumbai/Bombay.
16. Ursula Rao's chapter in this book describes the strong but often over-ridden wishes of local temple builders to keep their festivals in Bhopal from being hijacked by higher communalist politics.
17. One way of approaching this extravagance is through Freud's notion of negation. For Freud, to negate is to admit under a destructive, negative judgement, something that is desired but repressed. This could be extended to the negative admission of something that is lost but still deeply desired and repressed. The object in which the capacity for negative judgement is placed can also be desired affirmatively. Negation occurs precisely when these feelings are most acutely contradictory. Applying this thought, we need to have in mind on a social scale what is the agency of repression. It would be the equivalent of a superego or that part of the ego that acts as consciousness and judgement: the authority of the ancestors and of the rules of

gift, as well as the authority of the state. In the case of a festival, negation of a desired authority is achieved by displacement onto a 'lost' or otherworldly authority. It includes a repression of identification with and assumption of that very authority

18. Many thanks to Cosimo Zene, SOAS, for showing me a chapter of his forthcoming book (*Gift and Community in Central Sardinia*), in which he cites this proverb.

References

Ardener, Edwin. 1989. '"Remote areas": Some Theoretical Considerations', in Malcolm Chapman (ed.), *Edwin Ardener: The Voice of Prophecy and Other Essays*. Oxford: Blackwell, pp. 211–23.

Bristol, Michael. 1985. *Carnival and Theater: Plebeian Culture and the Structure of Authority in Renaissance England*. New York: Methuen.

Cohen, Myron. 2002. 'Commodity Creation in Late Imperial China: Corporations, Shares, and Contracts in One Rural Community', in David Nugent (ed.), *Locating Capitalism in Time and Space: Global Restructurings, Polities, and Identity*. Stanford: Stanford University Press, pp. 80–112.

Davis, Natalie. 1971. 'The Reasons of Misrule: Youth Groups and Charivaris in Sixteenth Century France', *Past and Present* 50: 49–75.

Feuchtwang, Stephan and Wang Mingming. 2001. *Grassroots Charisma: Four Local Leaders in China*. London: Routledge.

Freud, Sigmund. 1961 [1925]. 'Negation', in *Standard Edition of the Complete Psychological Works of Sigmund Freud*. London: The Hogarth Press, pp. 235–39.

Geertz, Clifford. 1980. *Negara: The Theatre State in Nineteenth-century Bali*. Princeton: Princeton University Press.

Gilmore, David D. 1998. *Carnival and Culture: Sex, Symbol, and Status in Spain*. New Haven: Yale University Press.

Haar, Barend ter. 1992. *The White Lotus Teachings in Chinese Religious History*. Leiden: E.J. Brill.

Hann, Chris and Elizabeth Dunn (eds). 1996. *Civil Society: Challenging Western Models*. New York: Routledge.

Hsieh Jih-chang. 1985. 'Meal Rotation', in Hsieh Jih-chang and Chuang Ying-chang (eds), *The Chinese Family and its Ritual Behavior*. Taipei: Institute of Ethnology, Academia Sinica Monograph Series B, No. 15: 70–83.

Humphrey, Chris. 2001. *The Politics of Carnival: Festive Misrule in Medieval England*. Manchester: University of Manchester Press, pp. 9–22.

Le Roy Ladurie, Emmanuel. 1980. *Carnival: A People's Uprising at Romans 1579–1580*. London: Scolar Press.

Lin Meirong. 1986. 'Yu jisutuan lai kan caotunzhende difang zuzhi' ('From Ritual Sphere to Grassroots Local Organisation'), *Minzuxue Yanjiusuo Jikan (Journal of Ethnological Research, Academia Sinica, Taipei)* 62: 53–114.

Liu Tielang. 2000. 'Cunluo miaohuide chuantong ji diaozheng' ('Tradition and Transformation of a Village Festival'), in Guo Yuhua (ed.), *Yishi yu shehui bianqian (Ritual and Social Change)*. Beijing: Shehui kexue wenxian chubanshe, pp. 254–309.

Parry, Jonathan and Maurice Bloch. 1989. *Money and the Morality of Exchange*. Cambridge: Cambridge University Press.

Schipper, Kristofer. 1977. 'Neighbourhood Cult Associations in Traditional Taiwan', in G. William Skinner (ed.), *The City in Late Traditional China*. Stanford: Stanford University Press, pp. 651–76.

———. 1982. *Le Corps Taoiste*. Paris: Fayard.
Schnepel, Burkhart. 1987. 'Max Weber's Theory of Charisma and its Applicability to Anthropological Research', *JASO (Journal of the Anthropological Society of Oxford)* XVIII(1): 6–47.
Thompson, Roger R. (trans.). 1990. *Mao Zedong, Report from Xunwu*. Stanford, CA: Stanford University Press.
Underdown, David. 1985. *Revel, Riot and Rebellion: Popular Politics and Culture in England 1603–1660*. Oxford: Clarendon.
Weber, Max. 1947. *The Theory of Social and Economic Organisation*. New York: Free Press.
Weller, Robert. 1987. *Unities and Diversities in Chinese Religion*. London: Macmillan.

Part IV

Religious Options and Identitary Claims

Chapter 9

Allies and Subordinates: Religious Practice on the Margins between Buddhism and Shamanism in Southern Siberia

Galina Lindquist

'The power of religion consists in its special and surprising message and in the bias which that revelation gives to life. The vistas it opens and the mysteries it propounds are another world to live in; and another world to live in ... is what we mean by having a religion.' This quotation of Santayana, from 'Reason in Religion', is an epigraph to Clifford Geertz's essay 'Religion as a Cultural System'. This essay, although much criticised, made a great impact on the anthropology of religion. But, for all its valuable insights, Geertz's essay reiterates the reification of 'religion' as a coherent, closed system of meanings and cultural expressions, hedged off from the mundane world – 'another world to live in' – that has been prevalent in Western scholarship since Durkheim, echoed by the Durkheimian distinction between the sacred and the profane. This view of religion as a 'world in itself' is tenacious, even though it has been criticised by a number of scholars who have shown how misleading it is for the understanding of ideas and practices in non-Western contexts. It has been argued that this way of seeing religion as an abstracted and universalised subject of study parallels attempts to achieve coherence in doctrines and practices which have historically marked Western Christianity (Asad 2002 [1993]: 116). Such universalisation and abstraction, however, are characteristic of a particular form of religion (institutionalised clerical Christianity) rather than real life. Thus, Asad proposed that 'religion' should be seen rather as a concrete set of practical rules attached to specific processes of power and knowledge (ibid.: 122).

The present volume starts from the assumption that to understand practices that, for lack of a better term, we call 'religious', we are better advised to proceed not from the centre of a coherent, closed ideational system that is built on belief, commands obedience and creates an idiosyncratic world (as Geertz would have it). Instead, the suggestion that inspired this volume was that we look at the margins between 'religion' and mundane life: folk practices that draw loosely on dogma and canon, where religious systems overlap and blend, and where people pick and choose from the repository of symbols offered by established religions. On these margins, the practices are aimed less at 'worshipping the sacred' than at attaining more immediate human purposes. Their rationale has been aptly summarised as the creation of a pragmatic, makeshift order and the securing of life (Ruel 1997).

Buddhism and Shamanism in Post-Soviet Tuva

This chapter considers the case of Tuva, a small country in the southern Siberia. Tuva is an autonomous republic within the Russian Federation, bordering Mongolia in the northeast, and Altai and Khakassia, two other autonomous republics of the Russian Federation, in the north and west. After perestroika, Buddhism and shamanism in Tuva were given the status of 'traditional' religions. Although treated as two separate institutional and ideational domains by both scholars and politicians, Buddhism and shamanism are nonetheless inseparable in the everyday life of Tuvans. A large part of what, for the lack of a better word, could be called the 'religious' life of Tuvans, takes place 'on the margins' between Buddhism and shamanism. These margins, more precisely, are a shared space between Buddhism and shamanism, whose practitioners respect, tolerate and challenge each other, and whose practices parallel and complement each other, overlap and intermingle.

There are social actors on the Tuvan official arena who identify themselves with either Buddhism or shamanism, vehemently rejecting the other. Thus, the founding father of 'Tuvan shamanism' as a religio-political movement after perestroika, Mongush Barakhovich Kenin-Lopsan, repeatedly declared that Buddhism in Tuva was an import of foreign origin, alien to Tuvan 'tradition'. Likewise, I heard some of the newly-converted, devout Buddhists (as well as born-again Christians influenced by Western missionaries) say that shamanic practices come from the Devil. Such people make their moves on the political arena and/or construct their identities in the name of one of these 'religions', and the exclusion of the other is part of their strategies. This might create the impression that Buddhism and shamanism can be studied separately. In this chapter, I shall try to show that this way of viewing religious life in Tuva is misleading: the sphere of Buddhist and shamanic practices share semiotic codes, the logic of ritual design, problems to solve, and non-human beings who are involved in solving them. To characterise these 'margins' between Buddhism and shamanism in Tuva, I shall describe the practices in which both lamas and shamans are engaged, and discuss the similarities and differences between them. While the similarities are due to the fact that shamans and lamas inhabit the same social and natural universe of humans and spirits, the differences are based on the positioning of the practitioners with respect to both human institutions and non-human agents. The authority of lamas pivots on the centres of ideological and institutional power, while shamans act as individuals who are, in many respects, intrinsically marginal.

'State Religions': Recent History of Buddhism and Shamanism in Tuva

It is said that Buddhism reached the territory where Tuvans lived as cattle-breeding nomads in the late seventeenth century, long before the consolidation of the national state. As a state, Tuva was from the beginning squeezed between the Manchurian and the Russian empires, and early in the nineteenth century it opted for the latter orbit. With the growth of Russian influence, Tuvans were introduced to Russian Orthodoxy. Russian Orthodox Christianity, however, sat ill with Tuvan cultural styles and habits, which had evolved through contact with neighbouring Mongolia, Buryatiya and Kalmykia. When Tuva attempted to become independent, at the end of the eighteenth century, Buddhism became a 'state' religion. As one of the 'great', and, to a large extent, 'globalised' religions, Buddhism provided the state with an ideological basis for its centralising endeavours, conferring a distinct identity that defined Tuva as possessing a cultural affinity with its most significant neighbours. In the half-century to follow, Buddhism flourished in Tuva. Monasteries were established throughout the country, communities where monks lived, prayed, studied and performed their rituals in traditional yurts as well as in wooden structures of intricate architecture. These monastic establishments owned land and cattle, trained new lamas, developed art and scholarship, and provided the inhabitants of the surrounding areas with the requisite ritual services. In distant settlements and at herders' stations (*aal*), single lamas could be found, individuals who had received some training and could perform services for the local people for smaller fees. But, apart from these individuals, a significant part of the Tuvan Sangha of the time was institutionalised, concentrated in several well-known places, and easily identifiable. This made the Tuvan lamas an easy target when the Bolshevik anti-religious campaigns started in the early 1920s.

The Communist campaigns struck Tuva as fiercely as they did other states built on the same ideology. Commissars came to *khurees*, local monasteries, and burned them to the ground, executing lamas on the spot, or sending them to certain death in prison. A local story tells about the Bolshevik executioners who descended on the biggest Tuvan monastery, Chaadan *khuree*, and took all its lamas to be shot in the capital town of Kyzyl, some three hundred kilometers away. It was the middle of darkest winter, in the excruciating cold, and the ageing lamas were made to walk all the way through the mountains. At an *art*, a pass over a crest, the lamas refused to move any further, stopping to read sutras in order to meet their deaths in an enlightened state of mind. The commissars started to shoot, but the bullets bounced back on the perpetrators. The terrified executioners allowed the lamas to complete their reading; when they finished reading, they died all together, in quiet dignity.

This story, while acknowledging the spiritual power and moral superiority of the Buddhist lamas, bears witness to an historical fact, still painful for Tuvans: Buddhism in Tuva was completely eradicated, at least as a social institution. The *khurees*, the loci of the Buddhist tradition and the wellsprings of Buddhist knowledge, ceased to exist.

About sixty years later, after perestroika, Buddhism in Tuva started to revive. There are stories about wise lamas who lived as secular persons among their kin, clandestinely keeping Buddhist knowledge alive, but the chain of formal instruction had been effectively broken. This sense of Buddhist knowledge as a preserved but inaccessible treasure is reflected in the stories of wise lamas who hid their sutras and ritual paraphernalia in caves deep in the mountains of the Tuvan taiga. According to local lore, these treasures were protected by a magic that instantly killed any unauthorised person who ventured even to touch them. Usually these treasures are said to belong to a particular grand- or great-grandchild of the wise lama who hid the treasures, this person him- or herself a practising (or aspiring) lama or shaman. The heir dreams of undertaking an expedition, similar to that of the quest for the Holy Grail, to recover the treasures that will make her even more powerful in her calling or her special abilities, such as healing or seeing the unseen. Such abilities are considered to be the assets of the practising local shamans (and other practitioners who do not call themselves shamans). Some lamas are also known to possess these abilities, but, unlike shamans, they acknowledge them and make use of them only grudgingly – situationally and selectively – to offer help in urgent situations, not as the tools of personal power.

Practices that can be broadly labelled as 'shamanic', and practitioners of renowned power and spectacular performance, have been part of Tuvan life from times immemorial. Students of 'shamanism' are familiar with the classical Russian ethnography of Siberian shamanism, with its rich descriptions of ecstatic shamanic performances, with shamans wildly drumming and dancing, falling into trance, foaming at the mouth, their faces contorted. During my own fieldwork with shamans in Tuva I almost never witnessed anything of the kind.[1] No matter whether and in what way their consciousness is altered, the major part of the shamans' work in Tuva requires enormous concentration, very likely involving shifts in the modalities of awareness, possibly approaching slight trance (however it may be defined), of which they are always in control. Shamans in Tuva are certainly dependent on direct, experienced communication with the non-human inhabitants of their natural and social universe (and so they can, strictly speaking, be referred to as 'shamans'). Apart from these terminological queries, the Russian word that the Tuvan practitioners use for self-designation is 'shaman', and scholars generally agree that 'shamanism' originated in Siberia, and that it is in Siberia, if anywhere, that 'real' shamans are to be found.

Shamans in Siberia were persecuted from the Tsarist times: first, more mildly, by the Christian missionaries, and later, cruelly, by the Bolshevik regime. In Soviet times, shamans everywhere in Siberia were arrested and sent to prisons and labour camps, or ruthlessly killed on the spot. As a result, shamanism was eradicated in the majority of Siberian small nations. Tuva is an exception in this respect. Many shamans were indeed killed, but others, when threatened, took to their horses and moved to the taiga, to remote villages or to herders' stations belonging to their kinsmen, where they could survive and even teach their grandchildren some of their craft. This makes Tuva unique among the Siberian titular nations as a country where shamanism survived as a more or less unbroken tradition. When, after perestroika, religious freedom together with the ideological vacuum and the search for an authentic tradition of national identity-building opened the way for 'traditional religions' to enter the public arena, people emerged from the shadows, claiming to belong to 'the unbroken shamanic tradition'. As a promised land of the authentic shamanism, Tuva attracts Russian and foreign scholars, as well as tourists, journalists, film-makers and spiritual seekers in search of shamanic exotica. Among the local practitioners, there is a certain division of labour between those catering for foreigners and those who deal predominantly with local clients, although this is in no way a hard and fast distinction: the masters of shamanic performances, sought after by outsiders, also treat local people. By the same token, many of those who, by dint of their efficacy, are considered 'strong shamans' by the locals, would not mind working with foreigners since the pay is incomparable.

After perestroika, freedom of religion was proclaimed, and three religions were declared 'traditional' for Tuva. Russian Orthodoxy, which has been there since the times of Russian colonisation at the end of the nineteenth century, caters to the ethnic Russian population. In the years of post-perestroika devastation, industrial decline and anti-Russian ethnic riots of the early nineties, this group (about one-third of the population) has been culturally marginalised. Interest in the Church is rather weak, and so is the role of the Russian Orthodox Church in Tuva. Two other 'traditional religions', Buddhism and 'shamanism', vie for space on the local political arena, for representation at such public events as inter-religious congresses and cultural festivities (extremely popular in Tuva, complete with 'throat singing', national wrestling, horse racing, and costumed dancing), and for funds and private donations. Tuvan Sangha needs money to hold religious festivals, to support the lamas, to build new *khurees*, and to send young men to India, Mongolia and Buryatiya to study. Shamans need money to build 'centres', peculiar establishments combining the roles of a clinic, school and clearing house, where older, experienced shamans come from the villages to receive clients and earn money, while young aspiring shamans, local and foreign, come to study, clients come to receive services, and foreigners to witness performances. There are four such 'centres' in the capital city of Kyzyl, and to start and maintain such a centre, a considerable social influence and personal charisma are needed. There are many more shamans in Kyzyl, and in smaller towns and villages, who are not affiliated with any such centre, and they depend entirely on local clients for their subsistence.

Ritual Practices

Like many other peoples, Tuvans resort to the help of ritual specialists to mark important life occasions, and to control the uncertainties of existence. Both lamas and shamans are sought to prevent misfortune, and to avert or mitigate it when is has already occurred. People come to both lamas and shamans (and healers of other persuasions, such as those operating with Buddhist symbols as well as those who stay within the purview of Russian folk religiosity) when they are stricken by disease, unemployment, theft of cars or cattle, house burglary, rifts in the family and other misfortunes. They call for shamans and lamas to bless newly acquired property to protect it from damage, such as newly bought cars, apartments, offices in the town and yurts in the countryside. They seek ritual specialists to secure a project to be undertaken, such as a long journey, often when adolescent children go to study in other places. College education is highly valued and keenly sought after, promising a better life in the state sector, and people come to lamas and shamans to secure successful entrance exams for their children. They come to secure favourable outcomes in lawsuits, to consult on how to stop fights and achieve peace between spouses, to learn how to get or keep a job in the limited and crisis-ridden public sector, still the main source of employment for urbanised Tuvans. They also come to find out what is the most propitious time to undertake journeys, big purchases and weddings.

Much of this can be solved by consulting horoscopes, a craft in which both lamas and many shamans are extremely proficient. It would be fair to say that knowledge of the horoscope is the main prerequisite for being able to provide good services both as a lama and as a shaman. Most lamas I know master horoscopes to perfection, while I have met a couple of shamans who do not work with horoscopes and yet are very popular. Tuvans' lives are guided by a complex system of horoscopes, and many problems are remedied by simple rituals that are based on this knowledge. These rituals, that have nothing to do with 'worshipping supernatural forces' (which, purportedly, is the core of all 'religious' activity), are rather directed to what Malcolm Ruel (1997) calls 'the ordering of life': putting the life of an individual in tune with the general order. The horoscope-based rituals are essential parts of the majority of bigger ritual complexes that are part of the repertoire of both lamas and shamans.

In the Tuvan universe, time is ordered by the Chinese horoscope through twelve-year cycles, in which each year corresponds to an animal: a horse, a pig, a dragon, a monkey, a rooster. Each animal goes well with two others and badly with two more. Each year of the twelve-year cycle also corresponds to a Buddhist deity, a mantra, and a set of interdictions. Further, time is also ordered in cycles of eight years, each year corresponding to an element: water, earth, wind, iron, ether (or the cosmos), wood and fire. To each of them is attributed its own colour and a set of characteristics. Again, each element fits well with some, is neutral in relation to others and fits ill with still others. Finally, there is a cycle of five years, where each year corresponds to a set of a certain number of coloured dots, in Tuvan called *mengi*. Tuvans think of them as if they were marks inscribed on the body from birth, imparting the individual with certain emotional and cognitive dispositions, and governing her life in certain ways. Each person has thus three sets of qualities that form her personality and life circumstances – the animal of the twelve-year cycle, the 'seat' and the birthmark. At the same time, each year has similar attributions, being a year of a certain animal, a certain 'seat' and a certain *mengi*, which match or clash with those of the individual. The match between the individual's horoscopic signs and those of the year defines the circumstances of one's current life, and in this correspondence – match or mismatch – explanations are sought for things which go wrong. Interpersonal relations depend on the match between personalities, as well as on the correspondence between these and the characteristics of the current year, and if something goes wrong in the relational aspect, explanation is first sought in the relationships between the sets of horoscopic signs pertaining to the people in question. It should be noted that 'interpersonal relationships' are seen to affect individuals on a much deeper level than we are accustomed to, not only socially and emotionally but also physically. Thus, if a daughter is constantly ill, the explanation can be that she and her mother have the same *mengi*, and that perhaps they happen to be the same as the *mengi* of the current year. The same applies to spouses, who are also understood to affect each other directly and physically.

This is remedied routinely by a simple ritual of 'the separation of the *mengi*', when the wrists of the two protagonists are tied together with a thread of the colour corresponding to that of their *mengi* (or the *mengi* of the current year), and then the thread is solemnly cut, accompanied by whispering of spells, which can be sutras or imprecations to a Buddhist deity, if performed by a lama, or pleas to personal spirit helpers, if done by a shaman.

To put this in context, let me describe a typical ritual for dealing with a misfortune, performed by a shaman, and compare it with that performed by a lama. Both concern a person who comes to a ritual specialist, as is most often the case, with a whole set of diffuse and overlapping misfortunes.

In the case of a shaman, the session starts with the client and the shaman sitting opposite each other, the client telling the shaman what the problems are. The shaman might cast *xuvanak* – a Tuvan divination technique with the help of stones, used by most shamans but not by lamas – thus deepening the dialogue with the client by providing clues and eliciting more detailed and insightful answers. This dialogue parallels the initial therapeutic interaction used by healers everywhere. It has been described by Susan Whyte (1998) as 'articulating uncertainty': the client confirms some cues and discards others, while formulating problems and their possible solutions in interaction with the ritual practitioner. The shaman then inquires about the years of birth of the client and of her relations who may be the focus of her concern, and checks against the horoscope book. The shaman then gives the first preliminary explanation of the misfortune, possibly based on the mismatches between the *mengi* or the elements of the client and those close to her, and perhaps of those of the current year.

In interactions with shamans and with lamas, the parts which formulate a diagnosis, give misfortune a name, and indicate a possible cause. This first part is also similar to such sessions in many other places, for example in interactions between Moscow magi and their clients, who use Tarot or ordinary playing cards, or diviners in Western Uganda who use either percussion instruments to interact with the local spirits, or Arabic books to find answers in combinations of words and numbers (see Whyte 1998).

Similarities and Differences in Ritual Design

The Shaman's Ritual

In the Tuvan case, problems that are attributed to the aberrations of the individual's position in the temporal order are tackled through specific ceremonies, such as those of the separation of the elements or of the *mengis*, mentioned above, but the ways of dealing with these are idiosyncratic. On the table between the shaman and the client there is always a bowl of milk (one of the central elements of any shamanic ritual, always provided by the client), and a bunch of *artysh*, Tuvan juniper, the most sacred plant in the Tuvan universe.

The shaman pours the milk into the bowl, takes a thread of the requisite color from his purse, sometimes making a plait of several, and immerses the thread into the milk, burning *artysh* and reading incantations over it.[2] Sometimes the thread is left to soak in the milk throughout the subsequent work with the drum, thus adding more power and stronger healing qualities to it; at other times, a couple of minutes of soaking is considered adequate. This may be followed by the act which lies at the heart of any shamanic séance, a bout of drumming or '*kamlanie*'.[3] In this session the shaman calls in her non-human allies, the beings or entities who in Western neo-shamanism are called 'spirit helpers', but who in Tuva are rather conceptualised as 'masters', or 'teachers'. 'Helpers' would imply a somewhat subordinate relationship of 'spirits' to the shaman, which would not describe correctly the nature of this relationship for Tuvan shamans. The 'spirits' certainly are the shaman's allies, and most of what she or he knows in terms of ritual techniques and cosmological details is taught by spirits. But the cooperation of spirits in Tuva can never be complacently or routinely counted on, never taken for granted. The 'spirits' are stern and sometimes even cruel instructors, and they require from the shaman both obedience and constant demonstration of prowess and competence if they are to cooperate instead of working against her (or perhaps abandoning her altogether).

This somewhat capricious and unreliable character of the spirits is never explicitly commented on by the practitioners; rather, it is my conjecture from the observations that I cannot report within the scope of this text. Suffice it to say that most shamans refer to their 'spirits' as 'masters'. Or, to avoid implications of inequality, shamans often talk about their spirits as just 'my folk'. The word of the masters is a shaman's command, not only in terms of ritual instructions and cosmological information (which is articulated only rarely – for example after insistent enquiries by the anthropologist) but also in terms of everyday practical questions, such as which clients to work for, how much money to charge, and so on. This obedience seems to be the best way of ensuring the cooperation of 'my folk' when it comes to fierce fights with other spirits, both the spirits of nature, masters of specific places, hoards of evil spirits that hover everywhere in the landscape and the hostile spirits of other shamans who are constantly at war with one another, just as humans themselves often are.

This digression will perhaps assist us in understanding what happens at the ritual of *kamlanie*. The shaman puts on his garb and head-gear, takes up his drum and then drums and chants an *algysh*, the shamanic song, summoning his spirits, in order to use their powers in the blessing and purification of the client. The shaman usually drums for himself, in the centre of the room, in front of the client, calling forth his spirits and communicating with them, paying them homage in his chant and perhaps telling them what kind of help is needed. Their cooperation thus secured, the shaman positions himself behind the client and drums above his head and around his body, to 'purify' the client. This purification is done to take away what is referred to as 'dirt' or 'filth', harmful objects or evil beings. This 'filth' is sometimes made almost visible when the shaman brushes it off from the client's head, using his *orba* – drumstick with fur and bells – as a handy brush. Throughout the client sits holding the bowl of milk in his hands, and in the end the shaman sprinkles the milk over the client, spitting some especially on the crown of his head and behind his collar. The client takes a sip of the milk, and this completes the ritual.

No two shamans' rituals are exactly the same. Rather, they are embroideries on a certain pattern, improvisations on a certain theme. This is because each shaman acts on behalf, and with the guidance, of her 'masters' (her folk), closely following their instructions and disregarding them only at her own peril. Irrespective of the practitioner, however, there are recurrent elements in all such rituals. These include the use of juniper smoke and of milk for purification – and, as I have already mentioned, lamas use this for the same purpose; and the use of milk for purification. In this cattle-breeding country milk is seen to possess sacred life-giving qualities, which are strengthened by, and themselves strengthen, the force of the spells.

What makes such a ritual manifestly 'shamanic' is the act of the shaman herself, when she marks the shift of what I would call performance modalities (rather than 'consciousness', as shamanic scholars would have it). When she puts on her garbs, she indicates that she is ready and open to interact with her 'masters', with all the excitement, drama and danger that such interaction entails. The presence of spirits is marked and acknowledged, and the work is done by the shaman and 'her folk' together.

Buddhist Ritual

A ritual with a lama officiating usually takes place in a *khuree*, a Buddhist temple, but a lama can perform it anywhere else: in a client's house or yurt, at a certain significant place in nature or in a small room somewhere on the premises of local authorities, allocated to a lama to receive clients in small villages or towns. The client talks about her predicament, the lama consults the horoscope and perhaps his dice, and suggests the cause of the problem. The ritual of 'separating the elements' (or *mengi*) may then ensue. The main part, however, is reading the sutras. What the drum is for a shaman – the main instrument and the central defining symbol – the sutras are for the lamas. Sutras are chosen carefully, depending on the occasion. There are 'Protectors of the Faith' – Buddhist deities – who in Tuva are seen to be responsible for certain problems: for example I heard that the Green Tara takes care of growth of plants, cattle and human beings, and mitigates the consequences of natural catastrophes such as floods and forest fires; Avalakitechvara solves interpersonal situations, White Tara helps mothers in solving their children's problems, and Zhanraising is a forceful deity who assists soldiers in war, new conscripts, policemen and people who work in law-enforcement bodies. In general, and in the most difficult cases, the deity addressed is Lhamo, the Buddhist 'Protector of the Faith' who is considered to be the chief patron of Tuva, with the power and knowledge to solve the specific problems of the

Tuvan people. Sometimes, additionally or instead, these rituals address the *eezi*, the master of the locality.

The ritual consists of reading the sutras, taken piece by piece from the stacks, which are otherwise kept reverently folded in silk or brocade cloth. They are read in Tibetan, in a nasal sing-song that reverberates over the entire locality. The chanting is interspersed with the sounds of the numerous musical instruments in which Buddhist temples abound – several kinds of bells, cymbals, shells and other kinds of horns (such as a thigh-bone trumpet, procured in India) and occasional single beats on a drum, as well as simple hand-clapping. All of these sounds are signals to greet the deities that are evoked in the particular reading. At some points the lamas may cover their heads with their crimson robes and gesture to the clients to do the same, since the power of the deity evoked can be too strong and harmful for the unprotected.

The culmination of this ceremony is a *serdzhim*, a libation of vodka to the selected Protector of the Faith or Master of the Locality. The clients bring vodka (and sometimes milk), which the lama, after reading the sutras, pours into a special chalice. The client, his head covered, comes out into the courtyard, in a direction prescribed in accordance with his horoscope, and pours vodka on the ground. He then returns to the temple, and the reading continues, while those present receive rice or millet that they hold in the palms of their hands throughout the ceremony, to be imbued with the blessing power of the words of sutras.

A Buddhist ceremony is completed when, one by one, all the members in the client's group come to the lama, who pats them gently on the head with the pack of sutras, now carefully re-wrapped in their silk cover. By this blessing the beneficial powers of the sutras are transmitted to the bodies and persons of the supplicants directly – in Peircian terms, indexically, in the same way as the milk, imbued with the power of the shaman's spells, is spat onto the crown of the client's head and over his body. In the end, after having wafted themselves with *artysh* smoke, the clients go around the temple, their hands folded together in a gesture of reverence, bowing especially to the statue of Buddha and to the portrait of the Dalai-Lama, and leaving some money, as well as biscuits, sweets and other offerings on a plate in front of the altar. They leave the room walking backwards, to avoid turning their backs to the temple relics.

We can see now that the overlap between Buddhist and shamanic ritual activities is extensive. Not only are they used for many of the same purposes but the meaning and logic of these rituals is largely the same. In the ceremonies for blessing of a newly-bought car, the shaman wafted the burning *artysh*, sprinkled milk and drummed around and inside the car; while the lamas put the car-keys and the driver's leather vest right on their desk among the ritual implements, while reading the sutras, burning *artysh*, blessing the rice and greeting the deities with their musical instruments. The rationale was the same: the negative forces and evil spirits were cast away from these objects, while the objects themselves were imbued with the force of good imparted by the shaman's spirits, the Buddhist deities, the sacred plant *artysh*, the milk and the sutras. The same forces were at work here: the positive force which emanates from certain objects and substances that in Durkheimian terminology could be called 'sacred', but which are more effectively conceptualised in Ruel's terms as 'life-giving'. As we have seen, some of these objects and substances are the same for both categories (*artysh*, milk), while others are, so to speak, 'occupationally-specific', notably the drum and the sutras. The initial conversation of what in Western bio-medicine could be called 'anamnesis and diagnosing' is the same in both practices. The device used to pinpoint the human being's maladjustments in the temporal order, the horoscope, is the same, as are the rituals to remedy these maladjustments. Most importantly, both kinds of specialists work indexically, in the modality of what Taussig once called 'contact' (1993), the mode that in anthropology is associated with magic, rather than with religion. Its rationale is pragmatic, and the mechanisms of its action may be conceived not only symbolically (based on the shared knowledge of *what* actions and objects signify) but, first and foremost, indexically, based on the shared knowledge of *how* they signify (Daniel 1984; cf. Lindquist 2005). This is possible because lamas and shamans live in the same natural universe, inhabited by the same human and non-human beings. What differ are the non-human beings they interact with, and the practitioners' attitudes to these beings.

Cooperation, Competition and Division of Labour

The tasks of shamans and lamas overlap significantly, but they are not identical. The rule of thumb is that lamas are preferred when things are good and people hope to keep them so: when blessing rather than combat is called for. When a disaster has already occurred, shamans may perhaps be preferred, but lamas are resorted to as well. Shamans are usually not summoned to bless the newly-born or newly-wed, while lamas sometimes are;[4] and, importantly, lamas are not called upon to perform the ritual central to the life of the Tuvans, seeing off the *sunezin*, the spirit of the dead.[5] Apart from this, the choice of the specialist tends to depend not on the nature of the task, but on the personal persuasions of the clients, on their devotion to Buddhism, on their previous experience of working with shamans and on how much money they are prepared or can afford to invest in the matter. Lamas cost less, and it is not they who set the price: people give them what they deem appropriate.

Similar divisions of labour between lamas and shamans have been noted in other ethnographic contexts. In the rural Himalayas lamas read sutras, and other ritual specialists, called 'bombos', deal with the non-human inhabitants of their shared social universe in other ways (Holmberg 1989). In such contexts, lamas and shamans are engaged in a sort of cooperation, each dealing with their kind of task, acting towards their kind of non-human counterpart, but sharing a cosmology and an audience of human users, in both interaction and 'dialogue' (Mumford 1989). In his classical description of village Buddhism in Sri Lanka, Gombrich (1971) notes that the Buddhists have no doubts about the reality of 'spirits', since deities of all kinds inhabit the Buddhist universe everywhere (see also Samuel 1993). Gombrich remarks that Buddha himself lived in a universe inhabited by spirits, and that spirits were among those to whom Buddha preached and whom he converted. The existence of spirits was a part of the natural order, and for Buddhists neither interaction with them nor their behaviour has anything to do with 'religion' (Gombrich 1971). The Buddhist world is inhabited by various deities: Buddhas, Boddhisatvas, Protectors of the Faith and other beings, whose identities vary depending on schools, traditions and local lore, and who easily incorporate the local spirits into their ranks. In Tuva, considering the overlapping of tasks, one might expect the relation between shamans and lamas to be one of competition rather than division of labour and dialogue. In fact, both attitudes can be discerned. Co-existence between these two categories of ritual specialists is primarily marked by tolerance, tacit mutual acceptance and acknowledgement of the other's place, but there is also hidden tension and implicit hierarchy. Much depends on the personal dispositions and political stakes of the individual practitioner. The leading public figure in Tuvan shamanism, Mongush Barakhovich Kenin-Lopsan, is expressly negative to Buddhism, maintaining that it is a foreign invention that threatens to destroy the 'local tradition' of shamanism. A shaman I worked with once accompanied me to a Buddhist temple in a village. She examined the *tanki* (canonical pictures of Buddhist deities) on the walls and the altar decorations with vivid interest and with a hint of admiration, but left almost immediately, saying that 'her folks' forbade her to be in this place. Other shamans regularly interact with lamas, if only on a personal level: I know a lama who sometimes sends people to a certain shaman, although this is perhaps unusual. Sometimes a shaman goes to a lama on her own behalf, and in certain cases sends her clients to a lama.[6] Several shamans active in Kyzyl today have more than a perfunctory knowledge of Buddhism, having studied in lay Buddhist groups or in schools for lamas; some were devout Buddhists earlier in life, and some even consider themselves good Buddhists while practising shamanism professionally. Certainly, almost all who consider themselves devout Buddhists also go to shamans on various occasions, and see no contradiction in this.

The following story, told to me by a very popular lama with acknowledged healing and clairvoyant abilities, neatly illustrates this attitude. 'It became clear early on that I was the one in the family who had inherited my mother's healing gift', Omak said, 'and even though I most of all wanted to become a sports-coach, my mother told me that I had to make use of my abilities. She said that there were two trades where I could use them: I could become a shaman or a lama. Becoming a shaman, I would be charged with both helping and harming people; becoming a lama, only helping. So I decided to become a lama'. The shaman's gift always has a double edge, and both the users and the shamans themselves admit to this dangerous and destructive aspect of their craft. This aspect is indispensable and desirable, because the shamans' competitive advantage lies in their aggressive and cunning warfare against harmful forces, as well as in their firmness in dealing with beings not intrinsically harmful but dangerously unpredictable in their behavior, such as the Masters of the Locality and the spirits of the dead.

The Buddhist cosmos is crowded with all sorts of deities, and in Tuva those most often encountered are the Protectors of the Faith, the Boddhisatvas and the Buddhas of particular qualities, responsible for certain professions. Apart

Allies and Subordinates

from these Buddhist deities, the world outside the *khuree*, and outside the Buddhist system of knowledge and authority, is swarming with various beings. There are *eeler* (sing. *eezi*), the masters of the certain places in nature, mountain tops, mountain passes where they cross over the crest (*art*), shamanic trees,[7] rivers, springs and other localities in the taiga and the steppe. These masters sometimes become the allies of shamans. Sometimes shamans have to fight these spirits or negotiate with them with the assistance of their own allies, or to pay them homage by feeding them, drumming for them, singing *algyshtar* for them, and giving them milk, beer, food and other signs of attention. These masters in most cases have no canonical appearance. Different shamans see them differently, although they are most often men and women, of a certain age and disposition. There are some well-known lakes whose masters are known to be animals, such as a blue bull or a bear, and otherwise animals are sometimes among the forms in which shamans can see their own masters (allies) and the masters of the place.

Besides these beings, there are others, commonly known from the local lore. Examples include *diiren*, handsome young men with iron noses, or *albys* and *shulbus*, maidens with iron teeth, long copper-red hair and hanging breasts that they swing over their shoulders. Shamans sometimes see them among the spirits which they encounter in their rituals out in the wild; non-shamans as well can sometimes meet them while alone in the taiga. For a layperson, such a meeting is not a happy occurrence, an uncontrollable, wild and most likely unfriendly power.

Further, there are the spirits (souls) of the dead, the *sunezin*, who leave the body after death and dwell around the abode for the first seven days. It is of utmost importance to see the *sunezin* off on its last journey, on the seventh and then on the forty-ninth day, and it is almost always shamans who are asked to perform that hard and perilous task. The *sunezin*, although not evil in themselves, are angry and sad to leave the world, and this can spill over onto the shaman, causing her harm. Also, the sunezin tend to want to take their nearest and dearest with them, and it is the shaman's duty to prevent this. If the seeing-off is not done properly, and the sunezin fail to go away, they tend to become evil spirits; when this happens, they wander around, intervening in the affairs of the living, causing illness in people and cattle, and occasioning other misfortunes.

Finally, the third category of non-human entities inhabiting the Tuvan universe is the 'filth' of all kinds, diverse spirits of the disease and misfortune that some shamans perceive as taking up abode within the individual's living body, dancing around the dwelling in a troubled home, or ravaging in droves out in the nature. With all these forces the shaman deals directly, socially, or, in semiotic terms, indexically. It is only the shaman who is expected to 'see' these beings during the ritual. The others might well see something in the dramatic performances staged by the shaman, but they do not focus on what they see, and they are not happy about seeing it, because such seeing entails the responsibility to act on what has been seen. Indeed, if a person persists in seeing these entities, she is expected to be marked and sooner or later to become a shaman.

Lamas in their rituals also directly acknowledge the masters of the place, giving them food, in the same way the shamans do: putting food on the fire and letting it burn, the food to be consumed by the masters while the fire is consuming it. But the evocations of the beings of Buddhist cosmology are understood to protect the lamas, as well as all other present, from the dangers associated with the tricks capricious and unpredictable masters can play. Much as Buddha once converted the spirits, lamas say that the masters are converted during the reading of the sutras and become the protectors of the faith or other *sagyzyn*, beings of the Buddhist pantheon. In this way they become subordinate to other Buddhist deities as well as to lamas, their earthly representatives. In contrast, spirits and shamans are on a par with each other. They can be allies or rivals or bitter enemies, but the outcome of this single combat is never known in advance. As equals, spirits communicate with shamans, and sometimes happen to disclose the information important to the lay participants, which adds drama and the excitement of the unexpected to the ritual if conducted by a shaman.

Thus, even in the cases where lamas' and shamans' tasks overlap (such as asking for blessing, protection, healing or other problem-solving), in the shaman's case the shared universe recreated in ritual acquires a living, vibrant character, conveyed by this immediate interaction between humans and spirits who have to be mindful of each other. In semiotic terms, this interaction is presented indexically, where the spirits are signified by the physical signs of their presence (spurts and spits of fire, gushes of wind, movements of rain and clouds, sounds and sights of birds and animals, and the like). In Buddhist rituals, however, the imaginary universe of the Buddhist cosmology is always over and above the natural universe of weather and landscape, the Buddhist deities controlling the angry spirits. This allows the human participants to feel secure, which takes away the anxiety but also, perhaps, the excitement of the shamanic ritual. The symbolic domination remains symbolic – effected through a shared knowledge of the meaning of signs, which also includes the awareness of the hierarchy of powers and beings involved. Accordingly, lamas need not be 'strong' and 'tell the truth', even though there are lamas with gifts of seeing and healing, thoroughly appreciated and widely popular. What is required from a lama is not primarily his personal charisma (although it may be important to an extent), but, rather, that he performs the ritual correctly, chanting the sutras, sometimes for hours, resorting to requisite paraphernalia at requisite times.

While the lama's chief virtue is knowledge and discipline, the shaman's is strength and audacity.[8] Lamas are incorporated into an ordered, hierarchical system of power positions, where knowledge is imparted from outside and learned by formal instruction, and where devotion and discipline are the prerequisites for such knowledge. Proper monastic Buddhist education is an issue of major concern for Tuvan lamas, who are painfully aware that Buddhist knowledge was destroyed and must rebuild, through years of study, privation and hard discipline in the monasteries of Buriatiya and India.

Shamans, however, learn the basics of ritual practice not through formal instruction but, rather, by practicing themselves, following the instructions of their 'folk'. This on-going 'contact learning' produces knowledge that is always open to revision and amendment, and supreme authority always lies with the shamans' spirits. This ritual and cosmological knowledge is in fact semi-secret for shamans – they can communicate it to a field-working anthropologist if they trust her, but they disclose this information by many caveats: 'this is how I see it ... but never tell this to any other shamans!'

*

This exposition of what, with some reservations, can be called 'the religious life' of the Tuvans, fits poorly with the Durkheimian/Geertzian view of religion as a closed system, hedged off from the mundane world. Most of the efforts of the religious specialists in Tuva are aimed at solving the problems of this world, at 'the securing of life' (quoting Ruel 1997) in the type of conditions where other means, more familiar to Westerners, are lacking. In this rendering, 'religion' is not 'another world to live in', but, rather, a tool to help life in this world. This pragmatic use of the symbolic apparatus of 'religion' tends to be seen by theologians and devout lay intellectuals in the West as 'folk practices', a form of 'corrupted' religion. In the terms of this volume, these are activities 'on the margin of religion'. In Tuva, however, these margins seem to be much vaster than the 'core activities' based on the shared dogma and practices imported from centres of traditional Buddhism (such as the construction of mandalas or the building of stupas, performed or supervised by Tibetan or Buryat monks, which also take place in Tuva). These margins notwithstanding, Tuvan practices of Buddhism can, after all, can be seen as a 'religion' in the Geertzian sense – as a coherent system of transmitted knowledge, based on institution building and official hierarchical structure.

Shamans, however, are always loners, constantly recreating their world through dialogue and interaction with spirits – their allies as well as opponents – even though some of them are sometimes forced to work together with other shamans within the specific post-Soviet institution of the shamanic clinics or centres. Therefore, even if it is politically expedient to class 'shamanism' as 'religion', attributing to it some apposite adjectives such as 'traditional' or 'State', the entity of 'shamanism' seen as an abstraction in isolation from the individual activities can be considered as only this – an abstraction, whose analytic or taxonomic usefulness is rather doubtful. Shamans as individuals are always centres of their own universe, always on the margin of established social worlds, positioned precariously until their rivals oust them or their allies (human or spirit) fail them. If we are to use 'shamanism' as an analytic term at all, we should be aware of its status on the margins of the institutions and systems of knowledge that we call 'religion'.

Notes

1. One scene that remotely resembled these descriptions pertained to a performance for a team of Italian journalists, and I have doubts about its relevance for 'Tuvan shamanism' as a whole.

2. The smoke of *artysh* is also used to 'feed' the *eeriner* – protective spirits contained in special amulets that shamans use for their own sake as well as for their clients.
3. *Kamlanie* comes from the Tuvan word for shaman, '*kham*' or '*kam*', and means literally 'shamanic work' or, more precisely, 'shamanising'.
4. Before the wedding, lamas are often asked to consult the horoscope, to indicate an auspicious day for the wedding.
5. This differentiates Tuva from many cultures defined by Tibetan Buddhism, where taking care of the departed is one of the central tasks of the lamas.
6. I do not know of a lama who goes to a shaman for his own sake.
7. Shamanic trees are trees of two kinds which grow from the same root.
8. 'Strong' lamas are highly appreciated as well. 'Strength' here is defined in the same way as for shamans – namely, in terms of the clarity of seeing and the efficiency of healing.

References

Asad, Talal. 2002 [1993]. 'The Construction of Religion as an Anthropological Category', in Michael Lambek (ed.), *A Reader in the Anthropology of Religion*. Oxford: Blackwell Publishers, pp. 114–32.

Daniel, Valentine. 1984. *Fluid Signs: Being a Person the Tamil Way*. Berkeley: University of California Press.

Geertz, Clifford. 1973. 'Religion as a Cultural System', *The Interpretation of Cultures*. New York: Basic Books, pp. 87–125.

Gombrich, Richard. 1971. *Precept and Practice: Traditional Buddhism in the Rural Highlands of Ceylon*. Oxford: Clarendon Press.

Holmberg, David. 1989. *Order in Paradox: Myth, Ritual, and Exchange among Nepal's Tamang*. Ithaca: Cornell University Press.

Lindquist, Galina. 2005. *Conjuring Hope: Magic and Healing in Contemporary Russia*. Oxford: Berghahn Books.

Mumford, S.R. 1989. *Himalayan Dialogue: Tibetan Lamas and Gurung Shamans*. Madison: University of Wisconsin Press.

Ruel, Malcolm. 1997. *Belief, Ritual and the Securing of Life: Reflexive Essays on a Bantu Religion*. Leiden: E.J. Brill.

Samuel, Geoffrey. 1993. *Civilized Shamans: Buddhism in Tibetan Societies*. Washington: Smithsonian Institute Press.

Taussig, Michael. 1993. *Mimesis and Alterity*. New York: Routledge.

Whyte, Susan. 1998. *Questioning Misfortune: The Pragmatics of Uncertainty in Eastern Uganda*. Cambridge. Cambridge University Press.

Chapter 10

On Celibate Marriages: Conversion to the Brahma Kumaris in Poland

Agnieszka Kościańska

Poland is predominantly a Roman Catholic country. Catholicism has played an extraordinary part in national history. Under the conditions of partition in the nineteenth century, the Church supported pro-independence activities. Similarly, and even more significantly, the Church supported anti-Communist opposition in the second part of the twentieth century. Under the repressive communist regime, the Church provided citizens with the space for an independent exchange of thoughts. As well as spiritual and intellectual support, the Church supplied resistance activists with essential material goods during the time of economic shortage. Moreover, the Polish anti-Communist movement, *Solidarność*, operated under Catholic patronage and drew heavily on both religious and nationalist symbols of the Catholic Church. Immediately after the downfall of the socialist regime in 1989, the Church supported the new governing elite with its symbolic power and gained an overwhelming influence over public discourse as well as over legislative processes. The Act ordering religious education in public schools and the restrictive anti-abortion law were the most spectacular achievements of the Church's influence over the public sphere in Poland in the first part of the 1990s. However, it is important to note that the Polish Roman Catholic Church is not homogenous. Rather, internal diversity has become significantly visible since 1989. This is most apparent in the ideological distance between, on the one hand, the progressive Catholic intelligentsia, and on the other, the fundamentalist movements focusing on the defence of national and religious identity and integrity against European secular influences. These latter movements are situated on the radical political right and recently have gained strong social support.

Religion also constitutes a very important element in the construction of individual and collective identity. I would like to consider briefly the ways in which Catholicism constructs gender identities, especially women's identities, in the Polish context. The basic model of female identity is build around motherhood, epitomised by *Matka Polka* (the Polish Mother), a notion which derives from the nineteenth century and is connected with the participation of women in the Polish struggle, including the military struggle, for independence after the downfall of the Polish state in 1795. *Matka Polka* constitutes an important element of Polish Romantic poetry; she is 'an admirable and delightful creature, good, caring and fertile, but also a patriot, one who gives birth to and brings up sons for the homeland, one who takes care of national values' (Monczka-Ciechomska 1992: 95, my translation). Moreover, she is strongly intertwined with the Catholic imagery of the Madonna.[1] Mary is the ideal of self-sacrifice.

In order to serve the national community, the Polish Mother sacrifices her own needs. In that context the concept of the motherhood goes far beyond biological reproduction, nurturing and feeding the family. It consists of women's duties towards their husbands, families and national community. During the nineteenth-century struggle for independence many women of the higher social strata were forced to take on their husbands' obligations to their families as well as to the national community, as their men were killed during uprisings or persecuted for participation in the resistance. Thus, the Polish Mother is a heroine who is able to rise to every occasion and who is totally devoted to sustaining the nation. Since that time the *Matka Polka*, who sustains religion and nation, has been the dominant female role model, offering women agency, social prestige and the possibility of taking an active part in the struggle against oppression, but with no choice and to the detriment of all other roles (on the Polish Mother see, for instance, Budrowska 2000; Pine 2001; Titkow 2001).

The Polish Mother survived the communist period. Although as a result of socialist state policy most women were employed in various sectors of economy, their labour was seen as a part of their maternal obligations. At the same time women were committed to household duties such as feeding the family, which during the years of shortage required an inordinate amount of time as well as quick wittedness and shrewdness. Women's double-burden is a part of the Polish Mother's self-sacrifice.

However, the economic and political transformation of the 1990s brought new role models for females. Women were presented as independent individuals. The topic of sexuality, under communism rarely evident, also appeared in public discourse. In the course of transformation, women were represented as having sexual needs and as being objects of sexual desires. The impact of Western popular culture, facilitated by the development of mass media, has been highly sexualised. Here again, Catholicism became a core of resistance, this time against the expansion of Western influences such as visible sexuality and individualism, or feminism. Catholicism (not only the radical right movements but more generally as well) is against not only pornography and the legalisation of prostitution but also sex education in public schools and the promotion of contraceptives. Sexuality is only acceptable within marriage. Within this public discourse, the notion of the Polish Mother has re-appeared, and again she is being called upon to protect national and religious integrity.

In this paper I focus on certain alternative modes of female identity and agency which stand in opposition to both the Polish Mother and the sexualised popular culture. I consider the case of the Brahma Kumaris – a movement rooted in the Hindu tradition which has been present in Poland since 1982. Members of the Brahma Kumaris spend most of their time on spiritual development. To be successful in this endeavour, they must fulfil very strict requirements, which totally reorganise both their own everyday lives and those of their families. Most of the Polish Brahma Kumaris members live with their families, not on ashrams. Raja Yoga, a meditation technique of the Brahma Kumaris, requires, aside from other practices, early morning meditation (starting at 4 a.m.), celibacy and strict vegetarianism.

In this paper I analyse life stories of female converts to the Brahma Kumaris; I am especially interested in their re-definitions of womanhood, motherhood and wifehood. I examine the way that commitment to the Brahma Kumaris reorganises both gender identities and the family life of converts. As most of the members are middle-aged women, wives and mothers of families, a very important term for this paper is 'motherhood'. 'Motherhood is as much about *doing* as about *being*' (Pine 2001: 61, original emphasis), Frances Pine notes in relation to rural regions of Poland; this also seems to be applicable in urban conditions. I use the term motherhood here in order to describe a certain mode of female identity, which goes beyond the biological fact of being a mother, and which comprises all commitments towards a family. My approach to gender is inspired by social construction theory and, in this paper, I show how motherhood is redefined after conversion, and how a woman's new identity and performance, based on purity and spirituality, influences her family kin networks and work place, and engenders new forms of social life.[2]

'Sind's Celibate Wives': Formation of the Brahma Kumaris

The World Spiritual University Brahma Kumaris is a transnational organisation which aims to transform the world. The founder of the organisation, wealthy diamond merchant Lekhraj Khubchand Kirpalani, who lived in Hyderabad, Sind province (now part of Pakistan), received a powerful vision of Shiva in 1938. As a result of this experience he ended his engagement with worldly matters, took the name Brahma Baba and organised the spiritual school. Even though his teachings were deeply rooted in Hinduism, he introduced several innovations which shocked his family and neighbours.

First, he redefined the Hindu cycle of time. According to his doctrine: 'The cycle is of 5,000 years which is divided into four equal periods of 1,250 years for the Golden, Silver, Copper and Iron Ages. In the Golden Age there is a maximum of eight births; Silver Age, 12 births; Copper Age, 21 births; and Iron Age, 42 births; with one spiritual birth in the Age of Confluence' (New Beginnings 1996: 95).

The cycle is understood literally. The Age of Confluence is a period of transition, in which the world is to be destroyed, and in which we are now living. Since Brahma Baba's vision all horrifying events (including the Second

World War and September 11) have been interpreted as proof that his vision was correct. At the same time, however, Brahma Baba's followers have been anticipating a forthcoming Golden Age, and all their rules of behaviour and meditation practices are directed towards the new paradise.

A second innovation, more practical than but closely related to the first, concerned gender and sexual relations. Brahma Baba focused on the empowerment of women. His revelation showed him that 'women play a crucial role in a transformation of the world'. Thus, he organised a committee of young girls, virgins (*kumaris*), and encouraged them to manage the community on both the spiritual and the organisational levels. The basic rule of the spiritual community was celibacy, and not only unmarried women but also wives followed Baba's path. This call for universal female celibacy aroused very strong anti-Baba sentiments; Brahma Baba's opponents accused him of abnormal sexual behaviour. A reporter for *The Illustrated Weekly of India* entitled his 1938 article on the Brahma Kumaris 'Sind's Celibate Wives. Truth about the Hyderabad Strike'; in the article one can read that 'A delicate problem for a number of husbands in Hyderabad (Sind) has been set by their wives who have joined a new religious cult and taken vows of celibacy' (quoted in Hodgkinson 1999: 23).

Although sexual abstinence is a deeply rooted tradition in India, only about 10–15% of the ascetic population are women (see Khandelwal 2001). The general path of high caste Hindu spirituality consists of four stages: an adolescent period of abstinence (*brahmacharya*); married life (*grihastha*); a forest-dwelling transition state (*vanaprastha*) and complete renunciation of worldly life (*sannyasa*) (Khandelwal 2001: 160). Women were associated with household life while the three other stages were designed for men.[3] Moreover, women who decide to embrace the ascetic life do not marry. For instance, a *sadhin* (female form of *sadhu*) must be a virgin (Phillimore 2001: 31; on female celibacy in India see also Gutschow 2001). In that context, therefore, the gender politics of Brahma Kumaris, in their insistence on the celibacy of wives as well as of unmarried women, seems to be revolutionary. Perhaps it is not surprising that opponents of such innovations organised an anti-Baba committee.

During her stay in Poland, one of the Brahma Kumaris teachers – Sister Vedanti – shared her story[4] with Polish followers. She told them how she had been looking for God since she was a little child. She had worshiped different Gods and Goddesses and studied Hindu philosophy, but she claimed that she had not found the Truth. Finally, she had a dream of the real God, and then some time later her dream came true. She met Brahma Baba, but her father refused to permit her to join the ashram. Conflict between Vedanti and her family lasted for a very long time. Finally Brahma Baba met her father and said to him 'Let her stay Kumari',[5] and Vedanti's father gave her permission. Vedanti dedicated her life to spiritual development. She become a powerful spiritual leader and organised the activities of the Brahma Kumaris throughout Africa. Her teachings concern, among other things, gender relations. However, she also broke all her earthly links with her parents – when they died she did not go to her family hometown to attend the funerals. Her story illustrates two sides of agency which can be achieved by the Brahma Kumaris: the possibility of going beyond traditional social roles (which are especially important in the case of women) and commitment to work on transformation of the world, and the total detachment form earthly matters (attachment is considered to be a vice which makes contact with God impossible).

Chaste Saints: Female Celibacy in the Polish Tradition

Before I move on to details of the development of the Brahma Kumaris in Poland, I would like to make some brief points about the female celibacy tradition in the country. In the course of the development of Christianity, vows of celibacy were often a source of power and agency for women: members of the first Christian communities, saints of the Middle Ages (the most famous European examples are Katherine of Sienna, Margery Kemp, Julian of Norwich, Hildegard of Bingen) and Shakers in the nineteenth century, to list only the most important ones. However, even a cursory overview of this phenomenon goes beyond the scope of this paper and therefore in this section I draw attention to some forms of female chastity in the Polish context alone.

The unquestionable prototype of female celibacy within Christianity is the Virgin Mary. Mary not only led a chaste life but also became pregnant without having sexual intercourse. Feminist theologians often stress Mary's virginity, and argue that renunciation was the main source of her power and agency (Adamiak 1997: 93–99). However, within Polish folk and popular religiosity Mary is venerated as a mother rather than as a virgin.

Undoubtedly Mary was an inspiration for many female saints. The thirteenth century provides some interesting examples. The first is Jadwiga of Silesia. Of German descent, she was the wife of the Piast prince Hendryk the Bearded – a powerful ruler during a period of regional partition of Poland. Although married, Jadwiga took vows renouncing sexual intercourse temporarily. Before deciding to remain permanently celibate, however, she gave birth to an heir to the throne (altogether she bore at least seven children). She also encouraged her husband to undertake vows of chastity. Due to her chastity she managed to organise her marital relations to give her relatively broad autonomy – her spiritual role was a source of power and agency she was lacking within her gendered role. Jadwiga was engaged in political activity and wielded a great influence over her husband's decisions, both political and personal. Her cult was very popular in Poland, and still remains so.

Jadwiga's ideas had great influence on the lower strata of the society, as well as on the elite. She was also a model of identity for other royal women in the region. For instance, Saint Kinga (Kunegunda), the daughter of the Hungarian king and the wife of the Piast prince, Bolesław the Shameful,[6] managed to convince her husband to renounce sexual intercourse permanently. Kinga and Bolesław remained chaste for the whole of their lives and they had no children, which was certainly against the interests of the Piast dynasty – the continuity of the Piasts as a governing family depended upon their producing heirs to the throne. Kinga was active in Polish politics; indeed, chroniclers emphasised that she was more talented in that field than her husband. After 1715 she was made a patron saint of Poland and Lithuania and she is still venerated today, especially within popular and folk religion.

In the cases of both Jadwiga and Kinga, chastity was a part of an ascetic lifestyle which included maintaining a vegetarian diet, frequently fasting, and wearing penance cloths. Both women were concerned with the plight of the poor and were engaged in charity. Not only did they distribute food among the poor but they also influenced their husbands to pass legislation to improve the lot of the lowest strata of society. Both were venerated by their contemporaries, but they were also criticised. On the one hand, ascetic life gave them power and let them act in the male-dominated political sphere, while on the other, their families often complained about their improper diet and dress, sometimes because it was felt that these could be dangerous for their health, but mainly because they were seen as inappropriate for their noble status (on thirteenth-century royal and holy women in Poland see Michalski 2004).

These and similar examples of radical female religiosity at times of political and economic uncertainty in Polish history are interesting to consider in relation to contemporary counterparts. It is worth noting, for instance, that currently some forms of sexual chastity are again becoming popular within a certain socio-religious milieu in Poland, such as the group which encompasses lay elite Catholics, who place high value on virginity before marriage as well as on temporary chastity within marriage itself, and the group including New Age seekers, who often have already 'tried sex', but have decided to pursue different kinds of sensual as well as spiritual experiences, for instance meditation (Pessel 2003).

'Look How These Women Are Treated by Society': Development of the Brahma Kumaris in Poland

After Brahma Baba's death in 1969 the Brahma Kumaris movement expanded to the West. The first Polish Sister – Halina – encountered the Brahma Kumaris in Canada in the 1970s. After three years of intensive meditation practice, she decided to come back to Poland and organise the Brahma Kumaris meditation centre. It was November 1981, just a few weeks before Martial Law[7] was declared in the country. Currently, the Brahma Kumaris have meditation centres in the Polish capital, Warsaw, as well as in the cities of Gdańsk, Łódź and Katowice. Polish meditation centres are in everyday contact with other centres all over the world. The Brahma Kumaris have their own newsletters, and leaders of the organisation (*Dadis* – older sisters) give lessons to the followers via the Internet. Also, Brahma Baba's teachings – since his death he continues to instruct his children regularly through one of his disciples who serves as a medium – are sent to all ashrams via the Internet (concerning the development of the Brahma Kumaris in Poland see Doktór 1991; Kościańska 2002, 2003; Zimniak-Hałajko 2003).

In Poland, as in other Western countries, the Brahma Kumaris place greater stress on social activity (for example courses for positive thinking and self-esteem) than on teachings about the Golden Age, knowledge of which is reserved for dedicated students. Thus, general teaching is focused on transformation in a more worldly sense and is addressed primarily to New Age seekers. This has generated two types of participation in the movement. Apart from dedicated members (Brahmins or students, as they call themselves), there is a large group of sympathisers (friends) who are not so deeply involved either in the activity of the organisation or in meditation practice.[8] Unlike in India, where Brahma Kumaris live on the ashram, in Poland the Brahma Kumaris live with their families (on adaptation of the Brahma Kumaris to Western conditions see, for example, Howell and Nelson 2000, Walliss 2002).

In Poland, as in other countries, most of the people interested in the Brahma Kumaris activity are women.[9] They come from different social strata; however, the percentage of practitioners with a higher education degree is high. Moreover, especially among sympathisers, there can be found people with prestigious and (especially after 1989) well paid professions, such as artists, journalists, psychotherapists, businesswomen and fashion designers. They usually come to know about the Brahma Kumaris through networks of friends and kin or through New Age circles.

The Brahma Kumaris often discuss women's general position within society. In the course of my fieldwork I was frequently told that in Polish society women are expected to take care of their families and to be subordinate to men. Sometimes women have to work, it was said, but it was pointed out that they earn less than a man doing the same job.

> The contemporary world, the realm of material things, provides a full offer of objects, which are beautiful, colourful, luxurious, and fashionable meant first and all to be indispensable for every woman in her effort to catch the necessary man in her life. Advertisements and the fashion industry promote the image of a woman as a plaything who is beautifully dressed or undressed and is surrounded by numerous material goods including a luxury car, all of which creates a complete package for a successful male life. (my translation, 'A real woman' 1994: 3)

The Polish Brahma Kumaris women stress that women who transcend this model are persecuted by society. Therefore, they see it as their task to empower other women and to help them to contribute to the transformation of the male-dominated world.

Aspects of their endeavour to transform the male-dominated world have led, perhaps inevitably, to conflict between the Brahma Kumaris women and the male authorities of the local Catholic parish. A very important factor determining development of the Brahma Kumarism in Poland is that the movement built their main meditation centre in very close vicinity of a Catholic church. The parish priest of this church took advantage of the anti-cult atmosphere in Poland (Kościańska 2004) to organise an anti-Brahma Kumaris campaign. Thus, the Brahma Kumaris have been labelled 'a dangerous sect' and accused, among other things, of abnormal sexual behaviours, kidnapping, contributing to ecological pollution, and so on. These accusations, publicised by the priest, local newspaper and anti-cult organisations, limited the activity of the Brahma Kumaris.

'She is Not My Wife Anymore': Conversion to the Brahma Kumaris

The process of becoming a Brahma Kumaris student is long and has many stages. The first step is to attend courses in positive thinking and the Raja Yoga meditation. This usually takes seven weeks. During that time a prospective member learns about basic principals of the Brahma Kumaris and gets to know about requirements of purity. A person who wants to attend everyday morning classes, called *murli*, has to renounce impure food, impure substances like alcohol and cigarettes, and sexual intercourse.

Most of my informants stress that it is quite easy to give up all worldly pleasures. Usually their first experiences of meditation are very intense.[10] One of them confessed in the interview:

> At the very beginning of the meditation course I experienced that I am a soul. I knew it before, but I couldn't experience that. I remember that evening. I went out from the meditation room. Streets were wet after the rain. And I wanted to scream: 'I am a soul, I am a soul', I wanted everybody to know, how wonderful I felt.

At that time she gave up smoking. 'I inhaled a cigarette, and I felt sick, that was my last cigarette'. She also started to follow restrictions concerning food. These rules significantly changed the organisation of her family live. Brahmins are allowed to eat only pure food. Meat, fish and eggs are prohibited. But the more significant factor is not what one eats, but rather how the food is prepared. The Brahma Kumaris student should eat only food which has been prepared by a person who practices meditation. A cook should be ritually pure (i.e., should have a bath before cooking; menstruating women are also considered impure) and should wear freshly washed clothes. Pots used by Brahmins should never be used for cooking meat. A cook has to concentrate on the action, and should do so while remembering God. Persons who are not Brahmins cannot use the kitchen at the same time. One set of cutlery and dishes is used in the process of preparing food, and another for eating it. When the food is ready, it should be offered first to God, and only then can it be served. Meals should be eaten with concentration. Household members who are not Brahma Kumaris may eat with those who are, but generally Brahmins, if they eat at home, prefer to eat on their own. They avoid sharing a table with a person who is eating meat at that time. Food belonging to the Brahma Kumaris and non-Brahma Kumaris members of the household is stored separately. Sharing food, cooking for somebody else, is an act of 'tying karmic accounts' and according to the Brahma Kumaris doctrine is considered as 'an attachment' – a vice which makes spiritual development difficult.

Meals, especially *obiad* – a meal which consists of soup, a main dish and a dessert, usually served around 2 p.m., and particularly celebrated on Sundays – are eaten together and are considered to be a very important part of family life in Poland. It is the duty of the woman, the mother, to bring the whole family together at the table. When the mother of the family becomes a Brahma Kumari, this part of family life ceases to exist. All my informants described processes of destruction of their domestic kitchen-table life. One of them, a 68-year-old physiotherapist, committed to the Brahma Kumaris for more than twenty years, told me: 'Gradually I started to cook for myself, and I stopped cooking for my husband. So he started to prepare meals for himself or ate at a canteen.' Husbands and children did not appreciate these decisions. A 60-year-old biologist who has been a member of the organisation for almost twenty years said: 'I stopped preparing meat dishes, and my son and my husband didn't like it and they still hold a grudge against me. In the beginning they even didn't want to eat what I cooked without meat in order to resist my vegetarianism.' Extremely difficult for my informants were Christmas and Easter, which are traditionally spent with family in Poland. Another informant, a 51-year-old woman who runs a small business and has been involved in the Brahma Kumaris since the beginning of the 1990s, said in the interview:

> There was a tradition of sharing the eggs for Easter at my mother's house. And my mother couldn't imagine that we could share something else. That causes some family problems. So, I tried to do something about that and I brought bread. I baked it by myself, I did my best to make it delicious. And I thought sharing the bread is as valuable as sharing the eggs. Sharing is important itself. But, for my mother tradition is more important than anything else. We couldn't go through with it.

At the same time, eating together and sharing the food is very important within the Brahma Kumaris community. *Dadis* usually distribute food (usually sweet cakes called *toli*) after meditation. Every Thursday and Sunday students have breakfast together. Preparing and eating food, as well as exchanging recipes, are basic ways of constructing the Brahma Kumaris family.

However, despite the success of these processes of construction through consumption, commensality and reciprocity, sexual abstinence remains a requirement which presents great difficulties. A significant number of women belonging to the Brahma Kumaris are married. The act of conversion forces them to change their relations with their husbands.[11] The Brahma Kumaris believe that relations between husband and wife should be a 'marriage of souls', for example they should meditate together, communicate via telepathy and renounce sexual intercourse. Brahmins should treat all people as souls. This attitude is practiced during retreats; for instance during a workshop for Central-Europeans, members participated in an 'angelic walk' during which they were asked to walk around the meditation hall and look deeply into the eyes of others; everyone had a chance to make eye contact with every other participant. The goal was to look into the soul, not at the body, and also to develop telepathic skills. The doctrine of the Brahma Kumaris emphasises that these kinds of relations will be the way of living in the future Golden Age.

The Brahma Kumaris women want to establish 'marriages of souls' with their husbands. Undoubtedly, this is much more problematic than changing eating patterns. Usually, the alteration of eating habits and the reorganisation of the daily domestic timetable (early morning meditations, going to the meditation centre at 6 a.m., and as a result going to bed very early in the evening) caused conflicts. Moreover, most of the women I interviewed claimed that their relations with their spouses had been tense even before meeting the Brahma Kumaris. However, renunciation of sexual intercourse usually brings or adds a discord between husband and wife.[12] Often kith and kin also become engaged in the conflict. One of my informants told me : 'I remember a very sad story. My decision for sexual abstinence became public. My husband spoke about it to his whole family. She is not my wife any more – he told them. The family took his side. I said that at our age sex is not decent.' The speaker here was a 46-year-old woman. Next, she recalled, a friend of hers tried to persuade her that she should have sexual intercourse with her husband. This brought about the end of their friendship.

Another woman, Ania, a 53-year-old teacher from a city in northern Poland, told me her story of how she convinced her husband that her decision of sexual abstinence was irrevocable. When she gave birth to her children, several years before meeting the Brahma Kumaris – she says – she felt that she did not want to have sex anymore. Her husband tried to change her mind. He told her that frigidity is an illness and she should visit a psychotherapist. Finally she met the Brahma Kumaris, and she recounted to me how through them she found proof that sexual intercourse is an act of evil, and should not be considered a conjugal duty, as it is in Catholicism. She moved out from the bedroom she shared with her husband. In response, he tried to blackmail her, threatening that if she would not come back to his bedroom, he would take a mistress. He also argued that his colleagues – he works in an exclusively male environment – have 'good sex with their wives, and he also deserves that'. She decided to seek a divorce, and went to work in Siberia, among a Polish community there. When she came back, one year later, her husband gradually became used to this new form of conjugal relations.

'There is No Menstruation, No Sex in the Golden Age': Toward New Forms of Relations

Commitment to the Brahma Kumaris influences gender relations. The Brahma Kumaris, like nineteenth-century Shakers, may best be seen as examples of the realisation of utopian gender equality (Sered 1994: 209; Collins 2001: 144). The Brahma Kumaris members claim as Shaker writers did to 'have true equality between men and women, and we are convinced that celibacy is the secret of that' (Sister Jayanti, one of the leaders of the Brahma Kumaris, quoted in Hodgkinson 1999: 188). Equality is also often seen as a result of female leadership.

In the Golden Age human beings will be non-gendered, like souls, just as now in the Confluence Age gender matters. The transition period gives very special opportunities to women. Sister Vedanti explained this to me:

> I, myself, as a woman, know my own role in my world. And that is why I have accepted to work with society, not only at home, with my husband and children and with my family, and my role is to work with many families, with cities, with countries, with the society of the world. Because it is said that a mother is a teacher. And not just a teacher for family and the children, but a mother is a teacher for

everyone, because a mother has her own quality. If we check the history of the world of many, many years we never find a man for giving birth to a child. A man can be a father, a son, a brother, can be a teacher, can be a guru. Many roles a man can play, but the role of a mother is difficult for a man to play in society. But a mother can play the role of a mother, a teacher, a guru, a sister, and also a father.

Next she focuses on the leading role of women. In her view, only women can lead the 'global family' within the Golden Age. However, to do so, first women should be empowered via meditation and a life of purity.

> Women know how to serve and how to give. ... However, this quality of giving to others must be also balanced with qualities of courage, determination, clear thinking and self-respect. Too often women have a tendency to give to others and neglect their own spiritual needs. It is one of the major reasons women find themselves depleted and lacking in spiritual power. (Sister Sudesh 1993: 40)

This attention to their own spiritual needs, in accordance to the Brahma Kumaris doctrine, will give women the possibility to 'transform the man's world'.

Vieda Skultans, who carried out her fieldwork in Mt Abu, the Brahma Kumaris headquarters, also observed the very close relation between celibacy and women's power: 'Celibacy has been widely recognised as conferring spiritual power and social advantage. ... Complete abstinence enables a break to be made between the earlier social and domestic roles of women and their new religious roles' (Skultans 1993: 54). Skultans also argues that sexual abstinence helps women to organise 'varied relationships with men' (ibid.).[13]

'We are bringing the Golden Age', was a claim I often heard. By obeying all requirements, the Brahma Kumaris anticipate the state of incorporeality, which is characteristic of the Golden Age. One woman, an ex-member of the Brahma Kumaris, whose son is mute, told me that because of meditation she could communicate with him through telepathy. According to the Brahma Kumaris teachings, the Golden Age starts within a single human soul – transformation of the world is preceded by a transformation of individuals – 'on the basis of self-transformation' (Sister Sudesh 1993: 45), and the path of the Brahma Kumaris is the only right way.

Keeping the very strict rules of purity may be seen as an act of resistance against the wider society. My informants were very critical toward the contemporary world, which they viewed as full of qualities such as greed, anger and sex-lust:

> There is no menstruation in the Golden Age. In the Golden Age children are born without sex, as a result of yoga. Menstruation is a result of overuse of sex. When a girl has her period for a first time she is terrified, she says that she is ill. That is a proof that it is not natural. Humankind has too much sex. It doesn't matter if you do it as a couple or during an orgy. This is an abuse ... violation against your own body and it causes numerous diseases like, for instance, breast cancer or prostate cancer.

Women I interviewed often claimed that following a path of spiritual development gave them independence and increased their level of self-esteem. This reflects on both their family relations and their professional careers.

Although the practical dimension of the conversion of one member of a household to the Brahma Kumaris involves total separation,[14] new forms of family life are worked out. One of my informants, who has not had sexual intercourse with her husband for nearly twenty years, says: 'Now, our relations are very gentle, much better that before ... It can be characterised as an everyday life based on integrity and dignity. ... My husband is in the mountains now, he went skiing. He calls me everyday, and asks what I am doing. He says that he misses me.' At the same time, sexual abstinence, which previously might have been a trouble spot in a family conflict, can become a topic of harmless jokes. The husband of my informant quoted above, when kissing her good-bye, said to her: 'I kiss you as a statue!'

This woman also reorganised her relations within her wider kinship network: 'Originally, during meetings with our relatives, I had tolerated it when my husband put smoked meats on the table, I had sat and suffered. But finally I started to prepare vegetarian recipes for them, and everyone was amazed. Now, there are only vegetarian recipes in my house.'

Another informant (the biologist quoted above), described how her son and husband, who in the beginning did not accept her vegetarianism, gradually have changed their attitudes: 'Now they eat what I cook with pleasure, they have their favourite dishes and they want me to cook it for them.'

Moreover, finally they also approved her life choice in more general terms:

> Now I see that my husband and my son appreciate what I do, my way of life, my behaviour towards them ... Maybe they are not very happy about what I want to tell them, especially my son, but they know why I say it. They appreciate it because they know that I say is for their own good ... They just like to spend time with me.

Some of the Brahma Kumaris, especially those who call themselves friends, work in very prestigious professions, frequently as freelancers. Often the Brahma Kumaris doctrine was a support in dealing with problems of economic transformation. Many women told me that they lost their jobs as a result of the changes which began in 1989. The spiritual power and self-esteem, as well as a new social network, helped them to find a new profession or show that they are effective and irreplaceable employees. Comparing stories of the Brahma Kumaris women to stories of unemployed women collected by Pine at the beginning of the 1990s in Łódź[15] (Pine 2002), it seems that the Brahma Kumaris doctrine helps them to operate within this new reality.[16]

At the same time, the rule of celibacy and, more generally, gender relations promoted by the organisation, are also very important arguments used against the Brahma Kumaris in the context of their conflict with the local community. During my conversation with the priest of the neighbouring Catholic parish I heard, as a major accusation, that 'they are against marriage'. A local newspaper also published an article presenting sexual abstinence of the Brahma Kumaris as unnatural and degrading. A comment of an ex-member was quoted: 'Members should renounce sex-lust, because sex-lust is the worst sin and vice. All feelings of love and friendship, also to a spouse, are considered as vices, called 'attachment'. All these feelings should be replaced with indirect love' (Życie Warszawy, 26/1/2000: 4–5).

Although many men and women appreciate participation in the movement, in my research I observed that what they call detachment often turns into total rejection of the outside world and isolation from social life. At the same time regulations concerning everyday life – rules of purity – are only a small part of the total codes of behaviour. These aim at engendering the Golden Age, although they may cause life within the Brahma Kumaris community to be highly controlled, as a utopian idea of equality can be replaced with internal hierarchy. As an ex-Brahmin remarked: 'That was a great time. But gradually I was losing a sense of belonging to the wider society. Politics did not exist to me, or social relations. Only me and my path. ... Being a Brahma Kumaris is like withdrawing from life.'

Conclusion

Commitment to the Brahma Kumaris causes transformation of identity and social relations. Gradually women redefine their roles as wives and mothers. A new way of motherhood is practised – spiritual motherhood, which goes beyond nuclear family and kinship network. All maternal obligations and skills, like feeding, nurturing, loving and many others, are used to serve a global family. Family and kinship relations are mainly reorganised by new ways of cooking and eating. Moreover, the rule of sexual chastity builds a new practice of marital relations. Finally, the stress put on self-realisation and self-esteem influences converts' activity beyond the private domain.

Therefore, the character of the Brahma Kumaris' teachings is also significant. Female leadership and a belief in the special mission of women, as well as strong emphasis on self-realisation, are crucial for new identities of members. They are also significantly different from those of mainstream religion in Poland. However, although rooted in Hinduism, the Brahma Kumaris are also responding to a Polish tradition of female celibacy. Moreover, the very high value of motherhood in Poland, on one hand, creates space for spiritual motherhood, but on another, causes tension around its redefinition. This is especially the case insofar as it is not connected to Catholicism. Conversion to the Brahma Kumaris is only one of numerous manifestations of the tension between women's individual personhood, their encompassing gendered roles as mother and wife (*Matka Polka*) and their sexualised image in mass culture, which is present in both private and public domains in Poland.

Notes

I am grateful to Frances Pine for her critical input and editorial assistance.

1. In Polish Mary is called *Matka Boska*, which means 'the Mother of God', but can also mean 'the Divine Mother'.
2. The ethnographic data on which this article is based were collected in the course of fieldwork carried out between June 2001 and December 2002, and in spring 2005. I conducted in-depth interviews with a focus on life-stories, as well as participating in the Brahma Kumaris lectures and workshops organised by the Warsaw meditation centre. I also attended retreats in Bukowina Tatrzańska (in the Polish Tatra Mountains) and at the movement's headquarters in Mt Abu, Rajasthan, India. Other very important sources included Brahma Kumaris publications and newsletters.
3. Khandelwal notes that 'this does not mean that women did not participate in the system's institution.' But even women she interviewed (sannyasisnis) see themselves as exceptions (Khandelwal 2001: 161). She also discusses female temporary celibacy; she concludes 'Female chastity, as the properly regulated expressions of sexuality, allows – even requires – temporary and intermittent periods of sexual abstinence, but the ideology of gender relations leaves it far removed from the historically male pursuit of celibacy' (Khandelwal 2001: 163).
4. Sharing stories, i.e. telling personal stories, concerning amazing events caused by Baba is a main preaching technique of Brahma Kumaris teachers.
5. This statement is related also to the relatively high status of virgins, unmarried daughters in the Sind region in that period (Babb 1984).
6. His sister Salomea also lived within a celibate marriage.
7. Martial Law was established on 13 December 1981 – the army took control over the state; the *Solidarność* movement, which had almost ten million members, was de-legalised and around 10,000 of its activists interned or arrested.
8. The number of dedicated members is very low (e.g. around 100 in Warsaw) but the number of sympathisers is much higher.
9. It is important to note that the Brahma Kumaris movement is not exclusively a women's organisation. Although marginalised (Skultans 1993), men are present in the movement, but they hardly ever gain leadership positions. They are encouraged to get rid of qualities which are considered male, and to learn 'female qualities' such as humility and patience. Meditation is a way to achieve that.
10. The importance of altered states of consciousness in commitment to the Brahma Kumaris is discussed by Julia Day Howell (1997).
11. All of the Brahma Kamaris men I met in the course of my fieldwork who were married, were married to other Brahma Kumaris.
12. Conversion to the Brahma Kumaris can also cause a divorce, but in this paper I focus on couples who decided to stay together. It is also important to note here that in Poland the divorce rate is relatively low.
13. For more on the Braham Kumaris female leadership see Puttick 1997; Howell 1998.
14. One of my informants even used this term describing relations with her husband.
15. In the course of my fieldwork I also interviewed the Brahma Kumaris students from Łódź.
16. This refers to both well-educated and non-educated members. In her teachings, the Brahma Kumaris Polish leader focuses on fighting against typical, in her view, Polish (*sanscara* – in the Brahma Kumaris terms) like lack of resourcefulness, helplessness and laziness, and also fear of the new.

References

Adamiak, E. 1997. *Błogosławiona między niewiastami. Maryja w feministycznej teologii Catheriny Halkes*. Lublin: Redakcja Wydawnictw Katolickich KUL.
Babb, L.A. 1984. 'Indigenous Feminism in a Modern Hindu Sect', *Signs: Journal of Women in Culture and Society* 9(3): 399–416.
Budrowska, B. 2000. *Macierzyństwo jako punkt zwrotny w życiu kobiety*. Wrocław: Wydawnictwo Funna.
Collins, P. 2001. 'Virgins in the Spirit: The Celibacy of Shakers', in E.J. Sobo and S. Bell (eds), *Celibacy, Culture, and Society: The Anthropology of Sexual Abstinence*. Madison, WI: University of Wisconsin Press, pp. 104–24.
Doktór, T. 1991. *Ruchy kultowe: Psychosocjologiczna charakterystyka uczestników*. Kraków: Zakład Wydawniczy 'Nomos'.
Gutschow, K. 2001. 'The Women Who Refused to Be Exchanged: Nuns in Zangskar, Northwest India', in E. J. Sobo and S. Bell (eds), *Celibacy, Culture, and Society: The Anthropology of Sexual Abstinence*. Madison, WI: University of Wisconsin Press, pp. 47–64.
Hodgkinson, L. 1999. *Peace and Purity. The Story of the Brahma Kumaris: A Spiritual Revolution*. London: Rider Books.
Howell, J.D. 1997. 'ASC Induction Techniques, Spiritual Experiences, and Commitment to New Religious Movements', *Sociology of Religion* 58 (2): 141–64.
———. 1998. 'Gender Role Experimentation in New Religious Movements: Classification of the Brahma Kumaris Case', *Journal for the Scientific Study of Religion* 37(3): 453–61.
Howell, J.D. and P.L. Nelson. 2000. 'The Brahma Kumaris in the Western World, Part II: Demographic Change and Secularization in an Asian New Religious Movement', *Research in the Social Scientific Study of Religion* 11: 225–39.
Khandelwal, M. 2001. 'Sexual Fluids, Emotions, Morality: Notes on the Gendering of Brahmacharya', in Elisa J. S. and S. Bell (eds), *Celibacy, Culture, and Society: The Anthropology of Sexual Abstinence*. Madison, WI: University of Wisconsin Press, pp. 157–80.
Kościańska, A. 2002. 'Brahma Kumaris w Polsce czyli duchowość w peerelu', *Maszyna interpretacyjna* 1(3): 11.
———. 2003. 'Poles, Catholics and the *Brahmins*: New Religious Movements in the Transitional Society', *Nord Nytt* 20 88: 59–75.
———. 2004. 'Anti-cult Movements and Governmental Reports on "Sects" and "Cults": The Case of Poland', in J.T. Richardson (ed.), *Regulating Religions. Case Studies from Around the Globe*. New York: Kluwer Academic/Plenum Publishers, pp. 267–78.
Michalski, M. 2004. *Kobiety i świętość w żywotach trzynastowiecznych księżnych polskich*. Poznań: Wydawnictwo Poznańskie.
Monczka-Ciechomska, M. 1992. 'Mit kobiety w polskiej kulturze', in S. Walczewska (ed.), *Głos mają kobiety*. Kraków: Fundacja Kobieca 'Efka'.
Pessel, W.K. 2003. 'Wstrzemięźliwy bon vivant: Między ascezą, agamią i nowym celibatem', *Res Publika Nowa* 16(6): 25–31.
Phillimore, P. 2001. 'Private Lives and Public Identities: An Example of Female Celibacy in Northwest India', in E.J. Sobo and S. Bell (eds), *Celibacy, Culture, and Society: The Anthropology of Sexual Abstinence*. Madison, WI: University of Wisconsin Press, pp. 28–46.
Pine, F. 2001. '"Who Better than Your Mother?" Some Problems with Gender Issues in Rural Poland', in H. Haukanes (ed.), *Women After Communism: Ideal Images and Real Lives*. Bergen: University of Bergen, 51–66.

———. 2002. 'Retreat to the household? Gendered Domains in Postsocialist Poland', in C.M. Hann (ed.), *Postsocialism: Ideals, Ideologies and Practice in Eurasia*. London: Routledge, pp. 95–113.

Puttick, E. 1997. *Women in New Religions: In Search of Community, Sexuality and Spiritual Power*. New York: St. Martin's Press.

Sered, S.S. 1994. *Priestess. Mother. Sacred Sister. Religions Dominated by Women*. Oxford: Oxford University Press.

Skultans, V. 1993. 'The Brahma Kumaris and the Role of Women', in E. Puttick and P.B. Clarke (eds), *Women as Teachers and Disciples in Traditional and New Religions*. Lewiston, N.Y.: Edwin Mellen Press, pp. 47–62.

Sudesh, Sister. 1993. 'Women as Spiritual Leaders in the Brahma Kumaris', in E. Puttick and P.B. Clarke (eds), *Women as Teachers and Disciples in Traditional and New Religions*. Lewiston, N.Y.: Edwin Mellen Press, pp. 38–45.

Titkow, A. 2001. 'On the Appreciated Role of Women', in M. Ingham, H. Ingham and H. Domański (ed.), *Women in the Polish Labour Market*. Budapest: Central European University Press, pp. 21–40.

Walliss, J. 2002. *The Brahma Kumaris as a 'Reflexive Tradition': Responding to Late Modernity*. Aldershot: Ashgate.

Zimniak-Hałajko, M. 2003. *Raj oswojony. Antropologia nowych ruchów religijnych*. Gdańsk: słowo/obraz terytoria.

Brahma Kumaris Sources

New Beginnings. 1996. Mount Abu, Rajasthan, India.

A real woman. 1994. 'Sprawozdanie z programu "Prawdziwa kobieta". Łódź', 20–22 maja. (Unpublished Report from the Brahma Kumaris program).

Part V

Modernity and the Transmission of Religion

Chapter 11

Elders' Cathedrals and Children's Marbles: Dynamics of Religious Transmission among the Baga of Guinea

Ramon Sarró

Baga Parents and Susu Children

In 1954, French anthropologist Denise Paulme and ethno-musicologist André Shaeffner were among the first social scientists ever to visit the coastal mangroves of Guinea, an area inhabited by different groups of rice farmers known as Baga, and the first to produce scholarly work about these people (Paulme 1956, 1957, 1958; Schaeffner 1962, 1964).[1] At that time the Baga were famous in the West for their art and ritual objects, but the social context of the objects stored in Western museums was not well known. Unfortunately, Paulme and Schaeffner could only make a few short visits and were unable to find out much about the ritual context of Baga objects. In fact, Paulme wrote that many of her interviewees were starting to feel detached from their own past. For instance, upon asking a young Muslim man about the culture of his elders, in which he expressed a distinct lack of interest, Paulme was told: 'Our fathers were Baga, but we are Susu' (Paulme 1956: 102). The Susu, who speak a completely different language to the Baga, are a neighbouring ethnic group; they have been spreading over the Guinean coast since at least the eighteenth century, encroaching on other peoples, in a process normally called 'Susuisation', which involves the others adopting the Susu language as well as converting to Islam and abandoning their previous religious identity.

Paulme took her young interviewee's statement to mean that Baga culture and society were disappearing. Accordingly, she wrote some rather pessimistic articles announcing their imminent dissolution. Whilst her articles show a lucid understanding of the tensions Baga were experiencing under French rule, her prediction proved wrong. Baga people did *not* disappear, although it must be said that only two years after her visit, in 1956–1957, the internal tensions that she so perceptively noted led to an iconoclastic movement that completely changed their religious culture. In 1996, a year before she passed away, Paulme told me how surprised she was to know that the Baga were still alive and kicking, and she became very interested in the work that Frederick Lamp, Marie-Yvonne Curtis and I were producing about Baga topics (Lamp 1996, Curtis 1996, Curtis and Sarró 1997).

And alive and kicking they certainly are. However, in 1999 an elderly man, a Christian schoolteacher, was talking to me about the past of the Baga Sitem (the subgroup among whom I conducted my fieldwork), precisely around the time when Paulme was there, when men were initiated in the sacred bush, when people did not tell lies, and when overall – he clearly thought – *everything* was better. He had been initiated when he was twelve years old, in 1948, in what was the last manhood initiation of the Baga Sitem in his village (in other Baga Sitem villages, the last manhood initiation took place in 1952). Like Denise Paulme fifty years before, the man finished his discourse with a rather pessimistic statement: 'This is the past. Our generation was the last one to be initiated. This is why we say that we are Baga, but our children are Susu'.

This was a statement about the loss of cultural values. Indeed, Baga elders view their Susu neighbours very negatively. They claim that the Susu lack moral education; that the Susu do not know what 'Baga' means and that they 'cannot keep secrets', an essential feature of any grown-up Baga man or woman. According to the Baga, the Susu are mostly liars and, properly speaking, they do *not* grow up. Thus, when a child is very tall for her age, Baga elders will say humorously that 'she is growing up like a Susu', meaning that there is no correspondence or equilibrium between her physical growing up and the process of becoming a thoughtful adult human being (which is, according to many, what the word 'Baga' means). She is growing up *too fast*.

The statement that the elders are Baga and the children are Susu is quite a common one, and the occasion I have just recalled is only one of many in which I have heard it. Men and women repeat it often in conversation, always with reference to a lack of moral integrity and the inability to keep secrets. 'A Baga knows how to shut up, a Susu does not' an elderly woman told me in April 2001. Indeed, secrecy seems to be at the core of the generation gap between youth and elders and between Baga and Susu. But secrecy is here to be understood not only as the unwillingness or prohibition to talk about one's inner convictions. It is also the *impossibility* of verbally discussing what has been lived through. 'We have our way of doing things', an old man said, 'which the young cannot understand'. He was not referring to things they know, not even really to things they do. Rather, he was talking about the *way* things are done by the elders, a *habitus* that only time and growing up can provide. Interestingly, the expression 'our way of doing things' (*kiyo kosu*) was sometimes translated as 'our secrets', thus supporting Bellman's point that secrecy has more to do with the way things are done than with a corpus of knowledge to be set apart (Bellman 1984). However, it is not my intention to support the view that secrecy is form only with no content. As I will discuss below, the concept of *tolom* (pl. *molom*), which can be translated as 'mask' or as 'secret', gives a very substantial content to Baga notions of secrecy.

Contrary to what one would probably expect, the youths, too, are quite convinced about the Baga-Susu divide. Even if they speak Baga, and even if they think that there is an objective cultural and historical difference between their community and the Susu's, most Baga young people agree with their elders that they are becoming Susu. 'Our elders had a *tolom* [cult] called *amanco ngopong* that made them Baga; we do not have it anymore and we do not know our customs' a forty-year-old man told me in 1999, referring to the cult of *amanco ngopong* (see below) and placing it at the core of the difference between elders and youths. Seniority is thus a fundamental aspect of Baga Sitem identity. The very word *sitem* stems from the root *tem*, which means 'old' or 'elder'. Thus, the Baga Sitem say that all the Baga are Baga but that they alone are the *abaka atem* (sing. *wubaka wutem*) the 'elderly Baga'. Looking at it from this point of view, not only are the Susu seen as junior and inferior but even other Baga are looked down upon as not being as elderly – and therefore not as *Baga* – as the Baga Sitem.

Being (or becoming) Baga is a process of maturation. From a Baga point of view, those who do not achieve it are just 'Susu'. Probably Paulme's mistake was to take the statement about the Susu-ness of youngsters too literally, as though 'Baga' and 'Susu' could only be used as ethnonyms (which is the case in our Western languages). When Baga claim that their youngsters are Susu, not Baga, they probably do not mean by 'Susu' the same thing we do, and therefore we should not conclude too hastily that the coast is Susu-ising without further examining the contested meanings and re-semantisations of these concepts we use exclusively to designate 'ethnic' groups.[2]

As with many an African society, the 'becoming-a-Baga' process involved, in the past, an initiation cycle composed of many stages. An individual started when he or she was very young and was gradually initiated into a series of cults (*tolom*, pl. *molom*). The last *tolom* for men was *kebere amanco* or *kidi amanco* (literally 'to join *amanco*', or 'to eat *amanco*'), an initiation whose full content was never revealed to me, but in which the participant was told that once he had 'eaten' *amanco* he could be considered a proper *wubaka*, that is, 'Baga'. Women had a counterpart cult, *ateken*, but their initiation into it did not made them become *wubaka*, rather it opened up the possibility for them to produce Baga people. I have elsewhere explored the structural opposition between these two cults (Sarró, in press). The initiatory cycle was called *kidi molom*, literally 'to eat *molom*'. The concept of *tolom* is quite difficult to translate as its semantic field does not match that of any Western concept, and as it happens with the 'empty' concepts so common in all religious cultures (Boyer 1986) it is more oriented towards provoking a reaction than to transmitting encyclopaedic bits of knowledge (see Berliner 2002 for a cognitive analysis of similar concepts among the Bulongic). For our purposes, it could sometimes be translated roughly as 'secret', other times as 'cult' and other times as 'ritual object'. In an interesting conversation I had in 1996, an interviewee glossed *tolom* as 'pain', and pain was indeed an essential component of most initiations of the cycle. When speaking in French, Baga translate *kidi molom* either as *manger les secrets* or, more commonly, as *initiation*.

From a Baga point of view, then, 'initiation' is not just a learning process, but one in which knowledge is eaten and embodied. We should not rule out the possibility that the *kidi molom* cycle included a final stage in which initiates literally ate the ritual objects, either smashed or burned to ashes. Although we do not have evidence to sustain it, we know that such is a common practice in other West African initiation cycles. When men had accomplished the whole cycle of initiation they became *alipne* (sing. *wulpine*, 'he who has finished'). I do not know whether in the past there were *alipne* in all Baga Sitem villages, but today the institution of the council of *alipne* exists only in the village of Bukor.

All these initiatory cults were abandoned in 1956, mostly as the outcome of the iconoclastic movement led by the Muslim charismatic preacher Asekou Sayon Keira.[3] This iconoclastic event marked a transformation in Baga society and especially in its religious culture. It is therefore legitimate for Baga elders, especially those who lived in pre-iconoclastic times, to think that people born since 1957 are not as well versed in the 'mysteries' of being Baga as *they* are. However, if we look at the context in which the old village schoolteacher told me that he and his contemporaries were Baga while their children were Susu, we can see that this context itself nuanced the very lack of cultural transmission he was talking about. Indeed, there was the old man recalling his memories for me, with the children in front of us, listening to the elderly man (their teacher), and thus indirectly learning about their past as well as about how adults introduce themselves to strangers like me. In short, they were growing up and, inevitably, becoming Baga.

Both in 1954 – when Denise Paulme was doing her fieldwork – and today it seems that the elders claim *they* are Baga while their children are Susu (a claim shared by the children, both in Paulme's days and today). There is a structural continuity in this generational-cum-ethnic divide, but there is also a major difference, because the end of initiations in the late 1950s resulted somewhat in a structural transformation. Being an adult in today's Baga Sitem society consists not only of having been initiated but also of having gone through those traumatic events of 1956 that mark such an important watershed in the historical imagination of the Baga. Indeed, it is quite rare to discuss Baga history or culture with Baga people without them taking 1956 as the starting point, whether it is to condemn the iconoclasts or to thank them for having got rid of 'evil things'. The generational divide between those who lived in the pre-1956 religious culture and those who did not is huge and it always revolves around the issue of secrecy. Many elders (*wubeki*, pl. *abeki*) consider those who were born after 1957 as youth (*wan*, pl. *awut*), even if they are over forty years old and married. However, it is clear that despite the secrecy and the lack of formal initiations, there is a basic religious culture which is passed down from generation to generation, not through 'initiations', since these have been abandoned, but rather through informal mechanisms such as games, songs, proverbs, overhearing or comments about the landscape.

Cathedrals and Marbles: The Margins of Religion and Religion in the Margins

In my research on Baga issues, begun in 1992, I have been equally interested in documenting the ruptures and transformations of Baga history as in showing the continuity of religious structures, both in knowledge and in practice. One fascinating thing about religious transmission among the Baga is that as an outcome of an iconoclastic movement in 1956/57 the transmission of some non-Muslim and non-Christian elements has moved from the 'centre' to the 'margins'. In fact, the centre has been 'colonised' by hegemonic Muslim and Christian religious cultures, and in order for us to search for previous religious elements, we must, as a huge body of recent anthropology has taught us, pay a close attention to mechanisms of cultural inheritance that go beyond the explicitly written or told.[4] Although I have been inspired by these contemporary authors, for the sake of the argument in this paper I want to follow an invitation made by Marcel Griaule almost seventy years ago. For several reasons, Griaule is an author I would normally follow with caution, if at all. Yet I must admit I was rather fascinated by a phrase I read in his book on Dogon games, when he stated that 'A revolution can destroy cathedrals, but one cannot see how it will deter children from playing with marbles' (Griaule 1938: 2). Having done fieldwork in a place where a revolution did destroy the big icons of religious culture, I found this quotation powerful for two reasons: on the one hand, it suggested that religious transmission could be achieved away from the centre of socio-religious activity (what Griaule metaphorically referred to as the 'cathedrals'), but it could also be achieved through a practical logic that pervaded the whole of society, including such 'marginal' things to religious activities as are children's games. On the other hand, it offered an *avant-la-lettre* agency to children, since in Griaule's times there were not many studies on the ways children's actions could transmit religious notions or practices.

For the Baga, the revolution that put an end to sacred bushes, icons and initiations happened in 1956, but its roots can be traced to much earlier than that, and certainly to the years when Denise Paulme conducted her fieldwork. She was, in fact, the first author who announced that Baga were in a complete state of anomie and that there were so many tensions in the society that it would sooner or later 'explode', to use her own words. The pessimistic impression of Baga society with which she was left in 1954 can be gauged in a few quotations:

> Baga society appears condemned by a lack of solidarity, by a lack of internal cohesion, and by a lack of natural pride too; neighbouring, healthier societies will soon have absorbed it. As it is now, one can still observe some institutions that the sociologist will regret not to have studied in more detail. (Paulme 1956: 102; my translation)

In another article, she expressed her perception of anomie by stating that:

A Baga can only conceive of his society in terms of divisions: the Bangoura against the Camara, the *asuto* against the *kulokinkaykosi*, youths against elders, men against women – the atmosphere is of a constant rivalry. Let a pressure from the exterior intervene and switch on this factor of internal disunity and the explosion will soon come. (Paulme 1957: 277; my translation; in Paulme's writings, the *asuto* and the *kulokinkaiyosi* were two categories of people: the asuto were first arrivals and wife-givers whereas the *kulokinkaikosi* were newcomers and wife-takers)

Muslim Youth vs the Tyranny of Custom

Let us see, albeit briefly, how all this 'exploded'. In pre-colonial and colonial times, Baga rice farmers were, from a strictly religious point of view, conspicuously non-Muslim and they were known for their rich ritual life and associations (sometimes referred to in the literature as 'secret societies'), most of them linked to unique forms of art and material culture. There are disagreements in the sources about the political structure in pre-French times. Some indicate that Baga were acephalous, while others seem to suggest that they had chiefs appointed by land-owning descent groups. Probably, the reality was an oscillation between these two modes of political organisation. What seems clear from oral history and regional comparison is that the prevailing system was based on what I call here an asymmetric settlement pattern, according to which groups of putative 'first arrival' (although this is a manipulable category) accumulated more land, people and power than those considered 'late arrivals'. Whatever the case, since 1886, Baga were ruled by a chief appointed by the French, sometimes referred to in colonial sources as the 'Baga king'. In 1922 the French created a 'Canton Baga' and until 1958 they continued to appoint elders to be 'traditional' or 'customary' chiefs of the canton.

The institution of traditional chieftaincy as promoted by French administrators soon became tyrannical. It reified notions of gerontocracy, patriarchy and ethnic territory that most likely had had a long history in the Upper Guinea Coast, but that had probably never been as rigidly applied as it came to be in colonial times, when it was sanctioned and enforced by French laws and officers. Under this regime, youths had to work hard at 'customary' celebrations of marriages, funerals, initiations as well as visitations of chiefs and colonial officials. For youths, Baga 'custom' became increasingly oppressive: not only were they to tap massive amounts of palm wine for all the celebrations but they were also subject to forced labour, 'rice campaigns' and other abuses that were channelled through the customary chieftaincy and therefore perceived – and today remembered – as part of 'Baga custom'. Under French rule Baga were enclosed upon themselves in their Canton Baga, which effectively worked both as a magnifying lens and as a fence: it amplified the local reality and avoided the entrance of other forces, particularly those of Islam, which since the early twentieth century had become a strong alternative voice in many other Guinean cantons. Traditional rituals legitimating the status quo in which chiefs and their relatives would enrich themselves and oppress the youths were clearly protected by the French colonialists, who were particularly worried about the anti-colonial content of some varieties of Islam. Interestingly, among Baga Sitem, Christianity became an unexpected ally of 'tradition'. Many landowning elders converted to Christianity in order to articulate an opposition to Islam, the strongest critical voice against tradition, palm-wine drinking, secret cults and unfair chiefs to be heard in the colonies.

After the Second World War, a refreshing wind was felt all around French West Africa. From 1946, the anti-colonial movement *Rassemblement Démocratique Africain* (RDA) fought for the full citizenship of Africans, as promised by De Gaulle at the Conference of Brazzaville (1944). Although at its beginning the RDA had links with European left-wing parties, in some parts of West Africa it eventually found that Islam was a secure medium to propagate the anti-colonial messages (Morgenthau 1964: 237). In much of West Africa, Islam became a strong agent in the modernising and opening-up of villages. Its followers proclaimed the establishment of a community based on universal values and denounced unfair chieftaincies as well as all those 'customs' that were keeping Africa backward: alcohol, masks, ritual elders and secret societies. Since the early 1950s, committees of the RDA were, in every Guinean village, a parallel and antagonistic institution to the increasingly obsolete 'customary chieftaincy' endorsed by – and in the Baga instance created by – the French.

Into this volatile situation, at the very end of French rule, appeared the iconoclastic *jihadi*st figure of Asekou Sayon (1956). Sayon marked the junction between two eras in Baga history, and he is remembered as a real agent of transformation, almost like a 'trickster' figure, as Charles Jedrej kindly pointed out to me. Sayon was a Muslim converter, a witch-finder, a 'fetish' destroyer, an RDA sympathiser, a dissatisfied people's leader (see Sarró 1999a for a whole description of this truly fascinating person). Almost immediately following the work of the *jihadi*st, President Sékou Touré deployed the state in a forceful campaign to establish the reality of a modern Guinean nation and identity, and to ban regional forms of either ethnic or religious identity (it was only possible to be Guinean and Muslim; local forms of Christianity were also accepted, but not so Western priests).

For all that, the deeds of Sayon, which overlapped with Sékou Touré's policies, are recalled today as a turning point in the history of the Baga. His movement was a complex one in which there were religious, political and other agenda at play. It was 'destructive' in that it did represent the end of some rituals and of the religious identity linked to them. The places where sacred bushes previously existed were now to harbour Muslim mosques, modern schools or plantations. You may object that I am not talking about destroying cathedrals but rather about building them, and certainly Sayon's movement could be analysed as part of the creation of a public Guinean space, much as Dozon, in a fine study on religion and politics, analysed the role that Harrist churches played in the making of the nation state in Côte d'Ivoire (Dozon 1995). There would be sound reasons to take such an angle, but in this chapter I want to concentrate instead on the destruction of the alleged 'Baga religious culture' and not on the making of this Guinean public space attempted by the RDA, Islam and the logics of modern state building.

In order to do so, I will build a narrative around one single 'thing': *amanco ngopong*. In colonial times, *amanco ngopong* was the most important spiritual agency in the Baga lived-world. Baga elders I interviewed, who had seen the huge *amanco ngopong* for the last time in 1948 or 1952 (when they were young initiates) claimed that *amanco ngopong* could take the form of a twenty-metre high wood-and-raffia construct with a bird-like headdress on its top. This huge construct used to appear in the village every time there was a manhood initiation, that is, every twelve to fifteen years. *Amanco ngopong* was a heavy palm-wine drinker (a clear objectification of anti-Muslim feelings), as well as the regulator of what could be done and said and the articulator of the differences between men and women, between elders and youth, and between the private knowledge only to be discussed in the secluded bush (*afan*) and the public knowledge to be openly discussed in the public sphere (*abanka*).

The Arrival of Sayon: Lessons on How to Sleep

The first Baga Sitem village that Asekou Sayon ever visited was Bukor, then in the *Cercle* of Boffa. It was at the end of July 1956 that the Baga of that village first heard of him, while he was performing *kalimas* (rituals of conversion to Islam and of destruction of evil things) in the village of Yampon, a bit farther south. Because he was a *sayon* ('born after twins') he was supposed to have 'second sight', that is, extra-sensorial abilities, and to detect evil-doers. He was also reported to be teaching some beautiful Sufi songs to the young people. Some Baga youths became very curious about it all. At that time, the youths were at odds with their elders for many reasons, but one of them seemed crucial and is typical of the accounts I gathered: that the elders did not want them to attend the *soirées dansantes* (dancing parties) of the *Jeunesse du Rassemblement Démocratique Africain* (JRDA). Because the elders had also prohibited the *soirées dansantes* of the recently introduced *Jeunesse Agricole Catholique* (an organisation that otherwise was rather antagonistic to the JRDA), the Catholic youths also joined in the rebellious team that wanted Sayon in the village.

Some young people of Bukor, angry at their despotic elders, went to attend the *kalima* at Yampon and invited Sayon to go to Bukor to perform the *kalima* there as well. Sayon agreed to their request and told them that in a few days he would be going to Bukor, provided they brought him enough wood and money. A crucial aspect for us to remember, and to which I shall return, is this. While Asekou Sayon was still in Yampon, one of the elders of Bukor is reported to have exhorted his age mates with these words: 'Asekou Sayon is coming to Bukor. Take care about the way you sleep, so that he finds you in a good sleeping position'. This genre of hidden speech is called *capafo* in Baga Sitem, and by its very nature a *capafo* has different readings. 'Take care about the way you sleep' can be a direct exhortation, since for the Baga it is at night that witches abandon their human bodies and go to celebrate 'cannibalistic' feasts in an invisible realm called *dabal*, which is also the realm of dreams. To find someone literally sleeping in a strange position might denounce his or her evil dreams. But the virtuosity of speaking in *capafo* is that the message conveyed can have different readings, and this one in particular has other meanings, as will be shown.

Asekou Sayon arrived in Bukor in September 1956 surrounded by the young men and women from Yampon singing religious songs. Sayon stayed in Bukor for about one month, performing the *kalima*, converting people to Islam, clearing the sacred bush, cutting down the big silk-cotton trees, destroying whatever non-Muslim objects or products were surrendered to him, inviting evil-doers to confess and acting with violence toward those accused of witchcraft who refused to confess. One of the leading men behind his official invitation and welcome in Bukor was Sheikh Amadou Haidara, the imam of the little mosque of the village. In 1956 the young Sheikh Amadou was not only a well-educated member of the Tijaniyya Sufi brotherhood but also a member of the RDA committee in Bukor. This confluence of religion and politics, although not always as clear as in the case of Sheikh Haidara, should not surprise us. In many ways, such a confluence was the very *zeitgeist* of the late colonial period, at least in that part of French West Africa where the RDA had the upper hand in local politics. I interviewed Haidara in 1994 and again in 2001. In both occasions he explained to me that he had invited Sayon to Bukor because the latter was, like himself, a member of the Tijaniyya and because he (Haidara) was horrified to live among so many *kafir* people.

Most of the discussions I had with my interviewees concerning Asekou Sayon's stay in Bukor inevitably revolved around the issue of whether he had destroyed *amanco ngopong* or not. Some elders recalled the first encounter between them and Sayon in the following anecdotal terms. As soon as Sayon arrived in Bukor, according to them, he asked the population to bring *amanco ngopong* to him. In a rather apologetic manner, someone explained to him that this would not be possible, since *amanco ngopong* was not a 'thing' that could be carried from one place to another, but rather a being with his own will, who came to the village whenever *he* wanted and not whenever *they* wanted. Sayon believed him, and let things go. *Amanco ngopong*, according to this version, still existed in the days I conducted the interviewees.

Yet this is by no means how Sayon himself presented things when I interviewed him in a series of talks in between 1993 and 1994, when he was more than seventy years old, and with a very clear memory. Sayon claimed that the first thing he did in Bukor was to go to the sacred bush and get in and out of it several times. Many observers were astonished because they thought that a non-initiated stranger could not go into the bush and return alive. He then invited the youth of the village to do the same thing and enter the sacred bush ('I always addressed the youths' he said to me at that point). Once such central space had been appropriated by him and his followers, Sayon started his destructive actions, particularly the destruction of *amanco ngopong* and the beating up of the ritual elders responsible for it. Sayon acknowledged that he was after *amanco ngopong*, of which he had heard long before reaching the Baga region, and he also claimed to have destroyed it. According to his description, inside the sacred bush there was a hut surrounded by human skulls and guarded by some very old men with long beards. It was inside this hut that *amanco ngopong*'s head was kept. Sayon gave orders to some of his followers to burn the head. In the village, he entered the ritual houses of different descent groups and took out many of their objects, including the rest of *amanco ngopong* (*amanco ngopong* had three parts, once described to me as the 'head', the 'trunk', and the 'feet', and each one of them was kept by a different descent group and therefore in a different ritual house). 'When I did that', Sayon recalled with a tone of victory, 'people said that the *Baga fe* [in Susu: 'Baga things', sometimes glossed as 'Baga culture'] were finished'.

It is worth emphasising this identification implicit in Sayon's words between *amanco ngopong* and 'Baganess'. Asekou Sayon clearly stated that he destroyed the 'Baga things' by materially destroying *amanco ngopong*. This identification was one of the few things on which Sayon's and Baga accounts agreed. Yet Baga interviewees most strongly sustained the opposite view: that Sayon could not have destroyed *amanco ngopong* and that he certainly did not. In fact, Sayon frankly acknowledged to me that the head of *amanco ngopong* was not burnt by him personally, but by his followers, who afterwards showed the ashes to him. But those were the ashes of what? Sayon seemed convinced enough that his followers were faithful to him and that he had persuaded them into his particular way of seeing things. But, as became apparent in my interviews with them, many of the youngsters who followed him back in 1956 did so reluctantly and with fear. On the one hand, they were eager for a change and for getting rid of sorcery, elders' abuses, tyrannical chiefs and many other things, but on the other hand they could not give up believing in the power of such spirits as *amanco ngopong*. This makes the historian's task difficult. More than a clear picture, we have an event and competing, even contradictory interpretations – a 'rashomonian' situation probably as complex as what really happened. In any case, what is clear to me is that reading the iconoclastic movement as a simple 'destruction' and conversion is simplistic. Underneath this stereotyped narrative, there lies a multilayered interplay between concealment and disclosure not easy to grasp. I shall try to unearth it, so let me return to Sayon's arrival.

The Events Revisited: Further Lessons on How to Sleep

We have already seen that while Sayon was in Yampon, an old man from Bukor exhorted his age fellows: 'Asekou Sayon will come to Bukor, take care about the way you sleep, so that he finds you in a good sleeping position'. The first time I was told this *capafo* my understanding of it was rather literal, as an invitation to abandon certain practices and beliefs. Yet, the *capafo* has other readings; an alternative interpretation was given to me by the very person who had told it in the first place, but one year later. According to him, what the old man had meant was that the Baga elders had to pretend to be sleeping while in fact being well awake; in other words, they would have to pretend to follow Sayon while still keeping their secrets. In a neighbouring village where I also conducted interviewees, I had a similar experience. The first time I gathered a narrative about Sayon's actions there, I was told: 'Asekou Sayon did not do any harm to us because he found that we were sitting properly'. In an identical pattern to that of Bukor, I was told that while Sayon was in a previous village, an old man went to spy on him and came back advising people 'to sit properly'. Only months later I was told that 'to sit properly' meant to be prepared not to let Sayon and the youths following him get away with their plans. In yet a third village I obtained an even clearer case of reluctance to follow Sayon. In this village, the head of the *Jeunesse Agricole Catholique* wrote a letter to the Catholic missionaries in September 1956 asking them to go to the French authorities so that Sayon's entrance to the Canton Baga would be forbidden. However, the French authorities did not do anything about it, and Asekou Sayon entered the Canton Baga and in six months he reached the village at stake. But six months is a long time to 'learn how to sit', if I may use the Baga *capafo* I just quoted. As it happens, the head of the JAC was also a member of the descent group who were in charge of *abol*, a female spirit sometimes described as '*amanco ngopong*'s wife'. Sayon, who knew it, immediately asked them to surrender *abol*. They accepted, but instead of giving him *abol*, they gave an ordinary piece of wood, slightly similar in shape to the real thing. Sayon and his followers happily burnt the object, probably thinking they were, once again, destroying the *Baga fe* when in fact they were just burning a piece of wood. Two questions may come to mind. First, what happened to the real *abol*, the one Sayon did *not* burn? Second, why did other people not reveal that someone was fooling Sayon?

The answer to the first question is that the real *abol*, like so many other objects that Sayon did not take away, was probably put somewhere safe. The answer to the second question is twofold. On the one hand, I think that many of Sayon's followers did not reveal the sheikh was being fooled because they were afraid of later punishments.[5] On the other hand, I think that many of them, being mostly youngsters, women and strangers, were probably as unaware of what the real *abol* looked like as Sayon himself.

* * *

Today, many people say that Sayon put an end to Baga culture and/or religion, and that it is a tragedy that a whole people decides to abandon their initiations and to live unaware of its tradition. Different degrees of this 'afro-pessimism' are found in scholarly views as well as among Baga people. My slightly more optimistic contention, however, is that what happened among the Baga was a translation from a visible religion with conspicuous icons in the public landscape ('masks', headdresses, objects, sacred bushes, silk-cotton trees, and so on) to the concealment of all non-Muslim or Christian religious elements. To put it in Baga words: Sayon could destroy the objects, but not the words you need to make the objects work, since the latter come out of people's bellies, and Sayon did not open them. According to the *alipne* of Bukor, the only reason why today there are no masquerades and objects in the public sphere is not because Sayon destroyed them, but because they (the *alipne*) do not allow it. Anybody who would want to go back to pre-iconoclastic public religion would be punished by them – or directly by *amanco ngopong*. According to this view, iconoclasm was one effective way to 'eat their secrets'. However, not even the *alipne* have a strict control on what people know or construct about their past, embedded as it is in the very world Baga live and talk about. Thus, in one Baga village where I conducted field research, one of the trees cut down by the iconoclastic youths was a silk-cotton tree that is still there, lying down yet not rotten, and from which nobody dares take wood; likewise, in this and other villages I noticed that even young non-initiated people knew very well that some stones, even if they were located near churches or mosques, had in the past a strong importance in the celebration of *amanco ngopong* masquerades and therefore they reacted with awe towards them. My friend Lamin (thirty-five years old in 1994), once told me that he had never seen *amanco ngopong*, but that some time ago the elders of the descent group had taken him on a tour around the village and neighbouring regions, and explained to him the meanings of each tree and of each rock and their relationship to *amanco ngopong*. But such 'explaining' is not always necessary. As someone else once put it, quite in an Austinian way, it is not what elders explained about *amanco ngopong* that made you feel fear, but the very way they pronounced the word *amanco ngopong*, a way that, he clarified, made you *not* want to know any more. And he added: 'it is like the chameleon: you say that it is not a dangerous animal and that we could touch it without any harm, but we do not want to waste our time verifying whether this is true or false; we hear the word "chameleon" pronounced by anyone and we simply avoid the place where the animal has been spotted'.

Today, then, Baga people no longer have initiations into manhood, but this does not mean a lack of transmission of knowledge. To start with, I think that to see initiation as a transmission of encyclopaedic knowledge and initiatory bushes as 'libraries' or as 'bush schools' is problematic, no matter how much these metaphors are used in African studies. Initiation is not a process of learning and storing information, but an experience.[6] Likewise, the iconoclastic rebellion was more a collective experience than a change in the cosmological premises. An experience that, today, opens a generational gap between those who went through it and those who did not. The destruction of the objects did not represent the end of any form of knowledge. Baga people today 'know' as much about *amanco ngopong* as Baga of the past. In fact, *amanco ngopong* seems to be equally powerful now that it has no physical support as it was in the days when it was – so they recall – represented by a twenty metre high headdress.

In 1957, Baga abandoned their 'animism'. However, in the mid-1990s and early 2000s *amanco ngopong* was still an object of constant fear, both to elders and to youths. You only had to live in a Baga Sitem village for a short time to realise that *amanco ngopong* lay behind an otherwise strictly Muslim or Christian religious landscape. But it was not really 'religion' that provided me with the evidence for this tenacity of a religious representation, it was a rather more 'profane' activity, namely, football.

Football, Carnivals and the Generation Game

Many things have happened in the Baga Sitem region since 1957. Amongst them, let us single out the creation of Kamsar (a mining port born in 1973, with more than 30,000 inhabitants today), the readmission of Catholic missionaries since 1984 (they had been expelled from Guinea in 1967), and the subsequent creation, linked to them, of football tournaments among the Baga villages.

The football tournaments were started in 1989 by the Catholic youths. Very much like Catholicism, football may appear as a globalising practice and discourse, and indeed it is so, but, very much like Catholicism too, it also has a Protean tendency towards 'inculturating' itself and collaborating in the everyday production of locality. Due to its own playful structure, the football tournaments generate territorial boundaries much stronger than vague notions of ethnicity or history.

Elsewhere I have discussed and analysed the history of these tournaments (Sarró 1999b). Suffice to recall here that at the beginning they were just a 'playful' activity that youngsters did far away from the elders. Accordingly, elders did not become too interested in it. However, as football became more and more important for the development of villages, for the image of the Baga in the Guinean state, and so on, the elders started to appropriate it. Little by little, football abandoned its aspect of 'game' to become something much more 'serious'. In doing so, the life story of the football tournament reminded us of the life story of some Baga cults. Indeed, in the past Baga used to distinguish between masks and objects called *powolsene* (lit. 'toys' or 'games') from those considered as *tolom*. Some cults I know of started as *powolsene*, simple things children played with, until the elders realised their power and, fearful of their children's agency, stole the 'toys' from them. In other cases the opposite was the case, and cults that belonged to elders were copied by children. Either way, the fact is that many a Baga mask or headdress had two distinct versions: one for adults (*tolom*) and one for children (*powolsene*). One of the cults I know of which was transformed from children's *powolsene* to adults' *tolom* was *tonkure*, a cult invented by the male children of Mare around 1945 and then taken to Bukor, where the male elders 'stole' it, although later it returned to the youths and, in fact, empowered them. The youths who had the *tonkure* in the 1940s and 1950s eventually became the respected *alipne* of today, constituting a council in charge of ritual activities and behind most political decision-making.

And it was Bukor, the very village we have already visited and revisited in this chapter, that had to host the annual football tournament in 1995. This particular tournament was prepared in a climate of fear. Not all the events surrounding it were 'playful'. Some of them were actually very tragic. In the previous year the tournament had taken place in Mare. That year (1994), a young boy who was observing one match fell from a tree and died. This death was said to be a sacrifice to *amanco ngopong* made by the people of Bukor in order to win the cup. The fact that subsequently Bukor *did* win the cup against all predictions reinforced this gossip about their witchcraft. Since Bukor was to organise the next tournament (1995) all these rumours had to be taken very seriously by the inhabitants of Bukor.

People from other villages were afraid of going to Bukor because of witchcraft actions and sacrifices to *amanco ngopong*, whose presence in Bukor is said to be stronger than in other villages anyway. Some young people from

Mare and other villages told me that they would not go to the tournament. 'People in Bukor do not understand that football is just a game', someone told me. People from Bukor had to take action against this predicament (the point of the tournament being of course to gather as many people as possible and not to scare them away).

To bypass the problem, Bukor *ressortissants* in Conakry[7] decided that in order not to let witchcraft attacks happen during the three weeks that the tournament normally lasts, they would let the *alipne* or council of initiated elders take care of the situation. The *alipne*, accordingly, performed the series of rituals known as 'the closing of the land'. These are very solemn actions that are very rarely performed and that theoretically make it impossible for people to die from witchcraft attacks. In the days when there were long initiation rituals, the closing of the land was linked to them and to the appearance in the village of *amanco ngopong* (*amanco ngopong* could only appear on a closed land). To my knowledge, the last time the land was closed was also in Bukor, in 1986, when a solemn sacrifice to *amanco ngopong* was made in the village to bless the *ressortissants* of Conakry. The closing of the land for the 1995 tournament had nothing to do with *amanco ngopong*, but rather with prevention of witchcraft during the tournament, but of course the association between the two elements (that is, this ritual and *amanco ngopong*) was in the minds of all Baga people. And the fact that the *alipne* of Bukor dared close the land in order to hold the football tournament did indeed frighten many people. The outcome was that some villages did not allow their children to compete in such a dangerous village. This may seem a bit contradictory, since such a closing of the land is nothing 'bad' in itself, but we have to take into account that the elders of these other villages were afraid that their 'irresponsible' kids would not know the importance of a closing of the land and they would not respect it, having to 'pay' deadly consequences later. When a village is ritually 'closed', for instance, unmarried people are not allowed to have sex, nor can any married person have illicit adventures. Yet, sex is obviously part of the fun youths search for on such occasions as a football tournament.

It was also decided that the *alipne* should be in charge of the preparation of the carnival, so that the outcome would be better than the poorly prepared *nimba* performance of the previous year in Mare. This year it had to be done properly. When the opening day arrived, there were a few dances and two masks: *nimba* and *saebondel*, which were danced under the direct control of the *alipne* and, as many people interpreted, 'in the old way'. But for the *ressortissants* of Conakry, these two masks were not enough. I remember talking to a few of them before the tournament took place. They insisted on the inclusion in their carnival of the old initiation dance (*kaekenc*), which had not been performed in the village since the early fifties. They sent a special commission to Bukor to discuss the issue with the *alipne*, who at first did not show an open opposition to the idea, and people in Conakry were very excited about it. I was somewhat hastily told by one of them that a group of young people had already been chosen by the *alipne* in order to be taught how to dance the *kaekenc*. But then, as the tournament approached, the *alipne* refused to teach the youths the secret *kaekenc*. They said that football is just a game and that in consequence only games can be played: *nimba* and *saebondel*, two headdresses that beyond any doubt fall into the category of *powolsene* and not to that of *tolom*. But even these toys had to be danced according to their strict directions. Despite the lack of the *kaekenc*, the outcome was a success of which the Baga of Bukor felt very proud, with the visit of the first lady of Guinea (the wife of President Conté, a Baga herself) and National TV coverage into the bargain.

Towards an End (or Maybe Not)

Where does religious transmission take place? We have seen in this paper that the religious field of the Baga and the institutional differences attached to it are built through an interplay between religiously 'marginal' activities (Islam and youth movements in the 1950s; football and carnivals in the 1990s) and a religious centre (cults in colonial days, Islam and Christianity today). Today, even if there are no longer initiations and therefore Baga no longer 'eat' their secrets, the fact remains that whenever they deem it necessary, they are quite able to perform rituals that had remained concealed for a relatively long time. By converting to world religions such as Islam and Christianity, they have created a religious landscape that, contrary to what a foreigner might think, conceals a rich activity of non-Muslim or Christian religious activity. Although interviewees often told me that the iconoclasts destroyed the religious landscape of the past because it was too 'pagan', my contention is rather that the main legacy of the iconoclastic movement was not an abandonment of Baga religious culture, but an increase of its secrecy and ambiguity and therefore of its manageability. In fact, one of the most difficult things to assess about Baga perceptions of their history is the degree to which they believe past activities and beliefs have been 'lost'. In my research I was always confronted with two parallel and antagonistic discourses: one according to which Sayon 'destroyed' Baga things (*e na leser mes mabaka*), and another one which claimed that he did not do any harm at all and that the *dabaka* (lit. 'Baga country') is still there (*dabaka deyi de*). Sometimes the same interviewee could say one thing first and the opposite one only a few minutes later. In general, elders who lived through the 1956 episodes tended to blame Sayon for having destroyed (*kileser*) Baga things in their first interviews. Yet many of them, in subsequent interviews, would reveal that in fact Sayon did not do that much harm, and that the Baga things, including many of the ritual objects, are still there, somewhere, well hidden and looked after. The youths I interviewed, on the contrary, and no matter how strongly they could also believe that the *dabaka* is somehow still there, blamed their elders for not passing it down to them: as we have seen, they admitted being 'Susu' and not Baga, but precisely by subscribing to this divide, as they already did in the 1950s, the youths were participating in the construction of this religious field in which secrecy and the management of ambiguity play such fundamental roles. I shall not be too surprised if one day I learn that my younger friends in the *dabaka* realise that they too are becoming Baga, and if I hear them contemptuously claiming that *their* children are 'Susu'.

Notes

1. This paper is a thoroughly revised version of an earlier one published in Spanish in Joan Bestard (ed.). 2002. *Identidades, relaciones y contextos*, pp 71–91. I thank Joan Bestard for giving permission to reuse here part of the material published in his edited volume.
2. I am grateful to Maurice Bloch for having made a comment in this direction when I gave this paper at the Halle Conference (April 2003). In a previous article I discussed the fact that the semantics of the words 'Baga' and '*wubaka*' (the word for 'Baga' in Baga Sitem language) do not quite match (Sarró, in press). Very often, the word we use to designate ethnic groups and to classify them is seen very differently if looked at 'from inside', as Richard Fardon cogently argued in reference to the Chamba of Cameroon (Fardon 1988).
3. Asekou is a transformation of Seku, the Mande equivalent of Sheikh (Muslim spiritual leader). 'Sayon' is the name given to any male or female individual born after twins. In most West African societies such a person is supposed to have 'second sight' and other mystical powers. Keira is a common Malinké family name.
4. See, for instance, Bloch (1998). The multiple ways cultural transmission is achieved beyond formal models of transmission and learning has recently been explored in areas very close to the Baga by two fine ethnographies on the Mende and the Temne of Sierra Leone (see, respectively, Ferme 2002 and Shaw 2002).
5. I was told there have been many punishments or revenge actions against those who followed Sayon and revealed to him where the sacred objects were located. Many of those who 'betrayed tradition', as my interlocutors put it, died afterwards in mysterious circumstances, while others had to leave the Baga Sitem villages and migrate elsewhere in order to avoid the punishments.
6. The distinction between doctrinal modes of religiosity based on semantic memory and iconic modes based on experience and episodic memory of traumatic events is central to the powerful theory of 'divergent modes of religiosity' proposed by Harvey Whitehouse and his followers (Whitehouse 2000). Whitehouse is well aware of formulating a difference that had been noticed by other scholars – although never as fruitfully and never as well knitted with scientific theories of memory and of transmission. Maybe one could place, in the genealogy of the 'DMR theory', no less than Aristotle, who in one of his apocryphal comments stated that the neophytes into Greek mystery cults suffered a transformation in their pathein (experiencing), but not in their *mathein* (thinking, learning) (Munz 1959: 67–68; Burkert 1987: 89–114).
7. *Ressortissants* are the natives of a village who live in a big city (mostly the capital, Conakry); they are quite instrumental as intermediaries between the village and the State.

References

Bellman, Beryl L. 1984. *The Language of Secrecy: Symbols and Metaphors in Poro Ritual*. New Brunswick, NJ: Rutgers University Press.

Berliner, David. 2002. 'Nous sommes les derniers Bulongic: sur une impossible transmission dans une société de l'Afrique de l'Ouest', Ph.D. thesis. Brussels: Free University of Brussels.

Bestard, Joan (ed.). 2002. *Identidades, relaciones y contextos*. Barcelona: Servei de Publicacions de la Universita.

Bloch, Maurice. 1998. *How We Think They Think: Anthropological Approaches to Cognition, Memory, and Literacy*. Colorado: Westview Press.

Boyer, Pascal. 1986. 'The "Empty" Concepts of Traditional Thinking: A Semantic and Pragmatic Description', *Man (N.S.)* 21(1): 50–64.

Burkert, Walter. 1987. *Ancient Mystery Cults*. Cambridge, Mass.: Harvard University Press.

Curtis, Marie Yvonne. 1996. 'L'art nalu, l'art baga de Guinée: approches comparatives', PhD thesis. Paris: Université de Paris I (Pantheon-Sorbonne).

Curtis, Marie Yvonne and Ramon Sarró. 1997. 'The Nimba Headdress: Art, Ritual and History of the Baga and Nalu Peoples of Guinea', *Museum Studies (Chicago)* 23(2): 121–33.

Dozon, Jean-Pierre. 1995. *La cause des prophètes: politique et religion en Afrique contemporaine*. Paris: Seuil.

Fardon, Richard. 1988. *Raiders and Refugees: Trends in Chamba Political Development, 1750 to 1950*. Washington: Smithsonian Institution Press.

Ferme, Marianne. 2002. *The Underneath of Things: Violence, History and the Everyday in Sierra Leone*. Berkeley: University of California Press.

Griaule, Marcel. 1938. *Jeux dogons*. Paris: Institut d'Etnologie.

Lamp, Frederick. 1996. *Art of the Baga: A Drama of Cultural Reinvention*. New York: Museum for African Art and Prestel Verlag.

Morgenthau, Ruth S. 1964. *Political Parties in French-speaking West Africa*. Oxford: Clarendon Press.

Munz, Peter. 1959. *Problems of Religious Knowledge*. London: SCM Press.

Paulme, Denise. 1956. 'Structures sociales en pays baga', *Bulletin de l'I.F.A.N.* 18(1–2): 98–116 (série B).

———. 1957. 'Des riziculteurs africains: les Baga', *Cahiers d'Outre-Mer* 10: 257–78.

———. 1958. 'La notion de sorcier chez les Baga'. *Bulletin de l'I.F.A.N.* 20(3–4): 406–16 (série B).

Sarró, Ramon. 1999a. 'Baga Identity: Religious Movements and Political Transformation in the Republic of Guinea', PhD thesis. London: University College London.

———. 1999b. 'Football et mobilisation identitaire en Guinée: la 'reinvention de la tradition' des jeunes bagas', *Politique Africaine* 74: 153–61.

———. (in press). 'The Throat and the Belly: Baga Notions of Morality and Personhood', *JASO (Journal of the Anthropological Society of Oxford)* 31(2).

Schaeffner, André. 1962. 'Musique et structures sociales', *Revue Française de Sociologie* (2nd year) 4: 388–95.

———. 1964. 'Musiques rituelles Baga', (6è) *Congrès International de Sciences Anthropologiques et Ethnologiques* 2: 123–25.

Shaw, Rosalind. 2002. *Memories of the Slave Trade: Ritual and the Historical Imagination in Sierra Leone*. Chicago: University of Chicago Press.

Whitehouse, Harvey. 2000. *Icons and Arguments: Divergent Modes of Religiosity*. Oxford: Oxford University Press.

Chapter 12

Geomancy, Politics and Colonial Encounters in Rural Hong Kong

Rubie S. Watson and James L. Watson[1]

During the last forty years, Hong Kong's rural hinterland has been transformed from a patchwork of green hills punctuated by fertile valleys into a hodgepodge of new, purpose-built cities complete with forty-storey apartment blocks. Many old villages dating to the 1600s are now surrounded by four-lane highways and train lines, by huge drainage canals, by fields that have been converted into storage depots and by massive housing estates. In a single generation, a once intimate, agrarian landscape has been transformed beyond recognition. In this paper we explore how a cosmology that Hong Kong people call *fengshui* (literally 'wind and water') informs local understandings of the environment. Specifically, we discuss the changing relationship between *fengshui* (or geomancy) practices and local politics from 1898, when Great Britain assumed control of the New Territories, until 1997, when sovereignty was transferred to the People's Republic of China.

Chinese geomancy encompasses a set of cosmological principles that manifest themselves in ideas regarding the flow of wind and water – of vital energy or *qi* – in the environment. It is the job of the geomancer[2] to place temples, houses, graves and villages in a positive relationship to this flow so that individuals, families and whole communities can benefit. There is good *fengshui* and bad *fengshui* – bringing fortune or disaster, depending on environmental circumstances. Buddhists, Daoists, Christians, atheists and followers of local gods all may observe the tenants of *fengshui*.[3] Among the people of Hong Kong's New Territories geomancy is deeply intertwined with the ancestor cult and can be considered integral to many local religious practices.[4] Geomancy not only allows humans to comprehend and take advantage of the forces of nature that surround them but also guides the creation and maintenance of landscapes. During the period under discussion here, a discourse of *fengshui* emphasised respect for the status quo – for the old ways and for those who believed that they embodied those ways. We also argue that *fengshui* facilitated interactions between colonial officials – agents of the British Crown Colony of Hong Kong – and New Territories' villagers until the 1980s.

Chinese Geomancy has been called a religion, a cosmological system, a feudal superstition, a form of divination and proto-environmentalism. The anthropologist Maurice Freedman, who studied *fengshui* in Hong Kong's New Territories in the 1960s, argued that geomancy is an amoral system founded on esoteric knowledge and complex techniques (1966). If knowledge and technique are sufficiently developed, he argued, benefits would follow as light follows darkness. In Freedman's view, *fengshui* is neither science nor religion but rather offers a mode of explanation resting upon a certain understanding of the cosmic order.[5]

Although geomancy can be found in some form among Han people almost everywhere in China, Chinese states from imperial times to the present have often been hostile to its popular practice.[6] Chinese geomancy, we argue, is highly localised, and we agree with Brun that disputes involving *fengshui* can and often do give voice to anti-authoritarian views. While this by no means explains everything we may want to know about Chinese geomancy, there is no doubt that a link between *fengshui* and anti-government protests exists and deserves attention (Brun 2003: 256, 259; see also Cheung 2001).

As Escobar (2001) had argued, the rise of global studies had led to a marked tendency to ignore or deny the salience of *place*. In this paper, we examine processes by which people make places for themselves – how landscapes are created and, once constructed, how they are protected in the face of radically altered political circumstances. We also endeavour to show why place and place-making deserve renewed attention (see also Bender 1993; Feld and Basso 1996; Casey 1997; Gupta and Ferguson 1997; Dirlik 2001; Feuchtwang 2004; cf. Appadurai 1996: 139–99). During the past two decades, there has been much insightful research on the conditions of 'placelessness' created by migration, diaspora formation and the collapse of time and space – the foundations of postmodernity. Here, we discuss the dramatic transformation of a place – a landscape – as well as the erosion of a form of geomancy that once guided, produced and articulated local understandings and appreciations of that place.

Geomancy, which guides the process by which spaces become places and environments become landscapes, is deeply implicated in the ongoing processes by which people constitute themselves as communities, neighbourhoods and localities. Geomancy offers a powerful and intimate form of local knowledge that arms its practitioners with the ability not only to diagnose a *fengshui wenti* (a geomancy problem) but also to overcome it – to change or modify what had been changed. A family that suffers economic loss might suspect that their good *fengshui* has been altered; perhaps someone has built in front of their grandfather's grave or a stream has been blocked near their home. A geomancer can confirm their diagnosis (or provide another) and offer a solution – move their grandfather's grave or redirect the stream so that wind and water can be propitiously reoriented. In Hong Kong's New Territories, each generation was responsible for understanding wind and water in order to safeguard family prosperity and health. Of course, Hong Kong's places were always changing – environmental transformation did not begin in the 1970s – and geomancy was always both active (emplacing) as well as reactive (countering the effects of emplacement), and was, therefore, part of the process by which people's attachment to place – locating themselves in the landscape – was created and re-created. Geomancy was a cornerstone of the practice of local geography.

The location of ancestral tombs was of utmost importance. Like many others in southeastern China, New Territories people practiced secondary burial.[7] After death, the deceased was interred in a simple, unmarked grave. On an auspicious day chosen by a geomancer (sometimes years after the initial burial), descendants retrieved and cleaned the bones of their ancestor. The bones were then re-arranged, placed in a pottery urn (or *jin ta*), a geomancer was hired to find a good *fengshui* site and a tomb was secured.[8] It is generally believed that descendants and ancestors interact through the medium of *fengshui* – thus connecting the living not only to the dead but also to sources of cosmic power (see, for example, Potter 1968, 1970; J. Watson 1982; for Taiwan see Ahern 1973: 175–90). Ancestral bones are thought to channel the generative forces of wind and water to male descendants through the medium of sacrificial pigs, which are offered at annual tomb rites. Major lineages staged (and some continue to stage) elaborate rituals at their founders' tombs, involving hundreds, even thousands, of descendants (see R. Watson 1988; J. Watson 2004).

Lineages claimed territory by burying their ancestors in new lands and, on occasion, in locales once held by rival kinship groups. '*Fengshui* towers', brick walls, trees, ponds or buildings may enhance or redirect the positive flow of wind and water – occasionally at the expense of neighbouring households or villages. The placement of ancestors within the landscape carried serious consequences for one's own well being and for one's descendants.

Geomancy and Colonialism

During the colonial era, New Territories people pulled government officials into a special dialogue based on geomancy. It was a dialogue, we argue, that recognised and at times reinforced certain entrenched privileges. Discussions based on geomancy both obscured and exposed the fault lines of a colonial relationship forged at the beginning of the twentieth century, when agrarian elites (wealthy members of powerful patrilineages) dominated the New Territories. Eventually, this dialogue was overwhelmed by economic and environmental changes as well as by new forms of colonial governance, although it was never completely silenced.

The ethnographic research upon which this paper is based was carried out in two villages located in Yuen Long District, northwest New Territories. We draw most heavily on work carried out in Ha Tsuen, a single-patrilineage village inhabited by descendants of a twelfth century pioneer surnamed Deng (all males born into this lineage community are surnamed Deng).[9] We lived in Ha Tsuen for fifteen months in 1977–1978 and have returned to the community on many occasions during the past twenty-nine years. Another single-patrilineage village, San Tin, also informs this essay (most of the people in that settlement are surnamed Man, Wen in Mandarin).[10] We lived in San Tin for seventeen months in 1969–1970 and have revisited the community periodically since the late-1970s.

Ha Tsuen and San Tin fell under British colonial control in 1898 when the Qing (Manchu) government in Beijing signed a 99-year lease granting the British Crown extraterritorial rights over a 365 square-mile section of Xin'an County in southern Guangdong Province. First called 'the new territory', this area was later renamed the New Territories. The local colonial administration was a unique, specialised bureaucracy devised to rule this small section of Chinese territory. Until 1997, when Hong Kong returned to Beijing rule, local government consisted of a colonial administration managed though a District Office. During most of the colonial period, Ha Tsuen and San Tin fell under the administrative control of the Yuen Long District Office. Villagers treated the local District Officer (D.O.) and his Cantonese-speaking staff as the face of government, and village politics were played out with the District Office firmly in mind.

In 1984, to the dismay and alarm of many in the New Territories, an accord between the Chinese and British governments was announced. The accord stated in clear terms that the New Territories (in fact, the entire colony of Hong Kong) would revert to Chinese control in mid-1997. During the 1980s the pace of political change quickened, new political institutions were created, the colonial administration changed form, and massive infrastructure and housing projects were implemented, one of the largest near the village of Ha Tsuen. When we first arrived in the New Territories, District Officers were young men from England and Scotland, often fresh out of Oxford or Cambridge, with degrees in classics or history. By the 1990s, District Officers were young Chinese graduates of Hong Kong University, with special training in public administration. During the run-up to Beijing control, new construction projects transformed the landscape of the New Territories. These projects had a profound impact not only on the place-based administrative apparatus and politics of the New Territories but also on the hills, streams, valleys, bays, temples, graves and villages that guided the flow of wind and water and, for centuries, had grounded the villagers of Ha Tsuen and San Tin in a landscape that sustained the local economy, gave a physicality to their history and connected them to their ancestors.

Colonialism, Quasi-Colonialism and Postcolonialism in Hong Kong

The people of the New Territories have experienced many forms of colonialism during the past 800 years. According to their own accounts, ancestors of New Territories people fled Jiangxi Province – 500 miles north of Hong Kong – just prior to and during the turmoil of the Mongol invasions (thirteenth century). Settling in the Pearl River Delta, they formed communities such as Ha Tsuen and San Tin that still exist today. In the seventeenth century, Han-Chinese rulers of the Ming dynasty (who had overthrown the Mongols in 1368) were themselves replaced by yet another foreign regime – Manchu overlords who ruled from 1644 to 1911. Manchu (Qing) rule ended early for the people of Ha Tsuen and San Tin when the New Territories was leased to the British in 1898.[11] British colonial rule was interrupted by a Japanese military occupation that lasted from 1941 to 1945, when Hong Kong returned to British colonial status. During the Cold War, Hong Kong was perched on the front line between capitalism and socialism; in many respects it was akin to Berlin. In 1997 Hong Kong and the New Territories reverted to China, and the people of the New Territories found themselves subject to yet another outsider regime. The Cantonese-speaking administrators of Hong Kong now 'watch the faces' of Mandarin-speaking Communist Party leaders in Beijing.

During the tenure of these colonial and quasi-colonial regimes, the residents of the New Territories have survived, and in many cases prospered (see, for example, Baker 1968; Potter 1968; J. Watson 1975, 2004; R. Watson 1985). In 1898 the designation *bendiren* (literally 'of the earth', perhaps best translated as 'local') became a protected category that conferred special privileges. Since 1997, the terminology used to describe this group has become a point of contention as post-colonial identities are reformulated. Space, the environment, place and geomancy provide arenas within which the battles over 'indigenous' rights have taken shape. In this paper, New Territories residents who trace descent to pre-1898 villagers are referred to as *indigenes* – a term that emphasises their 'local', historically grounded origins.

Britain Leases the New Territories

On 9 June 1898 in Beijing, Sir Claude MacDonald and Li Hung-chang signed the Convention Respecting an Extension of the Hong Kong Territory marking the Qing government's agreement to lease a part of Xin'an County to Great Britain for a period of ninety-nine years (see Wesley-Smith 1980: 1–3). This was one of a series of unequal treaties forced upon China in the aftermath of the Sino-Japanese War and the ensuing scramble for Chinese territory by Russia, Japan, Germany, France and Great Britain. Colonial officials and Hong Kong merchants (British and Chinese alike) had successfully argued for a buffer between Hong Kong Island, where government and business were conducted, and China, where Qing law was often conspicuous by its absence (Wesley-Smith 1980: 11–17). This buffer zone became the New Territories.

At first, the transition to British rule seemed to go smoothly, but as the handover date drew near tensions became apparent. During the Spring of 1899, British authorities were confronted by angry villagers protesting the disturbance of their 'wind and water'. On 3 April 1899, Captain F.H. May, with a small contingent of Sikh policemen and soldiers, tried to relieve two Indian constables who were erecting a temporary police station near the market of Tai Po. Nearby villagers were incensed and claimed that the station blocked the efficacious flow of geomantic forces to their families and ancestors. Words and bricks were hurled and after an uncomfortable night, as the British retreated to the safety of urban Hong Kong to await further instructions, the temporary station was torched (Wesley-Smith 1980: 59–60).

This was the first of many colonial encounters over 'wind and water'. During the next ninety-nine years, Hong Kong officials were to hear a great deal more about geomancy from rural elites and ordinary villagers alike. Eventually, geomancy became not only a framework for demarcating local interests in opposition to the colonial government but also, ironically, a method for educating colonial officers in the proper appreciation of local traditions. In 1898 the British were practiced colonials with experience not only in South Asia and Africa but also in Hong Kong. In 1842 they had wrested Hong Kong Island from China and in 1860 they added the Kowloon peninsula, thereby securing Hong Kong Harbour. However, the land that they leased in 1898 was different from these possessions. The 'new territory' was populated with long-settled villages and locally powerful elites, who owned sizeable parcels of land. And, of course, southern Xin'an County had been leased rather than ceded. In 1898 the fact that the British were leasors and had to contend with a long and arbitrary border with China contributed to the decisions they made regarding governance. The new regime had to confront and somehow co-opt local elites who were accustomed to taking care of themselves – thriving in a situation that, under the Qing, had been virtually devoid of state authorities.

James Stewart Lockhart was called upon to propose solutions to the problems presented by the new territory. Lockhart, a Scotsman, was not a typical colonial official. His biographer writes that because of his language ability and the small number of cadets in Hong Kong, he received a series of quick promotions after joining the office of the Colonial Secretary in 1882. As Registrar General he took on responsibility in 1887 for liaison with Hong Kong's Chinese merchants – part of his job was to see that British ordinances did not seriously contravene Chinese sensibilities. In 1895 he became Colonial Secretary, the Governor's most senior official, while continuing to hold the post of Registrar General (see Airlie 1989: 34–38). In 1898 the Colonial Office in London asked Stewart Lockhart to survey the leased territory and ascertain how revenues could be raised 'without exciting the suspicions or irritating the feelings and prejudices of the Chinese inhabitants'. In August he toured southern Xin'an County to gather information and explore the terrain. On 8 October 1898 Lockhart presented his report, in which he argued that local organisations should be retained as far as possible and direct British control limited (Wesley-Smith 1980: 46).

Lockhart argued for a degree of separation between the colonial government and the leased territory. Instead, a cost-saving compromise was reached by which the Colonial Secretary of Hong Kong (who happened to be Lockhart) was placed in charge of the Colony as well as the New Territories administration (see Airlie 1989: 97–98). The leased territory, it was decided, would be joined to the existing colonial government and local villagers would be subject to the laws of Hong Kong. There were, however, two important caveats: family affairs (marriage, succession, adoption and inheritance) and matters relating to land would continue to be governed by Chinese custom and Qing law. Section 13 of the New Territory Ordinance stated: 'In any proceedings in the Supreme Court or the District Court in relation to land in the New Territories, the court shall have power to recognize and enforce any Chinese custom or customary right affecting such land' (Wesley-Smith 1980: 91–103; see also Evans 1971).

Four basic principles governed colonial relationships in the leased territory. First, inscribed in the treaty, the British committed to 'no expropriation or expulsion of the inhabitants of the district included within the extension, and that if land is required for public office, fortification, or the like official purposes, it shall be bought at a fair price'. Second, the presiding Governor at the time of the lease, Henry Blake, promised in the New Territory Ordinance of 1900 that the colonial administration would not interfere with the 'usages and good customs' of territory residents. Third, the newly leased territory would be joined administratively and legally to the colony of Hong Kong, except, as noted, with regard to family and land law. And fourth, local (indigenous) organisations were to be utilised whenever possible. The recognition of New Territories residents (indigenes) as a special category different from the general population of Hong Kong was implied in these principles (see below), which were not without contradictions, although Hong Kong officials and the territory's residents learned to work around and within them.

Although the British took formal possession of the leased territory on 1 July 1898, they did not assume full control until the spring of 1899. They knew little about the territory and deemed it prudent to wait for Lockhart's report. Colonial officials also needed time to lay plans to survey and register land holdings and make decisions about boundary demarcation, customs and Chinese jurisdiction in Kowloon's Walled City (Wesley-Smith 1980: 46–55). The earliest days of British rule were unsettling. The 3 April geomancy protest at Tai Po turned out to be but one skirmish in what became a full-scale uprising. On 15 April Captain May, this time supported by a company of the Hong Kong Regiment, once again met protestors at Tai Po, but instead of a band of angry villagers he encountered more than a thousand organised Chinese who opened fire. Assisted by reinforcements from HMS Fame, British forces routed the insurgents, and the Union Jack was raised at Tai Po on 16 April 1899. Lockhart, dressed in his official uniform and accompanied by Commodore Powell, 400 men from the Hong Kong Regiment, and two fully dressed ships personally raised the flag to the sound of an artillery salute (Wesley-Smith 1980: 45). The next evening hostilities continued when the British camp at Tai Po was attacked. British troops (primarily Punjabi Sikhs) repelled the assault but another attack followed when they reached the village of Kam Tin. This, however, was the final battle. Local leaders apparently recognised that they could not defeat the British, and gradually conceded control to yet another set of occupiers, replacing Qing with British overseers (Wesley-Smith 1980: 61–63; see also Groves 1969). The newcomers, however, were to prove far more intrusive – and tenacious – than the emperor's officials.

Lockhart spent the final two weeks of April securing the New Territories, travelling from village to village, lecturing elders, arresting protest ringleaders and confiscating arms. Throughout the uprising, and after, the British remained deeply suspicious of the Qing government's encouragement of the rebels. But, as many scholars have pointed out, documents captured by the British clearly indicate that the resistance was spearheaded by indigenous militia organisations. The leaders came mostly from the wealthiest, single-lineage villages in the region (see, for example, Groves 1969: 43, 57).

Lockhart was furious with the resisters and argued for retribution. He wrote to Hong Kong's Governor: 'It will, I fear, tend to shake the belief of the people in British justice if the rascals who have created all the trouble are allowed to escape unpunished.' The Governor, however, disagreed: 'It is to my mind not improbable that in the future the leaders in the movement may be our most useful assistants in carrying out the local arrangements in the new territory' (quoted in Wesley-Smith 1980: 68–69). The governor won the day, but not before Lockhart, the 'old China hand', had built a string of police stations without any concessions to local geomancy sensitivities and torched the houses of three Ha Tsuen men, accused of murdering a fellow villager hired to post the official announcement proclaiming British sovereignty (Wesley-Smith 1980: 69–70).[12]

Hostility toward the British during 1898 and 1899 can be attributed to many factors but rumours regarding land confiscation and the desecration of tombs were certainly key (Wesley-Smith 1980: 84). Chinese land speculators, one of whom was said to be a confidant of Lockhart, were accused of feeding these rumours in hopes of buying cheap land (Wesley-Smith 1980: 70, 83–84). Local 'tax' arrangements also played a role. For generations, wealthy landowners and elite lineages had extorted 'revenue' through a taxlord system, whereby smaller villages and their residents paid fees (variously described as taxes, rents, protection money) to their wealthier and more powerful neighbours (Kamm 1977; Wesley-Smith 1980: 85–87; Palmer 1987: 16–23). There is no doubt that a great deal was at stake for local, landed elites, and it is no accident that their home villages became centres of resistance.

From 1900 to 1905 the British surveyed and registered all land in the leased territory and established a Land Court to settle disputed registrations. The new administration, as noted above, agreed to accept Chinese land law, which had been haphazardly applied in Xin'an County under the Qing. The taxlord system was not accepted, however. Acting Governor May set forth the policy that taxlord claims were to be evaluated by Chinese law (as reflected in Qing statutes and custom) at the time of the 1898 convention. In effect, this eliminated taxlords as a group, which further diminished the power and wealth of many elite lineage communities (Kamm 1977: 76–77; Wesley-Smith 1980: 96; Palmer 1987: 88–93).

In one of the many ironies of colonial rule in Hong Kong, British authorities did a more thorough job enforcing Chinese land law than China's imperial officials had ever managed. In the process, extractions by taxlords ceased,[13] land titles were allocated to people who could show proof of ownership, lineage land holdings (corporate ancestral estates) were recognised and managers of these estates were required to register with the new government. British readings of Qing law produced a land reform in everything but name (R. Watson 1985: 59–61).[14] Many small-scale owners were given full rights to their land, and some land owners, including lineages, lost properties to which they had long laid claim. The colonial government was keen, of course, to collect taxes, which they did with bureaucratic tenacity and zeal. However, after protests in 1905, they conceded that Crown Rents would not be raised for the duration of the 99-year lease (Wesley-Smith 1980: 98–99). Once the land question had been resolved and taxes assessed, the British were in a strong position from which to reach out to local elites, who became essential players in Hong Kong's version of indirect rule. Given the tiny staff of the New Territories Administration, some concessions to local power holders and village leaders were not only judicious but also necessary. The colonial administration determined that order and revenue collection were best achieved by cooperation rather than further confrontation. The processes of bureaucratic routinisation had begun and colonial rule was gradually established in the practice of everyday life.

Colonialism in Practice: The District Office

As noted earlier, New Territories residents were enumerated and recognised as a special category with significant privileges vis-à-vis not only their counterparts on Hong Kong Island and Kowloon but also those who migrated from China into the New Territories after 1898. These privileges, including the application of Chinese land law and family custom, were granted by the colonial government to those who were enumerated during the first New Territories census in 1911 (totalling approximately 100,000 people) and extended to their descendants. By means of this special status, village residents secured the continuation of certain practices, including patrilineal inheritance and succession, protection of corporate lineage estates, adoption rules, concubinage, rights to build village houses and burial customs that highlighted geomancy.

Endacott, an historian of Hong Kong, notes that the administrative structure of the New Territories evolved slowly. 'At first', he writes, 'the main problems were law and order and the land revenues.' In the early years a Chief Police Officer and two Assistant Land Officers coped with the 'main problems', while two districts – northern and southern – gradually took shape (see Endacott 1964: 268). In 1905 the position of District Officer was established for the northern region, which contained all the elite lineages in the leased territory. In 1909 the Land Officer became the Assistant District Officer and was placed under the District Officer's authority, and finally in 1910 a new administrative unit – the District Office – was created. A similar structure developed more slowly in the southern district, which included Hong Kong's islands (see Endacott 1964: 268–69).[15]

District Officers had wide-ranging responsibilities and limited power. In fact, a number of District Officers have compared themselves to Qing officials. Like the storied 'mother-father officials' (*fumuguan*) of late imperial China, District Officers were expected to settle disputes, handle land issues, attend ceremonies, know and abide by local forms of protocol as well as explain, and if necessary enforce, government policy. With regard to the latter, it appears that 'enforcement' often took the form of negotiation. James Hayes, who served many years in the New Territories Administration, refers to 'benevolent paternalism' and government by 'negotiation ad nauseum' (1996: 41, 194). Negotiation tended to focus on public works projects that required land. It was in this highly contentious arena that conflicts between the colonial government and indigenous villagers frequently arose and, not surprisingly, it was here that geomancy discussions and claims flourished.

Whenever a road was built, a drainage system constructed, or a village relocated, the government (in the guise of the District Officer) regularly entertained and paid compensation to *fengshui* claimants. Payments for environmental disturbances – as determined by geomantic principles – involved a well-understood process in which local interests and sensitivities were considered. The special customs of the indigenous New Territories population were accommodated whenever possible (Wesley-Smith 1992: 91–100). British colonial officials could not have been surprised by the *fengshui* protests they encountered during their early years in the New Territories.[16] Ole Brun provides a summary of many European encounters with *fengshui* as they tried to extend their commercial and missionary activities in China. *Fengshui*, he argues, 'could easily accommodate expressions of proto-nationalistic sentiments' (Brun 2003: 64). The degree to which the New Territories uprising of 1899 can be considered proto-nationalistic or a purely local attempt to protect entrenched privilege, or both, has yet to be examined in detail. But, what is clear is that the vehemence with which *fengshui* claims were thrust upon the new colonial rulers of the New Territories set the tone for later negotiations.[17]

In the late nineteenth century, the area that was to become the New Territories was peppered with tightly packed villages, many of which were walled.[18] Many villages were set among expanses of irrigated rice fields, others hugged the shores of rivers and bays, and some were built on terraced hills where farmers cultivated sweet potatoes and tea. Steep green hills marked off intensively farmed valleys, and everywhere water – in the form of streams, canals, bays and sea – influenced local life. Some of the cultivated land had been wrested from the estuaries and river deltas that gave the landscape its special shape and texture. Temples and shrines were protected by *fengshui* groves of litchi or banyan trees and villages were sited to capture the flow of the 'cosmic current', as Brun puts it (2003: 3). Farmers lived in small, often windowless houses with one door that was designed to direct and maximise this current. The hills were dotted with graves, bone urns and tombs – all of which interacted with the flow of wind and water.

The landscape that the British found in 1898 had been created during the Ming and Qing dynasties (1368–1911). It was fashioned by many human hands – Han migrants, local tribal people with whom the Han intermarried and eventually supplanted and state agents. The reclamations that turned marshes into fields, the irrigation systems that nurtured the rice paddies, the waterways that made inter-village communication possible were highly complex. Their maintenance was crucial and allowed many to survive and some to prosper. For hundreds of years, local geomancers and educated villagers had studied and mapped the contours of land and water. Specific formations were named and widely recognised: The Winking Elephant, Phoenix Landing, Dead Man's Gully (three prominent landmarks in the hills surrounding Ha Tsuen). Stories relating to these geomancy sites were deeply intertwined with family, lineage and local histories. Into this landscape the

British came, armed with ideas about land surveys and taxes, railroads and paved roads, harbour reclamations, district offices and police stations.

During the first decades of British rule, a skeletal road system, a railway between Kowloon and Guangzhou and government-licensed land reclamations were initiated and eventually completed. Most of these projects were located in Northern District, home of the largest and most powerful lineages (including those settled in Ha Tsuen and San Tin). A case in point is the 1930s *fengshui* dispute involving an ancestral tomb located near the present-day industrial town of Tsuen Wan, where the founder of many Deng lineage settlements in southern Guangdong Province, Deng Fuxie, was buried. The tomb is famous for its excellent *fengshui*; it looks out to the sea and is protected by a low rise of hills that produces a much sought after armchair effect. Deng lineage members claim that during the excavations for Fuxie's tomb, an ancient stone inscribed with a poem commemorating the glories of the site was found (see R. Watson 1988).

In the 1920s, the colonial authorities tried to have Fuxie's tomb moved to another location to make way for construction of a major road. The Deng immediately mounted a protest, citing Governor Blake's 1900 commitment to New Territories residents, which, they argued, guaranteed their right to practice local customs. Fuxie's tomb, they maintained, is sacred to all Deng in the New Territories, and they would not give up the grave's wonderful *fengshui* for an uncertain, untried locale, even if the government would bear the expense of relocation.

Although colonial land reform and the 1899 uprising had significantly affected many members of the New Territories elite, Deng villagers were still land rich and may well have been loath to allow or, perhaps more importantly, to be seen to allow colonial officials to interfere with their founding ancestor's tomb. For the Deng, this tomb represented irrefutable evidence of their long and illustrious history. For hundreds of years, good fortune had been captured and channelled to living Deng via their founder's tomb, and the colonial government could not have chosen a site that was more likely to stir up protest. Fuxie's tomb became a *cause celebre* among Deng peoples throughout the Hong Kong region; protestors came from as far away as Guangzhou. In time, Deng leaders and the colonial government reached an accommodation and the tomb remained untouched. However, because of its location near an emerging road system, it faced continuing threats of encroachment. During the 1930s the Deng formed a Tomb Protection Society, which eventually purchased the site surrounding Fuxie's remains. Colonial officials, it should be noted, had always claimed that the tomb was on government land. In the 1970s, the society leased part of the site to a non-Deng who operated a potted-flower business. This enterprise, Deng elders explained in 1978, would not disturb the tomb and showed 'the government that the land around the tomb is cared for and put to good use'. The tomb survived into the 1990s, but each year factories, apartment buildings and office blocks impinged, altering the *fengshui* that secures the prosperity of Fuxie's descendants. In recent years, there were negotiations afoot to remove the tomb, but no final decision has been made. Since the dispute over Fuxie's tomb in the 1930s, half a dozen 'New Towns' with populations of hundreds of thousands have been built in the New Territories – affecting many important tombs.

Post-World War Two Developments: Closed Border and Colonial Modernisation

In December 1941, the Japanese occupied Hong Kong and remained until 30 August 1945 (Endacott 1964: 300). The British resumed civil administration in 1946 and soon after, in an attempt to foster more representative forms of political organisation, began to establish Rural Committees in the New Territories. Members of these advisory bodies, elected by adult males who could claim indigene status, were organised to serve as channels of communication between the government and villagers. In time the Rural Committees evolved into important political institutions. The Chairmen and Executive Committee members met regularly with the District Officer and his assistants, and, not surprisingly, Rural Committee elections became hotly contested affairs (see R. Watson 1985: 139–42).

The New Territories (and indeed the entire colony) was just beginning to recover from the Japanese Occupation when, in 1949, the People's Liberation Army closed the Hong Kong border and the northern-most sector of the New Territories (which includes San Tin) was militarised by the British. During the Chinese Civil War (1945–1949) and the early days of the People's Republic of China, many thousands of Chinese streamed across the border into Hong Kong. The Korean War heightened tensions along the Anglo-Chinese border and once again (as in 1898) the New Territories became a buffer between the colonial government and wealthy merchants, on the one hand, and what were perceived to be the lurking dangers of socialism, threatening to spill over the Chinese border, on the other. To maintain order and protect business interests, the British once again needed good relations with the rural establishment. However, the New Territories was changing and the hold of the old elites was eroding. The instability created by the Japanese Occupation, increased presence of British military units, elections for the new Rural Committees and new economic opportunities during the 1950s and 1960s all lead to fissures in the control that indigene elites had exercised over both their poorer lineage mates and former tenants. New, 'up-from-the-ranks' leaders – men who had fought against the Japanese, or made small fortunes smuggling petrol and trucks to the People's Liberation Army across the border, or started new businesses in the booming market towns – began to challenge the hold of the old landed elite (see R. Watson 1985: 142–49). There were, however, two things about which all New Territories villagers could agree; they had privileges, which they expected the colonial government to respect, and they would defend their *fengshui* sites (around which their tombs, houses and villages had been aligned). Increasingly, *fengshui* became a means of pressing their claims for special treatment.

As Hong Kong's population skyrocketed in the post-occupation period,[19] water became a key resource. In an effort to increase water supplies, the colonial government initiated the Shek Pik Reservoir project on Lantau Island in the 1950s. James Hayes refers to the government-village negotiations over this reservoir as 'a classic of its kind' (1996: 31): 'the Shek Pik negotiation exemplified the Hong Kong government's desire to achieve its aims by negotiation ... All requirements – and they were legion – were negotiated from start to finish, never letting up and never allowing the villagers to get away from the negotiating table' (1996: 31). Shek Pik concessions, Hayes argues, were 'in line with the generally conciliatory policies pursued by the District Administration in those sensitive years, when urban needs called for the construction of major public works in the New Territories' (1996: 41). The colonial government was always asking 'the indigenous population ... to give up this or that landed property or customary entitlement in the interests of progress' and discussion rather than formal legal action seemed the most effective way of achieving development goals (Hayes 1996: 208). The Shek Pik project, which involved the destruction of villages, temples, ancestral halls and sometimes the surrounding hills and streams, was handled through discussion and compensation.

Geomancy was, of course, a key dimension of the Shek Pik project. In carrying out preparatory soil tests for reservoir construction, engineers exposed red earth in view of village homes. To the villagers, Hayes relates, '[t]his was a sign that the dragon's vein [an important local geomantic concept] ... had been cut and was 'bleeding', affecting the flow of beneficial influences in the locality'. After some debate, villagers' fears were calmed by protective rituals performed by a Daoist priest, with expenses paid by the District Office (Hayes 1996: 34). According to Hayes, the claims lodged during the Shek Pik project were complicated by the village's recent and troubled past. During the early decades of the twentieth century, in hopes of ending the population losses that they had suffered, Shek Pik residents had taken the drastic measure of moving their village to a new site, one with better *fengshui* (see Hayes 1996: 34–35). To ask them to relocate only a generation after this move was asking a great deal indeed.

The 'bleeding dragon' was by no means the only geomancy-related conflict. An excavation on a slope facing Shek Pik and the creation of a jeep track across the hills near a village neighbouring Shek Pik also involved protests and work stoppages. Sometimes villagers requested that protective walls and stands of trees be added to alleviate the dangers of a *fengshui* disturbance, or demanded that special rituals (*fasi*) be performed (Strauch 1980; Wesley-Smith 1992: 10, 25–26). These rituals were often accepted as legitimate claims on colonial coffers. In the case of the jeep track, government officials required that the contractor cease work after a geomancer hired by the government reported 'that he could only advise that no track be built' (Hayes 1996: 36). The removal of Shek Pik villagers to multi-storey apartment blocks in the industrial city of Tsuen Wan (compensation to which they had agreed) took place in 1960 after much negotiation over a 'lucky day' for the move and a series of *fengshui* claims and negotiations (Hayes 1996: 47–49).

In the Shik Pik project, it was the job of the District Office to negotiate the recovery of all private land (totalling 103 acres) necessary for the reservoir and to reach agreement with villagers regarding compensation and rehousing

(Hayes 1996: 38). But, Fan Pui, a small village neighbouring Shek Pik also affected by the reservoir project, refused to allow the removal of 'its *fung shui* hill' for reservoir construction until the entire village had been relocated (see Hayes 1996: 40, 43). Colonial officials had agreed to create a new settlement and fields, but Fan Pui villagers required an assurance with details of electricity, piped water as well as road, pier and outbuilding construction before agreeing to move (Hayes 1996: 44). After months of deliberations, the villagers agreed to the package, which included, according to Hayes, 'customary rituals associated with any village removal' (for a list see Hayes 1996: 44). The local District Officer had, however, forgotten to consult a geomancer when the new village was sited. Hayes writes: 'Mercifully, the site was acceptable to the [belatedly commissioned] geomancer' (1996: 45). Using three motor junks, five sampans and three lorries, villagers moved to their new village on 5–6 October 1959. Just prior to their move, Hayes reports, priests performed rituals in the old village 'and at the lucky hour the ancestral tablets of each household were moved to the new houses and installed there' (1996: 46). The engineers wasted no time and began work at the foot of the '*fung shui* hill' on 5 October and on the hill itself on 6 October. Hayes concludes the Fan Pui resettlement story: 'a few trees have been cut down and these by arrangement, have been picked up for firewood by the [departing] villagers, who, now that the issue of the hill had been settled, were nothing if not frugal and practical' (1996: 46).

Hayes notes that local *fengshui* disputes had an element of theatre, often hugely enjoyed by whole villages, but he does not consider geomancy claims to be 'hooey' as some colleagues and many contractors contended (Hayes 1996: 34–35). He attributes local geomancy and religious practices to '[f]ear of the elements, fear of disease, fear of bandits and sea robbers, and a general fear of the unknown ... The villagers felt it was vital to retain the goodwill of the gods of their locality ... such beliefs shaped their actions when faced with any family crisis or with sustained indications that life was out of kilter' (1996: 35). This kind of interpretation prevailed among many in the New Territories administration, although the interpretative range was broad and encompassed sympathetic as well as negative attitudes (see below).[20]

Austin Coates, also a one-time District Officer, writes in his memoirs about his own understanding (or perhaps lack of understanding) of geomancy. With regard to mining operations on one of Hong Kong's islands during the Korean War, Coates writes:

> Did the [village head] really believe the dragon had become malevolent? Or was it that, partly believing it, and knowing that government in the New Territories (where there was no Revolution of 1912) was more old-fashioned than in China, he considered he might use it as a convenient weapon or argument? Or was it that he did not believe it at all, but knew that Europeans thought Chinese did believe in such things, so that consequently, when a Chinese [village head] spoke of *fengshui*, it meant that a European official had to sit up and take notice?

These questions, Coates continues, recurred to him when he had to handle village *fengshui* cases, but 'I do not think I ever gave myself an answer which I could have sworn was correct' (1968: 170).

In 1960–1961 China suffered a devastating famine in which as many as forty million people lost their lives (see, for example, Bannister 1987: 85–86, 118; Yang 1996). In 1962, within the span of a week, border guards stood by as tens of thousands of refugees walked across the border between Hong Kong and China. Many found or made shelters in squatter settlements in or near Hong Kong's urban centres, but some stayed in the New Territories and joined the 'outsider' vegetable farmers who had migrated in 1949 and 1950. These poor, landless farmers rented fields from local owners who themselves were giving up agriculture in favour of emigration to Britain, factory work or small business operations. During the 1950s and 1960s, the pace of environmental change quickened. Reservoirs, squatter settlements, military compounds, new roads, garment factories and intensively farmed vegetable fields were replacing the once ubiquitous rice paddies. In most cases, the old villages with their tightly nucleated houses, *fengshui* groves and earth god shrines, protective walls and ponds remained, but the prospects – the views – from many of these villages were changing. Increasingly, familiar landmarks were disappearing and newcomers – refugee vegetable farmers, migrant factory workers, small-scale entrepreneurs – were making their presence felt. These new residents, it should be noted, were treated as intrusive minorities by both residents of Hong Kong's old villages and government officials alike.

Population growth and a hostile China had made the colonial government increasingly dependent on the New Territories for water, food and electricity. China was never completely out of the picture, however, because local suppliers could not begin to keep pace with what was needed. Mao's Cultural Revolution, launched in 1966, only added to what was becoming an immensely complicated and volatile mix. In 1967 serious rioting broke out in Hong Kong, Maoist propaganda groups crossed the border to perform 'loyalty dances' in Northern District villages (including San Tin), a colonial official was kidnapped and there were rumours that the British could not hold Hong Kong. They did, however, remain and in the aftermath of 1967 and the appointment of a new governor (Murray Maclehose) in 1971, the colonial government began ambitious programs that transformed its relationship with the indigenes of the New Territories (and the Hong Kong population in general). Colonial administrators were buoyed by the response of most residents, who had stood with the government (or at least did not participate) during the 1967 riots.[21] Hayes argues that in 1968 there was a realisation that the government could no longer depend only on elites and benevolent authoritarianism (1996: 281, 290).

In 1981 the heretofore separate administrative structures for Hong Kong Island/Kowloon and the New Territories were amalgamated into one unit – the City and New Territories Administration (Miners 1995: 169). In 1982 the Lands Department was formed and all land administration duties were transferred from the New Territories Administration to the new department (Ho 2004: 133). In rapid order the District Officers lost a key function – oversight of land transactions – and much influence.

In 1977 the Hong Kong government established New Territories District Advisory Boards, which included villagers as well as newcomer migrants (Hayes 1996: 278). In 1981 the Board structure (re-named District Boards) was extended to all of Hong Kong (Miners 1995: 169), and a year later District Board elections were first held.[22] In 1985 District Officers and other officials ceased being members of the Boards, although they continued 'to attend meetings by invitation to answer questions, give explanations, and present papers' (Miners 1995: 170). In many respects, District Boards were like Rural Committees (which continued to exist) in that, as Miners points out, they had no right to give instructions to government officials, no power to raise money ... and no authority to spend it' (1995: 176). However, they did make it possible for members to call attention to important social and economic issues and to be privy to valuable information.

Gradually, a new breed of government official – technocrats – were beginning to take over.[23] These men (and occasionally women), although they might be Hong Kong-born Cantonese, showed little interest in or appreciation of rural customs. Increasingly, villagers found it difficult to secure any benefits from the development projects that were altering their communities and affecting their futures. When land was resumed for development purposes, people were paid a sum that approximated the market value of their property. If they had to leave their homes, their removal expenses were compensated and they were usually rehoused, although not necessarily to their liking. But they played no active role in the planning of these large developments. Once a project was approved, they had no choice but to relinquish their land and move. One of the only ways for villagers to register their sadness, dissatisfaction and distress was to lodge complaints based on geomancy.

By 1980 the New Territories had already undergone considerable development: rural villas (small private houses) had sprung up like bamboo shoots and private as well as government-sponsored construction projects were increasingly visible. It is well to remember that for hundreds of years the Pearl River Delta, of which the New Territories is a part, has been a highly manipulated environment. The elaborate reclamation projects of Qing times that still survive from that era are testimony to the environmentally transformative agendas of eighteenth- and nineteenth-century Guangdong. However, there are significant differences between the low-tech conversion projects that characterised the delta until the 1950s (see, for example, J. Watson 1975; Siu 1989: 1–35) and more recent mechanised, high-speed reclamations that convert marshes or tidal lands into new cities in a matter of four or five years. The development projects of the 1980s and 1990s moved at what New Territories villagers perceived as lightening speed, and the consequences were increasingly disorienting for local people.

Housing and infrastructure development, which had added hundreds of thousands of residents to the New Territories, took an enormous toll on the local environment. 'One could say', Hayes muses, 'that development had tended to be in the New Territories rather than for the New Territories' (1996: 249). New Town projects, which often lacked coordination and clear impact analyses, created problems that could no longer be solved by the villagers themselves or their local organisations.

Geomancy, Protest and Development

Beginning in the 1970s, the informal pact between indigenous villagers and government – built on mutual need – began to unravel. Ha Tsuen provides an illustration of that unravelling process. In 1982 a New Town development was taking shape near the village of Ha Tsuen. The complex, known as Tin Shui Wai, was to be built on reclaimed land in an area that had been marsh, fishponds, brackish paddy and wasteland. Ha Tsuen's main ancestral hall had historically claimed the Tin Shui Wai area, but in the 1920s the Hong Kong government sold the marshland to outside speculators, arguing that the Deng had no proper title. In the 1970s, the land was resold to 'private developers'.[24] By 1980 a 448 hectare site had been acquired by Mighty City, a China-led consortium (see *SCMP* 26 March 1993). Mighty City proposed to create a New Town with a population of 500,000, but the Hong Kong Government quickly vetoed the plan as too ambitious. Eventually a high-rise complex for 135,000 residents was approved. There followed a period of wrangling between Mighty City and the government, occasioned by changes in Hong Kong's real estate market and disagreements concerning payment for the site's infrastructure needs, which were enormous.

By 1982, a new deal was struck in which the Hong Kong Government bought the site for HK$2.26 billion and sold back forty hectares (for HK$800 million) to private developers. This was the largest sum that the Government had ever paid for a parcel of land (paid, it should be noted, to Mighty City not to New Territories villagers). Furthermore, it was the first time that the government had bought land not earmarked for a specific project. Later, at the opening of Tin Shui Wai New Town, government officials proclaimed to the assembled press that the development represented a unique joint venture in which government and the private sector had cooperated from the origin of the project (*SCMP* 26 March 1993). (The extent to which PRC-dominated Mighty City could be considered 'private' is an interesting question.) In 1993, when the first residents moved into Tin Shui Wai, government sources reported that the venture had cost HK$10 billion, two-thirds of which was supplied by the Hong Kong Government. Government officials proudly announced that the massive construction had 'worked around a traditional *feng shui* sightline which bisects the town. Not even a footbridge has been allowed to cross this line' (*SCMP* March 26, 1993).

Prior to the creation of Tin Shui Wai, one could stand at the gates of Ha Tsuen's main ancestral hall, built in 1751, and see open land stretching into and beyond the marshes of the Pearl River estuary. Every day for generations elderly men have gathered at the great stone platforms that frame the hall's entrance to exchange news, pass the time and watch grandchildren. Today, when one looks out from the gates, the original sight line is blocked by enormous apartment towers. If there is a *fengshui* corridor, villagers say, only the planners can see it.[25]

From the 1950s to the 1970s, the locatedness of New Territories villagers – the common places of their everyday lives – remained largely intact. Even in the late 1970s, one could still see the fields near Ha Tsuen and San Tin that once produced rice, visit an old sugar refinery, sit in houses that had been built during the seventeenth century, walk along stone paths and make out the outline of reclaimed 'salt fields' (*han tian*) and canals that once served the local market. With the help of villagers it was possible to visualise the outline of a 'lived in past'. As the old men sat outside the gates of their ancestral hall talking about lineage history they pointed to historic sites and features of the landscape, imparting a physicality to the past that was deeply reassuring. Walks along village paths often occasioned stories about lineage feuds fought in the surrounding fields. Visits to ancestral tombs in the hills behind Ha Tsuen provided lessons in judging the attributes of well-known *fengshui* sites. In Lowenthal's words, the landscape, both natural and built, was very much part of the 'tangible past' (1985).

However, by the mid-1980s Ha Tsuen's recognisable and intimate environment was changing. Hills disappeared, huge drainage systems altered the flow of streams, rail lines snaked through nearby fields, and ship container parks[26] dotted the countryside. In 1993 and again in 1994, during return visits to Hong Kong, Ha Tsuen villagers and colonial officials discussed the question of a *fengshui* corridor passing through Tin Shui Wai New Town. Villagers, who pointed out that their access to the forces of wind and water had been blocked, expected the government to pay for a special ritual of placation (*fasi*). During our conversations with government officials, a sense of pride in the Tin Shui Wai development and what it had represented for Yuen Long District was evident. We were told that the flooding that had once been endemic in the Ha Tsuen area was no longer a problem because of the drainage network that had been constructed. Transportation had been greatly improved and no major villages, the officials noted, had been relocated. Ha Tsuen was, in their view, intact. Of course, the surrounding hills and fields had been tunnelled, huge drainage canals now passed through the village, and tens of thousands of 'outsiders' were now on their doorstep; but, we were assured, there had been no major residential disruptions to the villagers themselves.

As discussions with colonial officials continued, however, the language of the planner and business developer was increasingly interspersed with allusions to *fengshui*. In part this was due to our questions, but it also reflected the interests and enthusiasms of the officials themselves. Yes, they confirmed, a compensation payment for a *fasi* ritual had been made in 1991 after villagers claimed that tunnelling in the Ha Tsuen hills had ruptured the 'veins of the dragon'. Yes, a *fengshui* corridor was built in Tin Shui Wai.

The longer we talked the more it became clear that there was something more here than a concern with good government. These officials – Hong Kong born Cantonese with university degrees – claimed that *fengshui* was a kind of technology or science. 'There really is something to it,' they argued, 'it is environmentally sound.' In their view *fasi* rituals, dragons' veins and compensation payments are quaint, country ways of understanding what they believe to be more complex notions that underlie *fengshui*. They did not say: 'We urban, educated people understand these matters on a higher plane', but this was their implicit message.

Geomancy as practised in urban Hong Kong is different in important respects from the *fengshui* of New Territories villages.[27] The urban population consists primarily of (relative) newcomers, people who arrived in Hong Kong since the 1950s. Their tangible past, represented by squatter settlements, tenements and factories[28] of the early post-Cold War era, has been largely erased. Until recently, their identification with Hong Kong has been tentative, if indeed they thought about it at all (see Siu 1996; J. Watson 2006; Mathews 2001). For many émigrés, Hong Kong was indeed 'a borrowed place living on borrowed time' (Hughes 1968). Not surprisingly, the Chinese–British Accord on Hong Kong's reversion to Beijing set off an identity crisis that reached a peak just prior to 1997. During the late 1980s and 1990s, the colonial government sinicised their administration, poured vast funds into the university system, and made large contributions to local art, music and drama associations. New magazines and newspapers appeared and Hong Kong took on a kind of international cache during the last years of colonial rule. The formation of a Hong Kong identity ('we are different from those Chinese north of the border') required a past, but until the 1980s Hong Kong history had been badly neglected – the preserve of a few anthropologists and local historians.[29]

In the 1990s many in Hong Kong became keen preservationists whose 'tangible past' was encapsulated in a museum, a restored temple or a preserved ancestral hall. And, it should not be surprising that for many 'the past' came to reside in the New Territories. In this vision, *fengshui* was acceptable if it was cleansed of the political – anything that hinted at negotiation or stratagem. *Fengshui* had to be pure if it were to serve the social agenda of Hong Kong activists. For some intellectuals, *fengshui* is the 'opiate of the masses' (to quote one university professor). For others geomancy was one of the cultural elements that made Hong Kong unique. In the view of many urbanites, who pay the high fees that popular geomancers command, *fengshui* as it is practiced in the New Territories is superstition or, worse, extortion. Urban *fengshui*, by contrast, is technology ('it is like science'). It helps one live in the world that other people (governments, developers, planners) have created.[30] The 'wind and water' of the urban *fengshui* devotee does not course through an intimate, past-laden landscape. Rather, it allows urban apartment dwellers to position themselves – to arrange their apartments or offices – so that they can take advantage of new, rapidly changing opportunities or counteract danger from the built environment that surrounds them (see, for example, Rooney 2001: 66; Cheung and Ma 2005).[31]

Geomancy, Place and Identity

The relationship between Hong Kong urbanites and New Territories indigenes has been fraught in recent years. Each side lays claim to places deeply inscribed in the landscape but they share little else. Much of the approbation urbanites direct at rural *fengshui* is aimed at the New Territories power establishment, represented by a unique organisation called the Heung Yee Kuk. Roughly translated as 'rural consultative council', this organisation is composed of village leaders and political brokers who informally represent the old villages (the indigenes) of the New Territories. During the 1990s, members of the Heung Yee Kuk worked to retain the privileges granted to villagers by the British colonial administration in 1898. Leaders of the Kuk were well aware that colonial arrangements could not be imported wholesale into a future dominated by the Communist Party. To protect their special privileges, therefore, they had to redefine what it meant to be an indigenous villager. For much of the twentieth century, literate villagers made claims for a special kind of pioneer heritage founded in the competitive logic of Chinese history. They were *Tang-ren*, or the 'People of Tang Dynasty', and thus the living repositories of Han Chinese culture, which they proclaimed had disappeared in China itself (see Chan 1998). This was a claim that set local people apart from the aboriginal (non-Han) populations of the south and distinguished them from the Mongol and Manchu rulers who lived in north China.

However, in the 1990s New Territories leaders began to style themselves not as *Tang-ren* but as *yuanzhumin*, a term that translates literally as 'original-residing peoples'. In a full page ad appearing in Hong Kong's newspapers Heung Yee Kuk propagandists likened the New Territories *yuanzhumin* to the Maori of New Zealand and to North American Indians (*SCMP* 20 May 1994). This special status, they argued, entitled them to maintain traditional cultural forms and political privileges by right of their heritage. These customs – patrilineal inheritance, special rights to house lots, privileged access to government authorities, burial sites in the New Territories and greater control over local land use – were in their view sacrosanct. Their long residence in the New Territories, their resistance to the British in 1898 (valorised in the months prior to the 1997 repatriation ceremonies) and their distinct customs (ancestor worship, purification rituals or *jiao*, secondary burial and *fengshui* practices) led these villagers to expect special consideration from their new Communist masters. How deeply these particular claims resonated with ordinary villagers remains an open question. Many villagers of our acquaintance were either shocked or amused by the comparison between themselves and their putative allies in New Zealand and North America.

Leaders of the Heung Yee Kuk were not interested in crafting a new identity for everyone in Hong Kong. Their goal was highly restricted. They wished to reaffirm what it meant to be a New Territories indigene, but to do so they had to make claims to represent an entire category of people and to determine what was best for them. Urban intellectuals, in contrast, were concerned to create an inclusive Hong Kong identity, which built on carefully selected rural customs and architectural monuments. In doing so they came into conflict with the Hueng Yee Kuk leaders and other New Territories power brokers.

Conclusions

Hong Kong's space wars and identity battles are far from settled. Villagers continue to hire geomancers, to extract fees for placation rites, and to pay careful attention to the *fengshui* of their ancestral tombs. Nonetheless, much has changed. For some, geomancy is no longer a political resource; it now operates in the realm of personal meaning and local pride. Highly educated and well-travelled New Territories migrants regularly compare their ritual activities to the Muslim, Christian and (organised) Buddhist practices they see in urban Hong Kong and elsewhere. For them, geomancy is now perceived as a form of 'religion' (*zongjiao*) that is inseparable from their system of ancestor worship. Treated as a religious practice, *fengshui* is compartmentalised and detached from the mundane concerns of politics.

During our field research in the New Territories in the late 1960s, *fengshui* was closely interwoven with local politics. As the grandchildren of our Ha Tsuen and San Tin neighbours moved abroad or to new houses outside the old villages, their general vision of the New Territories also changed. In the case of San Tin, these ancient villages are no longer 'home' for a generation of diasporics born and reared in Britain, Germany, Netherlands, Belgium, Sweden and Canada (among other places). For these people, the New Territories represents a place of origin, a pilgrimage site where one can pursue 'roots' (J. Watson 2004). Ancestor worship rites and *fengshui* practices (encountered during brief visits to Ha Tsuen and San Tin) are interpreted through the lens of *ethnic* identity. 'These rituals are what makes me Chinese', said one 1990s pilgrim to San Tin (who speaks German and English, but not Cantonese). For this young man geomancy has nothing whatsoever to do with local politics, community organisation or space wars. For many in the Hong Kong diaspora, geomancy has become a personal resource that can be understood by consulting English language books and web sites, or by sending emails to Harvard anthropologists. It is no longer the 'lived-in' system that their grandparents took for granted and discussed in the metaphorical language of wind and water. Geomancy is still practiced in the New Territories, but for many it has moved from the centre of political life to what one might describe as the margins of religion.

For Ha Tsuen villagers, many of whom continue to live in the New Territories, *fengshui* remains important. There is pride in the auspicious setting of their ancestral halls and tombs, but the transformation of their surrounding landscape and their increasing inability to engage local officials in discussions of 'their *fengshui*' makes the heretofore familiar conversation one-sided. In fact, one might argue that they lack a conversation partner altogether as the Hong Kong government turns a deaf ear to their claims for attention.

After considerable debate, protest and behind the scenes manoeuvring New Territories indigenes have retained some of the privileges that they enjoyed under the British. At this writing (2005), they can still claim land to build village houses, although this privilege is now subject to modification and restriction. Ancestral halls and tombs continue to receive protection and patrilineal succession to ancestral estates is still recognised. Women, however, have been given inheritance rights to private (family) property, which was a bitter blow to many villagers (Chan 1997, 2003; Merry and Stern 2005).

The geomancer who 'sees *fengshui*' and the villagers who seek his services, we argue, created the landscape that the British encountered in 1898.[32] As that landscape took form, vested interests sought to maintain it. What were they maintaining? In *Sediments of Time*, J.R. McNeill places Chinese environmental history in global perspective. He argues that the 'Chinese agricultural landscape ... was thoroughly anthropogenic' (1998: 37). Because it was so heavily manufactured, McNeill continues, 'the Chinese landscape was unusually dependent on demographic and political stability, and unusually vulnerable to disruption by neglect' (1998: 37). In this regard, it is worth considering the creative role that geomancy played not only in manufacturing Chinese landscapes but also in sustaining them. Given an agricultural regime created by and dependent upon a complex and highly manipulated environment, geomancy practices may well have been a conservative force that protected the environmental status quo. There is no doubt that geomancy ultimately failed to block changes in the New Territories, as estuaries were reclaimed, streams were rerouted and hills were flattened. Nonetheless, as we have demonstrated, villagers did indeed resist – given that they had little to gain from these monumental changes.

Since the 1950s, the population of Hong Kong, which has nearly tripled to six million, has experienced good times (1980s and 1990s) and bad times (1950–1970). Most Hong Kong people are better educated, have access to a higher standard of health care, eat better, travel more easily and live in better housing than they did twenty-five years ago. These achievements, however, have come at a price, reflected in overcrowding (for many people apartments are costly, cramped and noisy) and in a form of competitive consumerism that is as alienating as it is incessant. Hong Kong's manufactured environment makes few concessions to the natural world. In what Hayes refers to as the 'transition from resident to citizen', indigene privileges have taken a beating (1996: 280, 296).[33] *Fengshui* no longer guides the creation of the New Territories landscape, neither geomancy practice nor discourse has the power to influence decisions about the local environment significantly. Whether in the future local geomancy practices can offer a creative response to the highly built environment in which many New Territories people find themselves seems unlikely. We do not claim special insights into the motives of villagers we have known since the late 1960s. Some clearly believed in the efficacy of *fengshui*, whereas others remained firmly agnostic and cynically manipulated the system for their own benefit. Geomancy does still guide tomb locations, but one suspects that unfettered access to the steep, green hills where ancestors and, in an important sense, the New Territories' past, are buried will become increasingly difficult.

Notes

1. Rubie Watson wishes to thank the Wenner-Gren Foundation and the American Council of Learned Societies for supporting research discussed in this paper. James Watson is grateful to the Chiang Ching-kuo Foundation for support of research in the New Territories in 1994. We are both grateful for the hospitality of the Department of Anthropology, Chinese University of Hong Kong for hosting us during our research in the Spring and Summer of 1997. Many thanks also to

Frances Pine, Wei-ping Lin, and Michael Szonyi for their comments on this paper and willingness to help us think about Chinese geomancy.
2. The task of the geomancer (*fengshui xiansheng*) is to 'see *fengshui*'. Brun notes, the geomancer 'scrutinizes his geomantic compass (*luopan*) and consults the traditional calendar (*nongli*) ... determines the location of the White Tiger (*bai hu*) and the Green Dragon [the active forces of geomancy] ... calculates the birth data of the owner [of the site] ... The actual techniques involved in rural *fengshui*-seing are simple' (Brun 2003: 4).
3. For a good discussion of *fengshui* in the New Territories that is sensitive to local terminology see Potter (1970: 140–42).
4. We understand geomancy to be a set of practices that exist within a complex and loosely organised conceptual frame. See Brun (2003: 2–32), who argues against the view that *fengshui* forms a coherent system.
5. According to Feuchtwang, Daoism and *fengshui* share 'a conception of the emergence of things from a great unity through the fertile balances of Yin and Yang' and 'is elaborated in a cosmology of flows of *qi* energies and substances, of destructive as well as constructive interaction of the five Elements, and of the astrological influence of stars, likewise harmful or benign' (2003: ix).
6. On occasion, however, officials did use local *fengshui* disputes for their own benefit, especially during Qing times (1644–1911) when state authorities attempted to limit foreign intervention (see, for example, Brun 2003: 9, 45–46, 65–71).
7. The very poor and those who died without descendants might be denied reburial.
8. Sometimes months or even years passed before urns were placed in tombs, and some urns were never entombed. One can see *jin ta* – often they are dug into ledges – throughout the hills of the New Territories.
9. Until the late 1980s the village of Ha Tsuen and the Ha Tsuen Teng lineage were largely coterminous. However, in recent years many Ha Tsuen villagers have rented their old houses to 'outsiders' (non-lineage members) and built new houses on the periphery of the original village complex.
10. The residents of these two villages speak a sub-dialect of Cantonese that is common in the Pearl River Delta of Guangdong Province.
11. Hong Kong Island became a colony of Great Britain in 1841, following the first Opium War.
12. For discussion of punishment of these men see Wesley-Smith (1980: 70–71).
13. Village security forces filled the vacuum left by taxlords and their agents. 'Fees' were collected from local farmers and commercial premises were 'protected' by village guardsmen who staked out territory after 1899. The guardsmen were recognised by colonial officials and allowed to carry firearms during the early years of British rule (see J. Watson 1989).
14. For a different perspective see Palmer (1987: 84–93).
15. In 1914 there were nearly 4,450 posts in Hong Kong's public service; by 1939 the total had increased to just over 10,000. Miners points out that this increase paralleled the colony's population growth from 462,422 in 1911 to 1,050,000 in 1939. Prior to the Japanese Occupation, many Europeans were employed (in both high and low positions) in the colonial service (11.6% in 1914 and 11% in 1930). Many of these Europeans served as 'ordinary constables in the police force, warders in the prisons, inspectors in the Sanitary Department, overseers of labour in the Public Works Department, and as clerks in all branches of the government' (Miners 1987: 79). They received higher wages than non-Europeans; for example, a British constable was paid seven times the wage of his Chinese or Indian counterparts (Miners 1987: 79). Disparities of this nature were justified, Miners notes, on the

'dubious evidence that European subordinates were more trustworthy and less corrupt than Chinese and were more efficient at their work' (Miners 1987: 80). Although pressure for more local hires increased over time, Miners points out that 'progress in replacing Europeans by local staff was slow' (1987: 83). Nevertheless, pressure from the Colonial Office in London and from Chinese and Portuguese members of Hong Kong's Legislative Council grew during the 1930s, but the number of Chinese staff increased only slightly (Miners 1987: 83-84).

16. For examples of *fengshui* disputes during the nineteenth century on Hong Kong Island see Eitel (1985: 1-2).
17. With the major exceptions of land registration, revenue collection and a Pax Britannica that accepted local control as long as id did not threaten British interests, New Territories people experienced considerable autonomy during the early years of Colonial administration. Village security forces continued to operate and male slavery and female domestic bondage continued until the 1920s (see J. Watson 1976; R. Watson 1991).
18. For another description of the New Territories in 1898 see Groves 1969.
19. Hong Kong's population increased from approximately 600,000 in 1945 to four million in 1970.
20. For a discussion of Chinese government and European observers' perspectives on geomancy see Brun (2003: 34-72).
21. J.S. Hoadley refers to Hong Kong's Chinese residents as 'willing subjects of a foreign government' (1970: 210).
22. The right to vote was extended to those who were twenty-one years of age or older, had lived in Hong Kong for seven years, and had registered. For a discussion of District Board elections in 1980s see Lau and Kuan 1987.
23. For discussion of Generalists-Specialists in Hong Kong's Colonial Service see Scott 1988.
24. For a discussion of private land investment companies in the Hong Kong area during the late nineteenth and early twentieth centuries see Palmer (1987: 40-52).
25. Yet another celebrated geomancy case, in which compensation was not the issue, involved not a government-inspired project but a private entrepreneur. The residents of Sheung Tsuen, a village in Pat Heung District, demanded that the developer of a massive, fifty million Hong Kong dollar columbarium (a bone ash depository) cease all operations. In 1992 and again in 1994 a coalition of villagers received a judgment from the Hong Kong Town Planning Board and finally the Town Planning Appeal Board against the project (and the developer, Treasure Base Development Company). The judgment required that the columbarium developer stop all work (*South China Morning Post* 28 May 1992; *SCMP* 9 October 1993). This case involved the active participation of Sheung Tsuen's *ah po* or 'old ladies' who literally 'womaned' the barricades and were the most visible protestors. Villagers also engaged in a march on the Town Planning Board on Hong Kong Island and orchestrated a very effective protest campaign in the local media. It is believed that the developer, who was well into the project when the protests began, lost nearly thirty million Hong Kong dollars.

Villagers argued that the site would destroy their *fengshui* and bring bad fortune on the community. A series of deaths in Sheung Tsuen, attributed to disturbances caused by the development, provided clear evidence, villagers claimed, that the local balance of wind and water had to be restored (see *SCMP* 9 October 1993). In 1991 villagers swore an oath before their temple god, refusing to accept compensation from the developer, which would have split the community. An 84-year-old village woman is reported to have said: 'you never know what the developers and the Government have come up with ... We are always kept in the dark and the last ones to know what is really happening'. She went on to say that she and about twenty other elderly villagers were spending most of each day at the building site to block the developers from entering. 'Whenever we see them approach', she said, 'we stand in a human wall and point our sticks at them and hit them. So all they can do is just leave' (*SCMP* 28 May 1992).

26. Many rice fields had been turned into storage fields where containers – the kind that transport goods on land and sea and from ships to trucks – were stacked four to five high. *Bendi* blamed 'outsiders' who had leased the fields but urbanites blamed *bendiren* for their greed.
27. For a discussion of *fengshui* in Hong Kong during the 1980s and 1990s see Waters 1997.
28. Most manufacturing and thus many factories moved to China during the 1980s.
29. For recent historical research on Hong Kong see, for example, Sinn 1989.
30. For most people in Hong Kong *fengshui* serves as a handy weapon in the arsenal that one needs to be competitive in a rapidly changing urban environment. These are the consumers of the geomancy magazines, handbooks and television programs hosted by *fengshui* masters that are now so much a part of the Hong Kong scene. Like the forms of *fengshui* practiced in the New Territories, urban geomancy is a technical and an amoral system devoted to optimising one's place in the environment. But, urbanites are more likely to begin their *fengshui* questions with 'how' rather than 'why'. 'How can I move my desk to improve working relations in my office? How can I create better *qi* (energy) in my factory so that my workers are more productive (and I can make more money)? How can I rearrange my apartment to enhance relations with my spouse or children?' Wind and water are perceived as natural forces, but in urban geomancy such forces operate within a highly built environment. Decisions regarding the location of apartments, factories or office buildings are not made by the occupiers of those spaces. Nonetheless, geomancy offers the people who must live in this built world an opportunity to secure their future by manipulating their personal spaces.
31. To be successful in business a geomancer might tell his client to 'move your desk here', 'place a fish bowl there', or 'put a mirror on the veranda'.
32. Lung (1980) provides a good illustration of '*fengshui* at work' in the creation of the walled village of Kat Hong Wai; see also Potter (1970: 142–43) and Knapp (1998).
33. For a general discussion of political participation in Hong Kong see Lam 2004.

References

Ahern, Emily. 1973. *The Cult of the Dead in a Chinese Village*. Stanford: Stanford University Press.

Airlee, Shiona. 1989. *Thistle and Bamboo: The Life of Sir James Stewart Lockhart*. Hong Kong: Oxford University Press.

Appadurai, Arjun. 1996. *Modernity at Large: Cultural Dimensions of Globalization*. Minneapolis: University of Minnesota Press.

Baker, Hugh. 1968. *A Chinese Lineage Village: Sheung Shui*. Stanford: Stanford University Press.

Bannister, Judith. 1987. *China's Changing Population*. Stanford: Stanford University Press.

Bender, Barbara (ed.). 1993. *Landscapes: Politics and Perspectives*. Providence: Berg.

Brun, Ole. 2003. *Fengshui in China: Geomantic Divination between State Orthodoxy and Popular Religion*. Copenhagen: Nordic Institute of Asian Studies.

Casey, E. 1997. *The Fate of Place*. Berkeley: University of California Press.

Chan, Ming K. and Alvin Y. So (eds). 2002. *Crisis and Transformation in China's Hong Kong*. Armonk, NY: M.E. Sharpe.

Chan, Selina Ching. 1997. 'Negotiating Tradition: Customary Succession in the New Territories of Hong Kong', in Grant Evans and Maria Tam (eds), *Hong Kong: The Anthropology of a Chinese Metropolis*. University of Hawaii Press, pp. 151–73.

———. 1998. 'Politicizing Tradition: The Identity of Indigenous Inhabitants in Hong Kong', *Ethnology* 37(1): 39–54.

———. 2003. 'Questioning the Patriarchal Inheritance Model in Hong Kong: Daughters, Sons and the Colonial Government', *Berliner China-Hefte* 24(May): 66–75.

Cheung, Sidney C.H. 2001. 'Land Use and Fung-shui: Negotiation in the New Territories, Hong Kong', *Cultural Survival* 25(2): 70–71.

Cheung, Sidney C.H. and Eric K.W. Ma. 2005. 'Advertising Modernity: Home, Space, and Privacy', *Visual Anthropology* 18: 65–80.

Coates, Austin. 1968. *Myself a Mandarin: Memories of a Special Magistrate*. Hong Kong: Oxford University Press.

Dirlik, Arif. 2001. 'Place-based Imagination: Globalism and the Politics of Place', in Roxann Prazniak and Arif Dirlik (eds), *Places and Politics in the Age of Globalization*. Lanham, MD: Rowman and Littlefield.

Eitel, Ernest J. 1985 [1873]. *Feng-Shui: The Science of Sacred Landscape in Old China*. 5th ed. London: Synergetic Press.

Elvin, Mark. 2004. *The Retreat of the Elephants: An Environmental History of China*. New Haven: Yale University Press.

Endacott, G.B. 1964. *A History of Hong Kong*. London: Oxford University Press.

Escobar, Arturo. 2001. 'Culture Sits in Places: Reflections on Globalism and Subaltern Strategies of Localization', *Political Geography* 20: 139–74.

Evans, D.M. Emrys. 1971. 'Common Law in a Chinese Setting – the Kernal or the Nut?', *Hong Kong Law Journal* 9.

Feld, Steven and Keith Basso (eds). 1996. *Senses of Place*. Santa Fe: School of American Research.

Feuchtwang, Stephan. 1974. *An Anthropological Analysis of Chinese Geomancy*. Vientiane: Vithagna.

———. 2003. 'Foreward', in Ole Brun, *Fengshui in China: Geomantic Divination between State Orthodoxy and Popular Religion*. Copenhagen: Nordic Institute of Asian Studies, pp. vii–xi.

Feuchtwang, Stephan. (ed.). 2004. *Making Place: State Projects, Globalisation and Local Responses in China*. London: UCL Press.

Freedman, Maurice. 1966. *Chinese Lineage and Society: Fukien and Kwangtung*. London: Athlone.

Groves, R.G. 1969. 'Militia, Market and Lineage: Chinese Resistance to the Occupation of Hong Kong's New Territories in 1899', *Hong Kong Branch of the Royal Asiatic Society* 9: 31–64.

Gupta, Akhil and James Ferguson (eds). 1997. *Culture, Power, Place: Explorations in Critical Anthropology*. Durham: Duke University Press.

Hayes, James. 1996. *Friends and Teachers: Hong Kong and its People, 1953–1987*. Hong Kong: Hong Kong University Press.

Ho, Pui-yin. 2004. *The Administrative History of the Hong Kong Government Agencies, 1841–2002*. Hong Kong: Hong Kong University Press.

Hoadley, J. Stephen. 1970. '"Hong Kong Is the Lifeboat": Notes on Political Culture and Socialization', *Journal of Oriental Studies* 8: 209–11.

Hughes, Richard. 1968. *Hong Kong: Borrowed Place, Borrowed Time*. London: Andre Deutsch.

Kamm, John Thomas. 1977. 'Two Essays on the Ch'ing Economy of Hsin-An, Kwangtung', *Hong Kong Branch of the Royal Asiatic Society* 17: 55–84.

Knapp, Ronald G. 1998. 'Chinese Villages as Didactic Texts', in Wen-hsin Yeh (ed.), *Landscape, Culture, and Power in Chinese Society*. Berkeley: Institute of East Asian Studies, pp. 110–28.

Lam, Wai-man. 2004. *Understanding the Political Culture of Hong Kong*. Armonk, NY: M.E. Sharpe.

Lau, Siu-kai and Kuan Hsin-chi. 1987. 'The 1985 District Board Election in Hong Kong: The Limits of Political Mobilisation in a Dependent Polity', *Journal of Commonwealth and Comparative Politics* 25(1): 82–102.

Lowenthal, David. 1985. *The Past Is a Foreign Country*. Cambridge: Cambridge University Press.

Lung, David. 1980. 'Fung Shui: An Intrinsic Way to Environmental Design with Illustration of Kat Hing Wai in the New Territories of Hong Kong', *Hong Kong Branch of the Royal Asiatic Society* 20: 81–92.

Mathews, Gordon. 2001. 'Cultural Identity and Consumption in Post-colonial Hong Kong', in Gordon Mathews and Tai-lok Lui (eds), *Consuming Hong Kong*. Hong Kong: Hong Kong University Press, pp. 287–317.

McNeill, J.R. 1998. 'China's Environmental History in World Perspective', in Mark Elvin and Liu Ts'ui-jung (eds), *Sediments of Time: Environment and Society in Chinese History*. Cambridge: Cambridge University Press, pp. 31–52.

Merry, Sally and Rachele E. Stern. 2005. 'The Female Inheritance Movement in Hong Kong: Theorizing the Local/Global Interface', *Current Anthropology* 46(3): 387–410.

Miners, Norman. 1987. *Hong Kong under Imperial Rule, 1912–1941*. Hong Kong: Oxford University Press.

———. 1995. *The Government and Politics of Hong Kong*. 5th ed. New York: Oxford University Press.

Palmer, Michael. 1987. 'The Surface-subsoil Form of Divided Ownership in Late Imperial China: Some Examples from the New Territories of Hong Kong', *Modern Asian Studies* 21(1): 1–119.

———. 1991. 'Lineage and Urban Development in a New Territories Market Town', in Hugh Baker and Stephan Feuchtwang (eds), *An Old State in New Settings: Studies in the Social Anthropology of China in Memory of Maurice Freedman*. Oxford: Journal of Anthropology Society of Oxford, Occasional Papers No. 8: 70–106.

Potter, Jack. 1968. *Capitalism and the Chinese Peasant: Social and Economic Change in a Hong Kong Village*. Berkeley: University of California Press.

———. 1970. 'Wind, Water, Bones, and Souls: The Religious World of the Cantonese Peasant', *Journal of Oriental Studies (Hong Kong)* 8: 139–53.

Rooney, Nuala. 2001. 'Making House into Home: Interior Design in Hong Kong Public Housing', in Gordon Mathews and Tai-lok Lui (eds), *Consuming Hong Kong*. Hong Kong: Hong Kong University Press, pp. 47–80.

SCMP. South China Morning Post (Hong Kong daily newspaper).

Scott, Ian. 1988. 'Generalists and Specialists', in Ian Scott and John P. Burns (eds), *The Hong Kong Civil Service and its Future*. Hong Kong: Oxford University Press, pp. 17–49.

Sinn, Elizabeth. 1989. *Power and Charity: The Early History of the Tung Wah Hospital*. Hong Kong: Oxford University Press.

Siu, Helen. 1989. *Agents and Victims in South China: Accomplices in Rural Revolution*. New Haven: Yale University Press.

———. 1996. 'Remade in Hong Kong: Weaving into the Chinese Cultural Tapestry', in Tao Tao Liu and David Faure (eds), *Unity and Diversity: Local Cultures and Identities in China*. Hong Kong: Hong Kong University Press.

Strauch, Judith. 1980. 'A Tun Fu Ceremony in Tai Po District, 1981', *Hong Kong Branch of the Royal Asiatic Society* 20: 147–53.

Waters, Dan. 1997. 'Foreigners and Fung Shui', *Hong Kong Branch of the Royal Asiatic Society* 34: 57–117.

Watson, James L. 1975. *Emigration and the Chinese Lineage: The Mans in Hong Kong and London*. Berkeley: University of California Press.

———. 1976. 'Chattel Slavery in Chinese Peasant Society: A Comparative Analysis', *Ethnology* 15(4): 361–75.

———. 1982. 'Of Flesh and Bones: The Management of Death Pollution in Cantonese Society', in Maurice Bloch and Jonathan Parry (eds), *Death and the Regeneration of Life*. Cambridge: Cambridge University Press, pp. 155–86.

———. 1989. 'Self-defense Corps, Violence, and the Bachelor Sub-culture in South China: Two Case Studies', *Proceedings of the Second International Conference on Sinology, Section on Folklore and Culture*. Taipei: Academia Sinica, pp. 209–21.

———. 2004. 'Presidential Address: Virtual Kinship, Real Estate and Diaspora Formation – The Man Lineage Revisited', *Journal of Asian Studies* 63(4): 893–910.

———. 2006. 'McDonald's in Hong Kong', in James L. Watson (ed.), *Golden Arches East: McDonald's East Asia*. Stanford: Stanford University Press, second edition: 77–109.

Watson, Rubie S. 1982. 'The Creation of a Chinese Lineage: The Teng of Ha Tsuen, 1669–1751', *Modern Asian Studies* 16: 69–100.

———. 1985. *Inequality among Brothers; Class and Kinship in South China*. Cambridge: Cambridge University Press.

———. 1988. 'Remembering the Dead: Graves and Politics in Southeastern China', in James L. Watson and Evelyn Rawski (eds), *Death Ritual in Late Imperial and Modern China*. Berkeley: University of California Press, pp. 203–27.

———. 1991. 'Wives, Concubines and Maids: Servitude and Kinship in the Hong Kong Region', in Rubie S. Watson and Patricia Ebrey (eds), *Marriage and Inequality in Chinese Society*. Berkeley: University of California Press, pp. 231–55.

Wesley-Smith, Peter. 1980. *Unequal Treaty, 1898–1997: China, Great Britain, and Hong Kong's New Territories*. Oxford: Oxford University Press, pp. 1–14.

———. 1992. 'Identity, Land, Feng Shui and the Law in Traditional Hong Kong', *University of Hong Kong Law School Working Paper Series*, No. 5, University of Hong Kong.

Yang, Dali L. 1996. *Calamity and Reform in China*. Stanford: Stanford University Press.

Chapter 13

The Sacrifices of Modernity in a Soviet-built Steel Town in Central India

Jonathan P. Parry

Daily they would vainly storm,
Pick and shovel, stroke for stroke;
Where flames would nightly swarm,
Was a dam when we awoke.
Human sacrifices bled,
Tortured screams would pierce the night,
And where blazes seaward spread
A canal would greet the light.
(Goethe, *Faust*, 11123–30, as translated in Berman 1983: 64).

Preamble

Until the mid-1950s, Bhilai was a small village in Durg district, in the Chhattisgarh region of Madhya Pradesh, central India. Chhattisgarh has since become a separate state and Bhilai is now a large 'company town', the site of one of the biggest steel plants in Asia. The construction of the Bhilai Steel Plant (BSP) was amongst those mega-projects of the post-Independence era that were key to Nehru's strategy for leaping over centuries of backwardness and kick-starting the Indian economy along the highway of rapid industrialisation. But the Nehruvian modernisers well understood that the creation of such a gargantuan industrial complex would require much sacrifice, as did the local peasantry whose land and labour were to be appropriated for the realisation of their vision. The suppositions of the planners and peasants about the kind of sacrifice involved were, however, different – and it is with this difference that my paper is largely concerned.

'Sacrifice' for the sake of the nation had been a leitmotif of the Independence struggle, the 'freedom fighters' offering their lives as *bali dan* that India might shake off the imperialist yoke. *Bali* is the standard term for animal sacrifice in

Hindu ritual discourse, and specifically for sacrifices intended (in the manner of Hubert and Mauss [1964]) to get rid of the 'bad sacred' – for which the British perhaps plausibly stood.[1] Alternatively, nationalist rhetoric deployed the word *kurbani* or some variant on *yagya* (respectively Urdu and Sanskrit for sacrifice), or the term *tyag*, which specifically evokes the renunciation of the Hindu ascetic. Being jailed in the nationalist cause became *deshyagna* ('sacrifice for the country') and in Surat answering the Congress Party's call to withhold municipal taxes – and thus risk the confiscation of property – was dignified as *bali dan* (Haynes 1991: 235, 227). Later, under the influence of Gandhi's disciple, Vinoba Bhave, the Rajasthan State Government was to optimistically establish its Bhoodan Yajna Board ('Board for the sacrificial donation of land') to oversee the voluntary redistribution of surplus land from an over-endowed rural elite to the landless poor (Oomen 1972: 45).

But despite its pervasive appropriation of the language of sacrifice, the nationalist movement in general, and Gandhi's style of religiosity in particular, were closely identified with a Hindu reformism that was hostile to blood offerings. True sacrifice is internal, a voluntary renunciation of the transient self for some transcendent goal. Through its association with reformist Hinduism, the modern Indian nation state is commonly assumed to discountenance the killing of animals (Fuller 1992: 101f.). At the time that the Bhilai Steel Plant was constructed, however, and as a paradoxical countercurrent to this 'new wind', the Chhattisgarhi peasantry were widely convinced that their government's development programme would require sacrifices of a more tangible kind on a massive scale – sacrifices not just of surrogate animals, but of the human beings for which they have always stood. From where, I want to ask, did such ideas arise and from where did they derive their rhetorical force? From a prescient perception of the evils of industrial modernity, or from an older stratum of beliefs about agricultural fertility and state-sponsored construction sacrifices?

The answer, I believe, is both. There is a family resemblance between this discourse about the sacrificial destruction demanded by modern industry and what in a different kind of setting the Comaroffs (1999) call the 'occult economy', which paradigmatically proposes a magico-religious explanation for the accumulation of capital in the hands of the few as the many are steadily impoverished. At least since Ardener's (1970) analysis of the changing witchcraft beliefs of the Cameroonian Bakweri (cf. Geschiere 1997), and Taussig's (1980) discussion of *The Devil and Commodity Fetishism in South America*, much anthropological writing has concentrated on the way in which these occult economies reflect contemporary politico-economic circumstance. Often – as with Taussig and the Comaroffs – the commentary they provide is held to reveal the way in which *capitalism* impinges on subaltern lives. Some elements of the sacrificial discourse I describe make sense, I suggest, in such terms; but (shades of Ardener) the template that underlies them does not. This seems to be made up of a set of core ideas that are strikingly similar to ones found in a variety of other cultural settings with very different types of political economy. The world over, for example, people have imagined it necessary to immure soft, mushy and transient human bodies in ostensibly solid stone or concrete foundations in order to render the *latter* permanent – to the modern mind at least a seemingly strange premise on which to base a construction business. Given the widespread distribution of such ideas across time and space, it seems plausible to suppose that they say at least as much about preoccupations of an existential sort that confront human beings more or less everywhere as about particular politico-economic conditions. Though I do not pretend that I am in a position to identify the ultimate source of such notions, in conclusion I offer some tentative suggestions about the kinds of concerns that inform them.

Bhilai as a Beacon of Modernity

Gandhi's antipathy to urban industrial modernity – which 'with its glittering baubles and trinkets (was) exactly what had first enslaved Indians to the British' (Khilnani 1997: 73) – is well known. So, too, is the eclipse of his ideological legacy by the economic policies championed by Nehru and his associates (ibid. Chap. 2). Investment in basic industrial infrastructure would allow India to pursue a course independent of more powerful nations. By absorbing surplus labour, rapid industrialisation would, moreover, relieve some of the pressure on the countryside; and would contribute to the reform of Indian society by blowing away some of the nastier cobwebs of the past, one of the thickest and nastiest of which was caste. Urban industrialism would act, that is, as a solvent to the old religiously enchanted world of status and collective identities, and usher in a more secular order based on the individual. In order to 'catch up' with 'advanced' industrial countries, India must 'modernise', and the shining new discipline of development economics would pilot its 'take-off' into a brave new world from which hunger, poverty and illiteracy would be extirpated. This is the 'modernity' to which my title alludes. In the spirit of it, the crucial Second Plan, drafted in 1954/5, gave clear priority to the development of heavy industry, and – in particular – to the construction of three large-scale public sector steel plants. The one at Bhilai was the first to be completed and has in the long term proved the most consistently profitable, and with the most harmonious record of industrial relations.

Now run by the Steel Authority of India, BSP was built with Soviet aid and technology under an agreement signed in 1955, and began production four years later. Originally designed for an output of one million tons, its capacity was steadily upgraded to four million tons over the next twenty years. Considerations of a social as well as technical kind had determined its location. Profits were secondary to employment in the planning priorities of the time, and Bhilai was situated in what was then regarded as a remote and 'backward' rural area. By 1987, BSP – along with its subsidiary mines – had 63,400 workers on its direct payroll. By 2003 that figure had fallen to 39,000 (though the plant was also providing employment to around 10,000 temporary contract workers each day on terms, conditions and rates of pay that were vastly inferior). 'Liberalisation' had begun to bite, and in sixteen years the jobs of some 24,400 permanent workers had been sacrificed to market 'imperatives'.

The plant itself covers an area of nearly seventeen square kilometres. In order to make way for it, for the spacious BSP township, for the mines and their townships and for the private-sector Industrial Estate, land from ninety-six villages was compulsorily purchased by the Government. Some of these villages disappeared altogether. Some have coke oven batteries or blast furnaces standing on top of them; others the BSP township. Yet others on its periphery lost some or all of their agricultural land, but the residential site was left intact. Most of the villagers remained and many eventually took jobs in the plant. Large numbers of outsiders moved in, and gradually most of these villages were swallowed up by urban sprawl. My fieldwork has focused on three of them.

As was intended, the plant has acted as a magnet for a good deal of private-sector industrial development, initially in the form of small-scale ancillary industries directly dependent on it. Some have grown into fairly large-scale enterprises, and the dedicated industrial estate on which many of them were relocated in the 1970s now houses around 200 factories. Aside from this development, the 40-kilometre belt between the district headquarters in Durg to the west and Raipur to the east is today a more or less continuous ribbon development of factories and housing colonies.

The modernising rhetoric of the pioneer days has taken deep root, not only in the managerial mind but also in the minds of many of the managed. Initiated just a few years after Independence and built with the fraternal aid of the 'anti-imperialist' Soviet Union, Bhilai epitomised the Nehruvian dream. A trail-blazer for the rapid development of the country, it was to serve as a beacon for modern India; 'a symbol and portent', as Nehru described it, 'of the India of the future', 'a temple of modern India'[2] (Srinivasan 1984: 58). A catalyst for a rejuvenated civilisation, it would provide a springboard for a giant leap into industrial modernity. No less than Stalin's Magnitogorsk (Kotkin 1995), its purpose was to forge not only steel but also a new kind of man in a new kind of society. But as those who had participated in India's struggle for Independence had made great sacrifices in the nation's cause, so new sacrifices were now necessary that it might enter this twentieth-century Shangri-la. If that meant the villagers sacrificing their land, then the plant would be 'mother and father' to them, and would provide its children with a new and brighter future.

One male member of every village household from which land had been compulsorily purchased was entitled to claim a BSP job. Initially, however, the take-up was disconcertingly small. The locals were notably reluctant to enter the industrial labour force, and the plant was in fact largely constructed and manned by migrant labour from other corners of the country, at least some of whom had the industrial skills and experience it needed so badly. Many of these immigrant workers eventually brought their families to join them and have put down permanent roots in the town.

Today, however, the local Chhattisgarhis bitterly complain about the disproportionate share of BSP jobs that these outsiders have taken. Organised sector industrial workers are an extremely privileged segment of the Indian labour force – in Bhilai none more so than those employed by the plant, who are its aristocracy of labour. The job is secure, the wages are high, the bonuses good and – despite recent in-roads on them – the fringe benefits still excellent. There is plenty of scope for illicit earnings 'on top' from innumerable scams and rackets, and significant numbers of workers make a not inconsiderable supplementary income from moonlighting occupations to which they devote as much time as they do to their jobs in the plant. As to the ex-villages on the periphery of the plant, say the Chhattisgarhis, just see how they have now become slums, and how all these 'foreigners' have corrupted our kids and run off with our women. And indeed there are significant numbers of unions between men of outside – and especially 'Bihari' – origin and local Chhattisgarhi women. Alcoholism does destroy many families, violence does hang in the air, *satta* (a numbers racket) has become an addiction and gangs of unemployed youths do mooch aimlessly about the streets at every hour of the day and night.[3]

In spite of all this, however, very few of my Chhattisgarhi informants appear to conclude that the Nehruvian dream of industrial modernity was really a chimera; or that Gandhi was right to suppose that all that it ever promised was baubles and trinkets. The resentment is rather that its self-evident benefits have not, in adequate measure, come their way; that it is they who made the sacrifices, but others who gathered their fruits. There is surprisingly little nostalgia for old village ways; and agricultural labour – even on fields of one's own – is for the most part regarded with complete disdain by those raised largely in town (Parry 1999a, 2003).

Sacrifices for Steel

When the construction of BSP started, there was little overt or organised resistance to it. Admittedly, some villages quibbled about soil qualities on which their rate of compensation depended. In Girvi and Patripar they grumbled loudly when their fields were taken in tranches, making it difficult to reinvest rationally, and the Nijigaon villagers blocked the main highway in protest when much of their previously requisitioned land was made over to the private-sector industrial estate.[4] But these were little local brush fires, and there was no coherent and unified opposition to the plant – far less one that stood on a principled objection to the project of modernity. So soon after the British, they now explain, people were not yet accustomed to the idea that they might gainsay their *sarkar* (government). And anyway this was a new and as yet largely unblemished *sarkar* – led, if not by knights in shining armour, then at least by saintly heroes in homespun with an unimpeachable record of self-sacrifice. When they called on the Chhattisgarhi peasantry to play their part, it was only theirs to obey.

In local newspaper articles, political speeches and BSP Public Relations' propaganda of the period, the theme of sacrifice (of *bali dan* and *kurbani*) is endlessly repeated. 'Sacrifice' is required to construct the plant. When it is constructed, it is in the name of their 'sacrifices' (*kurbani*) – and the *obligation* that government incurred on account of them – that local MPs demand a greater representation of Chhattisgarhis in its workforce.[5] When Nehru dies, BSP workers take a solemn pledge 'to consider no sacrifice great enough' to realise his dream of an 'economically self-sufficient India' and to bind 'our people together in secular bonds' (Mehta 1993 [1970]: 316). Though I do not suppose that the majority of villagers took this metaphorical discourse of sacrifice literally, it seems to me likely that the barrage of nationalist-inspired, and no doubt managerially orchestrated, rhetoric encouraged them to counterpose to it their own more familiar notions. They were in any event predisposed to believe that a project of this sort and scale required sacrifice; and they understood that to mean something other than the modernisers intended, and concluded quite logically that if there was sacrifice there had to be victims.

The Chhattisgarhis were, as we have seen, initially reluctant recruits to the plant. It is true that this was the era before the inflation of public sector wages, and that they could often earn as much, or more, working for a private contractor putting up quarters in the township. It is also true that, by the second half of the 1960s, many had overcome their qualms. They saw the outsiders returning from their shifts, saw the size of their now increasing pay-packets too, and had learned to desire consumption goods they had never dreamt of before. Then there were several years of chronic drought, and those still living off the land were forced to consider the alternatives. Crucially, however, the most immediate dangers of a job in the plant were by this stage deemed to have passed.

From my very first day of fieldwork, I was repeatedly offered – like a litany – the same two-part explanation for their original wariness. It is a discourse that seems over-determined; and – though apparently disconnected – I will suggest that there is a sense in which the two parts of the answer serve the same rhetorical purpose. I will also suggest that the fear of modern industry that constitutes the second half of the answer was more generalised, and that its exclusive attribution to the locals is motivated.

The first reason offered is that the local villagers' consumption demands were extremely limited, and that they saw no point in working harder than was required to meet them. Those who still had land preferred to farm it; those who now only had compensation money from BSP preferred to eat and drink at leisure and let tomorrow take care of itself, and those who were forced to work for wages preferred to earn them outside the plant. That is explained by the second part of the answer. To get such a massive plant started, thousands of sacrifices (*balis*; in dialect *pujvan* [or *pujai*])[6] would be necessary. New recruits were being set to work for a few days and then surreptitiously sacrificed – thrown into the foundations to make them bear the weight of such massive erections, into the furnaces to make them function. People were, of course, frightened for other more obvious reasons – frightened of the huge monster-like earth-moving machinery that they would watch from afar with fascinated awe but never approach. They said that the *poklin* (caterpillar tractors fitted with giant scoops) and *dozars* (bulldozers) were demons (*rakshas*) because they could shift more dirt in a day than a whole village could shift in a month. But chiefly they were frightened that they would be literally sacrificed to Nehru's dream of modernity; that their children would disappear into concrete if they did not hide them when long-trousered strangers came to the village.

Though it is hard to measure, all my evidence suggests that these stories had a real impact on actual behaviour. One index of it is that the Satnamis – the largest Untouchable caste in the region – have greatly benefited from what turned out to be such privileged employment (Parry 1999b). An important reason for this – though there are others – is that at the start they were generally less frightened of a job in the plant than their caste superiors, and therefore got into the BSP workforce early. As the poorest and most put upon segment of local society, in pre-BSP days Satnamis had constituted a large proportion of the Chhattisgarhi labour that had migrated to the jute mills around Calcutta, the rail centre at Kharagpur, the collieries of southern Bihar and the Tata steel town of Jamshedpur. When the plant was under construction, many returned to work on the site. For them modern industry held fewer terrors and they were apt to view these sacrifice rumours with more scepticism.

Others – like Khorbara, a Ravat-Herdsman by caste – were easier to rattle. He remembers standing in line at Power House to sign on for a BSP job. While he was waiting, a passer-by started screaming that they were like dumb animals queuing up to be *pujwan*. Two of the four lines simply melted away, and with them Khorbara himself. He would be safer hawking *channa-murra* (a mixture of chickpeas and puffed rice). 'But those who remained waiting', he ruefully reflects, 'have now become rajas, while I live on rent in this one-roomed hut ... But yes, some died. They were pushed into pits. Several thousand ended that way'.

There is at least a sense in which these stories are true. During those early days – and especially during its construction phase – working for BSP was very dangerous. A crude estimate, based on fatality figures published in *The Statesman* in early 1960, would suggest that for every thousand workers there were on average between one and two fatal accidents per year.[7] As if that is not chilling enough, what this average conceals is that the dangers were very much greater in some kinds of work than in others, and that there were undoubtedly segments of the workforce for whom the risks were several times higher.

Not that old-timers put much faith in press or plant statistics. Twenty or thirty would die, they say, and the company would claim that it was just two or three. And there was nobody to argue the toss since no proper records were kept of construction workers, and most were long-distance migrants with no family at hand to ask questions. It was easy to disappear. One characteristic story has seven or eight workers buried alive in the foundations of the Power Plant. On the order of the officers in charge, they dug out the corpse of the Russian engineer, but such was the urgency of the job that the rest were left where they were. A good deal of hyperbole has doubtless crept in, but I was endlessly offered supposedly eyewitness accounts of such accidents. Several dozen were immured when the banks of a huge reservoir that was being excavated caved in. A score or so were crushed by falling masonry when the roof and lining walls of an open-hearth furnace came down while it was under repair. My friend Somvaru was one of those sent in to retrieve the last of the bodies. The next day they summoned a Brahman priest who performed *puja*, smashed coconuts as *balis* to placate the furnace, and the job was re-started. The catalogue could go on, and – though on a much reduced scale – continues to be added to today. BSP is not a *karkhana* (a factory) but a *kal-khana* ('an abode of death'[8]), 'a well of mortality' (*maut ki kuan*), people still say. Nearly every worker from those pioneer days has stories about accidents witnessed or experienced, and not a few bear the scars. Some young dare-devils signed up in defiance of their families; some joined out of economic necessity, only to quit after a near-miss or two; but many more were discouraged from joining at all.

So it was that an accident rate that was dismal enough in reality assumed truly epic proportions on the village rumour mill[9] – feeding the conviction that there was more to these disasters than the Public Relations Department put out. Fact further 'confirmed' fantasy in that, at the time of construction, excavation-work was responsible for the largest loss of life.[10] Thereafter the highest incidence of serious accidents was in those shops that have the biggest furnaces (the Coke Ovens, the older of the two Steel Melting Shops and the Blast Furnaces). In other words, it was just where sacrifices were conventionally supposed to occur that actual fatalities were greatest.

In the light of all this it is hardly surprising that when Manohar Babu, who had just matriculated and got his first job with the Durg Employment Exchange in 1957, was sent round the villages in a jeep with a loud-hailer to encourage enlistment in the plant labour force, he lasted only a few days before desperately seeking a transfer to other duties. '*Marne ke liye kaun jaega? Vehan to bali dete hein …. pujvan hovat rahise*', 'Who will go there to die? They give sacrifices there', they would jeer, accusing him of being a *dalal* (commission agent) who ate the government's money in order to get them killed.

But becoming a *bali* was just one of the dangers. Most of my BSP informants remember the Russians with affectionate awe for their Herculean capacity for labour, their disregard for distinctions of status, and for leaving behind a plant of which India could be proud. Amongst bottom-of-the-heap casual workers, however, there was a more sinister side to their reputation. Pale-skinned, and 'with cheeks like tomatoes', they were known as *russi gorsa* ('Russian swallowers') because they devoured lone workers alive. True, it was a story to frighten the children from wandering too far from home; but it was also one with which adult contract labourers in the plant would frighten themselves.[11]

Though usually put down to 'illiteracy', local explanations of how these rumours gained credence are sometimes given a political twist. My Communist friends, but others too, often assert that they were deliberately fostered by the malguzars – the former landlords and revenue collectors of their villages, in which they exercised a truly autocratic power. The motives of these 'kulaks', as one well-versed union leader described them, were obvious. Their labour supply was threatened by the employment opportunities the plant provided. In support of this allegation I could find no evidence – though it seems a little more probable (and rather less repellent) than the analysis offered by a senior clerk in one of the Tehsil offices. His theory was that, in the early days when they were all outsiders, almost every BSP officer sought to strengthen the representation of his own region in the plant. The officer would truck in his countrymen, and set them to work alongside local labour. He would then chuck handfuls of coins into the excavations below, and while the Chhattisgarhis scrabbled for them, these outsiders would bury them alive. It wasn't a matter of sacrifice, but of 'ethnically cleansing' the labour force.

When I first encountered these ideas about *bali*, I was always given the impression that 'that was the way in which we simple Chhattisgarhi folk used to think, but now we know better and can see these superstitions for what they really are'. This history of redemption from the benighted ignorance of a less enlightened world is, I am sure, the way in which many people really think, and I do not doubt that today the majority take these sacrifices stories less seriously than they did in the past. But as what follows will show, there remain many others who still believe that sacrifices are necessary to start a *new* factory; some who think that even now they persist in a *sublimated* form in BSP itself, and a few who claim that they continue to be offered in much the same way.

Of this last school is D.K. Das, a refugee from East Bengal, who when I first met him was working as a carpenter on a large construction site on the Raipur road.

> Whenever they [re-]build one of BSP's tall chimneys, there has to be an inauguration ceremony [*udghatan*] at which they give blood. The Managing Director instructs that Rs. 10,000–12,000 is left on the top of the stack and some worker is told to retrieve it. But when he has reached the banknotes, they turn on the current – which flows through the metal lining of the chimney of course – and he falls to his death. The money they give to his family. But all that is known only to the MD and management. Even now, four to ten workers die every day. They fall from above, are 'cut' by a train ... whatever. But none of this news ever comes out. On BSP's order, they do not write it in the papers. They don't allow reporters in the plant. The CISF [Central Industrial Security Force] stand at the gate.

So had there been sacrifices on his present site? I wondered. 'It's not big enough to need them', he said. 'Anything that happens will be the fault of the engineers and the architect.'

In explaining what I mean by 'sublimated' sacrifice, I begin with a brief digression. Sometime in 1959, a Telugu worker in the Rail Transport Department had been crushed to death between two wagons at a spot near what is believed to be the old Shiva shrine of the village of Sonth, on which the Coke Oven batteries now stand. The shrine itself had been spared only by what was plainly divine intervention (the usual story, bulldozers that refused to go into forward gear, giant snakes that wrapped themselves around its steering column and so forth).[12] The accident was attributed to the deity's anger at the invasion of his space, and his shrine was now regularly tended. Then, on 6 January 1986, there was a massive explosion on the Coke Oven batteries in which nine people were killed and forty-five injured (twenty-five of them seriously). This disaster is commemorated annually by Coke Oven personnel in an elaborate *havan* ('fire sacrifice') and *abhishek* ('consecration ritual') at the shrine, which has now been expanded and re-built. The worshippers are divided over whether this more recent accident was caused by the deity's displeasure, or whether he is now worshipped just as a prophylactic against future disaster.

What *is* clear is that Kali causes accidents when she is offended and should be properly placated by sacrifice. In Chhattisgarh – as in some other parts (e.g., Brouwer 1988: 230) – the forge of the smith and the kiln of the potter is a form (*rup*) of the goddess. Unsurprisingly, so too are the giant furnaces of the steel plant. That is why, I was told, there is no danger in BSP of being molested by the ghosts of those who have died an untimely death in the plant. 'What ghost would have the audacity to remain in her presence?' As the hottest and fiercest of deities, Kali's association with furnaces seems symbolically appropriate, as does her routine demand for blood sacrifice.[13] But – as I said at the start – blood sacrifice was under major ideological threat, and in rapid decline, by the time that the plant was supposedly claiming so many sacrificial victims. Some measure of the aversion that many now have to it is that during the 'Nine Nights of the Goddess', Kanhaiya – a Patripar Satnami of conspicuous piety – refuses even to cut lemons as *balis*. This is because it is irresponsible to encourage her bad habits and cravings. But an addiction denied can have dangerous consequences for even innocent bystanders, and 'deities denied the sacrifices they want will wreak terrible revenge' (Fuller 1992: 102). It is not, then, surprising that people now say that Kali takes for herself – and probably with increment – what is no longer given her voluntarily. Industrial accidents, that is, are the result of her wrath (*devi ka prakop*) and her way of asserting her claims. In all likelihood, too, reformist zeal has exacerbated the slaughter.

Though in the Hindi spoken on the industrial belt, *bali* refers *both* to sacrifices voluntarily offered and to the victims seized by disappointed deities who have been denied their due, the local dialect makes a clear distinction. The former are *pujwan* and the latter are *bhakh*. *Bhakh*, that is, are victims forcefully *taken* by resentful deities because their worshippers have failed to fulfil their obligations[14] – as when a vow (*mannat*) has been made to provide a certain offering in exchange for a certain boon, and the supplicant fails to deliver on the bargain. 'Who takes the *bhakh*?' I would ask. The factory itself, or 'Earth Mother' (*Dharati Mayya*), I was generally told. 'But if so many *pujvan* were given when BSP was built, why are *bhakh* taken?' The answer I got was that there could never be enough offerings; and that is because the plant is so big and its machines are so many.[15]

This theory of sublimated sacrifice at least partly disposes of an obvious difficulty. Real sacrifices are accompanied by appropriate rites, including the ritual consecration of the victim, which should be physically unblemished, should give some signal that it is a willing offering and should belong to the sacrificer – be something of his to renounce. Though in one of the stories to come, the consecration of an intended victim did supposedly occur, I never heard it suggested that the mass sacrifices that are held to have accompanied the construction of BSP were in any way ritualised. We are, of course, dealing with rumours and it is perhaps not surprising if they are short on detail about ritual procedures. But as D.K. Das's testimony illustrates, the stories my informants tell suggest these are minimal. No priest presides; no rites of entry or exit appear to be prescribed (Hubert and Mauss 1964), and the focus is exclusively on the immolation of a generally anonymous victim.[16] What counts is that a life (*jiv*) is extinguished, and the method matters little – whether the victim falls from a height, is buried alive or its blood is shed. Neither is there any attempt to ensure that these *balis* are perfect physical specimens, nor the slightest suggestion that they were anything other than unwitting dupes or that the sacrificer relinquishes something he owns. If, however, they were in reality victims of the goddess's revenge for *not* receiving sacrifice, the absence of ritual – and indeed of consent or ownership – is no longer a problem.

Before I go further I should make it clear that most of the time most current BSP workers treat the space of the plant in religiously 'disenchanted' terms. Today, at any rate, they are far more likely to explain industrial accidents as the consequence of the callous incompetence or arrogance of their officers, of the ignorance and inexperience of the contract labourers, or – increasingly – of the production pressures imposed by economic 'liberalisation' and globalised competition in the steel market. We cannot assume, however, that these more secular explanations are any less ideological, or more 'objective', than the sacrifice theory. They are at least partly a product of partisan political agendas; and we should not discount the possibility that the *bali* version also contains a kernel of truth – the possibility that somewhere some industrial manager has supposed such measures to work. After all, the Indian press regularly carries reports of alleged cases of human sacrifice (twenty-five from western U.P. alone during the past six months, according to an article in the *Hindustan Times* in November 2003).[17] And even if every one were a fantasy,[18] there remain many accounts of kidnapped children being set to work in industries so hazardous that they die. They may not be offered as *balis*, but it is not hard to imagine how their deaths might come to be construed in such terms. Like rumours about children kidnapped for their organs that circulate among the poor of many countries, these sacrifice stories 'are true at that intermediate level between fact and metaphor' (Scheper-Hughes 1996: 5). They convey something real about the way in which the lives and bodies of the most vulnerable are seen as disposable.

The more secular explanations of accidents fit, of course, with a self-presentation in which all such superstitions have been left far behind. In May 1994, however, an interesting rumour spread rapidly through Girvi; and it made me realise that this repudiation of past credulity cannot entirely be taken at face value. A stranger had appeared in the 'village' and had tried to ingratiate himself with three village children by feeding them samosas. He promised to return next day with sweets – but it was to remain their secret. It did not, and when the stranger reappeared he was beaten unconscious by an angry crowd of villagers who then called the police. They demanded to speak to the children, but nobody could – or would – identify them; so the prisoner was released. Thus far consensus. Thereafter accounts diverge – most significantly with regard to the stranger's origins and motives.

One striking feature of such rumours is the extraordinary velocity with which they circulate. Another is their timing. They appear to peak in *Jyesth*, the *hottest* month in the year when Kali is presumably thirstiest for blood, when the goddess is at her most hyperactive (see Babb 1975: 28), and when the earth is ploughed and violence is done to Dharati Mayya (the goddess with which it is identified). Most striking, however, is the supposed identity of this perhaps entirely imaginary malefactor, and his purpose. He was definitely a 'foreigner'. One possibility was that – like others of his kind – he was intent on taking advantage of a simple Chhattisgarhi maiden. He was trying, it was said, to use the children to entice a supposedly 'mentally retarded' village girl on whom he had sexual designs. The background to this has already been hinted at. Many male migrants with wives and children at home – a significant proportion of them 'Biharis'[19] – have contracted secondary unions with local women. The more prevalent version, however, was that the stranger was searching for sacrificial victims for a new factory that was being built in the area. That, in this theory, the Girvi kidnapper was perhaps a 'Bihari' is significant, in that – in the Chhattisgarhi mind – 'Bihari' is more or less synonymous with 'gangster'. That he was perhaps a south Indian from Patripar caused me some discomfort in that my research assistant was a conspicuously dark-skinned south Indian from that neighbourhood. In either event, the ne'er-do-well was an archetypal outsider – perhaps even the anthropologist's alter ego.

Generally, the kidnappers are imagined to be merely agents – for the factory owners, for the big contractors or even for the government itself. I was sitting one day with Santu Satnami, his wife and their neighbour, Dukalu. The former had just returned to Patripar from the village in which they own land, and his wife was complaining about a recent crime wave in that area. 'Don't the police do anything?' I innocently asked. 'What will they do?' she said. 'They are all thieves for the government.' And she went on to explain that they scour the countryside in their jeeps, kidnapping children to cull in the cause of population control. 'No, no', protested Dukalu (who had just retired from BSP), 'they take them as *balis* for some new company, or for a bridge or a dam'. When I then asked why companies need them, I was told – with much circumstantial evidence – that it is

> because you can't set up a good one without ... Without *balis* you cannot make anything at all. You make a bridge and it falls down. You build a dam and it bursts. You install a machine and it will not run. And if you do not give, 'these people' [he meant the deities] will take. And that was how it was in BSP. Thousands of people were buried in the earth.

Government complicity is again clear from the following fragment from my fieldnotes. It is Jagdish's mother who does the talking. We had been discussing the many deaths caused by the local deity, Rajarav, when his territory was taken for the iron-ore mines at Rajhara, and she had been describing a meeting the villagers had called. The god had possessed one of them and through him announced that he would have no *kudali* (small pick-axes) or *dozars* (bulldozers) on his land. Though they had removed his image from the village, he was still living on the hillside from which ore was to be extracted, so nobody should work there. After performing *bhumi pujan* ('worship of the ground'), however, some outsiders did. To a man all of them died – 'all six *kauri* [120]. Not immediately, but slowly slowly. Even those who just went to watch also died. A family from Arjunda ... all six dead'. And when they started to dig the foundations for BSP itself, she went on, the government again organised a big *bhumi pujan*.

'There was a big fire sacrifice (*havan*) there, into which they offered many fistfuls of sesame seed. But even then, people did not believe what would happen.'

'What did happen?'

'Somewhere some fell to their deaths. Somewhere people were buried. Think how many seeds there were in all those fistfuls. That many died.'

'You mean that the number of sesame seeds offered was the number of *balis* that had to be given?'

'If you resolve in your heart and offer one flower in the sacred fire, then you will have to give one *bali*.'

'Who offered the sesame?'

'Who would offer it? Nehru came from Delhi. The Russians came.'

'You mean Nehru Ji offered the seed?'

'Nehru would hardly offer himself. With him came big, big pandits. Those people would have seen that without so many *balis* the factory would not stand up.'[20]

'Who takes these *balis*?'

'The *devi-devatas* (gods and goddesses). Who else? Durga, Sitala, Kali ... those people.'

'But people say that the goddess is our mother. How can a mother kill her own children?'

She launches into a heartrending story about a priest at the Mahamaya temple whose small son got accidentally locked in the temple one night. They had found him dead in the morning. 'If the goddess had thought, "this is my child", would she not have saved him? Would she have taken his life? Crying, crying the priest went mad'.

'So does it mean that we are not God's children?'

Everybody laughs. 'Get away with you, brother. I cannot give you an answer.' She gets up to resume her interrupted chores.

But the public sector and the government do not maintain a monopoly. Private enterprise too has its needs, even if these are not on such a large scale. In February 1998, a local newspaper published a long investigative report under the banner headline, 'Suspicious Death of Young Worker: Village Discusses Secret Sacrifice'.[21] It relates to a large rice mill near Samoda, on the main road between Dhamdha and Durg. A thirteen-year-old Satnami boy had gone there to work, but had never returned. His distraught mother enquired after him throughout the bazaar, but to no avail. A sympathetic crowd gathered and decided that they should check out the mill. The owner was shifty, said the boy had left hours ago, but was eventually persuaded to let two delegates in for a cursory check. There was no sign of Santosh Kumar, but one of them did spot some clothing they thought might be his. When they demanded to look in the big storage bunker, the owner refused and saw them off the premises. The crowd made its way to the local police station, but it was not until they had blocked the traffic on the main road outside that the police took an interest. And when they did return with the villagers to the rice mill and opened the bunker, there sure enough was the body. The crowd's first reaction was to demand compensation, and clutching the corpse they *gherao*-ed ('encircled') the factory owner until he had promised the mother Rs. 50,000.

But was it an accident? Not in the view of the villagers, nor – judging by the tone of the article – in that of the journalists either. Now other young boys from the village had come forward to tell how the rice mill owner had tried to persuade them to come to his factory at night. And one deaf-mute lad (of whom a large inset photograph) managed to tell the reporters – partly through signs and partly through writing – that when he had gone there to work, the owner had placed a *tilak* (mark of consecration) on his forehead. He immediately fled in terror, and never went back. Added to this damning testimony was the circumstantial evidence that there had been problems with that bunker from the start.

The article had implied that the police were complicit in a cover-up, and when I returned to Bhilai in 2000 I learned that the two reporters were now themselves facing court cases on account of it. Through the good offices of friends on a rival newspaper – which had more soberly carried the story as a case of child labour that had ended in tragedy – I tried to arrange an interview with the senior reporter involved. But he had got wind of what I wanted to talk about and never showed up for our appointments. My friends, however, assured me that though the villagers may well have genuinely believed it to be a case of *bali*, it was very unlikely that the journalists did so. One loyal colleague on the same paper claimed that the *bali* slant was a strategy to force the police to investigate the case properly and the owner to pay adequate compensation; though others supposed that it was just another instance of freelance blackmail from which only the journalists would benefit. But while my middle-class friends could credit the credulity of the crowd, I am not convinced that we should take that for granted. Their reaction, remember, was to demand financial recompense from the capitalist rather than lynch him – suggesting, perhaps, that a sacrificial victim would better loosen his purse-strings than other possible constructions on the death.

In any event, the story played on an entirely conventional theme – recalcitrant machinery that refuses to function because it has been disabled by deities hungry for sacrifice. 'The deities ride the machines and won't let them work'. 'They demand *balis*', which have to be provided 'to keep the gods happy'. Often, they make their requirements known by appearing in the dreams of the owner. And sometimes they demand a price he is unwilling to pay. There was a paint factory on the Bhilai industrial estate that had to close down because its owner had learned that the offering required was his only son. But the deities are usually more reasonable, and it is probably wise to indulge them. If their demands are unmet, one fatal accident follows another. In *bali* there is usually just one victim, so in the end human sacrifice is more economical of human life. It's almost a safety measure. At least that was the view that one group of workers in a large private-sector engineering firm explicitly put to me. 'So have there been *balis* in all of the 200 factories on the industrial estate?' I asked. It seems not. They mostly take place in those that have very big boilers, furnaces and chimneys.

The Samoda rice mill case, the Girvi kidnap rumour and the reception that Manohar Babu received when he went round the villages with a loudhailer all suggest a real sense of outrage. But this rather phlegmatic view of industrial sacrifices as sensible risk management and an inevitable price of progress is at least as characteristic of the tone my informants would adopt when we talked of such matters (cf. Fürer-Haimendorf 1944). As Madan Lal nonchalantly put it (playing cleverly on the word *kal* that can mean both [see n. 9]), 'no machine came without death'. Their detachment I attribute largely to the fact that nobody I know claims to know personally *anybody* who was *actually* offered as a *bali* (as opposed to a *bhakh*, see n. 17). But perhaps it also stems partly from a philosophical resignation to the ambiguity of power. Rulers properly make sacrifices *on behalf of* their subjects, but that often turns out to mean offering their subjects *as sacrifices*. That's the way of the world, and what can we do?

Sacrifices: Ancient and Modern

Much of this data is uncannily familiar from ethnography elsewhere in the world. For example, Drake (1989) identifies for Borneo a complex of kidnapping panics associated with construction sacrifices in which the state, acting through the agency of frightening outsiders who prey on local victims, is complicit. Dayak groups, believed by outsiders to hunt heads, in turn believe that outside agents of the state take *their* heads for dams, bridges and oil wells (Tsing 1993: Chap. 2). In much the same way, 'tribal' Chhattisgarh has – as we shall see – a fearsome reputation for human sacrifice while Chhattisgarhis suppose themselves likely victims of state-sponsored sacrifice. A pattern very similar to the Borneo one recurs in Flores (Erb 1991; Forth 1991 and Barnes 1993) and has close parallels on other continents. I will return to these cross-cultural continuities at the end, but for now my question is more limited. Do these *bali* rumours reflect a deep unease with industrial modernity and a profound distaste for the modern state, which appears all too ready to sacrifice its citizens? Are they, in others words, and as Drake claims for Borneo, a kind of 'ideological warfare' in a situation of 'socio-political stress and cultural conflict', a manifestation of 'brooding resentment' at the loss of autonomy, and a set of stories 'good-to-tell' because they powerfully express the way that people feel about the state? Or are they – as Barnes (1993) argues – a transposition to a new context of old ideas and associations that find credence amongst those who are otherwise largely uncritical of their rulers?

Posed in this way, the answer *at first sight* seems obvious. Only the context is new. As one Saurashtra Brahman told Pocock (1973: 73), 'You can't have a foundation ceremony without a blood sacrifice, it's essential and that's that'. And when the foundations are sufficiently important, it is an ancient idea that a human victim is called for. Thus, the stories of *bali* I have recounted evoke a set of very old legends involving rajas immuring innocent children in the foundations of forts and bridges in order to give them strength. In Chhattisgarh, and neighbouring regions, such tales abound and these sacrificial practices are held to have continued throughout the British period and into the present. Two years back, there was – as the workers interpreted it – a sublimated sacrifice on one of the larger construction sites on which I spent time. Three drunken BSP workers returning home at night had been roaring down the road on a powerful motorbike, missed the bend on the corner and smashed right through the wrought-iron grill on the gate to the site. *Bhakh* had been taken. As many of my informants tell it, however, there is hardly a bridge, a dam or an irrigation canal within a hundred kilometres of Bhilai which can have been constructed without a real *bali*,[22] and the new fly-over by Durg station required several, as Prakash confirmed. He works with the survey department of the municipal authority and should know. For other parts of India too, there are many reports from the colonial period: human sacrifices for the sinking of the Burmah Oil Company's wells; rumours of kidnappings in Bombay for a bridge in Baroda, resulting in violence in which there were more than twenty deaths; reports of Calcutta taxi-drivers killed on suspicion of procuring victims for the Kidderpore docks (Hutton 1946: 249f.).

Animal sacrifices for the fertility of the fields are routine in remoter parts of rural Chhattisgarh, and – though my informants are now reluctant to admit it – were until recently offered in the area around the plant. Today coconuts are smashed and fire sacrifice given in lieu. In the village on the Maharashtra-Chhattisgarh border in which Amit Desai worked, however, the offering of a human victim – paradigmatically of a *lamsena*, an uxorilocally resident son-in-law who is unprotected by his own kin – is widely supposed still to be practised in the more *jungli* villages around, to release the blocked up fertility of the fields.[23] Again in Bastar, to the south, where it is uncertain whether human sacrifice was actually practised,[24] it was nevertheless supposedly sponsored by the state in order to secure the harvest, and at key moments in the history of the kingdom, as when an heir to the throne was born (Sundar 1994: 164). The danger was greatest during the month of *Jyesth* before the crops were sown – remember the Girvi rumour. Many of the same elements recur in Hill Reddy country (Fürer-Haimendorf 1944); and in the Kond areas of Orissa on Chhattisgarh's eastern border, where human sacrifice almost certainly *was* practised, and where it was again associated with agricultural fertility, as well as with solidifying the earth at the beginning of time and with averting calamities.[25] The victim of Kond sacrifice – an outsider – was kidnapped by outsiders; and the *pusaha* (a child stealer) who haunts the imagination of many of my Chhattisgarhi informants of rural origin is stereotypically also a stranger. Indeed, he sometimes appears in the guise of that archetypal outsider – the wandering ascetic.

In the myths of some tribal groups in central India, ironworking had its origins in human sacrifice, and mining and metallurgy have – as in many other parts of the world – been held to require it (Eliade 1978: 65–66). Around Bhilai, animals were – and still sometimes are – sacrificed for other purposes as well: for the birth of a child, for unloosening the tongue of a son unable to talk, or for promotion in the police. When small-pox threatened, goats were 'cut' for the goddess Sitala; and at the *Divali* festival pigs are *buried alive* in the cattle byre to ensure the wellbeing of the household's milch animals.[26] Sacrifice, in short, has long been a central channel of communication and influence in Chhattisgarhi dealings with the divine, and the requirement for human victims when the objectives are greatest is a long-standing assumption.

It therefore seems plainly implausible to see contemporary recensions of the same theme as a direct commentary on, let alone as a direct product of, the new relations of production towards which a reluctant Chhattisgarhi peasantry are propelled. The reference here is to Taussig's (1980) celebrated interpretation of the Faustian pact with the devil, into which some Columbian peasants supposedly enter, as an indigenous commentary on the evils of proletarianisation; and of their folklore about the magical fecundity of baptised banknotes as a proto-Marxian theory about the mystery of capital accumulation. The *bali* stories we are dealing with here would be hard to represent as the fruit of folk philosophising on the commodity form from the perspective of gift morality. Long before 'free' labour and 'capitalistic' profit existed on any scale in the region, victims were supposedly being sacrificed to the purposes of the powerful. That is not, of course, to say that these beliefs about *bali* and industry have nothing to tell us about the villagers' views of the forces that confront them. But what they seem to say is that whatever the productive regime, creative power is forced out of sacrificial destruction – and that it is the little fish who pay the price as victims.

It would I think be a mistake, however, to see only a seamless continuity with the past. There is something valuable to retain from the lead of those – like Taussig, Drake, Erb and others – who stress the way in which such stories are made compelling by current politico-economic circumstances, and who encourage us to focus on the way in which the new world is revealed through the play of old symbols. In the new world that the Chhattisgarhi ex-peasants-turned-proletarians of the Bhilai industrial belt inhabit, *bali* is no longer quite what it was. At least in its phantasmagorical 'industrial' form, it seems to have been almost totally stripped of any sense of proper ritual procedure. It has also become a highly secret practice; but at the same time is held to take place on a quite unprecedented scale. Is it too fanciful to see in these shifts a reflection of the actual experience of the neophyte proletariat? The old ritualism has indeed lost much of its grip. The world does seem a less transparent place and even to those who perform them industrial processes are often opaque. Machines do have an extraordinary productive power that must come from somewhere, and the mass production of steel in such a gargantuan complex does suggest a need for sacrifice on an entirely new scale. That these stories relocate the power of modern industry in a timeless ritual practice – indeed one that created the cosmos – should not obscure the fact that its procedures have actually been transformed.

It is certainly the case that while, in the villages around Bhilai, other forms of sacrifice – for crops, cattle or the restoration of health – have steadily declined since the steel plant was started, the idea that factories require victims persists with some stubbornness. It is as if the powers of dangerous creativity have been relocated from the countryside to the town, and from agriculture to industry. Sacrifice, as Eliade (1954, 1959) insisted, repeats cosmogony. It therefore occurs at, and remakes, the centre of the world. Today it is concentrated in the industrial areas, and – as seen from Bhilai – that reflects the contemporary reality. It is now they who live at the centre.

But what is perhaps most revealing is that if sacrifice is a way of coercing the deities and gaining access to divine power, then in the old world of the peasant economy each peasant did sacrifice for himself (even if the raja also – and on a grander compass – performed it on behalf of his kingdom). In the new world of industry it is done by the government or the capitalist, and never by the worker who is its most likely victim. If, that is, it is done at all. And if it is not, the deities will ungraciously seize for themselves – and with increment – what men should have given up graciously, and again it is the workers who suffer. Either way, it seems like an allegory of their loss of control over their own personal destinies, of the price *they* pay for modernity.

In classical variants of sacrifice, moreover, the victim must represent something of value to the sacrificer, his possession or purchase (Biardeau 1984). In modern industrial sacrifices, however, he is kidnapped or tricked. It seems like a sad reflection on the relationship between men and masters in the contemporary world and on the way in which the lives of the former have been devalued.

As a qualifying footnote to this, however, it needs to be said that the Chhattisgarh Mukti Morcha, in the recent past the most radical union in the region, has sought to re-appropriate and – as it were – 'proletarianise' the power of sacrifice. Shankar Guha Niyogi, its charismatic Bengali leader, continually invoked the self-sacrifice of the nineteenth-century 'Tribal' insurrectionary, Vir Narayan, who was hanged by the British – and well before his own assassination predicted that he too would be made a *bali* by the local Bhilai industrialists. The victims of the police firing at the captive BSP Rajhara mines in 1977, and at Bhilai Power House in 1992, are commemorated in songs and speeches as *balis* or *kurbanis* to the working class movement, and the union hospital at Rajhara is the Shahid ('Martyrs') Hospital. Capital and the state have not had a complete monopoly on the creative potential of sacrifice, and the rhetoric of the Mukti Morcha is shot through with its imagery.

Sacrifices: True and False

What must not be lost sight of is that most of the time most of my informants – both locals and outsiders – now insist that the stories about the sacrifices that supposedly started the plant are untrue. Their scepticism takes several forms. At the less radical end of the spectrum is the claim that though the government never *gave balis* to build BSP, the deities *took bhakh* on that account. Alternatively, many – under the influence of Hindu reformist ideas – insist that theses rumours must be false since the deities do not really desire blood sacrifice. Though a government led by the heroes of the Independence movement would certainly know that, some concede the possibility that a few deluded owners of private factories might suppose otherwise. A twist on this view is that although 'real' *devi-devatas* are repelled by blood offerings, there are plenty of ghosts (*bhut-pret*) who are not. The deities do not want *balis*, even if these are sometimes solicited by the low-grade supernaturals who impersonate them. But such fence-sitting theories are less common than outright rejection. What most sceptics say (in a Nehruvian secularist spirit) is that there was no substance at all to these rumours and that victims were neither given nor taken when the plant was built.

It is striking, however, that even those who scoff most at these tales invoke them constantly. They almost invariably do so, moreover, in tandem with the other conventional explanation for the Chhattisgarhis' reluctance to join the BSP labour force – their limited grasp on the law of scarcity and restricted consumption demands. Is there some logic that links these two apparently disparate theories? Why, anyway, do the *bali* stories have such a hold on even those who profess to disbelieve them, and why is the fear of sacrifice so firmly attributed to the locals when the idea that large-scale engineering and industrial projects call for human offerings is common throughout the country? When kidnapping rumours blaze through the slum neighbourhoods that surround Bhilai, the panic is by no means confined to Chhattisgarhi parents. Indeed, when I first discussed them with Adhikari, a Telugu Catholic of 'untouchable' caste, a mission school graduate and now a railway worker, it was to him a novel idea that they might be anything other than true.

For many of the long distance migrants who arrived in Bhilai in the pioneer days, Chhattisgarh was a remote and savage land of jungles inhabited by 'primitive' Tribal peoples.[27] And their lurid stereotypes pre-eminently associated such people with the fearful practice of human sacrifice, and with a childlike propensity to live in the present and be content with little. The two theories that are held to explain the locals' unwillingness to work in the plant thus evoke the two key signifiers of 'Tribal' backwardness. Whatever these outsiders' own misgivings about the price that such a large project might exact from its labour force, they had come to earn a wage from a job on the site. But the locals had options provided by their fields or their compensation money; and – given the prevalence of human sacrifice in the region – could reasonably be expected to share their fears in magnified form. It is, in short, plausible to suppose that a terror of modern industry was a displacement of fears that were more generally shared onto a population that was imagined to be predisposed to them and pragmatically able to act on them.

Today these stories serve, I believe, other more significant ideological purposes. The idea of 'progress', of having embraced modernity and left rural darkness behind them, of belonging to a more 'educated' and 'civilised' world, has a powerful hold on the minds of BSP workers. For the Chhattisgarhis amongst them, what these now obviously childish fantasies about sacrifice show is the distance they have travelled along a path – illuminated by Nehru's beacon – that led from an illiterate and superstitious past to an enlightened and rational present. For such people, in short, it is the *falsity* of past beliefs that has real ideological salience and that needs to be continually asserted; and it is this that at least partly explains the continued currency that these tales of sacrifice have. And it is possibly here that their insistence on the present orientation of past beliefs also fits as the rhetorical antithesis to the future orientation of their present preoccupations with their children's career prospects and education. An inability to think for the morrow is, as we have seen, a defining attribute of '*jungli* primitives', and the gulf that now separates them from their past is emphasised by acknowledging (and probably exaggerating) the extent to which they had formerly lived for the moment.

As to the non-Chhattisgarhi outsiders, what both of these stories underscore is why *they* deserve the credit for dragging Chhattisgarh into the modern world. While those who now insist on their rights as the sons-of-the-Chhattisgarh-soil were cowering in their cottages for fear of *balis* and bulldozers,[28] and were boozing away their compensation money, it was *their* blood and sweat that was building Bhilai. The entirely imaginary sacrifices which so frightened the superstitious locals thus serve to highlight the *real* sacrifices that these outsiders made on the altar of Nehru's dream of modernity, and to explain why they have more right than anybody to enjoy its fruits and to fix jobs in the plant for their boys.

There is even, perhaps, a sense in which scepticism about these stories of *bali* may buttress belief in them. The more loudly the enlightened proclaim their falsity, the more plausible it is to conclude that there must be many others who give them credence, and a few who are likely to act on their superstitious beliefs. Take, for example, an alleged case of human sacrifice reported by the *Hindustan Times* in June 2001 from a part of Maharashtra not far from the Chhattisgarh border.[29] The death of the child-victim had at first been accepted as accidental, and it was not until an organisation called the Andha-Shradha Nirmoolan Samiti ('The Blind Faith Eradication Council') got the bit between its teeth that the 'truth' emerged. As a result of their painstaking investigations, an eleven-year-old girl would testify that the boy had been sacrificed by his grandmother. It further transpired that her own father had previously sacrificed a child. Reading between the lines of the press report, it is not hard to imagine how the complicity of a suggestible child might be secured. Nor is it difficult to see how the zeal of a 'secular' organisation dedicated to the extirpation of 'superstition', and to exposing the inhuman practices to which it gives rise, might have the unintended consequence of reinforcing the popular conviction that such practices really take place.

In summary, then, there are some who openly claim that large-scale factory production requires the literal sacrifice of human lives, but many more who – however watchful of their children when strangers appear in the neighbourhood – dismiss such stories as simply a myth. Though I am not in a position to offer a systematic epidemiology of such beliefs, my impressionistic evidence would strongly suggest that it is younger, better-educated workers with organised sector (and especially BSP) employment who are the most likely sceptics. Of a piece with that is that they are the ones most concerned to distance themselves from the antiquated notions of their illiterate 'thumb impression' (*angutha-chhap*) fathers. Those lower down the industrial hierarchy – many of whom have at some stage worked as contract labourers in the plant – are those most likely to admit to believing such stories. That is perhaps consistent with the fact that they are generally less schooled, less experienced and have a more limited understanding of industrial processes. Nor is it irrelevant that today – and by some considerable margin – a disproportionate number of fatal accidents in the plant involve contract workers. Most importantly, however, the pattern is exactly what one would predict on the premise that such stories represent – in the manner of Taussig – a kind of reflection on the character of modernity. Those who have benefited from it least are naturally prone to emphasise the price in human life that is paid for it; while those who have prospered most invoke the very same stories to proclaim its benefits by showing how it has done away with such nonsensical beliefs. From their own perspective, both are of course right.

The Big Issue: London Bridge is Falling Down

We have seen that there is a significant continuity between the human sacrifices that have in this region supposedly guaranteed the abundance of the harvest and those that supposedly enable large factories to function today. What is even more striking, however, is the close kinship between the latter and the construction sacrifices that have been reported in many other parts of the world. It is to these parallels that I turn in conclusion.

At least since Tylor (1871: 104–8), the wide distribution of foundation sacrifices – apparently premised on very similar ideas in very different cultures – caught the attention of our anthropological forbears. Legends and rumours of such sacrifices in connection with the building of bridges, dams, forts, monasteries, royal and chiefly dwellings, or city walls and gates were recorded from almost every continent.[30] 'London bridge is falling down' and its foundations must be bathed in the blood of small children (Opie and Opie 1951: 270f.). A young girl is immured in the walls of Copenhagen, one of St Columba's monks in the foundations of his cathedral on Iona, and when a new bridge was constructed at Halle in 1843 it was popularly supposed that it would only stand if a child was built into it. The Balkan countries have a ballad tradition of great poetic quality that celebrates such stories (Dundes 1996), and they provide the backdrop to compelling novels by two of the region's most celebrated twentieth-century writers (Kadare 1993 [1978]; Andrić 1995 [1945]). Even beavers, according to some native American groups, build one of their young into a new dam. Though modern anthropology has had little to say about such cross-cultural continuities,[31] it has continued to multiply examples (e.g., Hernandez 2002: 216–17) – including many that involve factories and mines.[32]

It is true that the details of the supposed sacrificial procedure vary – with regard, for example, to the preferred age and sex of the victim (there is often a preference for women, especially pregnant ones, or for children), and to the manner of immolation (most characteristically burial alive in the foundations). Often – though I never encountered this notion in Bhilai – the spirit of the victim stands perpetual guard over the building for which it was sacrificed. Almost invariably, however, human sacrifices are associated with mega-construction projects that smack of hubris and that rival the work of the gods. Unless such a sacrifice is offered the construction will collapse. Though the engineering problem seems transparent enough, what is less transparent – to the 'modern' mind – is the 'solution' proposed. How, as I asked at the outset, have people from so many cultures arrived at the apparently counter-intuitive conclusion that squelchy and corruptible human bodies make stone and concrete durable? Though it may make sense to argue that religious representations 'catch on' precisely because they are counter-intuitive and therefore attention-grabbing (Boyer 1994), that does not explain why this *particular* proposition recurs with such frequency.

Nor does politico-economic circumstance. One illustration of the operations of the occult economy that the Comaroffs (1999) offer is that of 'skulls built into the foundation of a new building to ensure a good business'. Such (real or imaginary) ritual practices, they acknowledge, have long been part of the ritual repertoire, but 'appear to have been relatively rare in the past'. Today they take epidemic form in response to the way that 'millenial capitalism' and 'the culture of neo-liberalism' impinge on the lives of the poor. At other points in their analysis, the Comaroffs stress that new situations produce new forms of magic, and that witchcraft beliefs mutate under 'the impact of large-scale transformations on local worlds.' Similarly, Geschiere stresses their volatility and the 'continuous innovation' to which they are subject (1997: 59). The general thrust of these analyses, then, is to suggest that cultural representations surrounding the occult economy are highly protean, and within rather wide margins malleable to politico-economic circumstance.

In the case I have documented, however, these margins seem narrow. True, I have argued that sacrifice is not what it was, and that the direction in which it has changed reflects the way in which neophyte proletarians experience the new world they encounter. But, as I have also shown, there is a core of ideas – including that power is created by sacrifice and that major constructions stand on account of it – that remain remarkably constant. This core, moreover, is found in a wide range of different cultures and in the context of very different types of political-economy. It does not therefore seem sufficient to say that these stories are 'good-to-tell' on account of that context (though that may be part of it). A significant part of their appeal – to say nothing of their core content – transcends specific material and political circumstance (cf. Niehaus 2005). I therefore assume that these stories also address problems of a more existential sort that confront people almost everywhere. It is this that explains their recurrence in such similar forms in such dissimilar material conditions, and much of their attention-grabbing quality.

At one level, I concede, both the 'existential' problem and its solution seem obvious. Life is risky, buildings fall down, workers get killed. In a religiously enchanted world, what better strategy than to get powerful deities on your side? The commonest way of doing that is to offer them sacrifice. In many such worlds, moreover, sacrifice is *the* supremely creative force and it is no surprise that its power is summoned in the building of buildings of major importance. The more ambitious the objective, the more valuable the offering must be. Human sacrifice is just sensible risk management, and deploys the standard technology of ritual power. It is therefore no mystery that people suppose it a necessary precursor to major public works.

What this fails to explain, however, is why these stories have a hold on the popular imagination even in circumstances in which the ideology of sacrifice is attenuated – as in much of Europe where such legends abound but where the ritual slaughter of animals (let alone of human beings) has not for many centuries been seen as a proper method of entering into contact with the divine. The problem is not so easy to dispose of. Not that I claim that I can satisfactorily do so, and the tentative suggestions with which I end are intended as no more than a beginning. I have two.

The first is that one of the conundrums such stories address is the effect of duration on the world we make. Without human sacrifice, the dam is breached, the bridge washed away, the factory chimney topples. In legend, what is built by day is destroyed by night. In reality that is true on a time-scale which is still unsatisfactorily short. An obvious solution is to suspend time and that is what construction sacrifice does. In such sacrifices, as Hubert and Mauss (1964: 10–11) saw, instead of being symbolically equated with and standing in for the person sponsoring the sacrifice, the victim is identified with the object to which the benefits of the sacrifice accrue. Indeed, the two are so inseparably fused that the victim literally becomes part of the building. Since now they are one, and since duration ends for the victim with his or her death, time stops for both. It does so, moreover, at precisely the point at which the power that sacrifice unleashes is at its most intense and the victim is maximally sacred. It is as if, by walling it up, that power is bottled up in the building. Immured forever within it, the victim is the remains of the sacrifice, its characteristically regenerative element that is the seed of new life and a guarantee of continuity.[33] The building is not only the tomb of the victim but also a womb that contains it as a kind of embryo in a state of perpetual gestation – making it symbolically appropriate that small children and pregnant women are often the ideal oblations. This power is what gives the bridge or the dam its seemingly *supernatural* capacity to withstand *natural* forces, or (as in the case of a blast furnace that turns ore into metal) to transform nature in a seemingly magical way. The deities associated with nature are not unnaturally apt to be angered by such hubris, and sacrifice is represented not only as a quasi-automatic mechanism that allows such marvels to be accomplished but also as the propitiatory price that must be paid for them.

This hubristic quality of the engineering projects for which human sacrifice is imagined to be essential is, I think, crucial. Through such constructions, mortals attempt to defy and master nature, appropriate divine powers of creation and immortalise themselves by accomplishing immortal feats. What these stories tell us – and the second unpalatable truth that I suggest they address – is that none of this can be done by mortal men unless they are willing to sacrifice human lives in their quest to objectify human creativity. Immortal deeds have a price; superhuman accomplishments only come at human cost. In sum, human beings everywhere face the ephemeral and transient character of their own creativity and recognise that ordinary mortals can only accomplish immortal deeds by transcending their mortal limits and making an oblation of human life. On that at least the two different discourses with which I started this paper share common ground.

Notes

1. In local parlance, at least, the composite term *bali dan* – literally, 'the gift (*dan*) of a sacrificial victim (*bali*)' – generally evokes the notion of *self*-sacrifice in a way that by itself *bali* does not.
2. The phrase is a conscious or unconscious echo perhaps of *The Communist Manifesto*: bourgeois industry 'has accomplished wonders far surpassing ... Gothic cathedrals'

(Marx 1977 [1848]: 24). It acquired considerable currency and was generically applied to the state-sponsored mega-industrial projects of the period – like Bhakra-Nangal dam (on which see Khilnani 1997: Chap. 2) and the Damodar Valley project (on which see Kligensmith 2003). Its authorship is generally attributed to Nehru himself, though it was actually the then Congress President, Sanjiva Reddy, who is recorded as having described Bhilai as 'a modern temple of Indian prosperity' (Srinivasan 1984: 54).

3. I have elaborated elsewhere on the various points contained in this paragraph (Parry 1999a, 1999b, 2000, 2001, 2003 and 2005).
4. Girvi, Patripar and Nijigaon are pseudonyms for the three ex-villages-cum-labour colonies on which much of my fieldwork has concentrated. I also use pseudonyms for individual informants.
5. See, for example, *Deshbandhu* for 26 October 1966.
6. Throughout the industrial area, the Hindi word *bali* is today routinely used to refer to such sacrifices. My older Chhattisgarhi informants tell me, however, that in pre-BSP days only the dialect terms had currency. As I understand it, however, *bali* and *pujwan* are not quite synonymous. While *bali* might refer to the sacrifice of a non-sentient surrogate (like a lemon), the latter always involves the taking of 'a life' (*jiv*).
7. *The Statesman*, 22 February 1960, reported thirty-six fatalities in the previous ten months, and an estimated 167 since the plant began. Of these almost all would have occurred since the start of 1956. My estimate of the rate per thousand is necessarily crude because the precise number of construction workers on site is unknown. In 1960, there were calculated to have been around 30,000 of them, and at that time the number of directly employed company production workers was in the region of 10,000–12,000. In earlier years, however, the combined total would have been appreciably smaller. Unfortunately, the only official plant accident rate statistics that I have been able to obtain for the first fifteen year's of BSP's operation are for a later period (1966–1969), and are from this point of view anyway unilluminating. What they record is an 'accident frequency rate' and a 'severity rate'. The first is a measure of the number of injuries per 100,000 man-hours worked, by which yardstick BSP's safety record was poorer than those of the two directly comparable public sector steel plants at Rourkela and Durgapur. The second is a measure of the number of man-hours lost due to accidents.
8. *Kal* not only means 'death' but 'time' (and also machine). Though there is, as we are about to discover, a strong association between the BSP furnaces and the fierily destructive goddess Kali, no explicit link is made between the factory and the *kali yuga* (our present degenerate world epoch) of the sort that Pinney (1999) has so elegantly unravelled for another company town in central India.
9. Even today, false rumours of some serious accident in the plant spread like wildfire.
10. One reason, I have been told, is that in the earliest days they would dig vertically down. It was only after a number of accidents that it became standard practice to excavate at a slight oblique angle to reduce the risk of a cave-in.
11. Of course she had been warned against 'Russian swallowers' as a child, Radha told Ajay (my research assistant). 'But it wasn't until I was big that I saw one. Where? In your house. Where else?' She meant of course me.
12. It is in fact doubtful that this Shiva shrine was there in pre-BSP days. At least a couple of displaced Sonth villagers I managed to trace denied its existence. Nearby, however, had been a small shrine to Bajrang *Bali* (Hanuman), whose image was incorporated in the new Shiva temple. There is, however, an old – and now flourishing – village Hanuman temple that abuts onto the walls of the main BSP hospital in the township and about which an elaborate mythology has also

developed. Generally, however, and notwithstanding the story of Rajarav I come to later, few locals seem to have lost much sleep over the fate of their temples at the time that the site was levelled. As old Baisakhu explained, 'we were endlessly wandering here and there for the compensation money for our fields, and nobody could spare much thought for the deities. And when we were paid, we had never seen so much money. Everybody was so happy and in Girvi we walked up to our ankles in the canisters of expended fireworks.'

13. Every shop floor has several images or pictures of Visvakarma ('the divine architect of the universe') who is the patron of artisanal and industrial production. But he appears to be an entirely benevolent deity who only accepts vegetarian offerings. 'Only Mother is given blood', I was told. 'But isn't Visvakarma the god of iron?' 'Brother, in the factory there are furnaces. Furnaces are the form (*rup*) of Kali. Before we had never heard the name of Visvakarma.' Except at his annual *puja* on 17 September, most BSP workers pay him no attention at all (though he is regularly worshipped in private-sector factories). His immigrant outsider status was brought home to me when I asked my friends in the Coke Oven Heating Group why his festival was fixed by the Roman, rather than by the Hindu, calendar. After some discussion, it was decided that since foreign lands had factories first, his annual *puja* must have been borrowed from abroad.

14. I was offered the Sanskritised Hindi *bhakshan* as a synonym. *Bhakshan* means 'food' in the specific sense of food consumed by malevolent and vengeful supernatural beings. Traffic accident black spots are said to take *bhakh*, as are certain tanks which demand *tin salla* – one death by drowning in every three years, though some say three deaths in three years.

15. Management or the unions, it might seem, could easily allay the workers' fears of becoming *balis* or *bhakh* by sponsoring the sacrifice of animal surrogates. Partly because of Hindu reformism, and partly because of the spirit of Nehruvian secularism that still hangs in the air, I judge that to be an ideological and political impossibility. Coconuts are indeed often smashed as non-sanguinary *balis* to bits of equipment and infrastructure, but it seems unlikely that anybody who takes these stories seriously would suppose such paltry substitutes sufficient to ensure their safety. Though I am not sure whether to believe his story, one contract worker I know, employed for some years by a big contractor in the plant, claims that his boss would always 'cut' four goats at their work site at the inception of a new contract. The only accident that they ever had involved one of his work-mates who, *through his own carelessness*, fell to his death. This is the only time that I have heard of animal sacrifice in the plant.

16. I say 'anonymous' because, with the exception of the case of Santosh Kumar discussed below, nobody seems to *personally* know anybody who suffered the fate of a *pujwan* in any factory in the area. Some, however, may well suspect that friends and relatives who died in plant accidents were taken as *bhakh*.

17. *Hindustan Times*, 1 November 2003. The commonest motivations for such sacrifices, claims the article, are childlessness, financial problems and illness. In the weeks that followed, several more cases were reported by the same newspaper.

18. Given the frequency of such reports, that is perhaps unlikely, and in 2000 the Delhi High Court felt confident enough to uphold the death sentence passed on a man and a woman found guilty of sacrificing a small girl (*Central Chronicles*, 22 October 2000).

19. In Bhilai, this identity embraces people from U.P.

20. In the village on the Maharashtra-Chhattisgarh border in which he has worked, Amit Desai (personal communication) recorded a very similar story about Indira

Gandhi offering sesame seeds into the sacred fire when she came to inaugurate a big dam project in the vicinity. Again, each seed stood for a victim.
21. *Dainik Bhaskar*, 9 February 1998.
22. For a different part of South Asia see Obeyesekere's (1989) extremely interesting analysis.
23. In that the sacrificer eventually dies on account of making it, this sacrifice is closer to a Faustian pact than the stories I recorded. The villagers tell of one field that had claimed not only his life but also those of two others who had subsequently tried to cultivate it (Desai, personal communication). There was no implication in any of the stories I heard that consequences of this kind would eventually catch up with those who offer *bali* for a factory.
24. Grigson (1949) and Sundar (1994), for example, are sceptical of the evidence for it. But Elwin (1950: 70–71) discusses a case from 1938 in which a pregnant woman had allegedly been sacrificed by a tank for the fertility of the fields it irrigated. More accurately, it appears to have been the foetus she carried that was the essential offering. The evidence seems to have been compelling, a conviction for murder was secured and the main protagonist hanged.
25. For accounts of human sacrifice amongst the Konds I have relied on Duff 1846, 1847 and 1848; Bailey 1958; Boal 1982; Stutchbury 1982; Padel 1995 and Hardenberg 2005.
26. Their burial alive parallels the way in which most *balis* to BSP supposedly died. These pigs are offerings to a *masan*. *Masans* attach themselves to certain households and make them rich, but rapidly bring ruin if neglected. They are only ever fleetingly glimpsed, and take different forms, but their distinctive characteristic is that they have pig-like bristles. When the steel plant started, most villagers with significant 'black wealth' (that is, several head of buffalo) would have offered such sacrifices. Few still do so. That is partly because large herds are no longer common and partly because they no longer consider sacrifice seemly and find they can get away without it.
27. In reality the majority of Chhattisgarh's population are not in fact 'Tribals'.
28. According to some outsiders, local fears of industry are still deeply entrenched. A Malayali neighbour recently assured me that even now the number of 'pure-bred' Chhattisgarhis with jobs in the plant is negligible; and when I demurred he explained how my impression to the contrary was based on an optical illusion. 'Chhattis-garh' is generally held to refer to the 'thirty-six forts' of former rulers of the region, but my informants from other states often (half-humorously) say that the real import of the name is that local women have thirty-six houses (i.e., husbands). The theory that my neighbour put to me (and he was entirely serious) is that as a result of their promiscuity the number of children of mixed parentage in the industrial belt is extremely large. Whenever there has been a hullabaloo about the under-representation of locals in the BSP workforce, it is these people who were 'brought forward'; and it is because of their outsider genes that they dare to work in the plant. BSP's Chhattisgarhi workforce is not really Chhattisgarhi at all.
29. *Hindustan Times*, 29 June 2001.
30. See, for example, Knight (1909), Westermark (1912) and Hartland (1913) from whom the examples given in this paragraph are taken. Drake (1989) usefully summarises several other early sources.
31. For some decades, the challenge of placing such stories in a more general comparative frame has been largely left to specialists in other disciplines. The folklorist, Alan Dundes (1996), has assembled a fascinating 'casebook' of

commentaries on variants of the 'walled-up wife' ballad from the Balkans and India. His concern is to stress the interpretative importance of looking at the 'Indo-European' corpus as a whole, but given the strong parallels this has to stories and legends from other regions, it is unclear why his comparison should stop there. From the perspective of comparative religion, Eliade (1954: 76; see also 1959: 51, 56) sees sacrifice in general as an act of (repeated) cosmogony, and construction sacrifice as one instance of this.

32. See, for example, Taussig (1995) on the human sacrifices required by a sugar mill in Venezuela. For the Andean region see Nash (1979), Taussig (1980) and Gose (1986) on the association between human sacrifice and modern mining, and between industrial accidents and the failure to sacrifice. For central Java, Wolf (1992: 129) reports popular beliefs about local spirits who cause deaths and disappearances because they were not properly propitiated when factories were built on their land. Dundes's casebook (1996: 54) includes a story about a Slav folk hero who sacrificed himself in a vat of molten steel in order to make it of the highest quality.

33. In Indian classical mythology, Sesa is both the remains of the sacrifice and the snake in whose coils Vishnu slumbers after the doomsday destruction of the cosmos and as a prelude to the start of a new cosmic cycle. Sesa's brother is Visvakarma, the divine carpenter who will construct the world anew (Malamoud 1996: 19).

References

Andrić, I. 1995 [1945]. *The Bridge over the Drina*. London: Harvill Press.
Ardener, E. 1970. 'Witchcraft, Economics and the Continuity of Belief', in M. Douglas (ed.), *Witchcraft Confessions and Accusations*. London: Tavistock, pp. 141–60.
Babb, L. 1975. *The Divine Hierarchy: Popular Hinduism in Central India*. New York: Columbia University Press.
Bailey, F.G. 1958. *Caste and the Economic Frontier: A Village in Highland Orissa*. Manchester: Manchester University Press.
Barnes, R.H. 1993. 'Construction Sacrifice, Kidnapping and Head-hunting Rumors on Flores and Elsewhere in Indonesia', *Oceania* 62(2): 146–58.
Berman, Marshall. 1983. *All That Is Solid Melts into Air: The Experience of Modernity*. London: Verso.
Biardeau, M. 1984. 'The Sami Tree and the Sacrificial Buffalo', *Contributions to Indian Sociology* 18(1): 1–23.
Boal, B. 1982. *The Konds: Human Sacrifice and Religious Change*. Warminster: Aris and Phillips.
Boyer, P. 1994. *The Naturalness of Religious Ideas: A Cognitive Theory of Religion*. Berkeley: University of California Press.
Brouwer, J. 1988. *Coping with Dependence: Craftsmen and Their Ideology in Karnataka (South India)*. Leiden: Karstens Drukkerij.
Burra, N. 1995. *Born to Work: Child Labour in India*. Delhi: Oxford University Press.
Comaroff, Jean and John Comaroff. 1999. 'Occult Economies and the Violence of Abstraction: Notes from the South African Periphery', *American Ethnologist* 26(2): 279–303.
Drake, R. 1989. 'Construction Sacrifice and Kidnapping Rumor Panics in Borneo', *Oceania* 59: 269–79.

Duff, A. 1846. 'The First Series of Government Measures for the Abolition of Human Sacrifice among the Konds', *Calcutta Review* 6(July–Sept.): 45–62.
———. 1847. 'Captain Macpherson and the Konds of Orissa', *Calcutta Review* 8 (July–Sept.): 1–51.
———. 1848. 'The Khonds: Abolition of Human Sacrifice', *Calcutta Review* 10: 273–341.
Dundes, A. 1996. *The Walled-up Wife: A Casebook*. Wisconsin: University of Wisconsin Press.
Eliade, M. 1954. *The Myth of the Eternal Return*, trans. W. Trask. Bollingen Series 46. Princeton: Princeton University Press.
———. 1959. *The Sacred and the Profane: The Nature of Religion*. New York: Harcourt Brace Jovanovich.
———. 1978. *The Forge and the Crucible: The Origins and Structures of Alchemy*, trans. S. Corrin. Chicago: University of Chicago Press.
Erb, M. 1991. 'Construction Sacrifice, Rumors and Kidnapping Scares in Manggarai: Further Comparative Notes from Flores', *Oceania* 62: 114–26.
Elwin, V. 1950. *Maria Murder and Suicide*. 2nd ed. London: Geoffrey Cumberlege, Oxford University Press.
Forth, G. 1991. 'Construction Sacrifice and Head-hunting Rumours in Central Flores (Eastern Indonesia): A Comparative Note', *Oceania* 61: 257–66.
Fuller, C. 1992. *The Camphor Flame: Popular Hinduism and Society in India*. Princeton: Princeton University Press.
Fürer-Haimendorf, C. 1944. 'Beliefs Concerning Human Sacrifice among the Hill Reddis', *Man in India* 24(1): 14–41.
Geschiere, P. 1997. *The Modernity of Witchcraft: Politics and the Occult in Postcolonial Africa*. Charlottesville: University Press of Virginia.
Gose, P. 1986. 'Sacrifice and the Commodity Form in the Andes', *Man* 21(2): 296–320.
Grigson, W. 1949. *The Maria Gonds of Bastar*. Rev. ed. Oxford: Oxford University Press.
Hardenberg, R. 2005. 'Children of the Earth Goddess: Society, Marriage and Sacrifice in the Highlands of Orissa', unpublished Habilitation thesis. Muenster: Westphalian Wilhelms University.
Hartland, E.S. 1913. 'Foundation, Foundation-rites', *Encyclopaedia of Religion and Ethics* 6: 109–15. Edinburgh: T. and T. Clark.
Haynes, D. 1991. *Rhetoric and Ritual in Colonial India: The Shaping of a Public Culture in Surat City, 1852–1928*. Berkeley: University of California Press.
Hernandez, M.T. 2002. *The Fantastic, the Demonic and the Reél*. Austin: University of Texas Press.
Hubert, H and M. Mauss. 1964 [1898]. *Sacrifice: Its Nature and Function*, trans. W.D. Halls. London: Cohen and West.
Hutton, J.H. 1946. *Caste in India: Its Nature, Function and Origins*. Cambridge: Cambridge University Press.
Kadare, I. 1993 [1978]. *The Three-arched Bridge*, trans. J. Hodgson. London: Harvill Press.
Khilnani, S. 1997. *The Idea of India*. Harmondsworth: Penguin Books.
Kligensmith, D. 2003. 'Building India's "Modern Temples": Indians and Americans in the Damodar Valley Corporation, 1945–60', in K. Sivaramakrishnan and A. Agrawal (eds), *Regional Modernities: The Cultural Politics of Development in India*. New Delhi: Oxford University Press, pp. 122–40.
Knight, G.A.F. 1909. 'Bridge', *Encyclopaedia of Religion and Ethics* 2: 848–57. Edinburgh: T. and T. Clark.

Kotkin, S. 1995. *Magnetic Mountain: Stalinism as Civilization.* Berkeley: University of California Press.

Malamoud, C. 1996. *Cooking the World: Ritual and Thought in Ancient India*, trans. D. White. Delhi: Oxford University Press.

Marx, K. 1977 [1848]. 'The Communist Manifesto', in D. McLellan (ed.), *Karl Marx: Selected Writings.* Oxford: Oxford University Press, pp. 221–47.

Mehta, V. 1993 [1970]. *Portrait of India.* New Haven: Yale University Press.

Nash, J. 1979. *We Eat the Mines and the Mines Eat Us: Dependency and Exploitation in Bolivian Tin Mines.* New York: Columbia University Press.

Niehaus, I. 2005. 'Witches and Zombies of the South African Lowveld: Discourse, Accusation and Subjective Reality', *Journal of the Royal Anthropological Institute* 11(2): 191–210.

Obeyesekere, G. 1989. 'The Myth of Human Sacrifice: History, Story and Debate in a Buddhist Chronicle', *Social Analysis* 25: 78–93.

Oomen, T.K. 1972. *Charisma, Stability and Change: An Analysis of the Bhoodan-Gramdan Movement in India.* New Delhi: Thompson Press.

Opie, I. and P. Opie. 1951. *The Oxford Dictionary of Nursery Rhymes.* Oxford: Oxford University Press.

Padel, F. 1995. *The Sacrifice of Human Being: British Rule and the Konds of Orissa.* Delhi: Oxford University Press.

Parry, J.P. 1999a. 'Lords of Labour: Working and Shirking in Bhilai', *Contributions to Indian Sociology* (n.s.) 33(1 and 2): 107–40.

———. 1999b. 'Two Cheers for Reservation: The Satnamis and the Steel Plant', in Ramachandra Guha and J.P. Parry (eds), *Institutions and Inequalities: Essays in Honour of André Béteille.* New Delhi: Oxford University Press, pp. 129–69.

———. 2000. '"The Crisis of Corruption" and "The Idea of India": A Worm's Eye View', in I. Pardo (ed.), *The Morals of Legitimacy.* New York: Berghahn Books, pp. 27–55.

———. 2001. 'Ankalu's Errant Wife: Sex, Marriage and Industry in Contemporary Chhattisgarh', *Modern Asian Studies* 35(4): 783–820.

———. 2003. 'Nehru's Dream and the Village "Waiting Room": Long Distance Labour Migrants to a Central Indian Steel Town', *Contributions to Indian Sociology* 37(1 and 2): 217–49.

———. 2005. 'Changing Childhoods in Industrial Chhattisgarh', in R. Chopra and P. Jeffery (eds), *Educational Regimes in Contemporary India.* New Delhi: Sage Publications, pp. 276–98.

Pinney, C. 1999. 'On Living in the Kal(i)yuga: Notes from Nagda, Madhya Pradesh', *Contributions to Indian Sociology* 33(1 and 2): 77–106.

Pocock, D. 1973. *Mind, Body and Wealth: A Study of Belief and Practice in an Indian Village.* Oxford: Blackwell.

Scheper-Hughes, N. 1996. 'Theft of Life: The Globalization of Organ Stealing Rumours', *Anthropology Today* 12(2): 3–11.

Srinivasan, N.R. 1984. *The History of Bhilai.* Bhilai: Public Relations Department, Bhilai Steel Plant.

Stutchbury, E.L. 1982. 'Blood, Fire and Mediation: Human Sacrifice and Widow Burning in Nineteenth Century India', in M. Allen and S.N. Mukherjee (eds), *Women in India and Nepal.* Australian National University Monographs on South Asia, No. 8, pp. 21–75.

Sundar, N. 1994. 'In Search of Gundar Dhur: Colonialism and Contestation in Bastar, Central India, 1854–1993', PhD dissertation. New York: Columbia University.

Taussig, M. 1980. *The Devil and Commodity Fetishism in South America.* Chapel Hill: University of North Carolina Press.

—. 1995. 'The Sun Gives without Receiving: An Old Story', *Comparative Studies in Society and History* 37: 368–98.

Tsing, A. 1993. *In the Realm of the Diamond Queen: Marginality in an Out-of-the-way Place*. Princeton: Princeton University Press.

Tylor, E.B. 1871. *Primitive Culture*. Vol. 1. London: John Murray.

Wolf, D. 1992. *Factory Daughters: Gender, Household Dynamics and Rural Industrialization in Java*. Berkeley: University of California Press.

Westermark, E.A. 1912. *The Origin and Development of Moral Ideas*. London: MacMillan.

Notes on Contributors

Simon Coleman is Professor of Anthropology at Sussex University. His main area of interest is the anthropology of religion and specifically of Christianity. He has written on *The Globalisation of Charismatic Christianity* (CUP, 2000) and *Reframing Pilgrimage* (ed. with John Eade, Rouledge, 2004). He is currently engaged in a project looking at hospital chaplaincy.

Grant Evans is Reader in Anthropology at the University of Hong Kong and currently Visiting Professor at the Ecole francaise d'extreme-orient, Vientiane, Laos. His latest publications are *The Last Century of Lao Royalty* (2006) and a revised version of his *A Short History of Laos: The Land in Between* (2002, published in Lao and Thai 2006).

Stephan Feuchtwang is Professorial Research Associate, Department of Anthropology, London School of Economics and Political Science. He has published books on Chinese popular religion, *feng-shui*, and (with Wang Mingming) on grassroots charisma in southern Fujian and northern Taiwan. His research interests are on the relations between politics and religion and on the anthropology of history, which he is currently pursuing by an enquiry into the transmission of grievous loss, in Taiwan, the Chinese Mainland and Germany.

Thomas Kirsch received his Ph.D. in social anthropology from the European University, Frankfurt/Oder in 2002 and has conducted extensive fieldwork on African Christianity in Zambia and, more recently, research on crime prevention in South Africa. His publications include *Lieder der Macht: Religiöse Autorität und Performance in einer afrikanisch-christlichen Kirche Zambias* ("Songs of Empowerment: Religious Authority and Performance in an African-Christian Church of Zambia" (1998) and "Restaging the Will to Believe: Religious Pluralism, Anti-syncretism and the Problem of Belief" (2004).

Agnieszka Kościańska is a Ph.D. candidate at the Institute of Ethnology and Cultural Anthropology, Warsaw University. Her research interests centre on gender, religion and social resistance, as well as on new religious movements in Poland. She is the co-editor of *Kobiety i Religie* (Women and Religions), Kraków 2006 and *Gender: Perspektywa Antropologiczna* (Gender: An Anthropological Perspective), Warszawa 2007.

Galina Lindquist is teacher and researcher at the Department of Social Anthropology, University of Stockholm. Her interests are in the anthropology of religion and medical anthropology, and in ritual and play. She has studied new religious movements in Scandinavia, healing and popular religiosity in urban Russia and, more recently, Buddhism and shamanism in southern Siberia. She is the author of *Shamanic Performances on the Urban Scene: Neo-shamanism in Contemporary Sweden* (1997) and *Conjuring Hope: Healing and Magic in Contemporary Russia* (2001) and co-editor of *Ritual in Its Own Right* (2005).

Jonathan P. Parry is Professor of Anthropology at the London School of Economics and Political Science. He has done field research in various parts of north and central India on various topics. His publications include *Caste and Kinship in Kangra* (1979), *Death in Banaras* (1994), *Death and the Regeneration of Life* (1982, ed. with M. Bloch), *Money and the Morality of Exchange* (1989, ed. with M. Bloch), *The Worlds of Indian Industrial Labour* (1999, ed. with J. Breman and K. Kapadia) and *Institutions and Inequalities* (1999, ed. with R. Guha).

João de Pina-Cabral is Research Coordinator at the Institute of Social Sciences of the University of Lisbon. His publications include *Sons of Adam, Daughters of Eve* (1986), *Os Contextos da Antropologia* (1991), *Em Terra de Tufões* (Portuguese edition 1993; Chinese edition 1995) and *Between China and Europe: Person, Culture and Emotion in Macao* (2002). He is co-editor of *Death in Portugal* (1984), *Europe Observed* (1992) and *Elites: Choice, Leadership and Succession* (2000).

Frances Pine is a Senior Lecturer at Goldsmiths College, University of London and a Senior Research Fellow at the Max Planck Institute of Social Anthropology, Halle/Salle, Germany. She is co-editor of *Surviving Post-Socialism: Local Strategies and Regional Responses in Eastern Europe and the Former Soviet Union* (1998), *Memory, Politics and Religion: The Past Meets the Present in Europe* (2004) and *Generations, Kinship and Care: Gendered Provisions of Social Security in Central Eastern Europe* (2005).

Ursula Rao is a Lecturer at the Department of Anthropoloy, University of Halle, Germany. Currently she is involved in a research project about the interactive creation of news in Indian journalism. She has worked extensively in the fields of Religious Anthropology and Performance Studies in India. Two recent publications are *Negotiating the Divine: Temple Religion and*

Temple Politics in Contemporary India (2003) and *Celebrating Transgression: Politics and Method in the Anthropological Study of Culture* (2006).

Ramon Sarró received his Ph.D. from University College London and is a Research Fellow at the Institute of Social Sciences of the University of Lisbon. He has carried out extensive fieldwork in Guinea-Conakry and is now working on African migration to the Lisbon area.

Cornelia Sorabji received her Ph.D. from Cambridge in 1989 and is an Honorary Fellow at the Department of Anthropology, University College London. She carried out fieldwork in socialist Bosnia in the mid-1980s. Her research interests include political ideologies, conflict and violence, religious belief, Islam, and the role of social sciences in policy making. She is currently a research analyst at the U.K.'s Foreign and Commonwealth Office.

João Vasconcelos is Junior Research Fellow at the Institute of Social Sciences and Ph.D. candidate at the Institute of Social Sciences of the University of Lisbon. He has carried out fieldwork in northern Portugal and in the Cape Verde Islands.

James L. Watson is Fairbank Professor of Chinese Society and Professor of Anthropology, Harvard University. His publications include *Emigration and the Chinese Lineage* (1975), *Class and Social Stratification in Post-Revolutionary China* (1984), (1988) and *Village Life in Hong Kong* (with Rubie S. Watson) (2004).

Rubie S. Watson is Curator of Comparative Ethnology, Peabody Museum, and Senior Lecturer in Social Anthropology, Harvard University. She is the author of *Inequality among Brothers: Class and Kinship in South China* (1985), the editor of *Memory, History, and Opposition under State Socialism* (1994) and the co-editor of *Marriage and Inequality in Chinese Society* (1990) and *Harmony and Counterpoint: Ritual Music in Chinese Context* (1996).

INDEX

A
Abraham 103
absolutism 39, 54n3
abundance 138–9
The Academy 34n50
Adamiak, E. 173
Africa *see* religious logistics in Africa
Aggrawals 85–6
agricultural fertility 234
Ahern, Emily 207
Ahmedl, Akbar 39
Airlie, Shiona 210
Alexander, Bobby 61
American Ethnological Society 47
American Ethnologist 46
American fundamentalism 54n8
American Society for Psychical Research 33n11
Ammerman, Nancy 55–6n24
ancestor worship 121, 132, 133, 224, 225
ancestral tombs and *fengshui* 207
Andalusia 145, 146, 148n14
Andha-Shradha Nirmoolan Samati ('Blind Faith Eradication Council') 252
Andrić, I. 253
Anglo-Chinese border tensions 216
animal magnetism 17
animal sacrifice 233–4, 248
animism and modern spiritualism 16, 22–8
Anthropological Theory 110n3
anthropology
 ambivalent intersections in 46–7
 animism and marginality 22–8
 anthropological taboos 42–4
 'going native' 43
 of religion 1–2
 rhetorical strategies 47–8
 shared intelligibility 45
 spiritualism and anthropology of religion 13–35
anti-communist movement in Poland 169
anti-government protest and *fengshui* 206
anti-religion in Hindu manipulation 88
Appadurai, Arjun 206
Ardener, Edwin 147n1, 234
Arendt, Hannah 9n3
Aristotle 8, 202n6
Asad, Talal 9n1, 20, 21, 42, 44, 153
Aubrée, Marion and Laplantine, François 35n61
Ayodhya, Ram Temple at 87, 89

B
Babb, L.A. 182n5, 243
Baga of Guinea 187–202
 Baga-Susi divide 188–9
Bailey, F.G. 258n25
Baker, Hugh 209
Bakhtin, M. 48
Bakker, Jim and Tammy 52
Bakr, Abu 101
Bannister, Judith 219
Barnes, R.H. 247
Barthes, Roland 48
Bastard, Joan 202n1
Beeri Chettiars 85
Bellman, Beryl L. 188
Bender, Barbara 206
bereavement ritual in Bosnia 103
Berliner, David 189
Berman, Marshall 233
Bhadakariya, Shyamlal 90

Bharatiya Janta Party (BJP) 87–8
Bhave, Vinoba 234
Bhilai
    beacon of modernity 235–7
    steel plant construction 233, 234, 237–8, 239
Bhilai Steel Plant (BSP) 233, 235–44, 247, 250, 251–2, 256n6, 256n7, 256n8, 257n13, 258n26, 258n28
    Chhattisgarhis
        attitudes to Russians 240
        as reluctant recruits 238, 240, 251
        dangers of working for 239–40
    Satnamis employed by 239
Bhoodan Yajna Board ('Board for the sacrificial donation of land') 234
Bhopal *see* contested spaces in Urban India
Biardeau, M. 250
Bible Believers (Ammerman, N.) 55–6n24
Bihari migration to Bhilai 244
Blake, Henry 211
Bloch, M. and Parry, J. 103
Bloch, Maurice 202n2, 202n4
Boal, B. 258n25
Boleslaw the Shameful 173
Bond, Virginia et al. 77n9
The Book of Jerry Falwell (Harding, S.) 46, 48, 51
Bosnia *see* neighbourliness in Bosnia
Bougarel, Xavier 99, 107
boundary making
    in rural China 138
    in urban India 82, 85
bounteousness and extravagance 146
    givers and receivers of bounty, asymmetry between 146–7
Bowen, J. 99
Boyer, Pascal 189, 253
Brahma Kumaris 182n9, 182n16
    Brahma Baba 171, 172, 174, 182n4
    character of teachings 181
    conflict with Catholic authorities 175
    conversion to 171, 176–8, 181
    development of 174–5
    formation of 171–3
    gender and sexual relations 172
    Halina, Sister 174
    Hindu cycle of time 171–2
    Jayanti, Sister 178
    Kirpalani, Lekhraj Khubchand 171
    meditation, experiences of 176
    Sudesh, Sister 179
    Vedanti, Sister 172, 178
Brass, Paul R. 87
Bringa, Tone 100, 102
Bristol, Michael 136

British Association for the Advancement of Science 27
British Folklore Society 25
British Society for Psychical Research 17, 22, 25, 33n11
Brouwer, J. 242
Brown, K. 104
Brubaker, R. 97–8, 100
Bruce, Steve 55–6n24
Brun, Ole 206, 214, 227n2, 227n4, 227n6, 228n20
Buckser, Andrew 61
Buddhism
    Buddhist knowledge 155–6, 165, 166
    death and commemoration in Lao Buddhism 119–23
    deities of Buddhist cosmos 164–5
    khurees in 155, 157, 165
    ritual of 161–3
    Royal Family Commemoration in Laos 115, 116, 119–23, 125
    as 'state religion' 155
    Theravada Buddhism 120, 122, 132n9
Budrowska, B. 170
Bulgarian Ethnic Model (BEM) 98–9
Burkert, Walter 202n6

C
Callon, Michel and Latour, Bruno 74
Cantrell, Reverend 46–7, 48–9, 55n20, 55n21
capitalism
    colonialism and 41
    impingement on subaltern lives 234
    millennial capitalism 209
    socialism and 209
carnival of football 200–201
Carsten, Janet 2
Casanova, J. 100
Casey, E. 206
Castañeda, Carlos 22
Catholicism 29–30, 53
    football and 199
    in Poland 169, 170, 181
    popular Catholicism 42
    sexual intercourse as conjugal duty within 178
celibate marriage in Poland 169–82
    anti-communist movement in Poland 169
    Boleslaw the Shameful 173
    Brahma Kumaris
        character of teachings 181
        conflict with Catholic authorities 175
        conversion to 171, 176–8, 181
        development of 174–5
        formation of 171–3

gender and sexual relations 172
Hindu cycle of time 171–2
meditation, experiences of 176
Catholicism in Poland 169, 170, 181
celibacy and gender relations 180–81
celibacy and social advantage 179
chastity and asceticism 174
economic and political transformation in Poland 170
equality and female leadership 178–9
family life, new forms of 180
female celibacy in Polish tradition 173–4
female identity, modes of 170–71
female religiosity in times of uncertainty 174
gender relations 178–9, 180–81
Hildegard of Bingen 173
Saint Jadwiga of Silesia 173, 174
Julian of Norwich 173
Katherine of Sienna 173
Kemp, Margery 173
Saint Kinga (Kunegunda) 173–4
kinship networks, new forms of 180
male-domination, transformatory efforts 175
'marriages of souls' 177–8
meals and family life 176–7
menstruation and purity 179
motherhood and *Matka Polka* (Polish Mother) 170, 171, 181
purity and meditation 179
relations, towards new forms of 178–81
religion and identity in Poland 169–70
sexual abstinence 172, 177, 178
sexuality 170
spiritual needs, attention to 179, 180
subordinate position of women in Poland 175
Virgin Mary, inspiration of 173
Central Chronicles 257n18
centrality and marginality, temple ritual in China 135–49
abundance, performance and vision of 138–9
authority, localism and the reconstruction of 147
boundaries of local loyalty 138
bounteousness and extravagance 146
celebratory enjoyment, gratitude and 146–7
centrality in China 135
charismatic leadership 136, 138–9, 144
Chen Decai 141, 148n10
Chen Wansheng 141–2, 148n10
democracy, charismatic authority and 144–5

democracy and rural civil society 136
divination and collective choice 136–9
Dragon assembly in Fanzhuang 138, 140, 142–4
givers and receivers of bounty, asymmetry between 146–7
imperial state, local temples within 140–41
local sovereignty, celebration of 144, 145
marginality, scale and perspective 135
mechanism of divination 137
Meifa village 136, 141–2
microcosm, merging with macrocosm 135
negation, Freud's notion of 148–9n17
pomp and extravagance 145–7
populism 145–6
public good, manifest in extravagant festivity (*renao*) 138–9
republican state, local temples within 140–41
ritual centrality 135
ritual selection of leaders 136–7
rotation, principle of 137–8
rural civil society, democracy and 136
territorial festivals in China 136–7
territorial liturgical associations 137–8, 139, 144–5, 147n4
territorial nature of temples and temple management 139–40, 147–8n5
vulgarity in festivity 145
Wang Mingming 141, 148n8
wealth as factor in ritual selection 137
Chakrabarty, Bidyut 87
Chan, Selina Ching 224, 225
charismatic leadership 136, 138–9, 144
charismatic ministry *see* Word of Life
Charuty, Giordana 35n67
chastity and asceticism 174
Chen Decai 141, 148n10
Chen Wansheng 141–2, 148n10
Cheung, Sidney C.H. 206
Cheung S.C.H. and Ma, E.K.W. 223
Chhattisgarh 233–4, 236–42, 244, 247–52, 256n6, 258n27
attitudes to Russians in 240
Mukti Morcha Union 250
peasantry of 234, 236, 237, 238, 239, 241, 244, 247, 248, 258n28
people as reluctant BSP recruits 238, 240, 251
China *see* centrality and marginality, temple ritual in China; geomancy in rural Hong Kong
Cho, Tracey 33n11, 33n14
Christ, Jesus 29

Christianity 3, 40–42
　Bible in 52, 76n1
　Christian fundamentalism 42, 46, 54n6, 55n16
　conservative Christianity 53
　evangelical Christianity 43, 46–7, 48–50, 52
　religious logistics in Africa 61–76
　and tradition in Guinea 193, 201
Christie, D. and Bringa, T. 109n2
Chukov, V. 99
Chulalongkorn Day 123
clairvoyance 28, 164
Claverie, Élizabeth 18, 31
Cliggett, Lisa 77n9
Coates, Austin 218–19
Cock Lane and Common Sense (Lang, A.) 34n41
Cohen, Myron 137
Coleman, S. and Carlin, L. 41
Coleman, Simon 5, 6, 8, 39–58, 263
Collins, P. 178
colonialism
　capitalism and 41
　and geomancy in rural Hong Kong 207–9
　hostility to British rule in Hong Kong 212
　and modernisation in rural Hong Kong 216–24
　New Territories, principles of colonial relationships in 211
　in practice in rural Hong Kong 213–16
　wind and water, encounters in rural Hong Kong over 209–10, 214–16
Colson, Elizabeth 64, 67, 68, 77n9, 77n10
Colson, Elizabeth and Scudder, Thayer 64, 66, 76n8
Comaroff, Jean and Comaroff, John L. 66, 234, 254
The Communist Manifesto (Marx, K. and Engels, F.) 255–6n2
Conakry, Guinea 7, 200, 202n7
Conan Doyle, Sir Arthur 15, 32n6, 33n11
consecration ritual 241
constitutional monarchy 115
　see also Royal Family Commemoration in Laos
construction sacrifices 234, 237–8, 239–40, 241, 246–7, 247–8, 255
contested spaces in urban India 81–95
　Aggrawals 85–6
　anti-religion in Hindu manipulation 88
　Bharatiya Janta Party (BJP) 87–8
　boundary making 82, 85
　bureaucratic power and temple approvals 84

　city planning and unpredictability of temple building 84
　Dali-movement 88
　divine intervention 82
　divine power and divine actors, temple location and 83
　divine self-manifestations 90
　divine will 89–90
　　bureaucratic intervention and 91–3
　Durga Temple, construction of 85–6, 88, 92
　government administration and temple building 83–4
　human agency, setting aside 90–93, 93–4
　illegal temple building 83–4
　India Union and Merger Movement 86
　law enforcement, divine intervention and 90–91
　legitimacy and temple building 83–4, 89
　Madhya Pradesh, Mahakaleshvar Temple at 91, 92
　modernity and freedom from religious conflict 87
　motivation 89
　multi-religious setting 81
　Muslim religious manipulation 88
　Nilkantheshvar Mahadev Temple in Maha Pratap Nagar 88
　planning and construction reality, gap between 82
　politics and religion 85–90, 93–4
　power and manipulation of religious issues 88–9
　religion and public life 81–2, 94
　religion and state, strict separation of 87
　religious activists, conflicts between 81–2, 84, 86
　religious appropriation of space 82–5, 93–4
　religious buildings, mapping of 82–3
　religious intentions of temple builders 84
　religious performances, historical friction between Muslims and Hindus 86–7
　religious tensions, egoistic politics and 87–8
　secularisation of Indian society 87
　self-interest 89
　Shiva Temple and Durga Temple, connection between 86
　Shrivratri procession in Bhopal 85–6
　social demarcations 81–2
　temple building, geographical considerations 83

untouchables 88
'Convicted by the Holy Spirit: The Rhetoric of Fundamental Baptist Conversion' (Susan Harding paper) 46
coronation and cremation rites in Laos 119–20
cosmic consciousness 17
cosmic current flow 214–15
Crapanzano, Vincent 46, 48, 52, 54n8, 55n20
Crehan, Kate 9n5
Croce, Paul Jerome 33n11, 33n14
Csordas, T.J. 48
Cultural Revolution in China 219
Curtis, M.-Y. and Sarró, R. 188
Curtis, Marie-Yvonne 188
Cushman, T. 110n3
custom
    and practice, accommodation to 214
    tyranny of 192–4

D

Dali-movement 88
Daniel, Valentine 163
Darwin, Charles 19
Das, D.K. 241, 242
Das, Veena 94
Davis, John 62–3
Davis, Natalie 136
Davis, Richard H. 90
Dayton Agreement (General Framework Agreement on Peace, GEAP) 106, 109n1
de-divinization 33n23
De Gaulle, Charles 193
de-spiritualisation 25
death and commemoration in Lao Buddhism 119–23
deities of Buddhist cosmos 164–5
democracy
    charismatic authority and 144–5
    and komšiluk in Bosnia 99
    and rural civil society 136
demons 18–19
Deng Fuxie 215
Denich, B. 110n3
Derrida, Jacques 9n6
The Devil and Commodity Fetishism in South America (Taussig, M.) 234
Dharati Mayya 242, 243–4
Dirlik, Arif 206
disenchantment 19–20
divination
    and collective choice 136–9
    mechanism of 137
    see also geomancy in rural Hong Kong

divine intervention 82
divine power, temple location and 83
divine self-manifestation 90
divine will 89–90
    bureaucratic intervention and 91–3
Dizdarević, Zlatko 110n9
Doktór, T. 174
Donia, R. 101
Donia, R. and Fine, J. 97
Dozon, Jean-Pierre 193
Dragon assembly in Fanzhuang 138, 140, 142–4
Drake, R. 247, 249, 258n30
Du Boulay, J. 104
Duff, A. 258n25
Dundes, Alan 253, 258–9n31, 259n32
Durga Temple in Bhopal, construction of 85–6, 88, 92
Durkheim, Émile 7, 9n8, 14, 24–5, 34n35, 110n8, 153

E

Earth Mother (*Dharati Mayya*) 242
Eckert, Julia 147, 148n15
economics
    political and economic reform in Laos 124–5
    political and economic transformation in Poland 170
    transformation (and deterioration) in Africa 65, 70
Eickelman, Dale and Anderson, John 61
Eitel, Ernest J. 228n16
Ekman, Ulf 45
Eliade, Mircea 248, 249, 258–9n31
Elwin, V. 258n24
Encounters with Nationalism (Gellner, E.) 54n11
Endacott, G.B. 213, 216
Enlightenment Puritanism 39–40
An Enquiry Concerning Human Understanding (Hume, D.) 27–8
Erb, M. 247, 249
Escobar, Arturo 206
ethno-nationalist Balkan politics 97–8, 100–101
ethnocentrism 1, 2, 8
ethnography
    ethnographic taboos 42–4
    fieldwork and 41, 42–4, 45–7, 49–50, 51, 54n3
    'gospel' texts and figurative usage 55–6n24
    language, problem of ethnographic and religious 51
    'other' in ethnographical strategy 48

preacherly and ethnographic languages,
Harding's merging of 42, 45–9, 51,
52, 55–6n24, 55n19, 55n20,
55n23
religion and, intersections between 51
evangelicism 47, 61
evangelical Christianity 43, 46–7,
48–50, 52
Evans, D.M. Emrys 210
Evans, Grant 6, 115–34, 132n5, 132n8,
132n11, 132n12, 133n15, 263
Evans-Pritchard, E. 40
exotiká 18–19
Experiencing Ritual (Mead, M.) 22

F
Fa Ngum, King of Laos 122–3, 125
Falwell, Jerry 42, 52, 55–6n24, 55n16,
55n23
family affairs, Chinese custom on 210, 211
family life, new forms in Poland 180
famine in China 219
Fan Pui village, relocation of 218
fantastic beings 18–19
Fanzhuang, Dragon assembly in 138, 140,
142–4
Fardon, Richard 202n2
Favret-Saada, Jeanne 31, 47, 54n12
Feld, Steven and Basso, Keith 206
female celibacy in Polish tradition 173–4
female identity, modes of 170–71
female religiosity in times of uncertainty
174
fengshui
coping tool in competitive environment
229n30
see also geomancy in rural Hong Kong
Ferme, Marianne 202n4
fetishism 26
Feuchtwang, Stephan 6, 135–50, 206,
227n5, 263
Feuchtwang, Stephan and Wang Mingming
139, 148n7
fieldwork
ambivalent participation 50–51
in ethnography 41, 42–4, 45–7, 49–50,
51, 54n3
language, central importance of 50
recollection of 55n20
Filandra, S. 101
fire sacrifice 241, 245
football tournaments in Guinea 199–200
Les formes élémentaires de la vie religieuse
(Durkheim, É.) 25
Forstorp, P.-A. 52
Forth, G. 247

foundation sacrifices 234–5, 238, 239,
247, 253–5
Freedman, Maurice 206
Freitag, Sandra B. 84
Freud, Sigmund 14, 24–5, 32
Friedman, J. and Robbins, J. 110n3
Fujian, China 136, 138, 140, 142, 143,
144, 147
Fuller, C. 234, 242
fundamentalism 39–40, 45–6, 48, 51,
54n1, 99, 169
American fundamentalism 54n8
Christian fundamentalism 42, 46, 54n6,
55n16
Hindu fundamentalism 87
Islamic fundamentalism 54n6
language of 46–7
rationalist fundamentalism 40, 44
religious fundamentalism 44, 53
Fürer-Haimendorf, C. 246, 248
The Future of Illusion (Freud, S.) 24

G
Gafijczuk, Dariusz 9n7, 9n8
Gandhi, Mohandas K. (Mahatma) 234, 235
Garton, Carole 32n1
Garvey, Brian 77n14, 77n17
Gazurov, Ilya 132n10
Geertz, Clifford 49, 145, 153–4
Geiss, P. 102
Gellner, Ernest 39–41, 43, 44, 45–6, 51,
54n2, 54n3
gender relations in Poland 178–9, 180–81
genealogy and status in Laos 122
generational tensions in Guinea 194–5,
199–200
geomancy in rural Hong Kong 205–29
administrative structures, changes in 219
ancestor worship 224, 225
ancestral tombs and *fengshui* 207
Anglo-Chinese border tensions 216
anti-government protest and *fengshui* 206
border closure 216–24
Chinese geomancy 205–6
colonialism
and geomancy 207–9
and modernisation 216–24
in practice 213–16
cosmic current flow, importance of
214–15
Cultural Revolution in China 219
custom and practice, accommodation to
214
dependence of Hong Kong on New
Territories 219
emigration to Britain 219

environmental change and *fengshui* corridors 221–2
environmental disturbances, payments for 214
family affairs, Chinese custom on 210, 211
famine in China 219
Fan Pui village relocation 218
fengshui 205–7, 214–19, 221–6, 227n2, 227n3, 227n4, 227n5, 227n6, 228–9n25, 229n30
geomancy in urban Hong Kong and *fengshui* in rural villages, differences between 223
Heung Yee Kuk 223–4
hostility to British colonial rule 212
Japanese occupation 216
Kowloon Walled City 211
land confiscation and tomb desecration 212
Land Court, establishment of 212
land law, British enforcement of 212–13
land matters, Chinese custom on 210, 211
land reclamations 215
landscape, fashioning of 214
local *fengshui* disputes 217–19
local geography, geomancy and 207
local life and land systems 214–15
local politics, *fengshui* and 225
local pride and geomancy 224–5
Manchu (Qing) government in China 208, 209, 211, 212, 213, 214, 224, 227n6
New Territories
  administrative structure 213–14
  British lease of 209–13
  District Advisory Boards 220
  generational responsibilities 206–7
  housing and infrastructure development in 220–21
  principles of colonial relationships 211
  reversion to Chinese control 208
original residing peoples (*yuanzhumin*) 224
personal meaning and geomancy 224–5
place
  identity and geomancy 223–4, 225–6
  salience of 206
planning, development and allusions to *fengshui* 222–3
population expansion, water problems of 216–18
post-World War II developments 216–24
postcolonialism 208–9
protest, development and geomancy 221–3, 225
quasi-colonialism 208–9
refugees from China 219
revenue raising in New Territories 210
Shek Pik Reservoir project 216–18
Sheung Tsuen village 228–9n25
space, place and geomancy 206–7
Tai Po geomancy protests 211–12
taxlord system 212, 227n13
technocratic administration 220
territorial possession 207
Tin Shui Wai New Town 221
Tomb Protection Society 215
transformation of rural Hong Kong 205
vehemence of *fengshui* claims 214
wind and water, colonial encounters over 209–10, 214–16
Georgieva, T. 99
Geschiere, P. 234, 254
Gifford, Paul 78n23
Gilmore, David D. 145, 146, 148n14
Glazier, Stephen 2
Goethe, Johann Wolfgang von 233
Gombrich, Richard 163, 164
Gose, P. 259n32
The Gospel According to Spiritism (Kardec, A.) 29, 30
Gramsci, Antonio 9n5
Gray, Richard 65–6
Griaule, Marcel 191
Grigson, W. 258n24
Groves, R.G. 211, 228n18
Guinea *see* religious transmission, dynamics among Baga of Guinea
Gupta, Akhil and Ferguson, James 206
Gutschow, K. 172
Gwembe Valley, Zambia 64–72, 75, 76n6, 76n8

H

Haar, Barend ter 143
Hackett, Rosalind 61
Hadžijahić, Muhamed 101, 110n5
Haidara, Sheikh Amadou 195
Halina, Sister 174
Handler, Richard 34n40
Hann, Chris 147
Hardenberg, R. 258n25
Harding, Susan 42, 45–9, 51, 52, 55–6n24, 55n19, 55n20, 55n23
Hartland, E.S. 258n30
Hastrup, K. 42, 49
hauntings 18–19
Hayden, R. 97, 99, 107–8, 110n3
Hayes, James 213, 217, 218, 219, 220–21, 226
Haynes, D. 234

Hazelgrove, Jenny 17
Headrick, Daniel 77n12
Heaven and Hell (Kardec, A.) 29
hegemony 2, 4, 9n5, 21, 30, 41, 42, 191
Hellman, Eva 87
Henkel, Reinhard 66, 77n12
Hernandez, M.T. 253
Hertiage USA 52
Hess, David 23
Heung Yee Kuk 223–4
Hildegard of Bingen 173
Hinduism 171, 181
 Hindu fundamentalism 87
 Hindu spirituality 172
 reformist Hinduism 234
 see also contested spaces in urban India; modernity, sacrifices of in an Indian steel town
Hindustan Times 243, 252, 257n17, 258n29
Hinn, Benny 62, 76n2
Hirohito, Emperor of Japan 115
The History of Spiritualism (Doyle, A.C.) 32n6
Ho Chi Minh 132n12
Ho Pui-yin 219
Hoadley, J.Stephen 228n21
Hodgkinson, L. 172, 178
Holmberg, David 163
Holy Spirit
 bodily incorporation of 72
 as evanescent entity 71–2
Hong Kong
 border closure against 216–24
 see also geomancy in rural Hong Kong; New Territories of Hong Kong
horoscopes, consultation of 158–9
household relationships in Bosnia 104–6
Howell, J.D. and Nelson, P.L. 175
Howell, Julia Day 182n10, 182n13
Howsam, Leslie 61
Hsieh Jih-chang 137
Hubert, H. and Mauss, M. 234, 242, 255
Hughes, Richard 223
human agency, setting aside 90–93, 93–4
human sacrifice 234, 243, 248–9, 251, 253, 255
Hume, David 27–8
Huntington, Samuel 94
Hutton, J.H. 248
Hypnotism and Spiritism (Lombroso, C.) 19

I
iconoclastic movement 188, 190, 191, 193, 196, 198, 201
Iliev, A. 99

The Illustrated Weekly of India 172
independence for Laos 115
India *see* contested spaces in urban India
industrial and construction sacrifices 234, 237–8, 239–40, 241, 246–7, 247–8, 255
Ipenberg, A. 77n14
Islam 2, 40, 53
 anti-colonialism and 193, 201
 Islamic fundamentalism 54n6
 Muslim religious manipulation in urban India 88
 Muslim youth and tyranny of custom 192–4
 and neighbourliness in Bosnia 101–3
 new trends in Islamic thought 110n10
 see also contested spaces in urban India

J
Saint Jadwiga of Silesia 173, 174
Jaffrelot, Christophe 84, 87, 95n9
James, William 13, 16–18, 25, 33n11
James Sr., Henry 33n11
Japanese occupation of Hong Kong 216
Jaspan, M.A. 68
Jayanti, Sister 178
Jeunesse Agricole Catholique (JAC) 194, 197
Jeunesse du Rassemblement Démocratique Africain (JRDA) 194
jihadism 193
Judeo-Christian tradition 2, 8
Julian of Norwich 173

K
Kadare, I. 253
Kali, sacrifice to 242
Kamm, John Thomas 212
Kandasami Festival in Madras 85
Kant, Immanuel 28
Kapferer, B. 110n3
Kardec, Allan 13–14, 15, 21, 22, 29–31, 32, 35n60, 35n61
Kariba Dam (and Lake Kariba) 64, 72
Karic, E. 101
Katherine of Sienna 173
Kaysone Phomvihane 119, 130, 132n12
Keane, Webb 47, 48, 50
Kemp, Margery 173
Kenin-Lopsan, Mongush Barakhovich 154, 164
Kerr, Howard 33n11
Keys, Charles F. 120, 122
Khamphin, Princess of Laos 123–4, 125, 131, 132n2
Khandelwal, M. 172, 182n3

Khilnani, S. 235, 255–6n2
Kideckel, D. 110n3
kidnapping and stories of sacrifice 243–4
Kim Il Sung 132n12
Saint Kinga (Kunegunda) 173–4
kinship networks 180
Kirpalani, Lekhraj Khubchand 171
Kirsch, Thomas 6, 61–80, 263
Klass, M. 54n1
Kligensmith, D. 255–6n2
Knapp, Ronald G. 229n32
Knight, G.A.F. 258n30
knowledge 188, 189, 190, 191, 198
  Buddhist knowledge 155–6, 165, 166
  cosmological knowledge 167
  discipline and 166
  double knowledge 43
  encyclopaedic knowledge 23, 198
  esoteric knowledge 206
  of genealogy 122
  hierarchy of 21
  of the horoscope 158
  initiation and embodiment of 190, 198
  intellectualist rationalisation 19
  knowledgeable cosmopolitanism 70
  legitimacy of 20
  legitimation by 29
  limit of acceptable 27
  local knowledge 206
  perfunctory knowledge 164
  personal experience of 42
  power and 153, 161
  private knowledge 194
  public knowledge 194
  religion as set of knowledge practices 4
  revelation knowledge 45
  scientific knowledge 14, 18, 20, 21, 25, 32
  shared knowledge 163, 166
  sources of 28, 35n62
Koljević, Nikola 100–101
komšiluk (neighbourliness, neighbourhood) 97–110
  concept of 97, 99–101
  costs and benefits of 104–6
  debate about 98–9
  democracy and 99
  derivation of 100
  emotional investment in continuance of 108–9
  'groupism' and 100
  inter-ethnic dimension 99–100
  intercommunal relations and 101, 104–6, 106–7
  significance of 99
Kościańska, Agnieszka 6, 169–84, 264

Kotkin, S. 236
Kowloon Walled City 211
Kremmer, Christopher 132n4, 133n17

L
Laidlaw, J. 110n8
Lal, Madan 246–7
Lam, Wai-man 229n33
Lambek, Michael 2, 33n23
Lamp, Frederick 188
land in rural Hong Kong
  confiscation and tomb desecration 212
  Land Court, establishment of 212
  land reclamations 215
  landscape, fashioning of 214
  law on, British enforcement of 212–13
  matters of, Chinese custom on 210, 211
Lang, Andrew 14, 25–6, 27–8, 32n4, 34n41, 34n44, 34n45
language
  body-language 52
  of fundamentalism 46–7
  imitation and plagiarism 55n23
  power of 51–2
  preacherly and ethnographic languages, Harding's merging of 42, 45–9, 51, 52, 55–6n24, 55n19, 55n20, 55n23
  problem of ethnographic and religious 51
  religious and academic ideologies, intersections of 51–2
  of sacrifice, appropriation of 233–4
  spiritual hearing 52
  terminological variation 14–15
  terminological variation in modern spiritualism 14–15
Lao Nation (Xat Lao) 117
Lao People's Democratic Republic (LPDR) 117–19, 125, 132–3n12, 133n20
Laos *see* Royal Family Commemoration in Laos
Latour, Bruno 20–21, 31
Lau, Sui-kai and Kuan, Hsin-chi 228n22
Launay, Robert 61
law enforcement, divine intervention and 90–91
Le Roy Ladurie, Emmanuel 136
Ledeneva, A. 104
legitimacy
  of knowledge 20
  and temple building 83–4, 89
Lett, James 33n30
Lévinas, Emmanuel 9n6
Li Hung-chang 209
Lin Meirong 137
Lin Wei-ping 226–7n1

Lindquist, Galina 6, 147, 153–68, 264
literalism
  Biblical literalism 41
  meta-literalism 53
  reality, textual dogmatism and 52–3
Liu Tielang 138, 140
localism
  authority and 147
  fengshui disputes 217–19
  life and land systems 214–15
  local geography, geomancy and 207
  politics, *fengshui* and 225
  pride and geomancy 224–5
  sovereignty in, celebration of 144, 145
Locke, John 107
Lockhart, James Stewart 210–12
logistics of the spirit 71–5
Lombroso, Cesare 16, 17, 18, 19
London Missionary Society 77n13, 77n14
Lowenthal, David 222
Lowie, Robert H. 33n33
Luang Phrabang 115, 117, 122, 125, 126, 127, 131
Ludden, David 94
Luhrmann, T. 43, 54n9, 56n28, 56n30
Luig, Ulrich 66, 68, 77n16
Luig, Ute 68, 77–8n22, 77n9, 77n20
Lung, David 229n32

M
Maass, P. 109n2
McCutcheon, R. 42
MacDonald, Sir Claude 209
Macek, Ivana 100, 110n6
MacIntyre, Alisdair 45
Maclehose, Governor Murray 219
McNeill, J.R. 226
Madan, T.N. 87
Madhya Pradesh, Mahakaleshvar Temple at 91, 92
Madras 85
Makambe, E.P. 77n9
The Making of Religion (Lang, A.) 25–6, 28, 34n44
Malamoud, C. 259n33
Malik, Aditya 94
Malik, Y.K. and Singh, V.B. 95n9
Malinowski, Bronislaw K. 42
Manchu (Qing) government in China 208, 209, 211, 212, 213, 214, 224, 227n6
manhood initiation in Guinea 188
Manilai, Crown Princess of Laos 118–19, 123, 125, 132n1
Mao Zedong 132n12, 140, 141, 219
Marcus, A. 102

Marcus, G. and Fischer, M. 48
Marett, Robert R. 33n33
marginality 2
  anthropology, animism and 22–8
  Buddhism and shamanism in Siberia, margins between 153–68
  centrality and 3, 4–5
  commemoration at the margins 131–2
  marginal forms, transformatory potential of 1
  margins, notion of 3, 4
  margins of religion in Guinea 191–2
  microcosm, merging with macrocosm 135
  power in 7
  psychical research within sciences 22
  relative marginality 135
  religion and 1, 3, 4, 5, 6
  religion in the margins 191–2
  religious practice on the margins between Buddhism and shamanism 153–68
  scale and perspective in China 135
  social marginalisation of spiritualism 14, 19
Marian apparitions 30, 35n63
'marriages of souls' 177–8
Martin, D. 53, 54n6
Marx, Karl 255–6n2
masabe healers 68, 69, 75, 77–8n22
Masowe, Johane 78n24
Matthews, Gordon 223
Max Planck Institute 3
May, Captain F.H. 209, 212
Mead, Margaret 22
mediums, psychism of 16, 17, 29, 30–31
The Medium's Book (Kardec, A.) 29
Mehta, V. 238
Meifa village, China 136, 141–2
memorial rituals in Laos 121–2
mengi, separation in ritual practice 158–9, 161
menstruation and purity 179
merit transference 120–21
Merry, Sally and Stern, Rachele E. 225
Mesmer, Franz Anton 17
mesmerism 17, 33n13
Michalski, M. 174
microcosm, merging with macrocosm 135
Mihaylova, Dimitrina 110n4
Mill, John Stuart 107
Miners, Norman 219, 220, 227–8n15
Mines, Mattison 85
Miracle, M.P. 76n7
miracles 27–8
missionaries in Guinea 64, 66, 67, 68–9, 76n8

Index

Primitive Methodist Missionary Society 64
Mittal, Kamla 86
modern spiritualism 13–35
  animal magnetism 17
  animism and 22–8
  animist hypothesis 16
  bafflement on, age of science and 19
  clairvoyance 28
  cosmic consciousness 17
  de-spiritualisation 25
  demons 18–19
  disenchantment 19–20
  exotiká 18–19
  fantastic beings 18–19
  fetishism 26
  hauntings 18–19
  marginality
    anthropology, animism and 22–8
    psychical research within sciences 22
    social marginalisation of spiritualism 14, 19
  mediums, psychism of 16, 17, 29, 30–31
  mesmerism 17, 33n13
  miracles 27–8
  modernity, techno-scientific 19–20
  mysticification, problem of 31
  naturalness of 'spiritic' facts 27–8
  obscurantism 29
  origins of 15–18, 19–20, 21–2
  pax moderna between science and religion and 14
  premonition 28
  proof and credibility 21–2
  proof and science in Kardec's spiritism 29–31, 32
  proof and scientific knowledge 18
  psychical research 15–18
  rationalisation and disenchantment 19–20
  religion, social function and 24–5
  religion and belief 20–21
  religion and science, homeless spirits in age of 18–22
  religious experiences 14
  science, state and church, domains of 20
  science and, homeless spirits in age of 18–22
  science and proof in Kardec's spiritism 29–31, 32
  scientific and common knowledge 21
  scientific experimentation 14
  scientific knowledge, proof and 18
  secularism 20–21
  spiritism 13–14, 15, 29–31, 32
  spiritist science 30–31
  'spiritual' phenomena 14, 16–17
  spiritualism, science and 13
  subliminal self, notion of 17
  supernatural
    naturalisation of the 15–18
    reality of the 17–18
  supernormal experiences 25–6, 28
  superstition 29
  symbolism 25
  terminological variation 14–15
  universal pan-psychism 17
  witchcraft 22, 23, 25, 31
  X-region and X-phenomena 25–6, 27
modernity 1, 3
  and freedom from religious conflict 87
  modernization through spirits 68–9, 70
  and sacrifice 249–50
  sacrifices of in an Indian steel town 233–59
    agricultural fertility 234
    Andha-Shradha Nirmoolan Samati ('Blind Faith Eradication Council') 252
    animal sacrifice 233–4
    animal sacrifices 248
    Bhilai, beacon of modernity 235–7
    Bhilai Steel Plant (BSP) 233, 235–44, 247, 250, 251–2, 256n6, 256n7, 256n8, 257n13, 258n26, 258n28
    construction of 233, 234, 237–8, 239
    Bhoodan Yajna Board ('Board for the sacrificial donation of land') 234
    Bihari migration 244
    BSP (Bhilai Steel Plant)
      Chhattisgarhis as reluctant recruits 238, 240, 251
      Chhattisgarhis attitudes to Russians 240
      dangers of working for 239–40
      Satnamis employed by 239
    capitalism, impingement on subaltern lives 234
    Chhattisgarh 233–4, 236–42, 244, 247–52, 256n6, 258n27
    circulation of sacrifice stories 243–4
    consecration ritual 241
    construction sacrifices 234, 237–8, 239–40, 241, 246–7, 247–8, 255
    creative power out of sacrificial destruction 249
    Earth Mother (*Dharati Mayya*) 242
    fire sacrifice 241, 245
    forms of sacrifice, decline in 249
    foundation sacrifice 247
    foundation sacrifices 234–5, 238, 239, 253–5

government cover-ups of sacrifice
    245–6
human sacrifice 243, 248–9, 251,
    253, 255
human sacrifices 234
ideological purposes of sacrifice stories
    251–2
industrial and construction sacrifices,
    phlegmatic view of 246–7
invocation of sacrifice stories 250–51
Kali, sacrifice to 242
kidnapping and stories of sacrifice
    243–4
language of sacrifice, appropriation of
    233–4
modernity and sacrifice 249–50
Mukti Morcha Union, Chhattisgarh
    250
peasantry of Chhattisgarh 234, 236,
    237, 238, 239, 241, 244, 247, 248,
    258n28
political rumour-mongering 240–41
productive power of machines 249
reformist Hinduism 234
rites and sacrifices 242–3
sacrifice
    and access to divine power
        249–50
    ancient and modern 247–50
    to dreams of modernity 238
    of freedom fighters 233–4
    of industrial destruction 234
    of industrial development 237–8
    to Kali 242
    in propaganda 237–8
    by recalcitrant machines 246
    for steel 237–47
    stories of 243
scepticism of sacrifice stories 250, 252
self-sacrifice 250
state-sponsored construction-sacrifices
    234, 244, 247
Steel Authority of India 235
sublimated sacrifice 241, 242
'Suspicious Death' or 'Secret Sacrifice'
    245–6
voluntary sacrifice 242
witchcraft beliefs 234
science and religion, conflict of 40
techno-scientific modernity 19–20
Monczka-Ciechomska, M. 170
moral environment, neighbourhood as 102
Morgenthau, Ruth S. 193
Moses 29
motherhood and *Matka Polka* (Polish
    Mother) 170, 171, 181

motorised proselytism 69–71
Msiska, A. 77n15
Mukti Morcha Union, Chhattisgarh 250
Mumford, S.R. 163
Munz, Peter 202n6
Myers, Frederic 17, 33n14, 33n15
mysticification, problem of 31

N
Nandy, Ashis 87
Narayan, Vir 150
Nash, J. 259n32
naturalness of 'spiritic' facts 27–8
Needham, Rodney 8, 33n11
negation, Freud's notion of 148–9n17
negative tolerance 107, 108
Nehru, Jawaharlal 235, 236, 237,
    255–6n2
neighbourliness in Bosnia 97–110
    bereavement, ritual of 103
    Bulgarian Ethnic Model (BEM) 98–9
    complexities of everyday life 107
    conversational artfulness 104
    ethno-nationalist Balkan politics 97–8,
        100–101
    household relationships 104–6
    ideological commitment to tolerance
        107–8
    individual relationships 104–5
    Islam and neighbourhood 101–3
    komšiluk (neighbourliness,
        neighbourhood)
        concept of 97, 99–101
        costs and benefits of 104–6
        debate about 98–9
        democracy and 99
        derivation of 100
        emotional investment in continuance of
            108–9
        'groupism' and 100
        inter-ethnic dimension 99–100
        intercommunal relations and 101,
            104–6, 106–7
        significance of 99
    moral environment, neighbourhood as
        102
    negative tolerance 107, 108
    neighbourhood relations 104–6
    physical space, neighbourhood as 102
    positive tolerance 107–8
    post-war neighbourhood relations 106–9
    principles and practice of tolerance
        107–8
    Ramazan 102–3
    re-integration 106, 107, 109
    relationships and *veze* networks 104–5

Sarajevo Bosniacs 98, 102, 108, 109, 110n9
  secrecy and suspicion in Balkan life 104
  social life and neighbourhood 102–3
  social ties and bonds 97–8, 104–6
  Socialist Self Management 105
  socio-economic circumstances, post-war 109
  strains on social ties and bonds 104–6
  symbolic nature of neighbourhood 102
  tolerance 106–9
  virtue of tolerance 108
  women's death ritual (*tevhid*) 103
Neitz, M. 56n26
Nelson, Geoffrey 32n6, 32n7
Neuffer, E. 109n2
New Territories of Hong Kong
  administrative structure 213–14
  British lease of 209–13
  District Advisory Boards 220
  generational responsibilities 206–7
  housing and infrastructure development in 220–21
  principles of colonial relationships 211
  revenue raising in 210
  reversion to Chinese control 208
  see also geomancy in rural Hong Kong 220
New Wine in Old Wineskins (Warner, R.S.) 49–50, 55–6n24
Niehaus, I. 254
Nilkantheshvar Mahadev Temple in Maha Pratap Nagar 88
nirvana 120
Niyogi, Shankar Guha 250
Nouvelles du Laos 115, 119
Nowotny, H. 97–8

O

Obeyesekere, G. 258n22
O'Brian, Dan 68
obscurantism 29
Oomen, T.K. 234
Opie, I. and Opie, P. 253
Oppenheim, Janet 16
original residing peoples (*yuanzhumin*) 224
origins of modern spiritualism 15–18, 19–20, 21–2
Oslobodenje 101, 110n9
Ottoman Empire 102

P

Padel, F. 258n25
Palmer, Michael 35n72, 212, 227n14, 228n24
Pandey, Gyan 84

Parry, Jonathan P. 7, 8, 233–62, 264
Parry, Jonathan P. and Bloch, Maurice 146
participation 4, 42, 68, 102, 121, 137, 145, 170, 175, 181
  ambivalent participation 50–51
  evangelical participation 51
  mass participation 140
  political participation 229n33
Paulme, Denise 187–8, 189, 190, 191n0–2
pax moderna between science and religion 14
peasantry of Chhattisgarh 234, 236, 237, 238, 239, 241, 244, 247, 248, 258n28
Pels, Peter 33n21, 34n52
Pentecostalism 53, 54n6, 54n7, 62
  Pentecostal Word of God Ministry 70
Percy, M. 52
perestroika 155–7
personal meaning and geomancy 224–5
personalised spiritual mediation 62
Peshkin, Alan 46
Pessel, W.K. 174
Phillimore, P. 172
physical space, neighbourhood as 102
Pina-Cabral, João de 1–10, 32n1, 41, 264
Pine, Frances 1–10, 109, 170, 171, 180, 181, 226–7n1, 264
Pinny, C. 256n8
place
  identity and geomancy 223–4, 225–6
  of religious transmission in Guinea 201
  salience of 206
planning
  and construction reality, gap between 82
  development and allusions to *fengshui* 222–3
Pocock, D. 247
Point de Vue 130
Poland *see* celibate marriage in Poland
politics
  political rumour-mongering 240–41
  and religion 85–90, 93–4
pomp and extravagance 145–7
Pope Pius IX 29–30, 35n64
populism 145–6
positive tolerance 107–8
possession cults (*masabe*) 68, 69, 75, 77–8n22
postcolonialism 208–9
Postmodernism, Reason and Religion (Gellner E.) 39–40
Potter, Jack 207, 209, 227n3, 229n32
Pouligny, B. 99–100
poverty 42, 70, 78n23, 235
power 9n3

bureaucratic power and temple approvals 84
creative power out of sacrificial destruction 249
divine power and divine actors, temple location and 83
knowledge and 153, 161
language of 51–2
and manipulation of religious issues 88–9
in marginality 7
productive power of machines 249
of religion 153–4
sacrifice and access to divine power 249–50
spiritual power of Buddhist lamas 155
Pragmatism (James, W.) 17
premonition 28
Preporod 101
Price, Neil and Thomas, Neil 67
Primitive Culture (Tylor, E.B.) 14, 23, 24, 26
Primitive Methodist Missionary Society 64
proof
credibility and 21–2
and science in Kardec's spiritism 29–31, 32
and scientific knowledge 18
protest, development and geomancy 221–3, 225
Protestantism
conservative Protestantism 43, 44, 45–6, 52, 53
psychical research 15–18
modern spiritualism 15–18
universal pan-psychism 17
see also modern spiritualism
public good, manifest in extravagant festivity (*renao*) 138–9
public memorial ceremonies 130
public statues of Royalty 122–3
purity and meditation 179
Puttick, E. 182n13

Q
quasi-colonialism 208–9

R
Ragsdale, John P. 77n15
rain shrines (*malende*) 67–8, 69
Rama V, King of Thailand 123
Ramazan 102–3
Ranger, Terence 77n18
Rao, Ursula 6, 81–96, 148n16, 264–5
Rassemblement Démocratique Africain (RDA) 193
rationalisation and disenchantment 19–20

rationalism 35n62
rationalist fundamentalism 40, 44
rationality 45
in science and religion 44
Ratsami, Princess of Laos 118, 123, 125, 132n1
Read, Gordon 64
Reddy, Sanjiva 255–6n2
relationships 9n7
relations, towards new forms in Poland 178–81
and *veze* networks in Bosnia 104–5
relativism 40, 44, 55, 147n1
Religião e Sociedade 32n1
religion
anthropology of 1–2
belief and 20–21
ethnography and, intersections between 51
faith, commitment to 43
freedom of religion 157
Holy Spirit as evanescent entity 71–2
and identity in Poland 169–70
importance of 2
marginality and 1, 3, 4, 5, 6
in the margins 191–2
margins of religion, concept of 5
missionaries 64, 66, 67, 68–9, 76n8
pax moderna between science and religion 14
power of 153
and public life in urban India 81–2, 94
as quasi-(social-)scientific view 45
religious activists, conflicts between 81–2, 84, 86
religious appropriation of space 82–5, 93–4
religious authority, evolution of 74
religious boundaries, recreation of 81–95
religious buildings, mapping of 82–3
religious discourses and practices, organisation and 62–3
religious experiences 14
religious fundamentalism 44, 53
religious geographies in Africa 65–9
religious intentions of temple builders in urban India 84
religious performances, historical friction between Muslims and Hindus 86–7
religious practice on the margins between Buddhism and shamanism 153–68
religious tensions, egoistic politics and 87–8
religious transformation in Africa 65
and science, homeless spirits in age of 18–22

science and 40
social function and 24–5
spiritual seclusion, need for 72–3
spiritualism and anthropology of 13–35
and state, strict separation of 87
'tradition' and 1
religious logistics in Africa
  ambivalence towards 63, 65–9, 73, 74–5, 75–6
  bodily incorporation of the Holy Spirit 72
  communities and 'spheres of influence' 66
  distances between congregations in Gwembe 77n21
  economic deterioration 70
  economic transformation 65
  evangelicism 61
  'filling station' enterprise in Gwembe 77n11
  Gwembe Valley, Zambia 64–72, 75, 76n6, 76n8
  Holy Spirit as evanescent entity 71–2
  infrastructure and development 64–5, 66, 67
  instrumentalisation of senior leaders 74
  intercongregational logistics 63, 73, 76
  Kariba Dam (and Lake Kariba) 64, 72
  logistics of the spirit 71–5
  masabe healers 77–8n22
  missionaries 64, 66, 67, 68–9, 76n8
  modernization through spirits 68–9, 70
  motorised proselytism 69–71
  personalised spiritual mediation 62
  possession cults (*masabe*) 68, 69, 75
  poverty 70
  propositional content 61–2
  rain shrines (*malende*) 67–8, 69
  religious authority, evolution of 74
  religious discourses and practices, organisation and 62–3
  religious geographies 65–9
  religious transformation 65
  roads and missions 67, 75
  roads and routes 64–5, 67
  social sphere, church leaders difficulties with 72–3
  socio-cultural transformation 65
  solitariness, need for 72–3
  spatial movements, need for recurrence of 72
  spirit manifestation 67–8
  spiritual quality, dissemination of 62
  spiritual seclusion, need for 72–3
  spirituality and logistics 63
  touring of branches (*kuswaya mbungano*) 74
truck-driving malignity 69–70
truck-driving religious leaders 63, 69–70, 71, 75
Zambia Electricity Supply Corp. (ZESCO) 70
religious transmission, dynamics among Baga of Guinea 187–202
  Baga parents 187–90
  Baga-Susi divide 188–9
  carnival of football 200–201
  Christianity and tradition 193, 201
  cultural values, loss of 188
  custom, tyranny of 192–4
  ethnic-cum-generational divide 190
  football tournaments 199–200
  generational tensions 194–5, 199–200
  Haidara, Sheikh Amadou 195
  iconoclastic movement 188, 190, 191, 193, 196, 198, 201
  initiation cycle, stages of 189
  internal tensions in Baga society 187–8, 191–2
  Islam and anti-colonialism 193, 201
  Jeunesse Agricole Catholique (JAC) 194, 197
  Jeunesse du Rassemblement Démocratique Africain (JRDA) 194
  jihadism 193
  knowledge, initiation and embodiment of 190, 198
  management of religious transmission 201
  manhood initiation 188
  margins of religion 191–2
  maturation process 189
  ministry of Asekou Sayon 193, 194–6, 196–8, 201
  Muslim youth and tyranny of custom 192–4
  place of religious transmission 201
  pretence in following of Asekou Sayon 196–8
  Rassemblement Démocratique Africain (RDA) 193, 195
  religion in the margins 191–2
  ritual context of Baga objects 187
  secrecy in Baga tradition 188
  secrecy of religious transmission 201
  seniority and identity 189
  socio-religious activities, practical logic and 191
  spiritual agency (*amanco ngopong*) 189, 194, 195, 196, 197, 198, 199, 200
  Susu children and Baga parents 187–90, 201
  Susuisation 187, 188

traditional chieftaincy, institution of 192
witchcraft and sacrifices 199–200
representation, 'thing' and 9n8
Rheubottom, D. 104
Rice, P. and Waugh, P. 48
The Rise and Fall of the New Christian Right (Bruce, S.) 55–6n24
rites and sacrifices 242–3
ritual centrality 135
ritual context of Baga objects 187
ritual design in shamianism and Buddhism 154, 159–67
ritual practices of shamanism and Buddhism 157–9
ritual selection of leaders in China 136–7
Rivail, Léon *see* Kardec, Allan
Rivière, Peter 41
roads
 and missions in Africa 67, 75
 and routes in Africa 64–5, 67
Robbins, J. 40
Roberts, Oral 47–8
Robertson, Roland 78n28
Rooney, Nuala 223
rotation, principle of 137–8
Royal Family Commemoration in Laos 115–33
 ancestral spirits, offerings to 132n9
 Buddhism 115, 116, 119–23, 125
 ceremony of *kathin* (offering of robes to monks) 125–8
 Chulalongkorn Day 123
 constitutional monarchy 115
 coronation and cremation, rites of 119–20
 death and commemoration in Lao Buddhism 119–23
 economic and political reform 124–5
 Fa Ngum, King of Laos 122–3, 125
 Gazurov, Ilya 132n10
 genealogy and status 122
 independence 115
 Kaysone Phomvihane 119, 130, 132n12
 Khamphin, Princess of Laos 123–4, 125, 131, 132n2
 Lao Nation (Xat Lao) 117
 Lao People's Democratic Republic (LPDR) 117–19, 125, 132–3n12, 133n20
 Luang Phrabang 115, 117, 122, 125, 126, 127, 131
 Manilai, Crown Princess of Laos 118–19, 123, 125, 132n1
 marginality, commemoration at the margins 131–2
 memorial rituals, post-cremation 121–2
 merit transference 120–21
 nirvana 120
 Point de Vue 130
 portraits of Royalty 132n10
 pretension to Royalty 133n19
 public memorial ceremonies 130
 public statues of Royalty 122–3
 Rama V, King of Thailand 123
 Ratsami, Princess of Laos 118, 123, 125, 132n1
 re-traditionalisation 125
 rebirth of *vinyaan* 121
 reciprocity in monkhood 121
 revival of fortunes 123–31
Royal Family Commemoration in Laos 115–33
Saisana, Prince of Laos 125, 129, 130
Satu Khamchan, supreme patriach of Luang Phrabang 127
Satu Mouk, abbot of Vat Phone Phao 123
Sauryavong, Prince Regent of Laos 130
Savang Vatthana, KIng of Laos 119, 127–8
Sethathirath, King of Laos 122
Sisavang, Prince of Laos 118–19
Sisavang Vatthana, King of Laos 117, 118–19, 128, 130, 131, 132n10, 133n22
Sisavang Vong, King of Laos 115, 116, 117, 118, 119–20, 122, 125, 126, 128, 131
Somsack Pongkhao 133n14
Soulivong, Prince of Laos 125, 129, 133n18
Souphanouvong, 'Red' Prince of Laos 133n20, 133n22
Souvanna Phouma, Prince and Prime Minister of Laos 117
Thanya, Prince of Laos 125, 129, 130, 133n18
That Haysokarath 117
That Luang in Vientiane 122, 124, 126
Theravada Buddhism 120, 122, 132n9
Tiao Soukthivong 127
unification of modern Laos 115–16
Vientiane Times 125
Vong Savang, Crown Prince of Laos 117–19
Rubel, P. and Rosman, A. 43
Ruel, Malcolm 154, 158, 167
The Rules of Sociological Method (Durkheim, E.) 9n8
rural civil society, democracy and 136
Russian Orthodox Church 155, 157

Index

S

sacrifice
  and access to divine power 249–50
  ancient and modern 247–50
  construction sacrifices 234, 237–8, 239–40, 241, 246–7, 247–8, 255
  to dreams of modernity 238
  forms of sacrifice, decline in 249
  of freedom fighters 233–4
  human sacrifice 234, 243, 248–9, 251, 253, 255
  of industrial destruction 234
  of industrial development 237–8
  to Kali 242
  in propaganda 237–8
  by recalcitrant machines 246
  scepticism of sacrifice stories 250, 252
  for steel 237–47
  stories of 243
  sublimated sacrifice 241, 242
  'Suspicious Death' or 'Secret Sacrifice' 245–6
  voluntary sacrifice 242
Saisana, Prince of Laos 125, 129, 130
Samuel, Geoffrey 163
Sanguin, A.-L. 98
Santayana, George 153
Sarajevo Bosniacs 98, 102, 108, 109, 110n9
Sarró, Ramon 7, 8, 187–203, 265
Satu Khamchan, supreme patriarch of Luang Phrabang 127
Satu Mouk, abbot of Vat Phone Phao 123
Sauryavong, Prince Regent of Laos 130
Savang Vatthana, KIng of Laos 119, 127–8
Sayon, Asekou 190, 193–9, 201, 202n3, 202n5
Schaeffner, André 187
Scheper-Hughes, N. 243
Schiller, Friedrich 33n23
Schipper, Kristofer 135, 147n4
Schneider, Jane 33n23
Schnepel, Burkhart 144–5, 147
science
  pax moderna between science and religion 14
  and proof in Kardec's spiritism 29–31, 32
  and religion
    conflict of 40
    homeless spirits in age of 18–22
  scientific and common knowledge 21
  scientific experimentation 14
  scientific knowledge 14, 20, 21, 25, 32
    proof and 18
  spiritist science 30–31
  spiritualism, science and 13

state and church, domains of 20
Science as a Vocation (Weber, M.) 19–20
The Scientific Aspects of the Supernatural (Lombroso, C.) 16, 17, 18, 19
Scott, Ian 228n23
Scudder, Thayer 70, 77n10
secrecy
  in Baga tradition 188
  of religious transmission in Guinea 201
  and suspicion in Balkan life 104
secularism 1, 20–21
  secularisation of Indian society 87
Sediments of Time (McNeill, J.R.) 226
self-interest 89
self-sacrifice 250
seniority and identity in Guinea 189
Sered, S.S. 178
Sethathirath, King of Laos 122
sexual abstinence 172, 177, 178
sexuality and celibate marriage in Poland 170
shamanism and Buddhism in Siberia
  Buddhism as 'state religion' 155
  Buddhist *khurees* 155, 157, 165
  Buddhist ritual 161–3
  clairvoyance 164
  co-existence, tolerance and 164
  colours and characteristics of time cycles 158
  communist atrocities 155
  competition between 163–7
  cooperation between 163–4
  deities of Buddhist cosmos 164–5
  division of labour between 163–4
  freedom of religion 157
  history of 155–7
  horoscopes, consultation of 158–9
  identification with 154
  interpersonal relations and time cycles 158–9
  life, ritual ordering of 158
  mengi, separation in ritual practice 158–9, 161
  non-human entities 163, 165
  overlapping tasks and lamas and shamans 166
  perestroika and revival 155–7
  persecution of shamans 156–7
  power of religion 153–4
  religious practice on the margins between 153–68
  ritual design, similarities and differences in 154, 159–67
  ritual practices 157–9
  shamanic performances 157, 159
  shamanism, ritual of 159–61

spirits of the dead 165
spiritual power of Buddhist lamas 155
strength and audacity of shamans 166–7
time, cycles of 158
'traditional religions' revival of 157
Tuva in post-Soviet context 154–7
virtue and discipline of lamas 166–7
Shaw, J.R. 77n15
Shaw, Rosalind 202n4
Shek Pik Reservoir project 216–18
Sheung Tsuen village in rural Hong Kong 228–9n25
Shils, Edward 73
Shiva Temple and Durga Temple, connection between 86
Shrivratri procession in Bhopal 85–6
Siberia *see* shamanism and Buddhism in Siberia
Sinn, Elizabeth 229n29
Sisavang, Prince of Laos 118–19
Sisavang Vatthana, King of Laos 117, 118–19, 128, 130, 131, 132n10, 133n22
Sisavang Vong, King of Laos 115, 116, 117, 118, 119–20, 122, 125, 126, 128, 131
Siu, Helen 220, 223
Skultans, V. 179, 182n9
Smith, Matthew 33n28
social demarcations 81–2
social life and neighbourhood 102–3
social sphere, church leaders difficulties with 72–3
social ties and bonds 97–8
 strains on 104–6
Socialist Self Management 105
socio-cultural transformation in Guinea 65
socio-economic circumstances in post-war Bosnia 109
socio-religious activities in Guinea 191
Solidarność 169, 182n7
Solioz, C. 98
solitariness, need for 72–3
Somsack Pongkhao 133n14
Sontheimer, G.D. and Kulke, H. 94, 95n7
Sorabji, Cornelia 6, 97–112, 147, 265
Soubirous, Bernadette 29–30
Soulivong, Prince of Laos 125, 129, 133n18
Souphanouvong, 'Red' Prince of Laos 133n20, 133n22
South China Morning Post (*SCMP*) 221, 224, 228–9n25
Souvanna Phouma, Prince and Prime Minister of Laos 117
space

place and geomancy in rural Hong Kong 206–7
spatial movements, need for recurrence of 72
Sperber, Dan 34n39
Spickard, J. and Landres, S. 43, 54n7
spirit manifestation 67–8
spiritism 13–14, 15, 29–31, 32
spiritist science 30–31
The Spirits Book (Kardec, A.) 29, 31
spirits of the dead 165
spiritual agency (*amanco ngopong*) 189, 194, 195, 196, 197, 198, 199, 200
spiritual needs in Poland 179, 180
'spiritual' phenomena 14, 16–17
spiritual power of Buddhist lamas 155
spiritual quality, dissemination of 62
spiritual seclusion, need for 72–3
spiritualism, science and 13
Spiritualist Alliance 32n6
spirituality and logistics 63
Srinivasan, N.R. 236, 255–6n2
Stalin, Josef 236
state-sponsored construction-sacrifices 234, 244, 247
The Statesman 239, 256n7
Steel Authority of India 235
Stewart, Charles 18, 40, 41, 42, 43
Stewart Michael 109
Stocking, George 34n44, 34n52
Strauch, Judith 217
Stutchbury, E.L. 258n25
sublimated sacrifice 241, 242
subliminal self, notion of 17
Sudesh, Sister 179
Sundar, N. 248, 258n24
supernatural
 naturalisation of the 15–18
 reality 17–18
 revelation knowledge 45
supernormal experiences 25–6, 28
superstition 26, 29, 91, 125, 206, 223, 241, 243, 252
Susu of Guinea 187–90, 201
Swedenborg, Emmanuel 28, 33n11
symbolism 25
 symbolic nature of neighbourhood in Bosnia 102
Szonyi, Michael 226–7n1

T
taboos, anthropological 42–4
Tai Po geomancy protests 211–12
Taiwan 136, 137, 138, 140, 142, 143, 145, 146, 147
Tambiah, S. 44

Index

Tannen, D. 47
Taussig, Michael 163, 234, 248–9, 259n32
taxlord system in rural Hong Kong 212, 227n13
technocratic administration in rural Hong Kong 220
territorial festivals in China 136–7
territorial liturgical associations 137–8, 139, 144–5, 147n4
territorial nature of temples and temple management 139–40, 147–8n5
territorial possession in rural Hong Kong 207
Thanya, Prince of Laos 125, 129, 130, 133n18
Thapar, Romila 94
That Haysokarath 117
That Luang in Vientiane 122, 124, 126
Theravada Buddhism 120, 122, 132n9
Thompson, Roger R. 140
Tiao Soukthivong 127
time, cycles of 158
Tin Shui Wai New Town 221
Titkow, A. 170
Tityakian, Edward 33n29
tolerance in Bosnia 106–9
Tomb Protection Society 215
Tomlinson, Matthew 55n22
Touré, President Sékou 193
touring of branches (*kuswaya mbungano*) 74
traditional chieftaincy, institution of 192
'traditional religions' revival of 157
Trinity Broadcasting Network 62
truck-driving
    malignity of 69–70
    religious leaders engagement in 63, 69–70, 71, 75
truth, uniqueness of 39–44
Tsing, A. 247
Tucker, Jennifer 35n67
Turner, Edith 33n31
Turner, Frank Miller 33n14
Turner, Victor and Turner, Edith 35n63, 73
Tuva in post-Soviet context 154–7
Tylor, Edward Burnett 14, 23–4, 25, 26, 27, 34n44, 253

U

Underdown, David 148n13
'The Uniqueness of Truth' (Ernest Gellner sermon) 39
universal pan-psychism 17
untouchables in urban India 88, 95n11

V

Valtchikova, Galia 147

Vanaik, Achin 87
The Varieties of Religious Experience (James, W.) 17
Vasconcelos, João 5, 8, 13–37, 265
Vedanti, Sister 172, 178
Veyne, Paul 35n71
Vickery, Kenneth P. 66
Vientiane Times 125
Viet-Minh 115
Vietnam War 116
Virgin Mary (*Matka Boska*) 29, 31, 170, 182n1
    inspiration of 173
virtue
    and discipline of lamas 166–7
    of tolerance in Bosnia 108
voluntary sacrifice 242
Vong Savang, Crown Prince of Laos 117–19
vulgarity in festivity 145

W

Wales, Quaritch 119
Wallace, Alfred Russell 14, 19, 25, 26–7, 34n50
Walliss, J. 175
Wang Mingming 141, 148n8
Warner, R. Stephen 49–51, 55–6n24, 56n27
Waters, Dan 229n27
Watson, James L. 7, 205–32, 265
Watson, Rubie S. 7, 205–32, 265
wealth as factor in ritual selection 137
Weber, Max 19–20, 21, 33n23, 136, 144
Weller, Robert 148n6
Wesley-Smith, Peter 209, 210, 211, 212, 214, 217, 227n12
Westermark, E.A. 258n30
Whitehouse, Harvey 202n6
Whyte, Susan 159
Williams, Bernard 107–8
Willis, Roy 33n31
Wilson, B. 45
Wilson, R. 110n3
Winch, Peter 45
wind and water, colonial encounters over 209–10, 214–16
witchcraft 22, 23, 25, 31
    beliefs in 234
    sacrifices and 199–200
Wittgenstein, Ludwig 3
Wolf, D. 259n32
women's death ritual (*tevhid*) 103
Word of Life 43, 44, 45, 54n8, 55n17
World Spiritual University *see* Brahma Kumaris

X

X-region and X-phenomena 25–6, 27

Y

Yang, Dali L. 219
Young, D.E. and Goulet, J.-G. 33n31

Z

Al-Zamakshari ('Jar Allah') 101
Zambia Electricity Supply Corp. (ZESCO) 70
Zambia *see* religious logistics in Africa
Zene, Cosmo 149n18
Zhao Xudong 148n11
Zhelyazkova, Antonina 99
Zimniak-Halajko, M. 174
Zycie Warszawy 181